VIZ GRAPHIC NOVEL

ANGEL OF REDEMPTION

A BATTLE ANGEL ALITA™ GRAPHIC NOVEL

STORY AND ART BY

YUKITO KISHIRO

C O N T E N T S

741.5
952
Kish

This volume contains
BATTLE ANGEL ALITA PART FOUR in its entirety.

STORY AND ART BY YUKITO KISHIRO

English Adaptation/Fred Burke & Toshifumi Yoshida
Touch-Up Art & Lettering/Wayne Truman
Cover Design/Viz Graphics
Managing Editor/Annette Roman
Senior Editor/Trish Ledoux
Editor-in-Chief/Hyoe Narita
Publisher/Seiji Horibuchi
Director of Sales & Marketing/Dallas Middaugh

First published as Gunnm by Shueisha, Inc. in Japan

Printed in Canada

Published by Viz Communications, Inc.
P.O. Box 77010 • San Francisco, CA 94107

10 9 8
First printing, March 1998
Eighth printing, November 2001

YUKITO KISHIRO GRAPHIC NOVELS TO DATE

BATTLE ANGEL ALITA	ANGEL OF VICTORY	ANGEL OF CHAOS
TEARS OF AN ANGEL	ANGEL OF REDEMPTION	FALLEN ANGEL
KILLING ANGEL	ANGEL OF DEATH	ANGEL'S ASCENSION

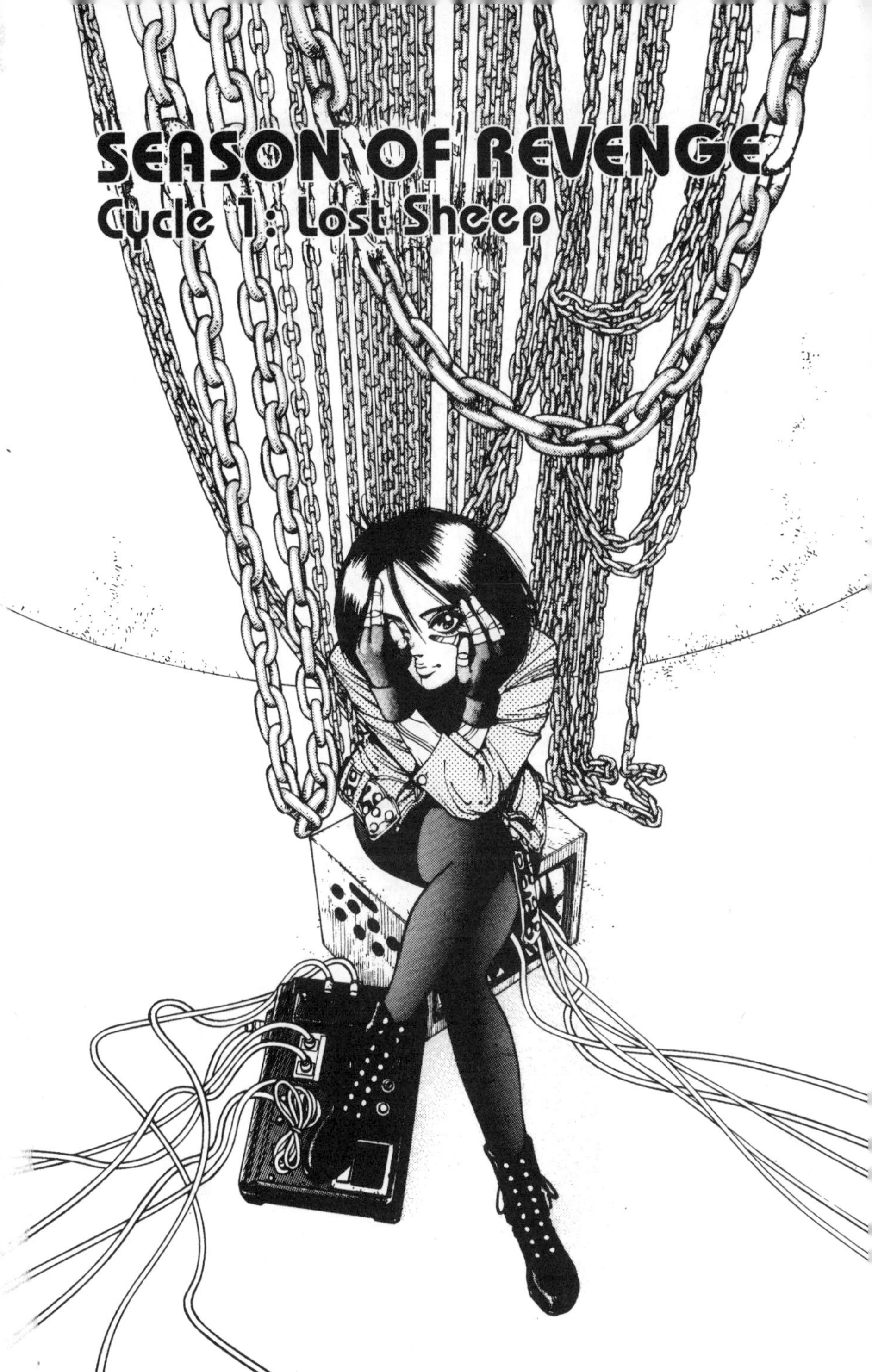
SEASON OF REVENGE
Cycle 1: Lost Sheep

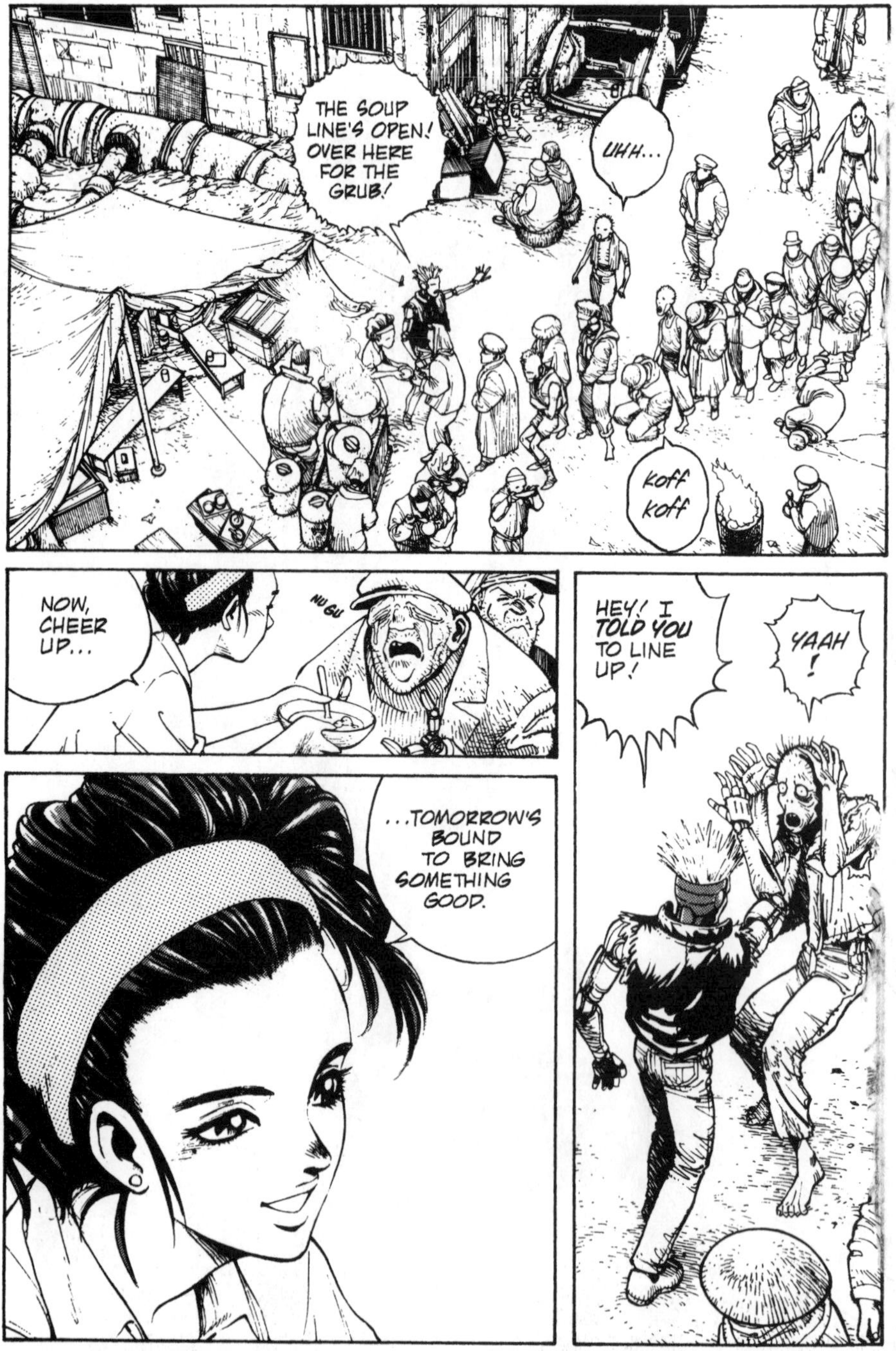
THE SOUP LINE'S OPEN! OVER HERE FOR THE GRUB!
UHH...
koff koff
NOW, CHEER UP...
NU GU
...TOMORROW'S BOUND TO BRING SOMETHING GOOD.
HEY! I TOLD YOU TO LINE UP!
YAAH!

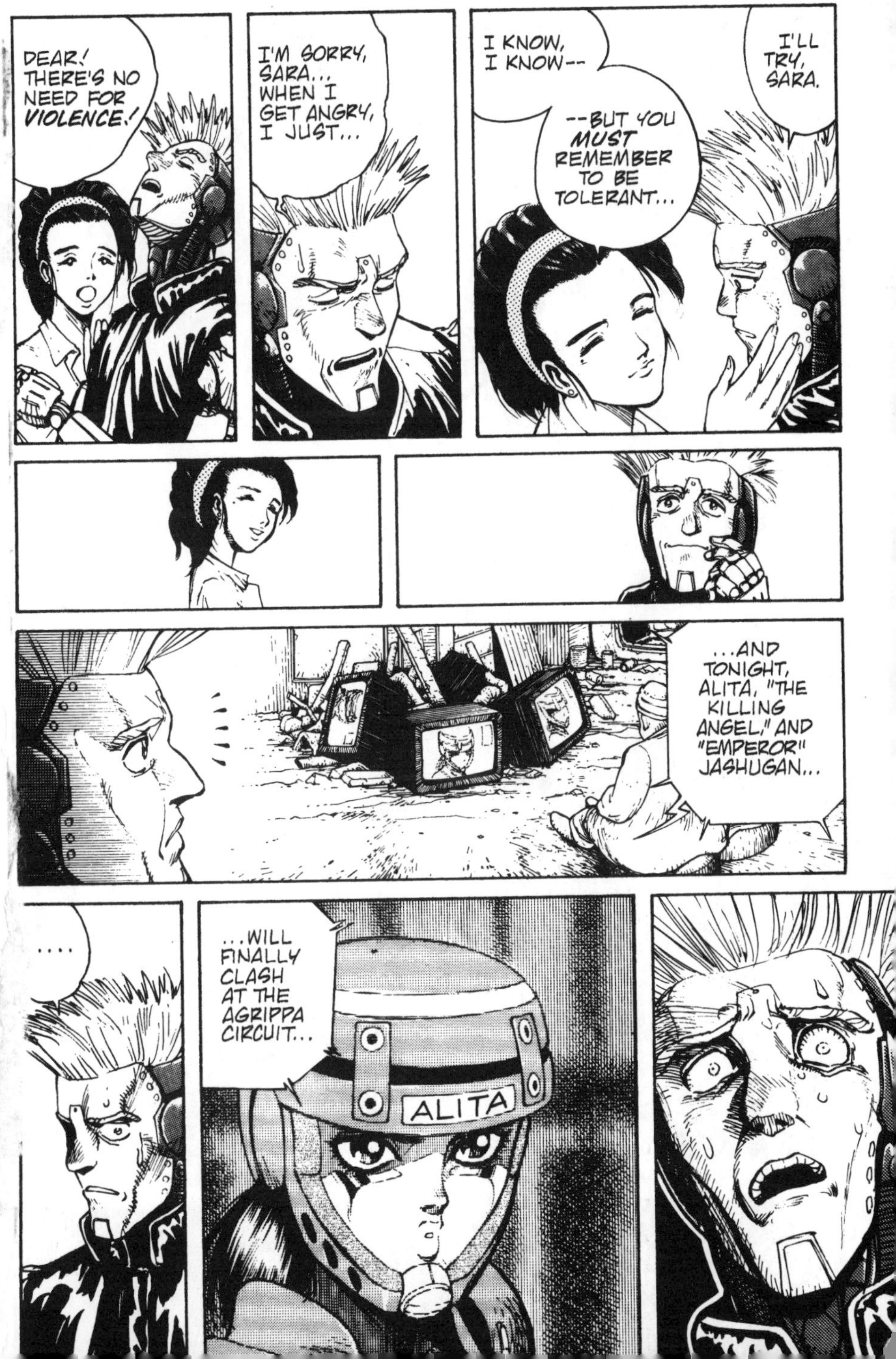
DEAR! THERE'S NO NEED FOR VIOLENCE!
I'M SORRY, SARA... WHEN I GET ANGRY, I JUST...
I KNOW, I KNOW--
--BUT YOU MUST REMEMBER TO BE TOLERANT...
I'LL TRY, SARA.
...AND TONIGHT, ALITA, "THE KILLING ANGEL," AND "EMPEROR" JASHUGAN...
....
...WILL FINALLY CLASH AT THE AGRIPPA CIRCUIT...
ALITA

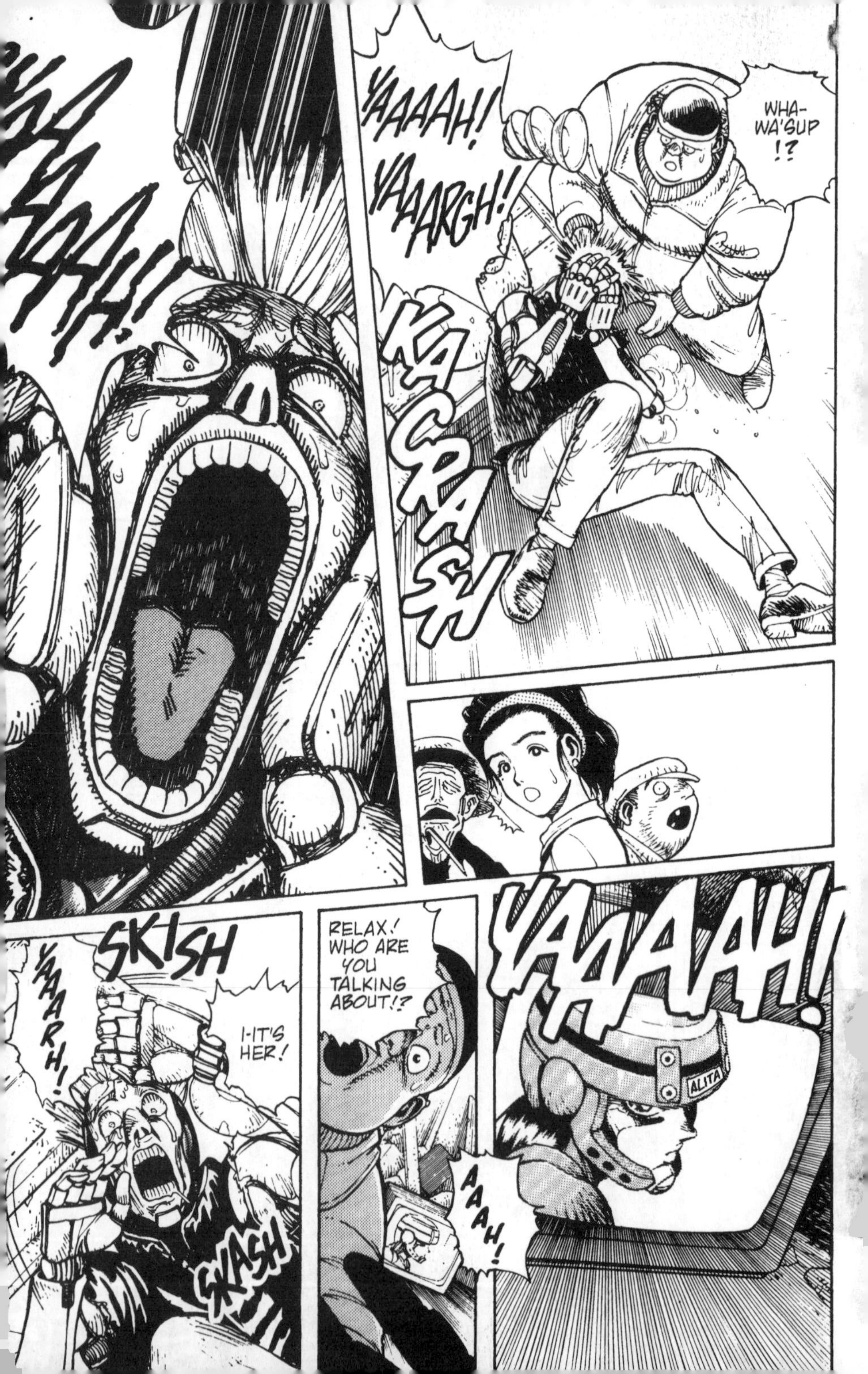

YAAAAAH!!
YAAAAAH!
YAAARGH!!
WHA-WA'SUP!?
KACRASH
SKISH
YAAAARH!
I-IT'S HER!
SKASH
RELAX! WHO ARE YOU TALKING ABOUT!?
YAAAAH!
ALITA
AAAAH!

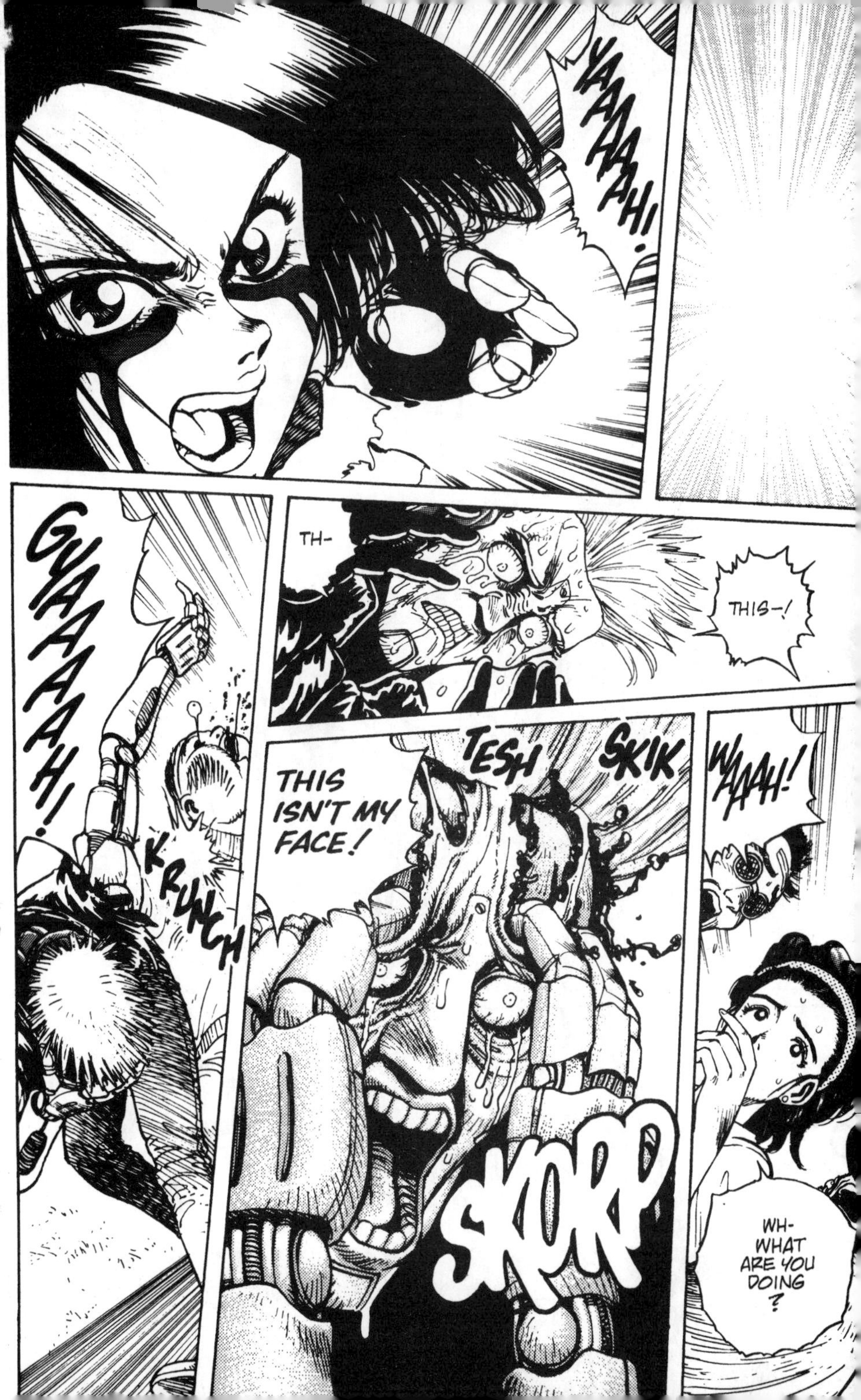
YAAAAAAH!
GUAAAAAAH!
KRUNCH
TH-
THIS-!
THIS ISN'T MY FACE!
TESH
SKIK
SKORP
WAAAH!
WH- WHAT ARE YOU DOING?

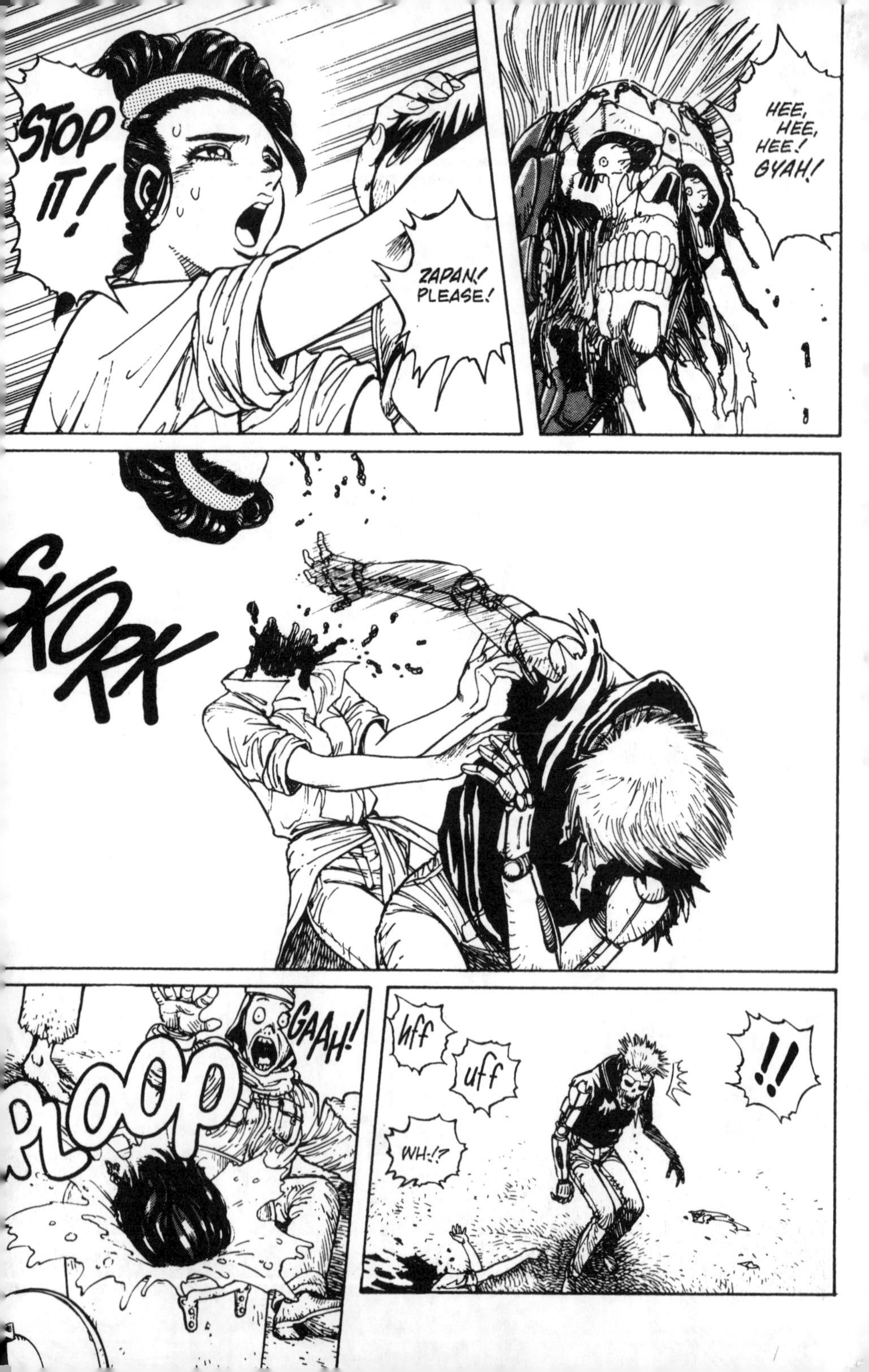
STOP IT!
ZAPAN! PLEASE!
HEE, HEE, HEE! GYAH!
SKORK
PLOOP
GAAH!
uff
uff
WH-!?
!!

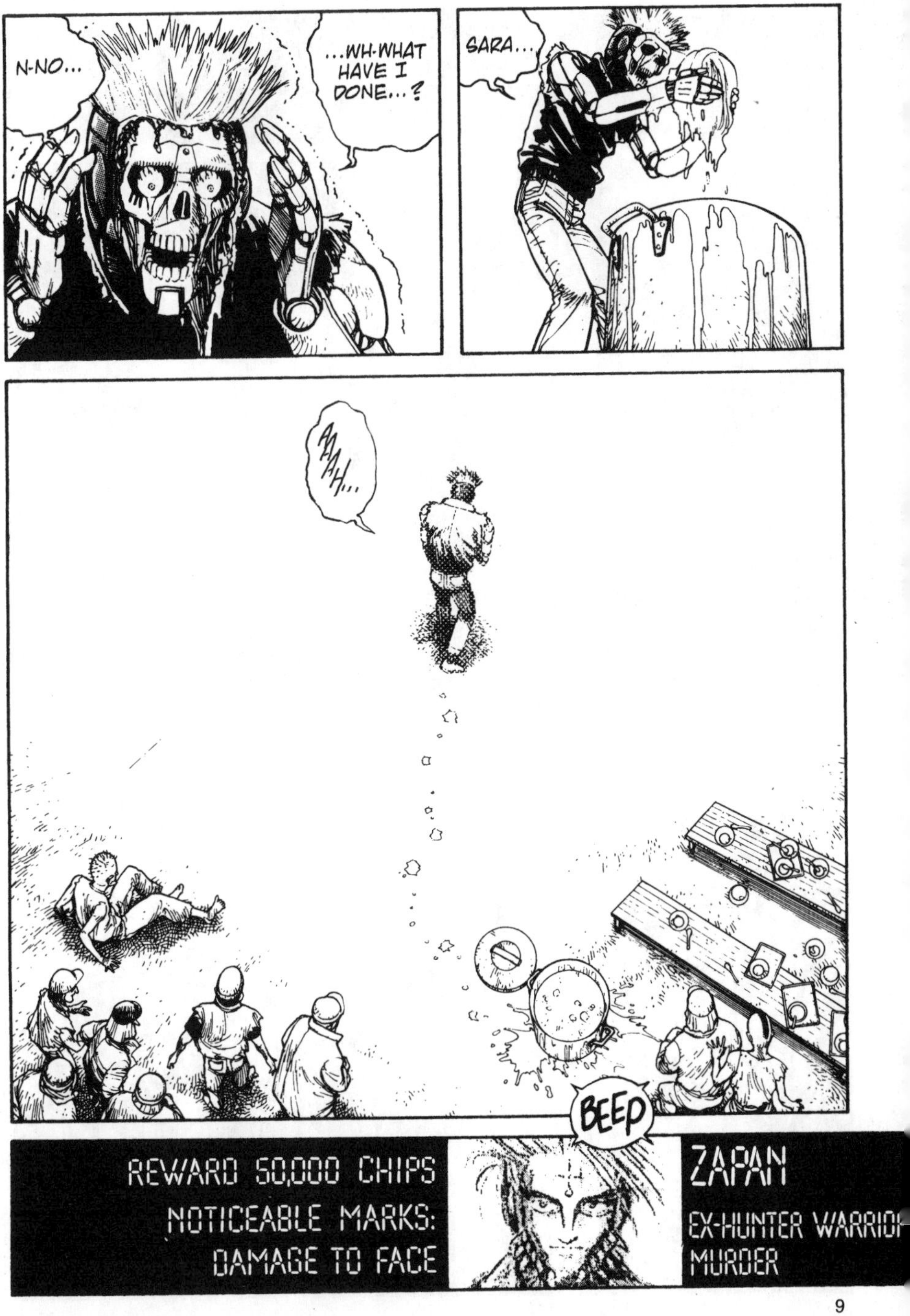
N-NO...
...WH-WHAT HAVE I DONE...?
SARA...
AAAH...
BEEP
REWARD 50,000 CHIPS
NOTICEABLE MARKS: DAMAGE TO FACE
ZAPAN
EX-HUNTER WARRIO
MURDER

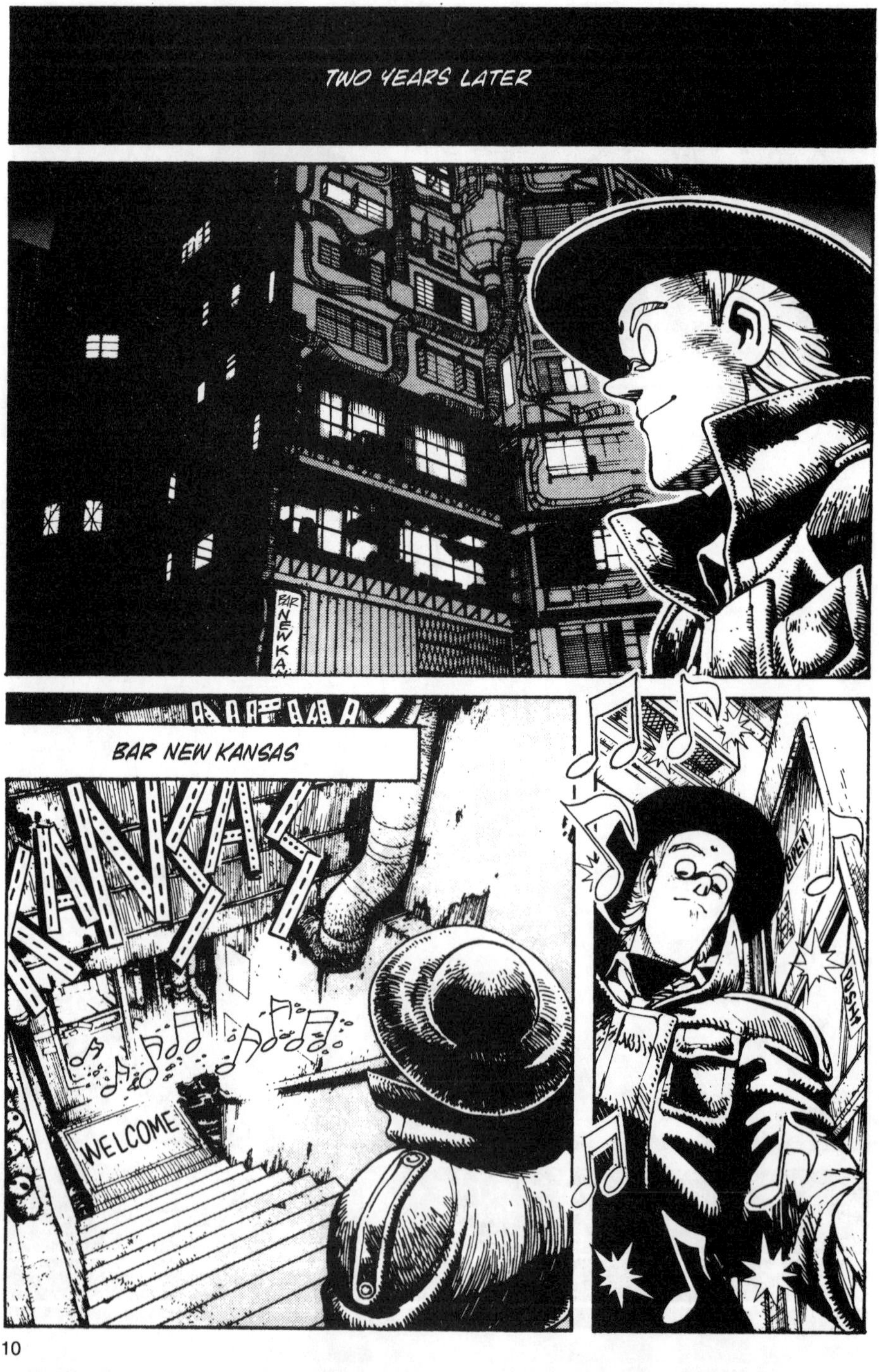
TWO YEARS LATER
BAR NEW KANSAS
WELCOME

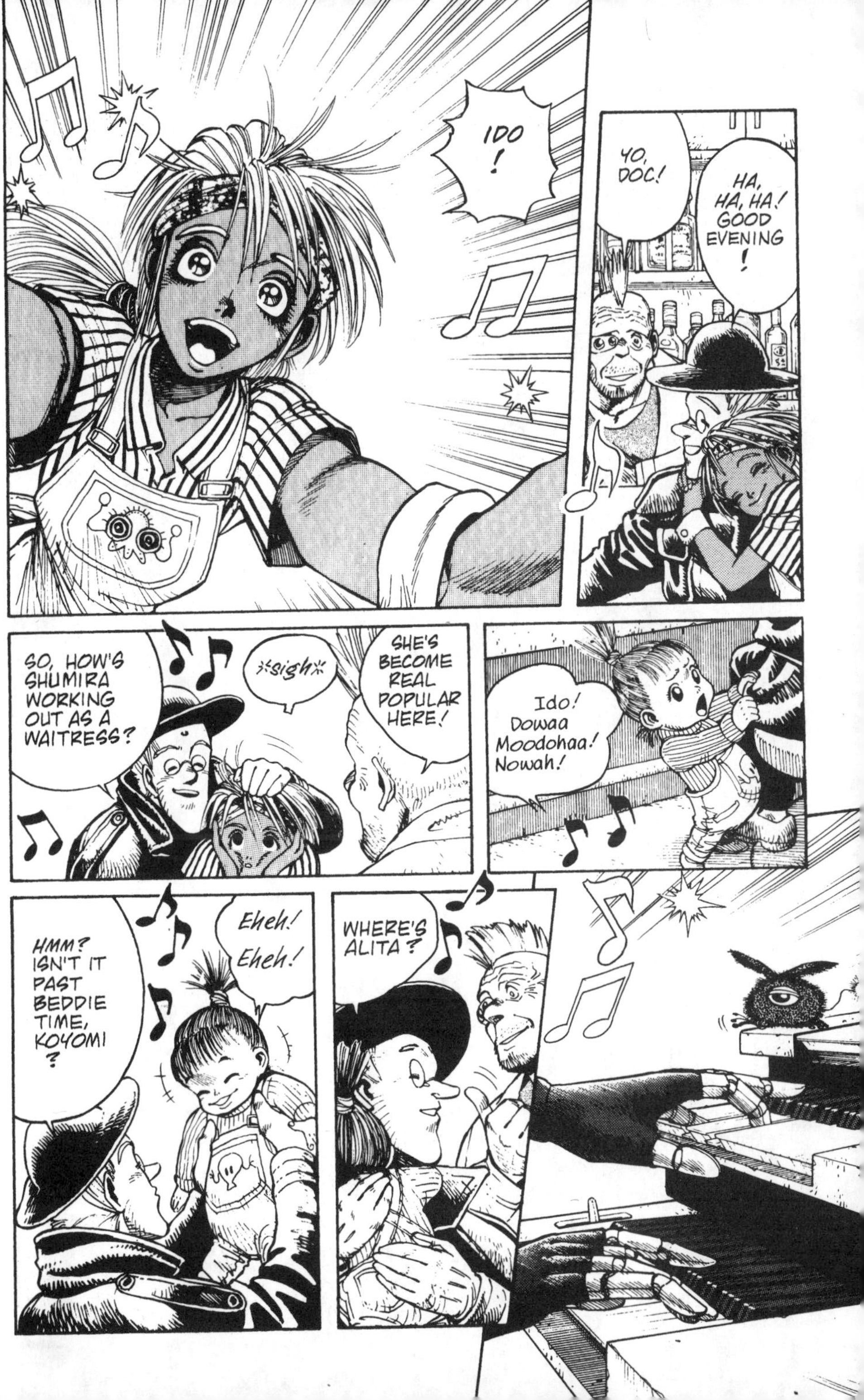
IDO!
YO, DOC!
HA, HA, HA! GOOD EVENING!
SO, HOW'S SHUMIRA WORKING OUT AS A WAITRESS?
sigh
SHE'S BECOME REAL POPULAR HERE!
Ido! Dowaa Moodohaa! Nowah!
HMM? ISN'T IT PAST BEDDIE TIME, KOYOMI?
Eheh! Eheh!
WHERE'S ALITA?

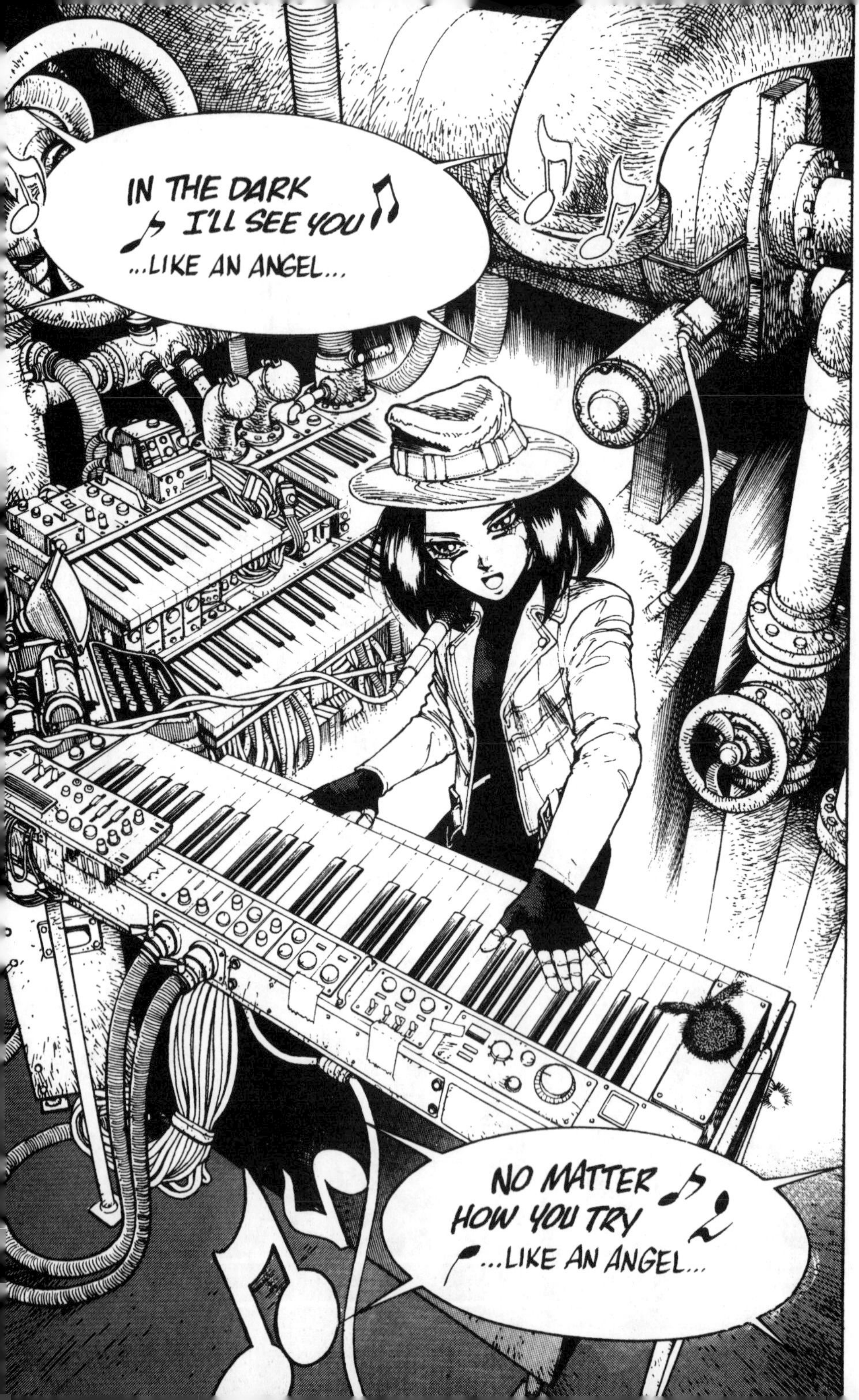
IN THE DARK I'LL SEE YOU ...LIKE AN ANGEL...
NO MATTER HOW YOU TRY ...LIKE AN ANGEL...

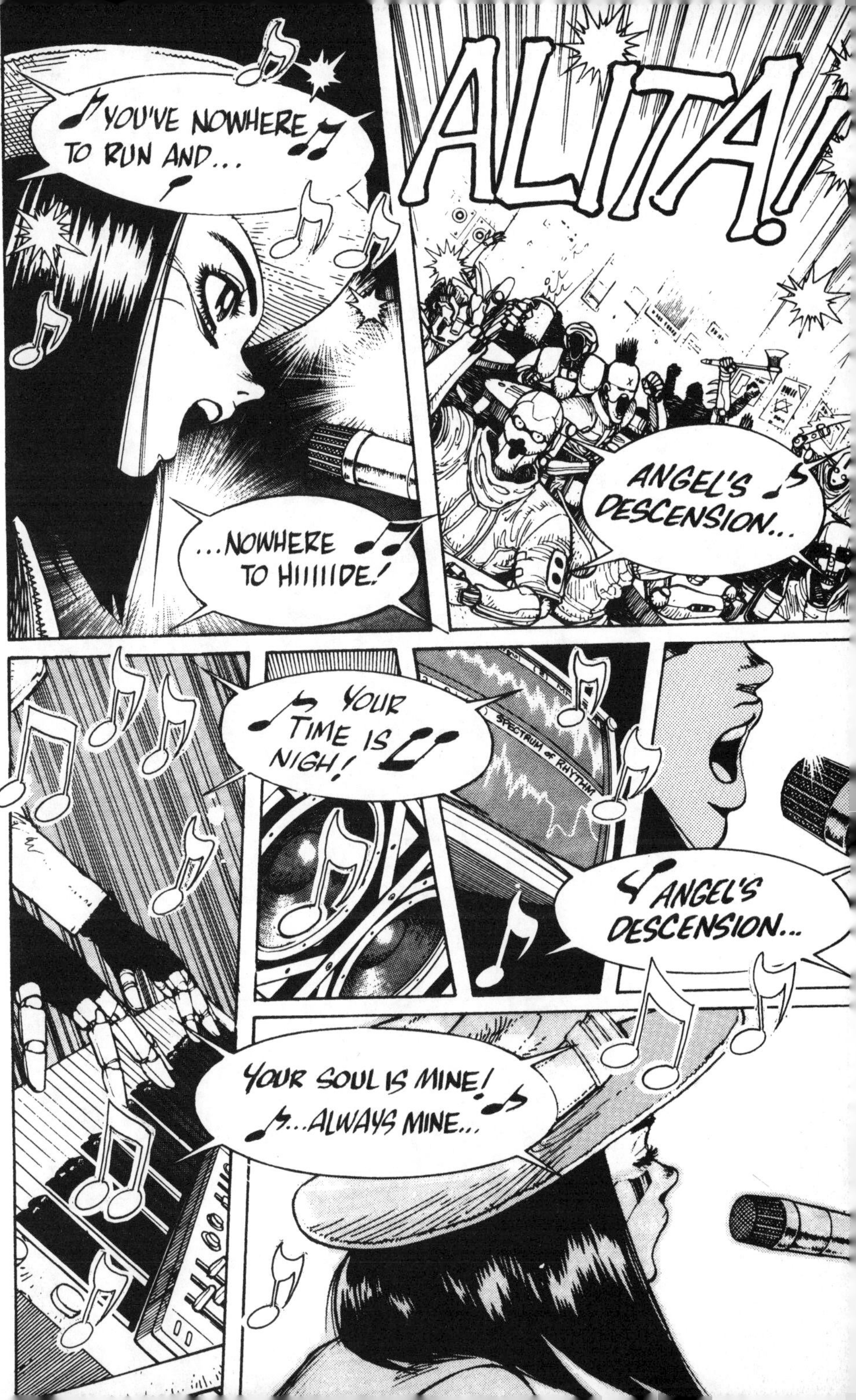
YOU'VE NOWHERE TO RUN AND...
...NOWHERE TO HIIIIIDE!
ALITA!
ANGEL'S DESCENSION...
YOUR TIME IS NIGH!
SPECTRUM of RHYTHM
ANGEL'S DESCENSION...
YOUR SOUL IS MINE! ...ALWAYS MINE...

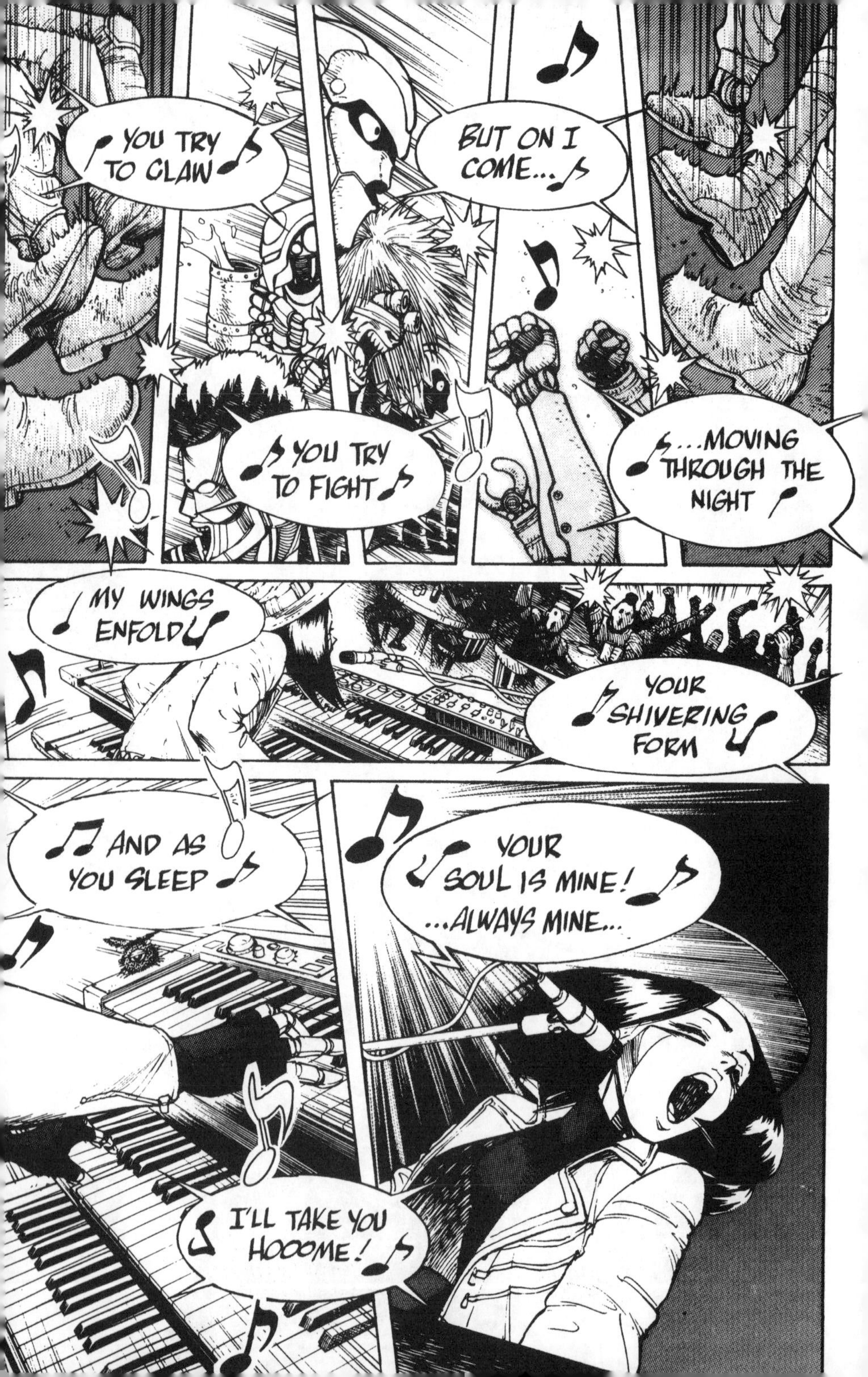
YOU TRY TO CLAW
BUT ON I COME...
YOU TRY TO FIGHT
...MOVING THROUGH THE NIGHT
MY WINGS ENFOLD
YOUR SHIVERING FORM
AND AS YOU SLEEP
YOUR SOUL IS MINE! ...ALWAYS MINE...
I'LL TAKE YOU HOOOME!

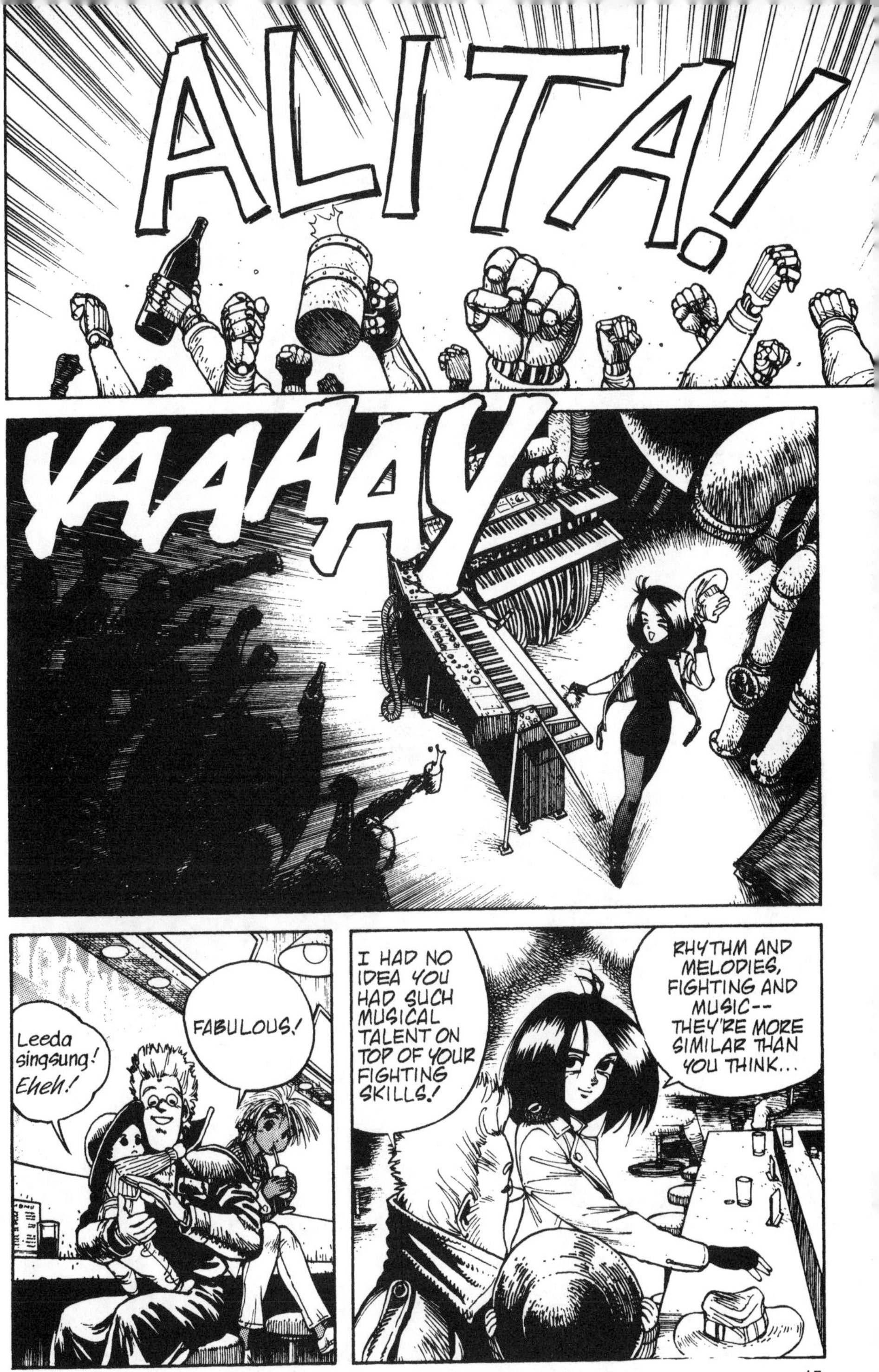
ALITA!
YAAAAY
Leeda singsung! Eheh!
FABULOUS!
I HAD NO IDEA YOU HAD SUCH MUSICAL TALENT ON TOP OF YOUR FIGHTING SKILLS!
RHYTHM AND MELODIES, FIGHTING AND MUSIC-- THEY'RE MORE SIMILAR THAN YOU THINK...

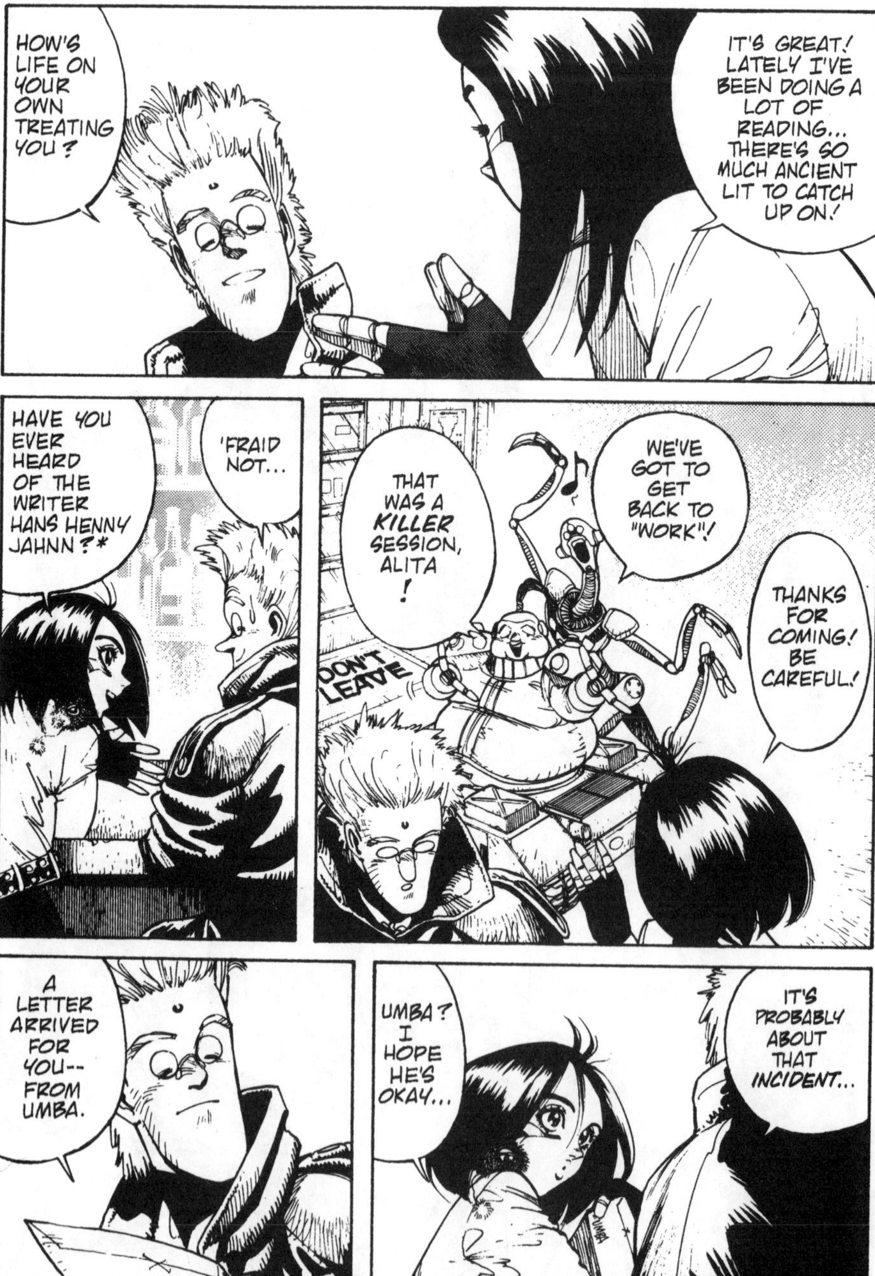
HOW'S LIFE ON YOUR OWN TREATING YOU?
IT'S GREAT! LATELY I'VE BEEN DOING A LOT OF READING... THERE'S SO MUCH ANCIENT LIT TO CATCH UP ON!
HAVE YOU EVER HEARD OF THE WRITER HANS HENNY JAHNN?*
'FRAID NOT...
DON'T LEAVE
THAT WAS A KILLER SESSION, ALITA!
WE'VE GOT TO GET BACK TO "WORK"!
THANKS FOR COMING! BE CAREFUL!
A LETTER ARRIVED FOR YOU-- FROM UMBA.
UMBA
UMBA? I HOPE HE'S OKAY...
IT'S PROBABLY ABOUT THAT INCIDENT...

*HANS HENNY JAHNN (1894-1959) GERMAN KNOWN TO SOME AS THE "GREATEST UNKNOWN AUTHOR"

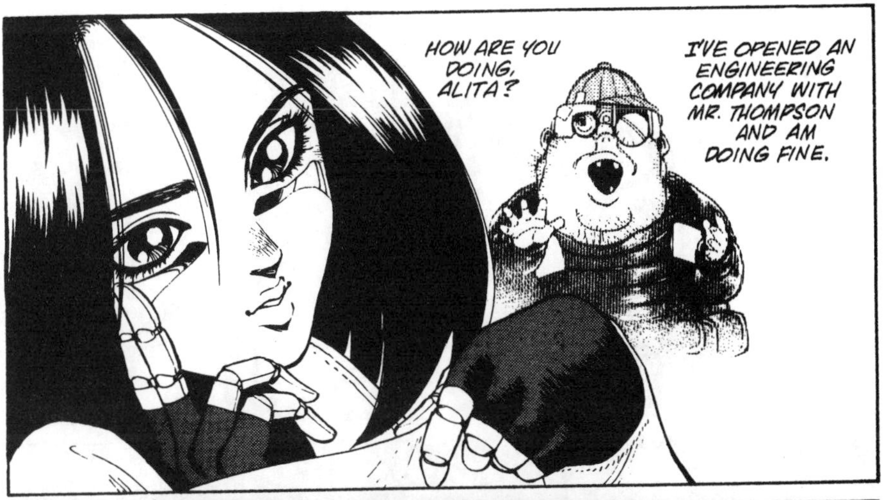
HOW ARE YOU DOING, ALITA?
I'VE OPENED AN ENGINEERING COMPANY WITH MR. THOMPSON AND AM DOING FINE.

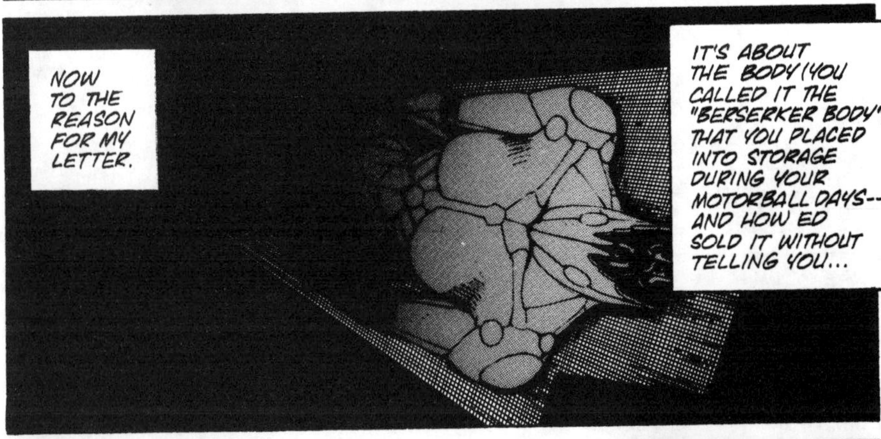
NOW TO THE REASON FOR MY LETTER.
IT'S ABOUT THE BODY (YOU CALLED IT THE "BERSERKER BODY") THAT YOU PLACED INTO STORAGE DURING YOUR MOTORBALL DAYS-- AND HOW ED SOLD IT WITHOUT TELLING YOU...

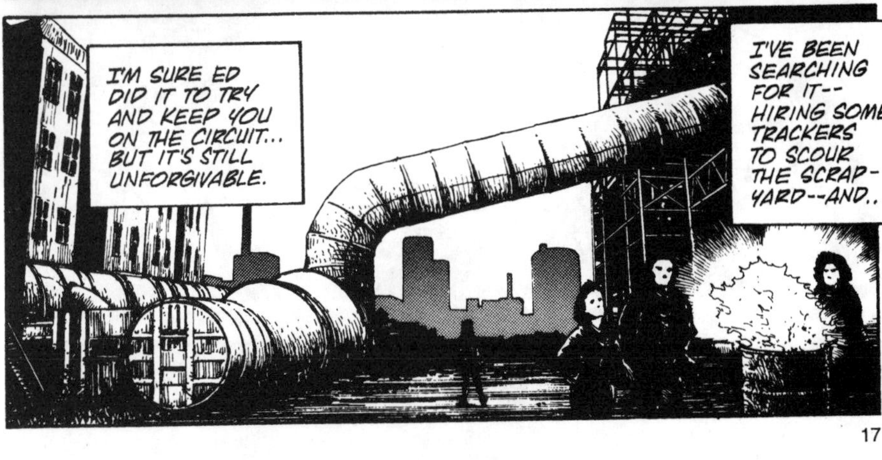
I'M SURE ED DID IT TO TRY AND KEEP YOU ON THE CIRCUIT... BUT IT'S STILL UNFORGIVABLE.
I'VE BEEN SEARCHING FOR IT-- HIRING SOME TRACKERS TO SCOUR THE SCRAP-YARD--AND...

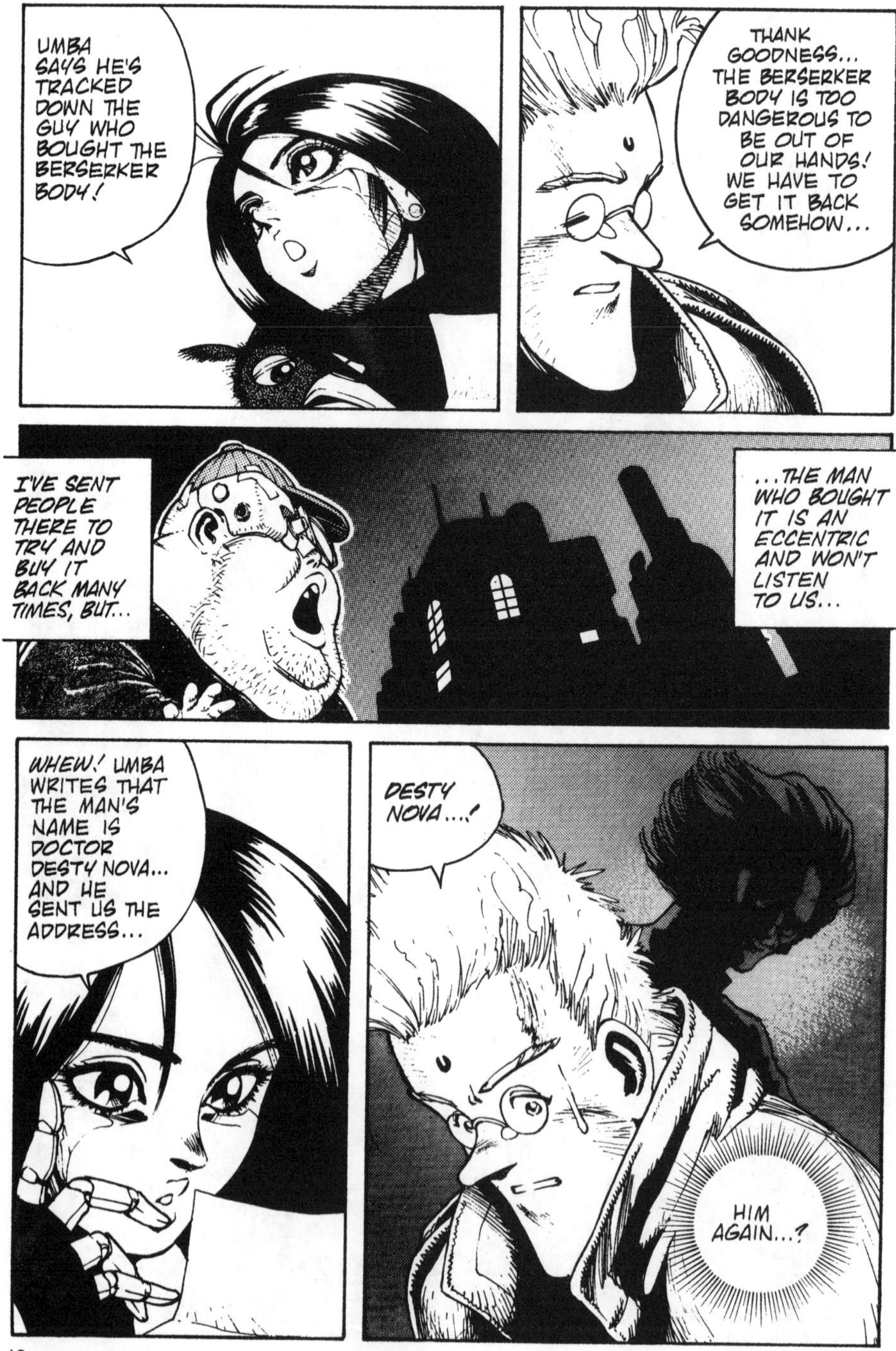
UMBA SAYS HE'S TRACKED DOWN THE GUY WHO BOUGHT THE BERSERKER BODY!
THANK GOODNESS... THE BERSERKER BODY IS TOO DANGEROUS TO BE OUT OF OUR HANDS! WE HAVE TO GET IT BACK SOMEHOW...
I'VE SENT PEOPLE THERE TO TRY AND BUY IT BACK MANY TIMES, BUT...
...THE MAN WHO BOUGHT IT IS AN ECCENTRIC AND WON'T LISTEN TO US...
WHEW! UMBA WRITES THAT THE MAN'S NAME IS DOCTOR DESTY NOVA... AND HE SENT US THE ADDRESS...
DESTY NOVA...!
HIM AGAIN...?

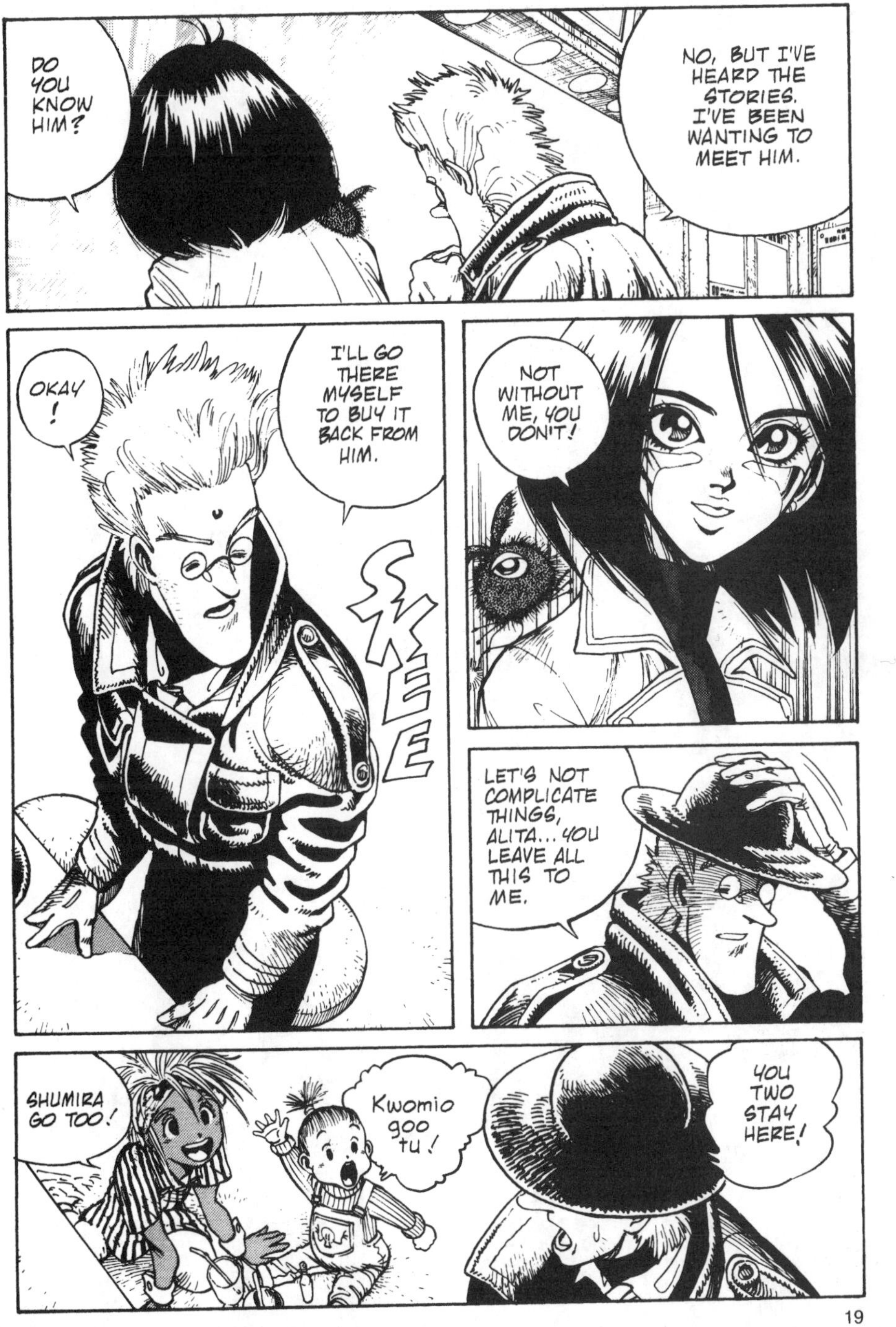
DO YOU KNOW HIM?
NO, BUT I'VE HEARD THE STORIES. I'VE BEEN WANTING TO MEET HIM.
OKAY!
I'LL GO THERE MYSELF TO BUY IT BACK FROM HIM.
SKEE
NOT WITHOUT ME, YOU DON'T!
LET'S NOT COMPLICATE THINGS, ALITA... YOU LEAVE ALL THIS TO ME.
SHUMIRA GO TOO!
Kwomio goo tu!
YOU TWO STAY HERE!

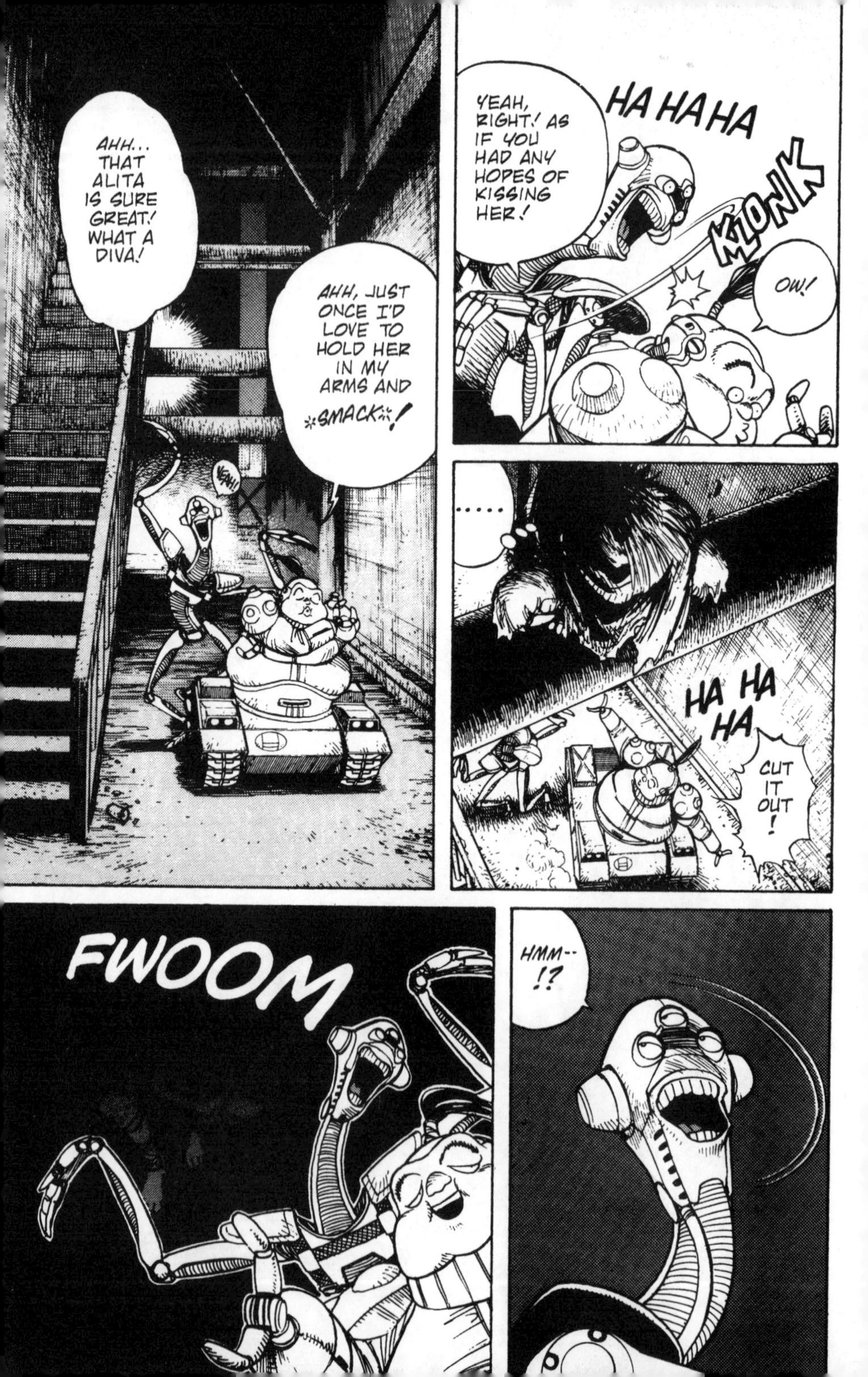
AHH... THAT ALITA IS SURE GREAT! WHAT A DIVA!
AHH, JUST ONCE I'D LOVE TO HOLD HER IN MY ARMS AND *SMACK*!
YEAH!!
YEAH, RIGHT! AS IF YOU HAD ANY HOPES OF KISSING HER!
HA HA HA
KLONK
OW!
.....
HA HA HA
CUT IT OUT!
FWOOM
HMM--!?

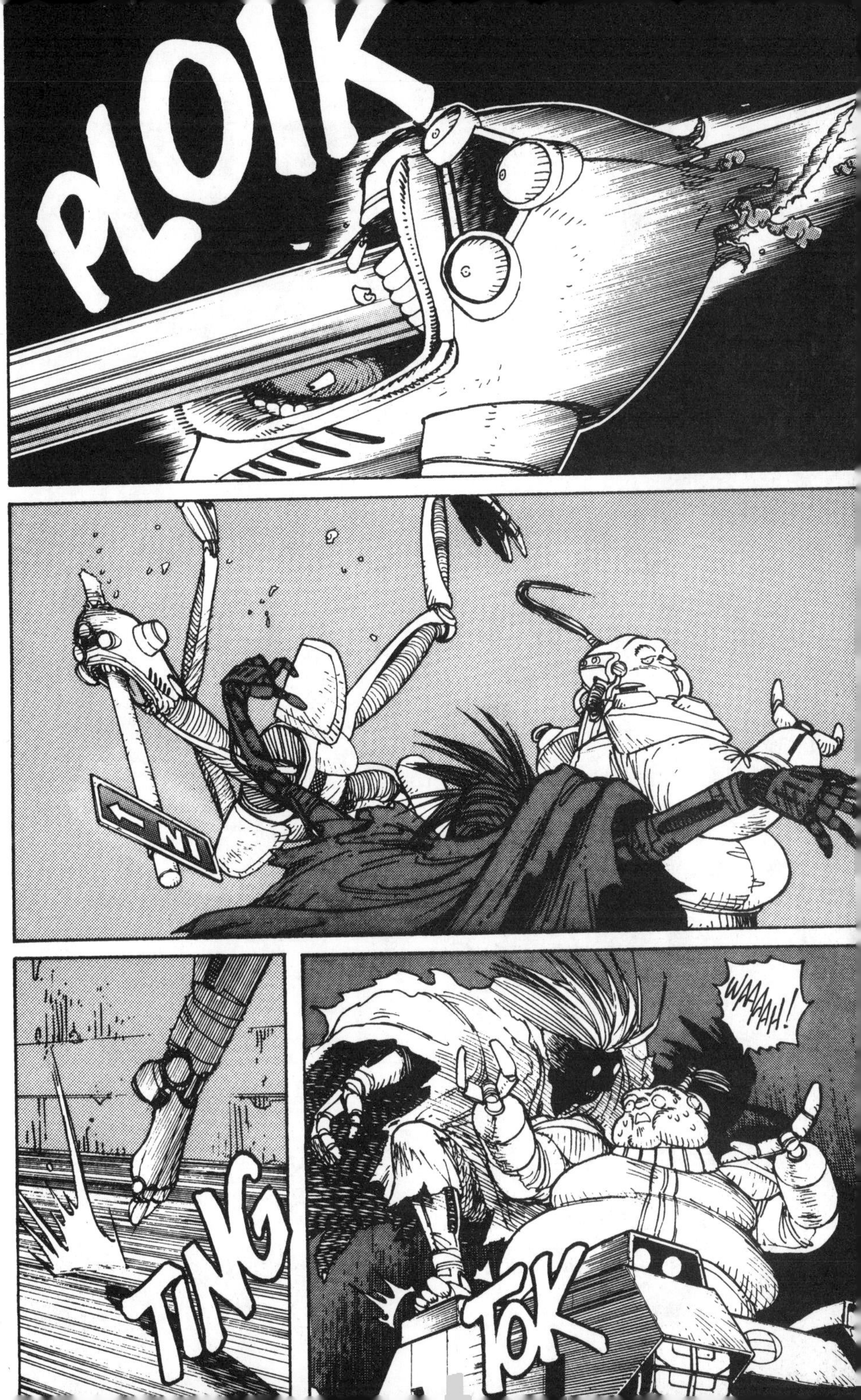
PLOIK
NI
WAAAAH!
TING
TOK

CHONG

BLAM

UNGH!

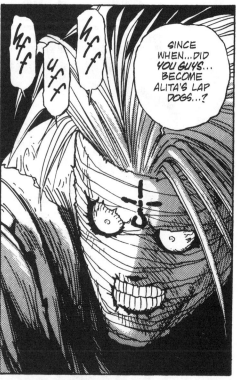

SINCE WHEN...DID *YOU GUYS*... BECOME ALITA'S LAP DOGS...?

hff hff hff

Y-YOU'RE...

Z-ZAPAN... YOU'RE *ZAPAN*, RIGHT...!?

I'M GLAD... YOU *REMEMBER* ME...

W-WHY ARE YOU DOING THIS?

GUH GUH

YOU'RE NOT STILL HOLDING A GRUDGE AGAINST ALITA, ARE YOU!?

22

YEAH... DOES THAT *GIRL* STILL REMEMBER...?

DOES SHE STILL REMEMBER WHAT SHE *TOOK* FROM ME? OR WILL I HAVE TO *REMIND* HER...?

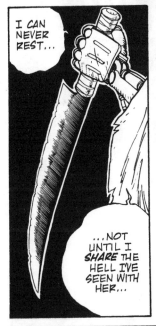

I CAN NEVER REST...

...NOT UNTIL I *SHARE* THE HELL I'VE SEEN WITH HER...

YOU'RE O-OUT OF YOUR MIND...!

DO YOU *SERIOUSLY* THINK YOU CAN DEFEAT ALITA...?

KANG

SHE'S THE BEST KILLER THE SCRAP-YARD'S EVER SEEN! WHO ELSE COULD'VE DEFEATED THAT MONSTER MAKAKU!?

HEH HEH HEH

COMPARED TO HER, WE'RE NOTHING BUT A BUNCH OF INSECTS...

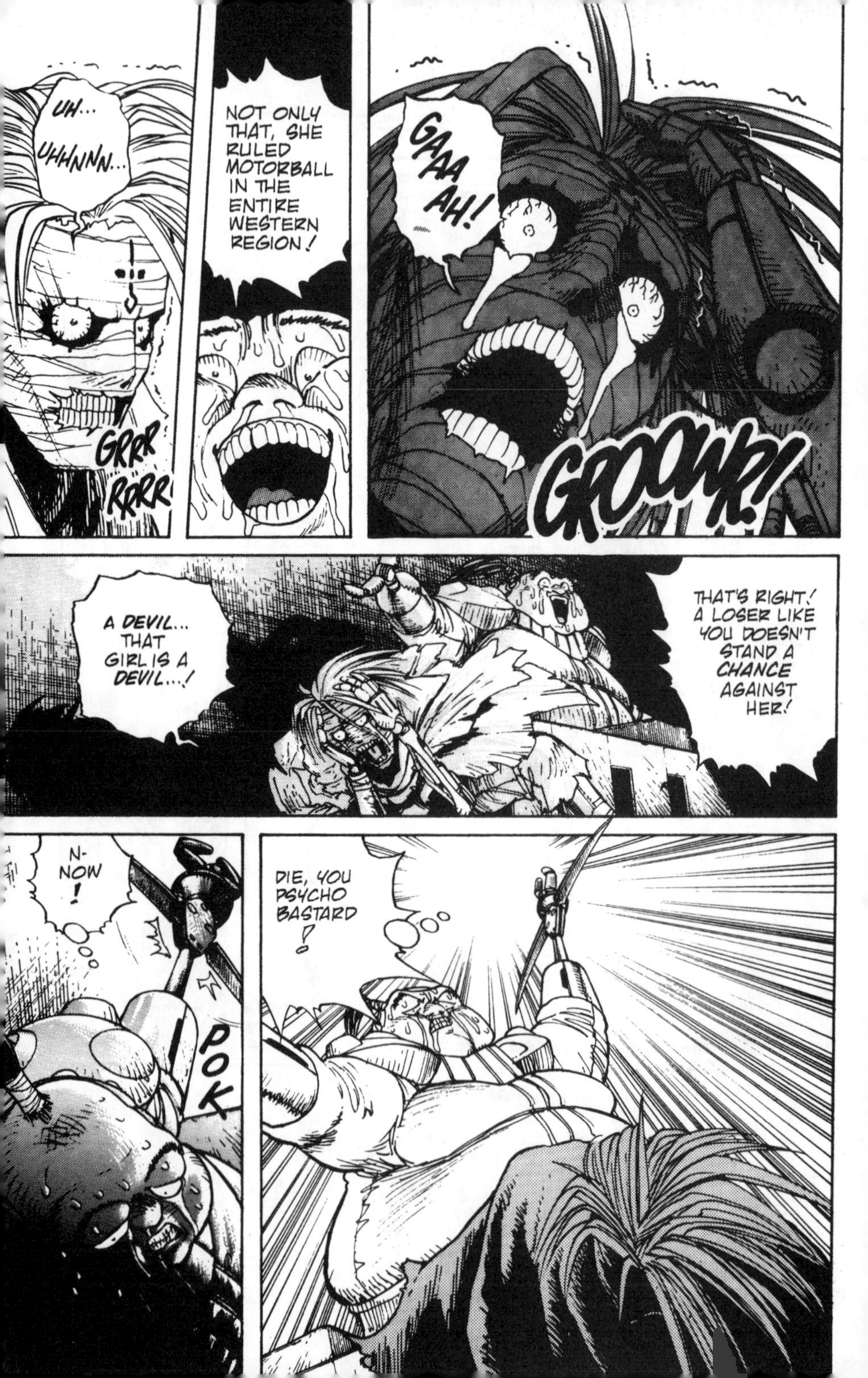
UH... UHHNNN...
GRRR RRRR
NOT ONLY THAT, SHE RULED MOTORBALL IN THE ENTIRE WESTERN REGION!
GAAAAAH!
GROOWR!
A DEVIL... THAT GIRL IS A DEVIL...!
THAT'S RIGHT! A LOSER LIKE YOU DOESN'T STAND A CHANCE AGAINST HER!
N-NOW!
POK
DIE, YOU PSYCHO BASTARD!

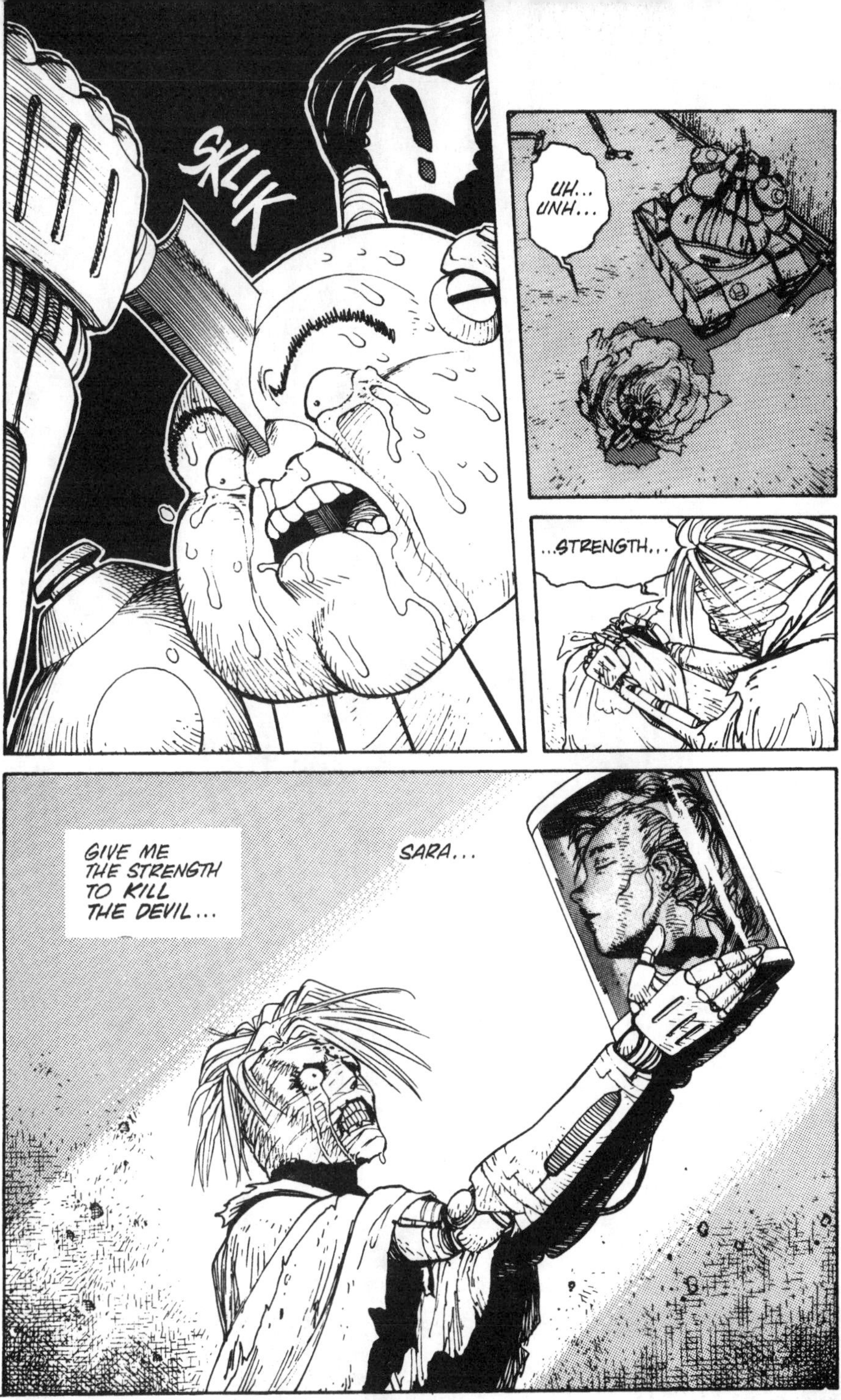
SKLIK
!
UH... UNH...
...STRENGTH...
GIVE ME THE STRENGTH TO KILL THE DEVIL...
SARA...

DOG MASTER
Cycle 2: Melody of Redemption

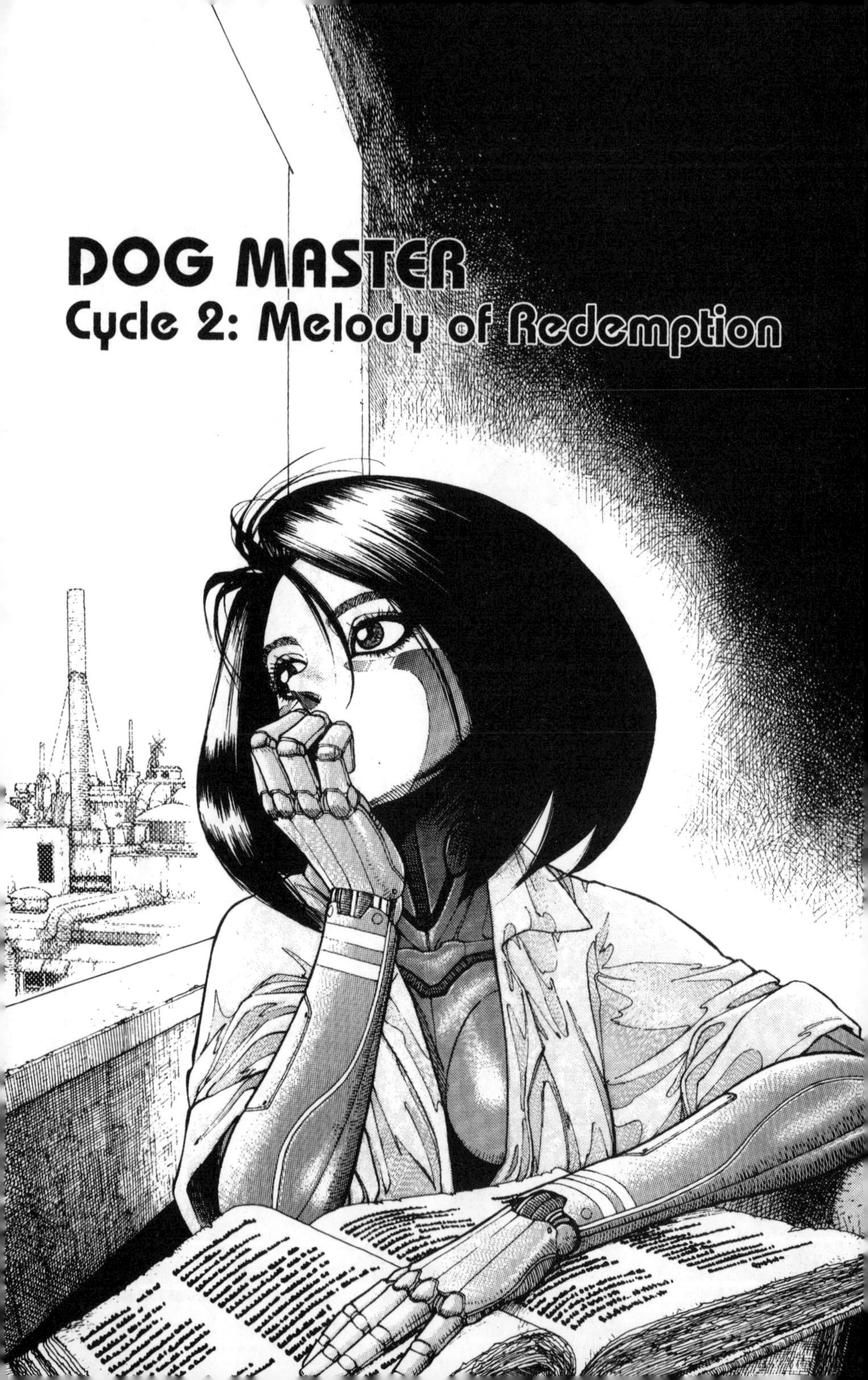

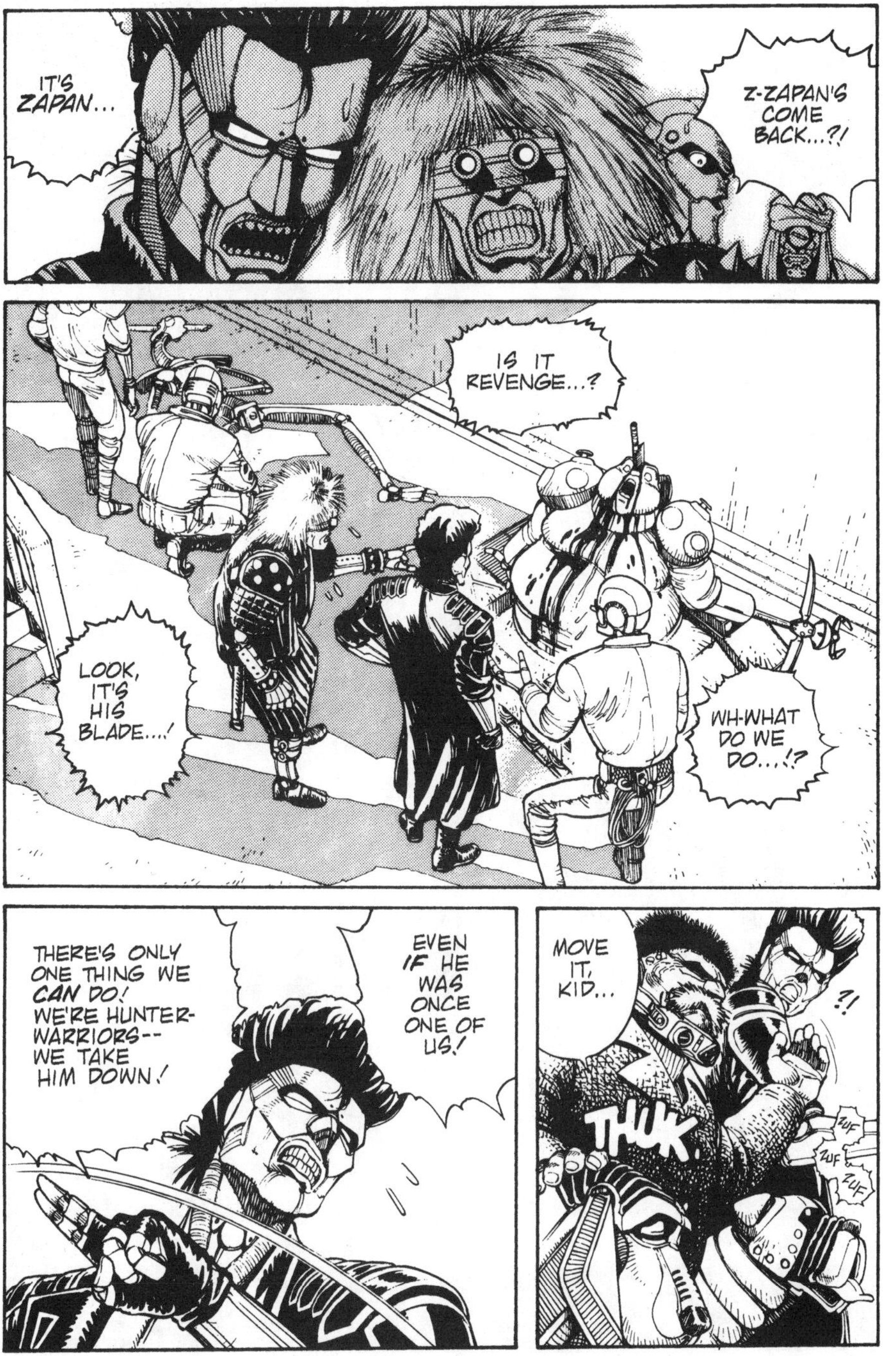
IT'S ZAPAN...
Z-ZAPAN'S COME BACK...?!
IS IT REVENGE...?
LOOK, IT'S HIS BLADE...!
WH-WHAT DO WE DO...!?
THERE'S ONLY ONE THING WE CAN DO! WE'RE HUNTER-WARRIORS-- WE TAKE HIM DOWN!
EVEN IF HE WAS ONCE ONE OF US!
MOVE IT, KID...
?!
THUK
ZUF
ZUF
ZUF

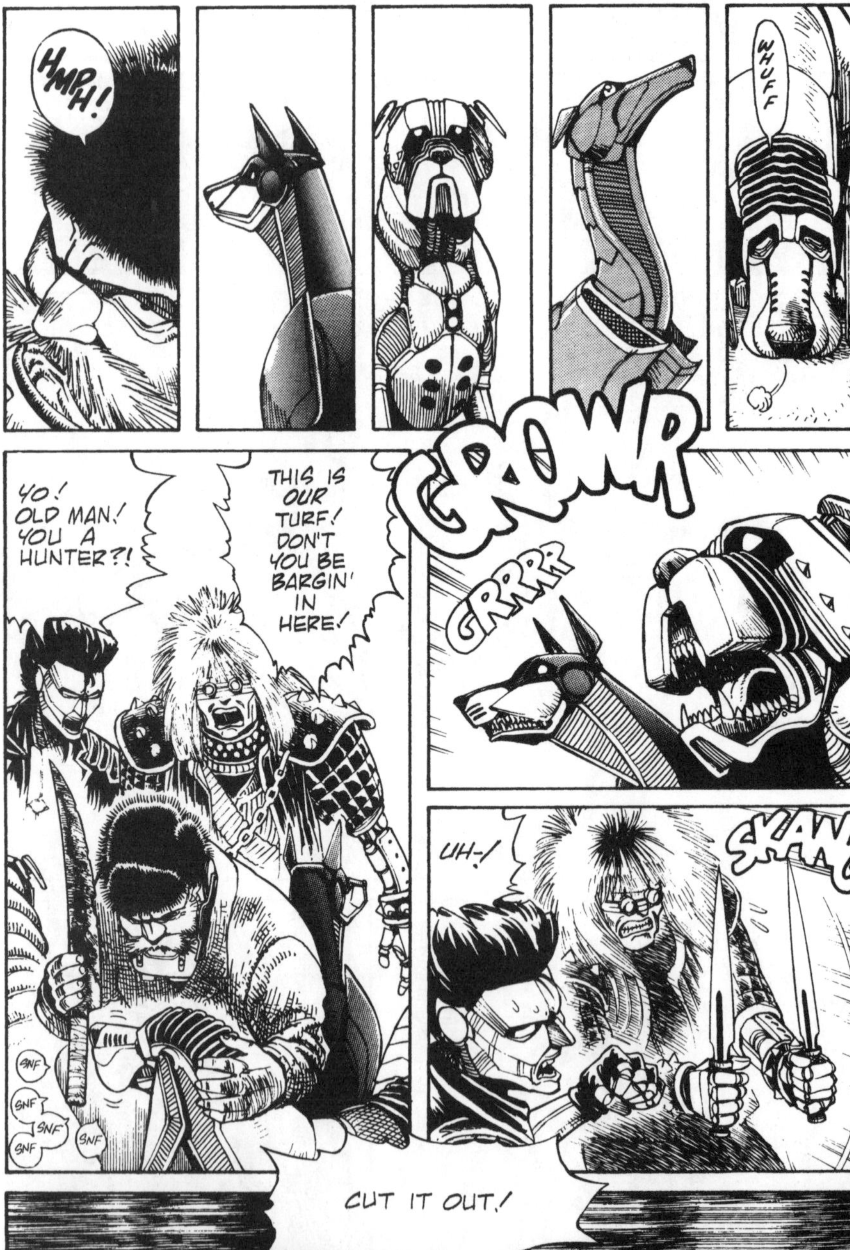
HMPH!
WHUFF
YO! OLD MAN! YOU A HUNTER?!
THIS IS OUR TURF! DON'T YOU BE BARGIN' IN HERE!
SNF
SNF
SNF
SNF
SNF
GROWR
GRRRR
UH-!
SKANG
CUT IT OUT!

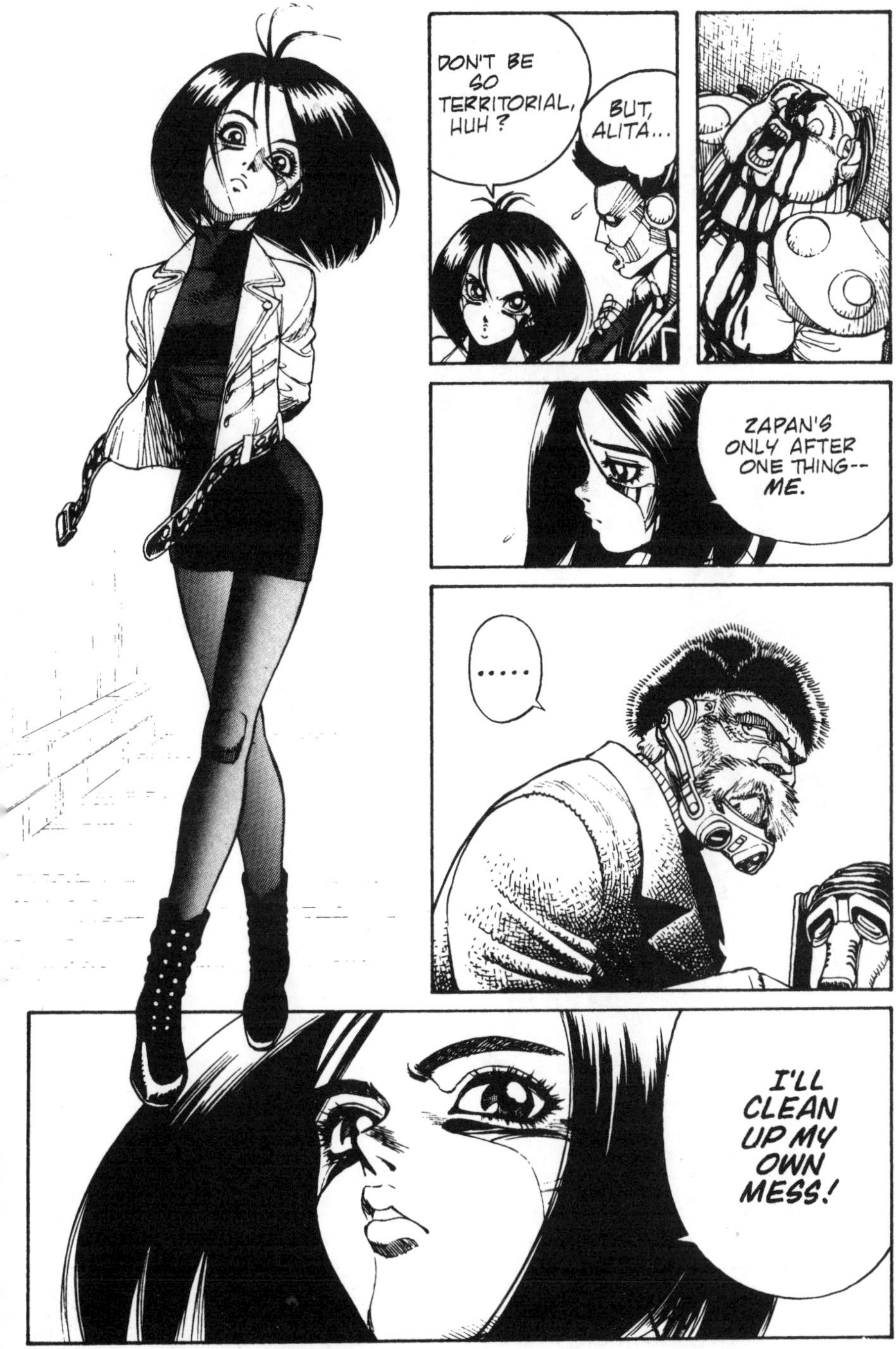
DON'T BE SO TERRITORIAL, HUH ?
BUT, ALITA...
ZAPAN'S ONLY AFTER ONE THING-- ME.
......
I'LL CLEAN UP MY OWN MESS!

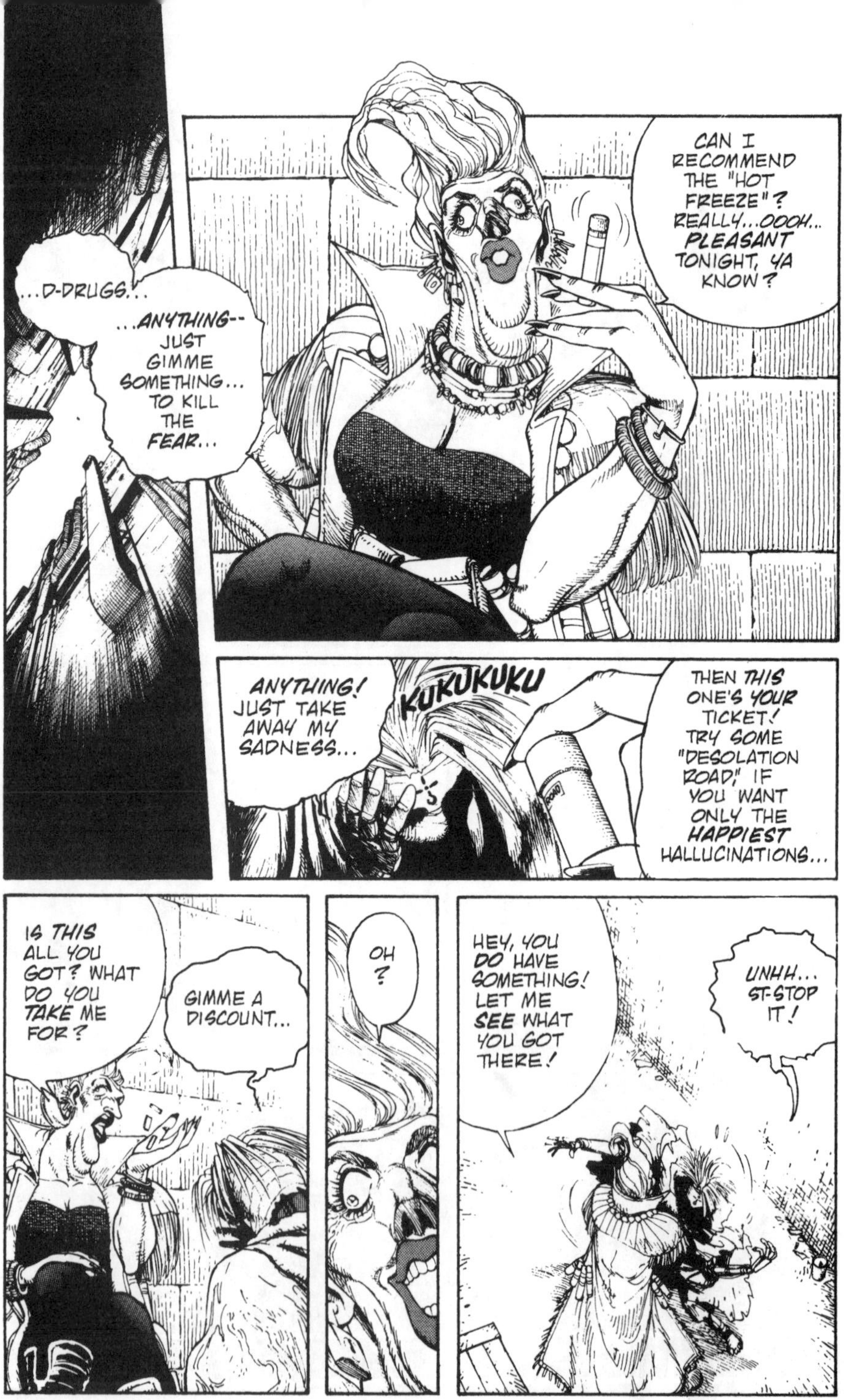
CAN I RECOMMEND THE "HOT FREEZE"? REALLY...OOOH... PLEASANT TONIGHT, YA KNOW?
...D-DRUGS...
...ANYTHING-- JUST GIMME SOMETHING... TO KILL THE FEAR...
ANYTHING! JUST TAKE AWAY MY SADNESS...
KUKUKUKU
THEN THIS ONE'S YOUR TICKET! TRY SOME "DESOLATION ROAD," IF YOU WANT ONLY THE HAPPIEST HALLUCINATIONS...
IS THIS ALL YOU GOT? WHAT DO YOU TAKE ME FOR?
GIMME A DISCOUNT...
OH?
HEY, YOU DO HAVE SOMETHING! LET ME SEE WHAT YOU GOT THERE!
UNHH... ST-STOP IT!

OH, MY! A HEAD IN A BOTTLE! HOW QUAINT!

YES, YES-- I *LIKE* HER! A TREASURE...

WHAT SAY I TRADE YOU THIS FOR THE DRUGS?

G-GIVE IT BACK...

LET YOU IN ON A LITTLE SECRET, MY PERVY FRIEND... DEAD BODIES *REALLY* TURN ME--

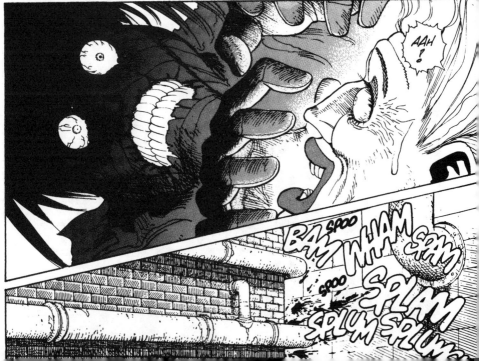

AAH!

BAM SPOO WHAM SPAM SPOO SPLAM SPLUM SPLUM

AAAAH...

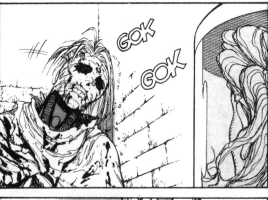

GOK
GOK

SARA...
I WAS A
LOSER--
DESERVED
TO BE
DEAD...

...JUST
LIKE ALL
THE
OTHERS
IN THE
SCRAPYARD...

SKRCH

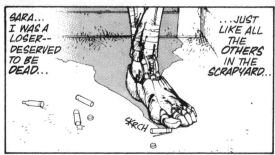

BUT
YOU...
TO
ME...

...YOU OPENED
YOUR ARMS
TO ME...
TRIED TO
SAVE ME...

WHY DID
YOU DO
THAT?
WHY!?

"ZAPAN...

"...YOU
THINK THE
SAME WAY
AS MY
FATHER..."

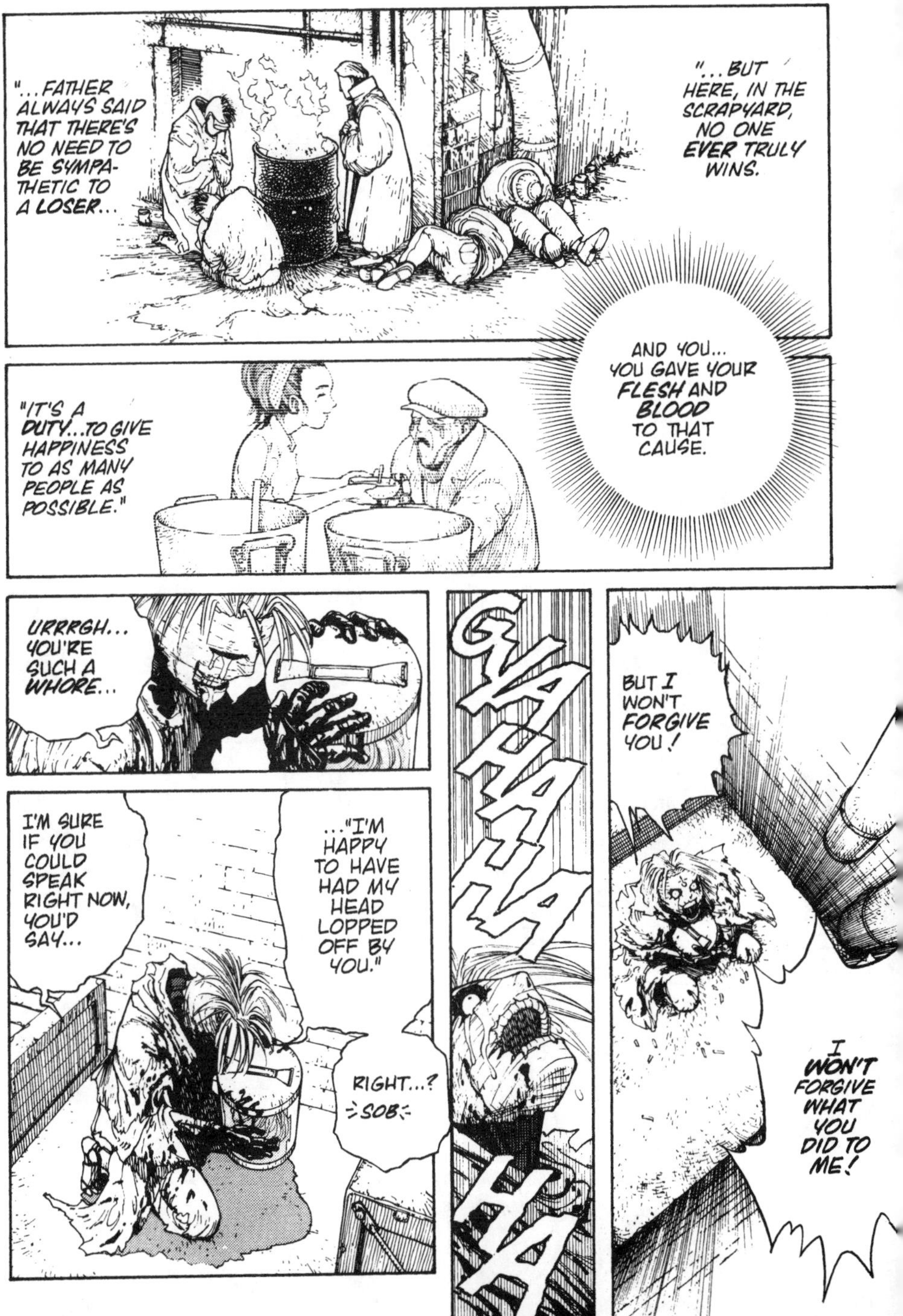
"...FATHER ALWAYS SAID THAT THERE'S NO NEED TO BE SYMPA-THETIC TO A LOSER...
"...BUT HERE, IN THE SCRAPYARD, NO ONE EVER TRULY WINS.
"IT'S A DUTY...TO GIVE HAPPINESS TO AS MANY PEOPLE AS POSSIBLE."
AND YOU... YOU GAVE YOUR FLESH AND BLOOD TO THAT CAUSE.
URRRGH... YOU'RE SUCH A WHORE...
I'M SURE IF YOU COULD SPEAK RIGHT NOW, YOU'D SAY...
..."I'M HAPPY TO HAVE HAD MY HEAD LOPPED OFF BY YOU."
RIGHT...?
SOB
GYAHAHAHA
HA
BUT I WON'T FORGIVE YOU!
I WON'T FORGIVE WHAT YOU DID TO ME!

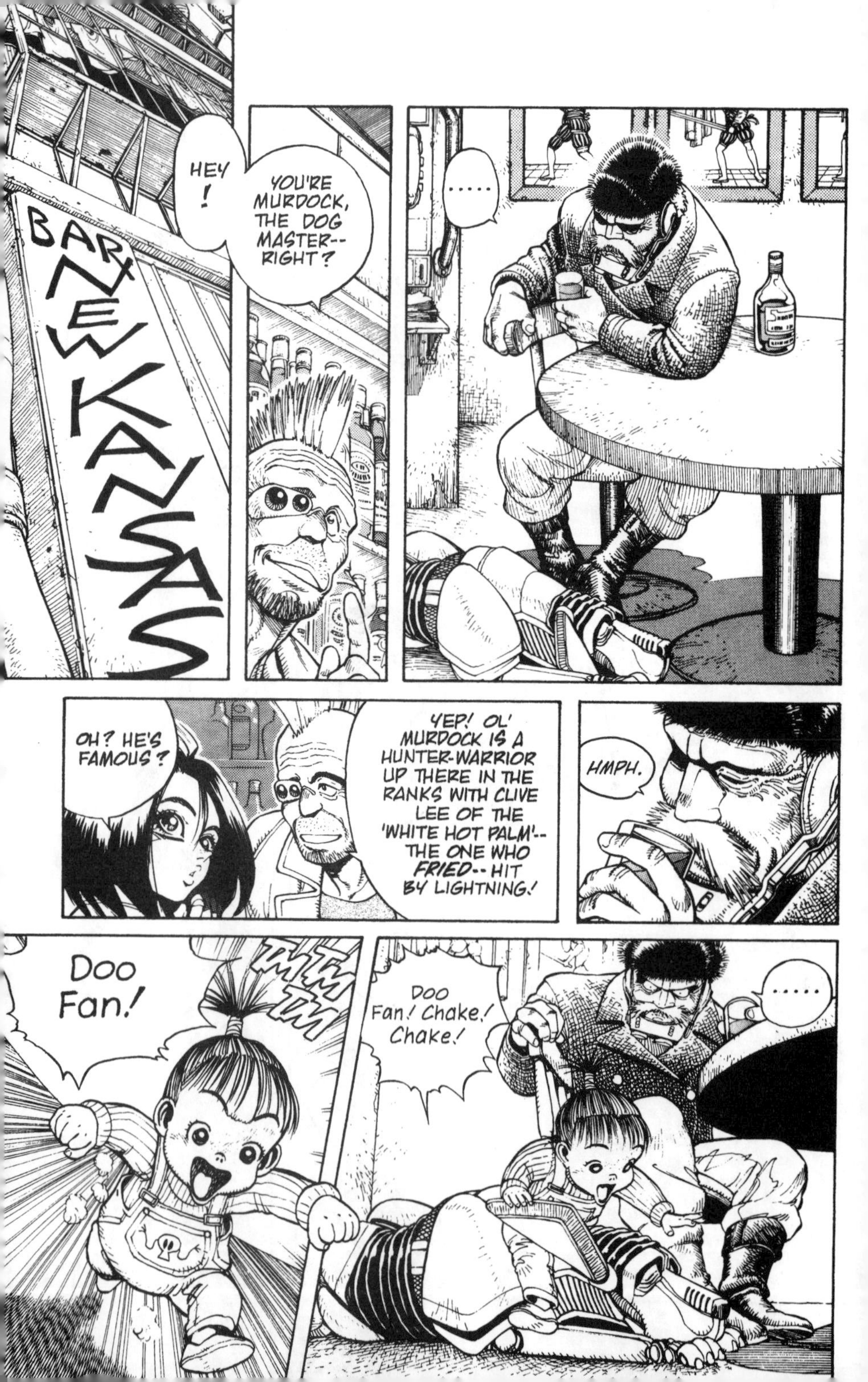
BAR NEW KANSAS
HEY!
YOU'RE MURDOCK, THE DOG MASTER--RIGHT?
......
OH? HE'S FAMOUS?
YEP! OL' MURDOCK IS A HUNTER-WARRIOR UP THERE IN THE RANKS WITH CLIVE LEE OF THE 'WHITE HOT PALM'-- THE ONE WHO FRIED-- HIT BY LIGHTNING!
HMPH.
Doo Fan!
Doo Fan! Chake! Chake!
......

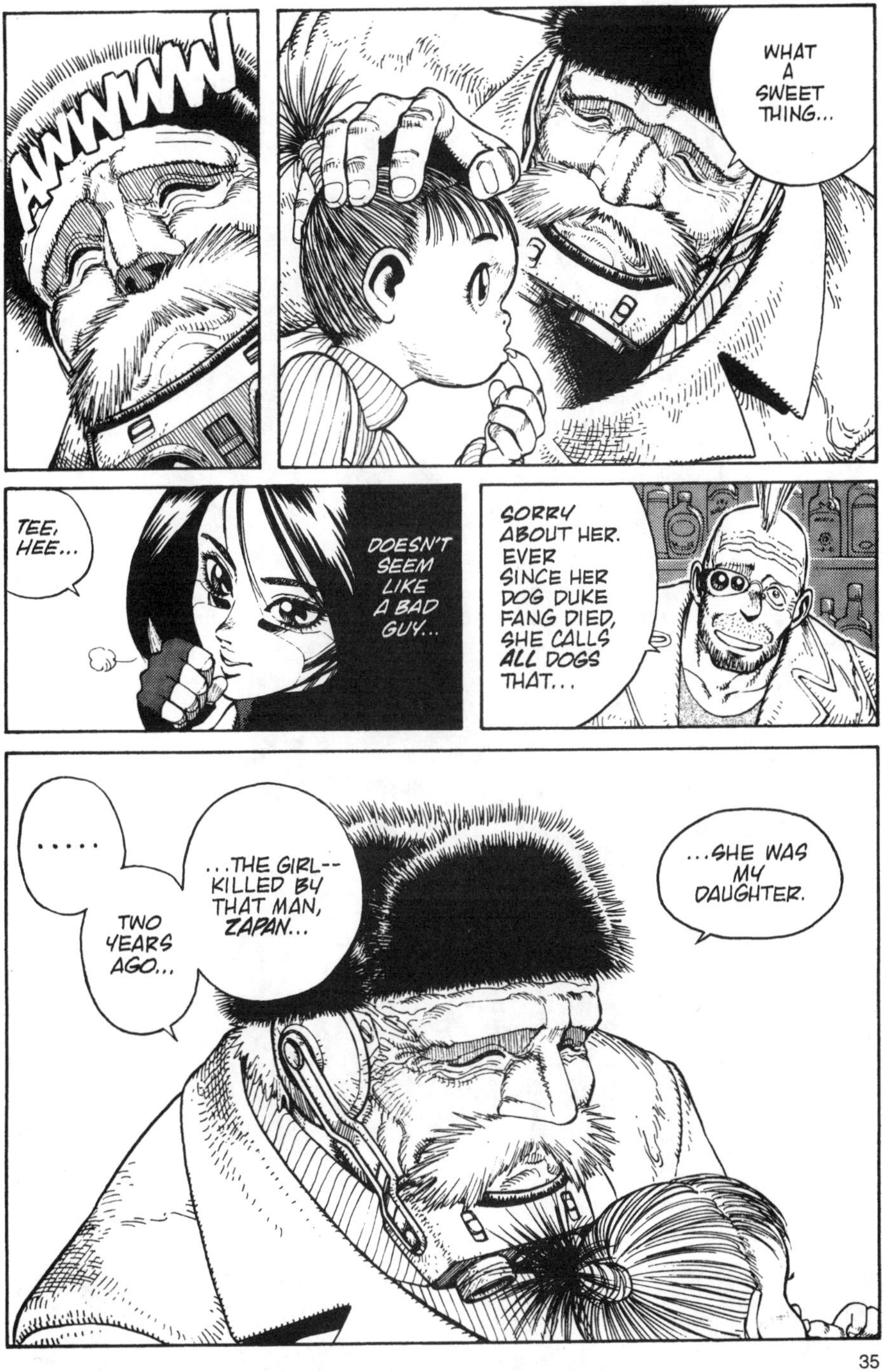
AWWWWW
WHAT A SWEET THING...
TEE, HEE...
DOESN'T SEEM LIKE A BAD GUY...
SORRY ABOUT HER. EVER SINCE HER DOG DUKE FANG DIED, SHE CALLS ALL DOGS THAT...
.....
TWO YEARS AGO...
...THE GIRL-- KILLED BY THAT MAN, ZAPAN...
...SHE WAS MY DAUGHTER.

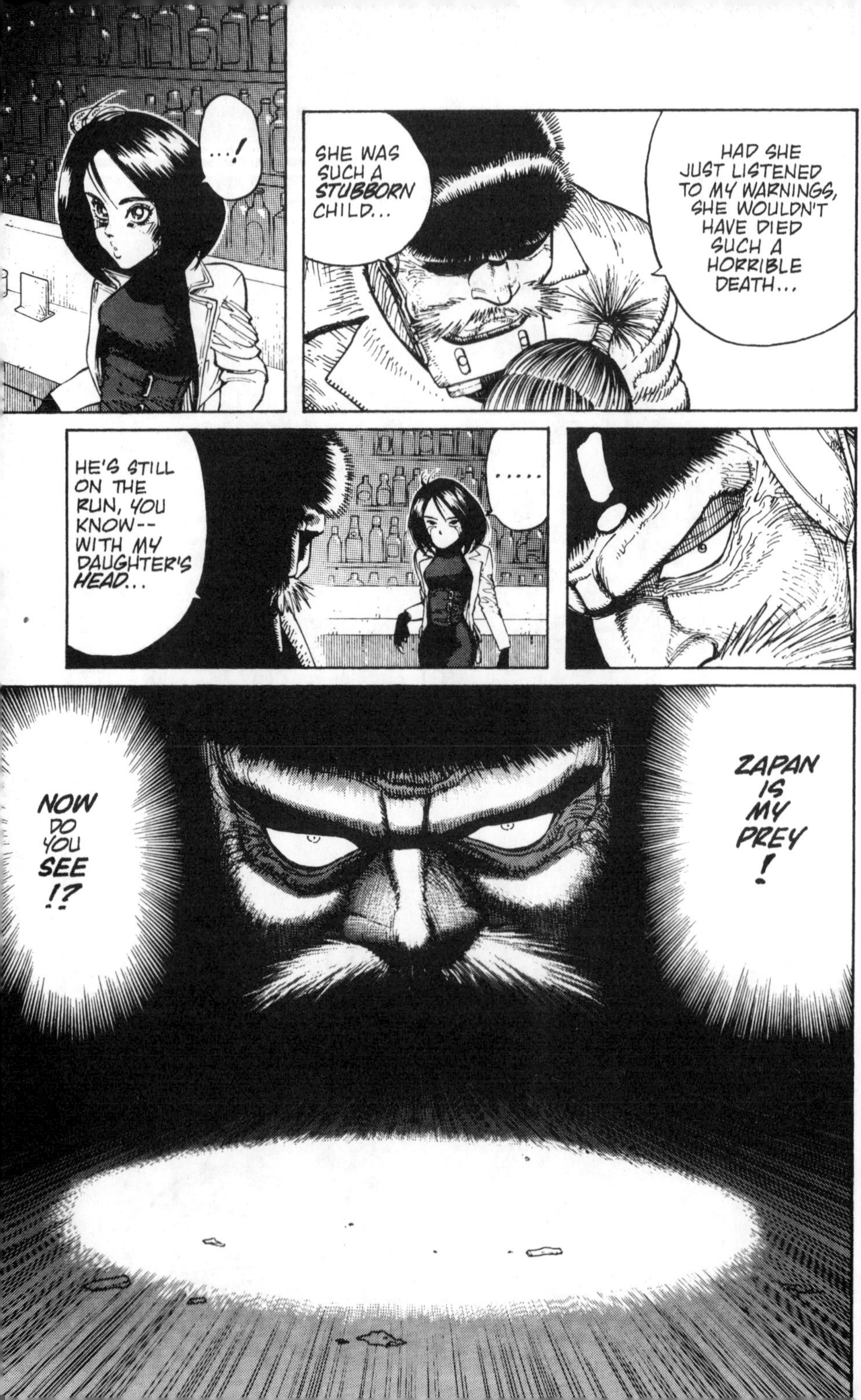
...!
SHE WAS SUCH A STUBBORN CHILD...
HAD SHE JUST LISTENED TO MY WARNINGS, SHE WOULDN'T HAVE DIED SUCH A HORRIBLE DEATH...
HE'S STILL ON THE RUN, YOU KNOW-- WITH MY DAUGHTER'S HEAD...
.....
NOW DO YOU SEE !?
ZAPAN IS MY PREY !

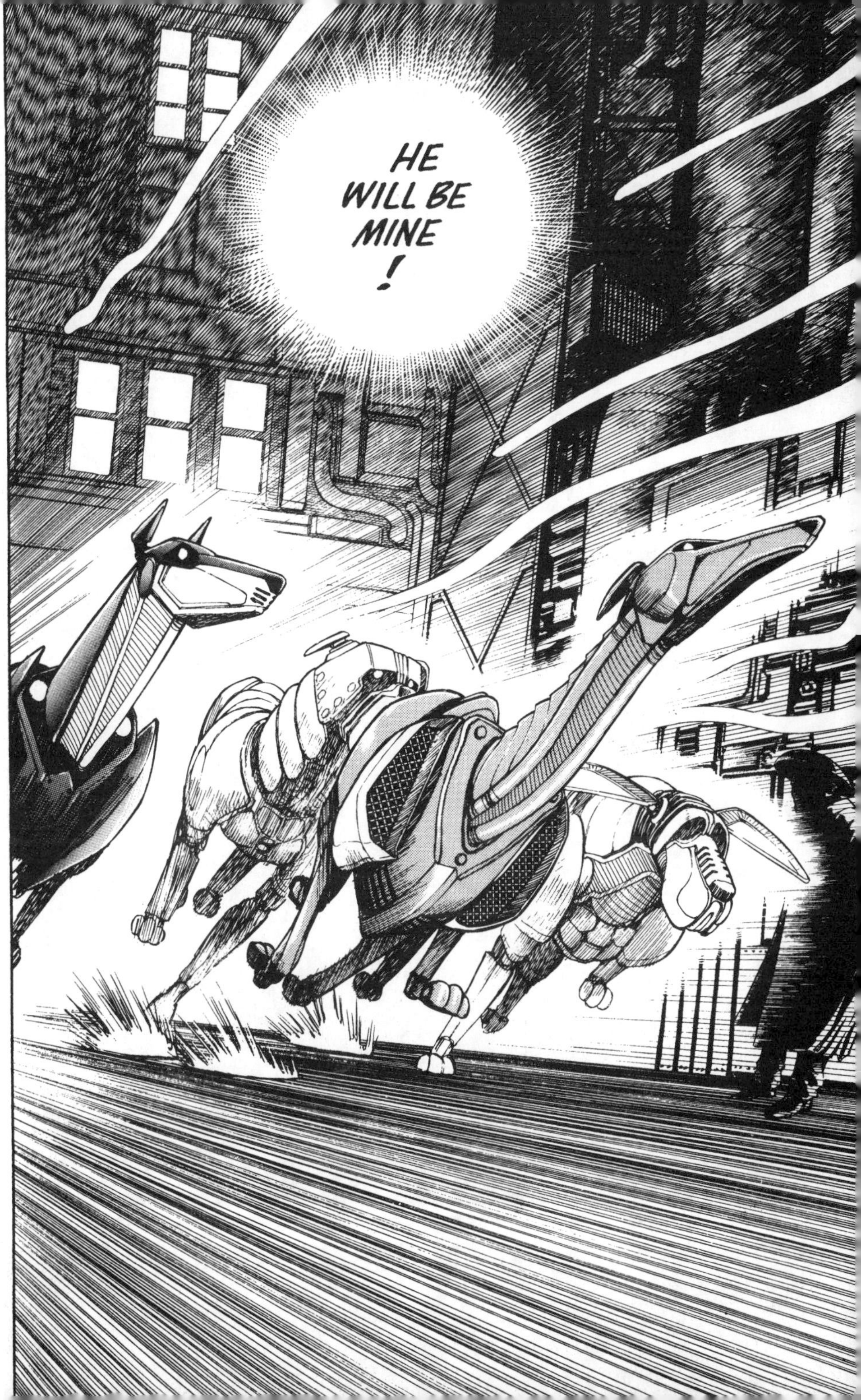
HE WILL BE MINE !

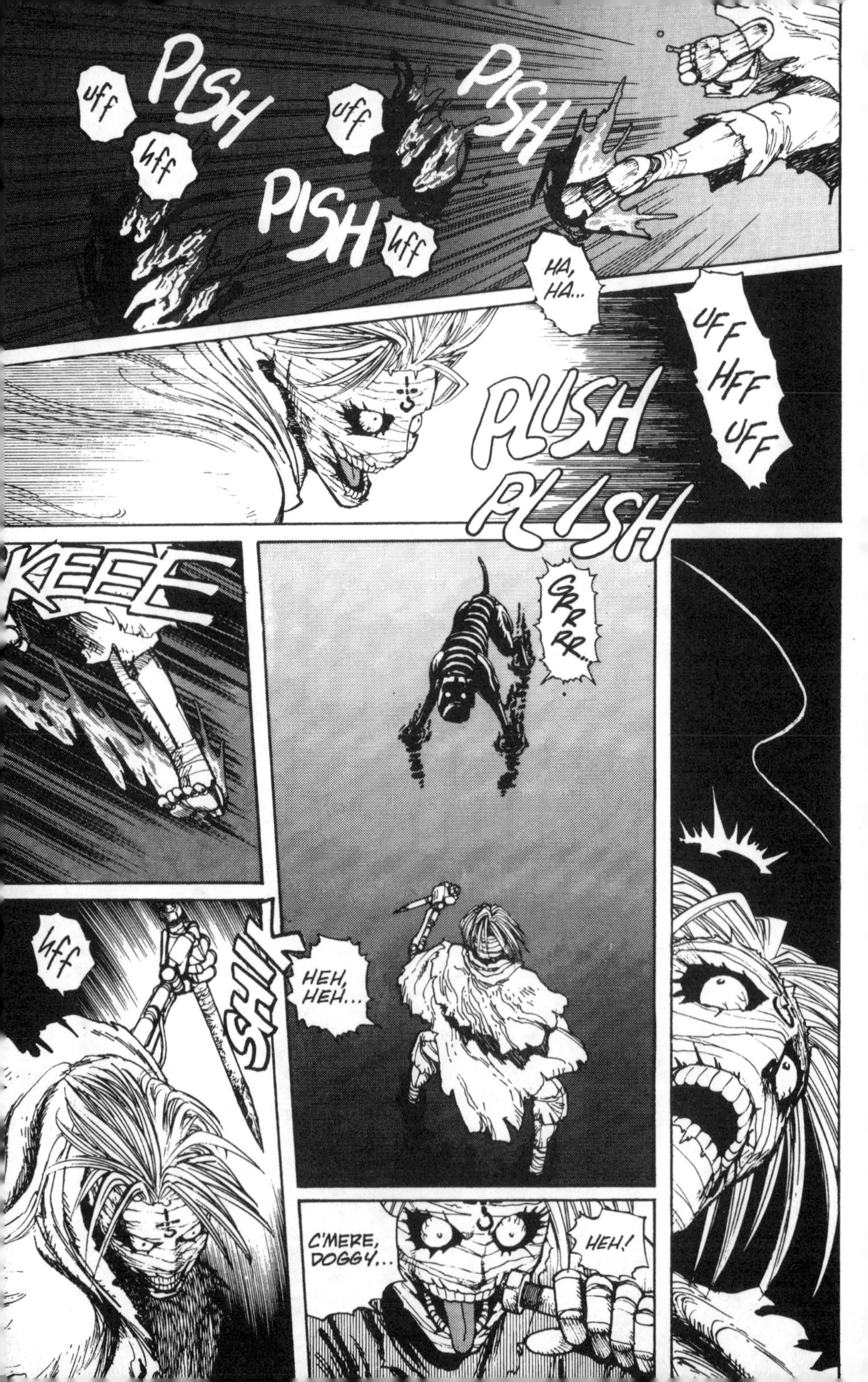
PISH
uff
hff
PISH
uff
PISH
hff
HA, HA...
PLUSH
PLISH
UFF HFF UFF
KEEEE
hff
SHIK
GRRRRR...
HEH, HEH...
C'MERE, DOGGY...
HEH!

IT'S BEEN A LONG TIME... ZAPAN.

YAAAH!

SPLOOSH

A. ALITA!

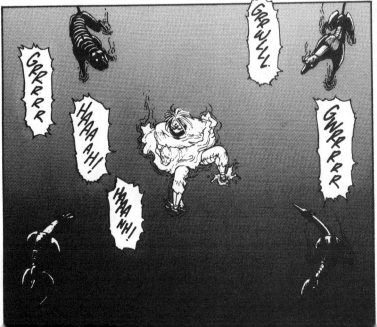

GRRRR

HAAAH!

HAAA NH!

GRRWLL.

GWRRRRR

ZAPAN! NOW I'VE GOT YOU...

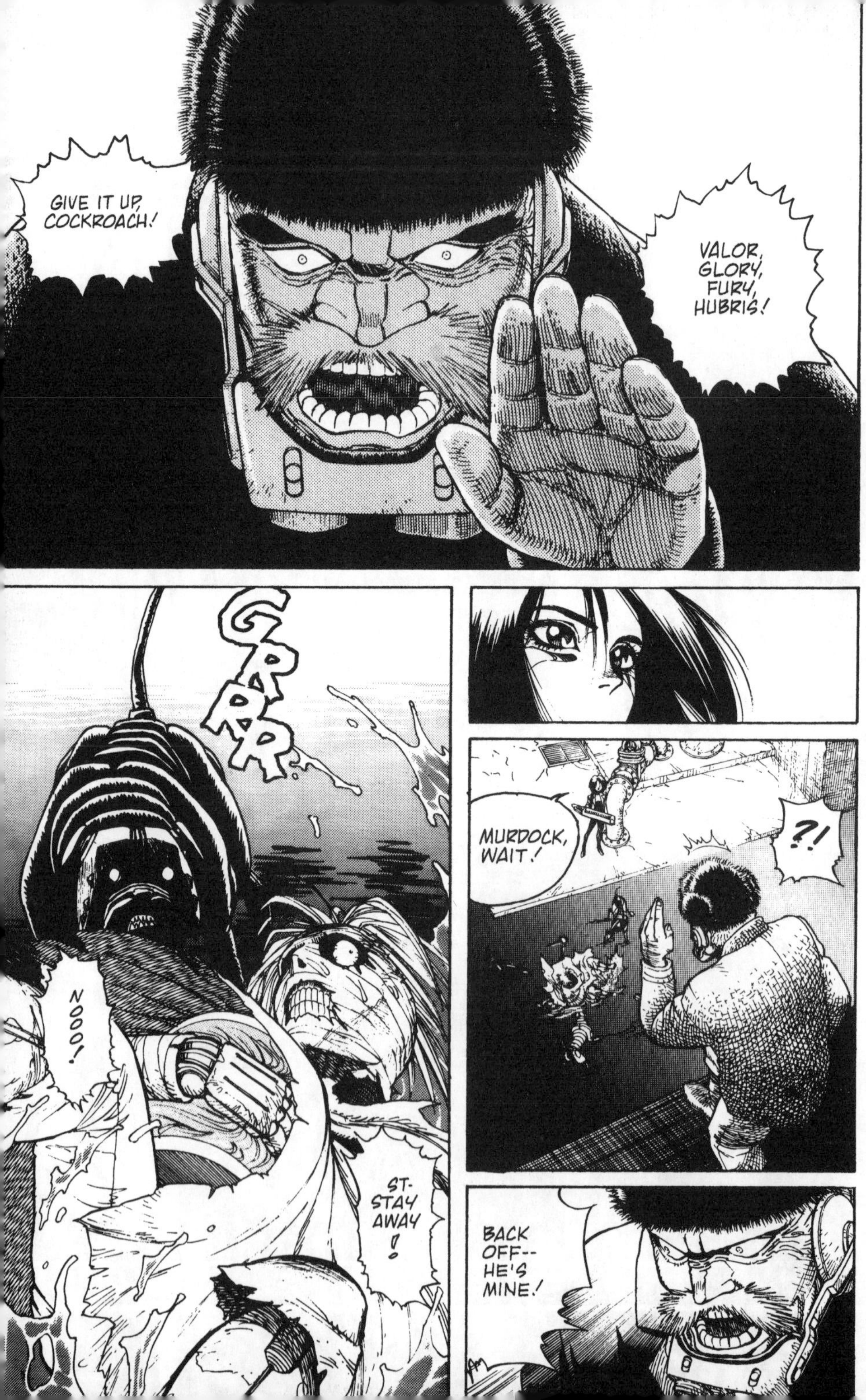
GIVE IT UP, COCKROACH!
VALOR, GLORY, FURY, HUBRIS!
GRRRR
NOOO!
ST-STAY AWAY!
MURDOCK, WAIT!
?!
BACK OFF-- HE'S MINE!

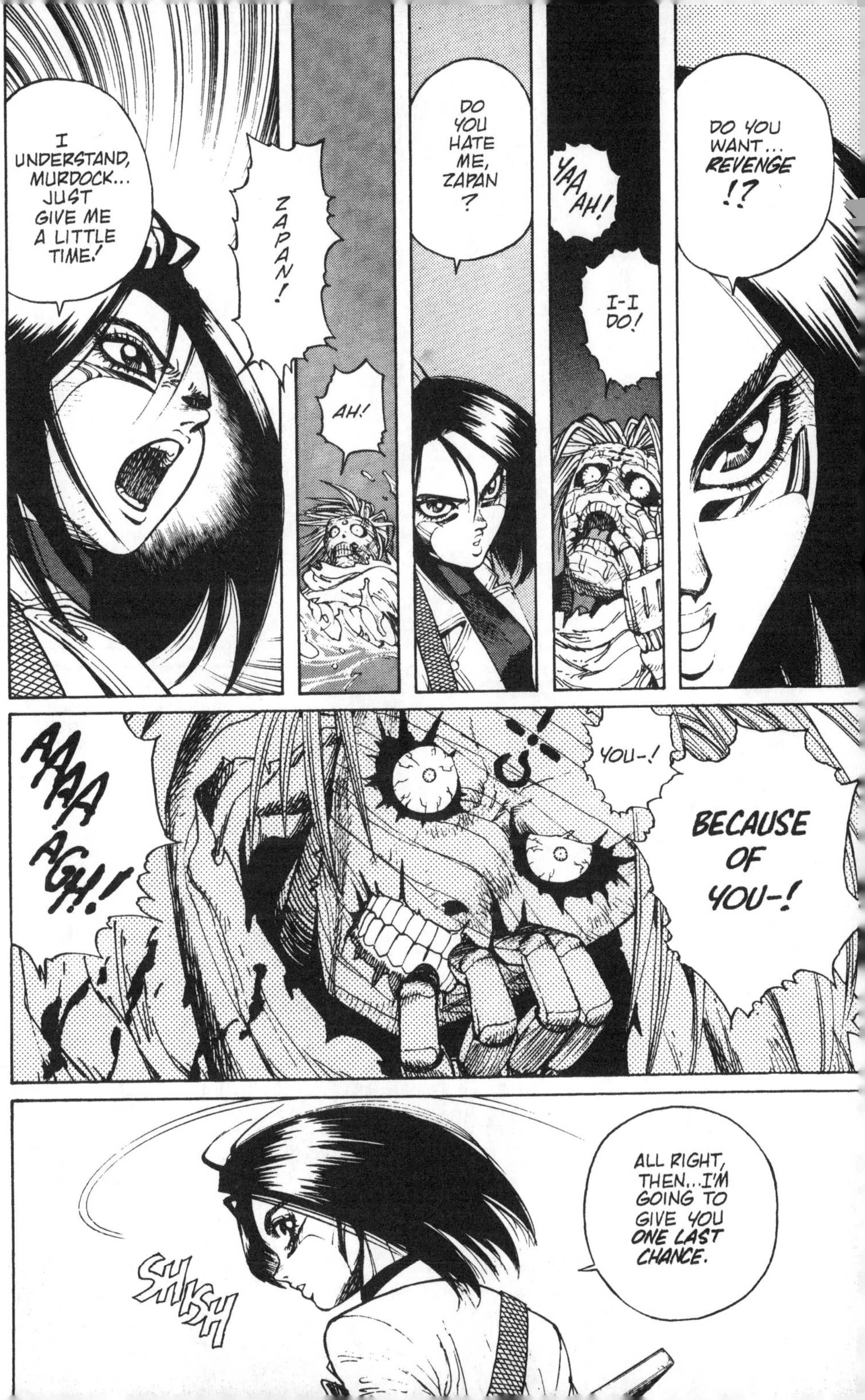
I UNDERSTAND, MURDOCK... JUST GIVE ME A LITTLE TIME!
ZAPAN!
AH!
DO YOU HATE ME, ZAPAN?
YAAAH!
I-I DO!
DO YOU WANT... REVENGE!?
AAAAAAGH!
YOU-!
BECAUSE OF YOU-!
SHHSH
ALL RIGHT, THEN...I'M GOING TO GIVE YOU ONE LAST CHANCE.

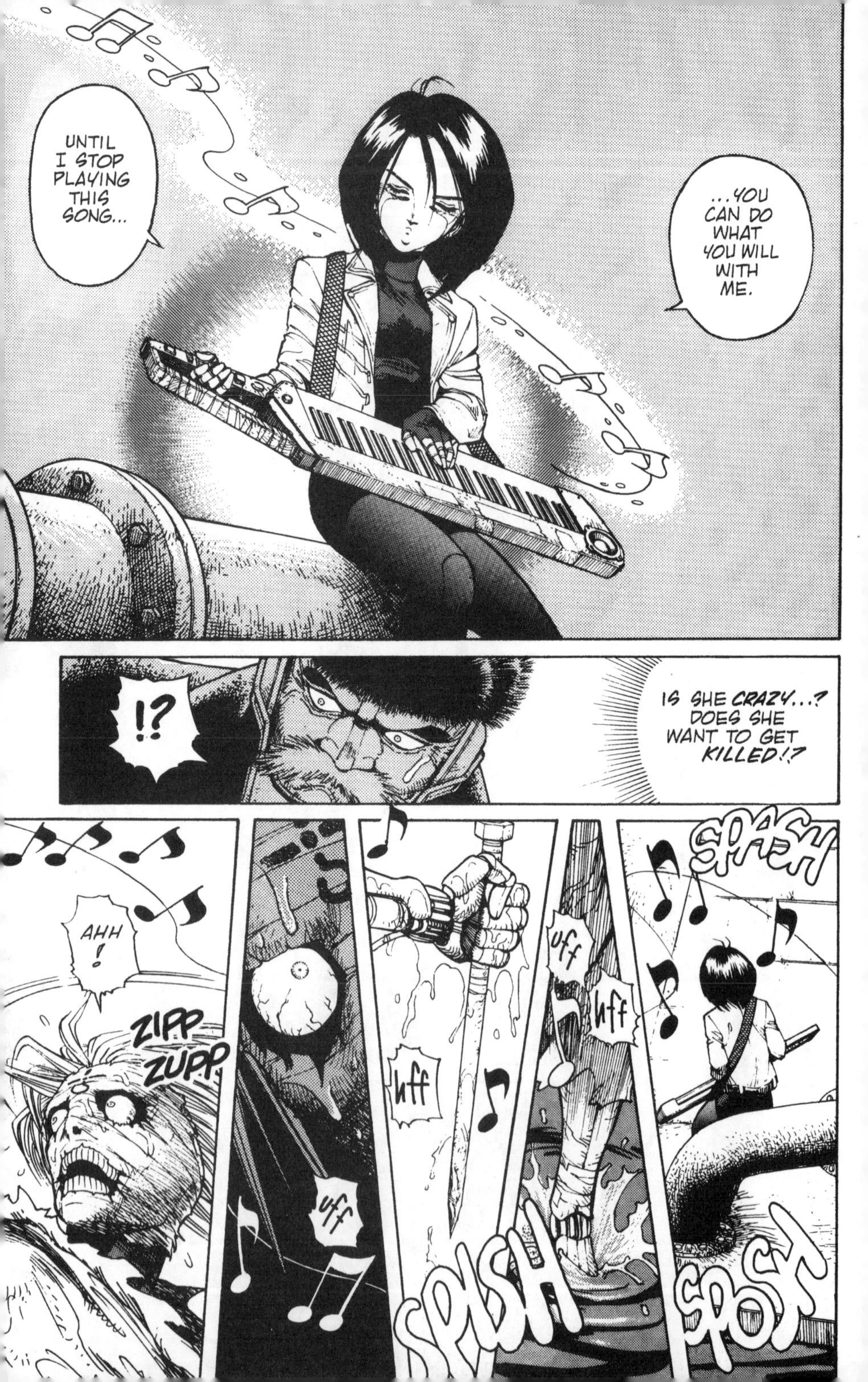
UNTIL I STOP PLAYING THIS SONG...
...YOU CAN DO WHAT YOU WILL WITH ME.
!?
IS SHE CRAZY...? DOES SHE WANT TO GET KILLED!?
AHH!
ZIPP
ZUPP
uff
uff
uff
uff
uff
SPISH
SPASH
SPOSH

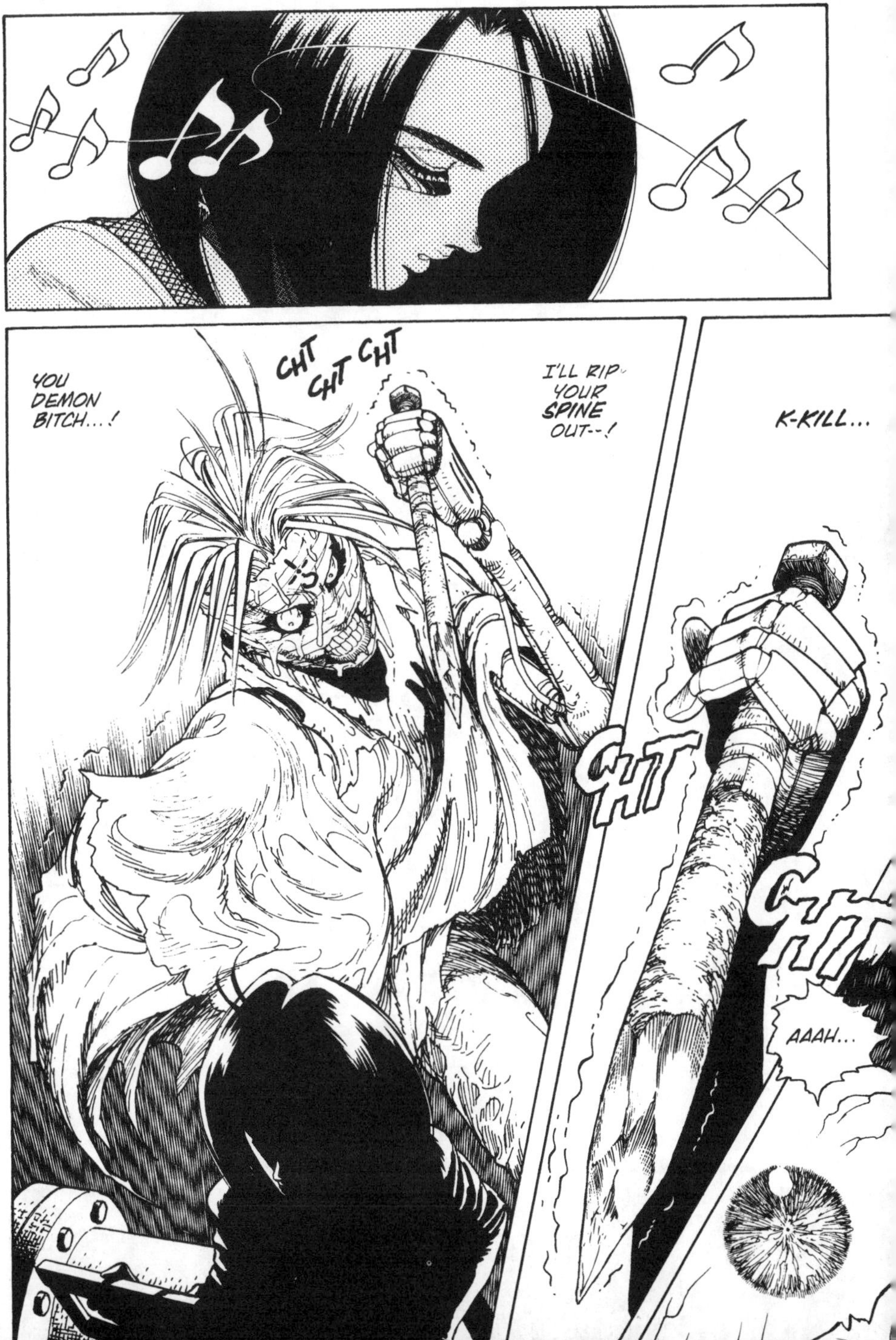
YOU DEMON BITCH...!
CHT CHT CHT
I'LL RIP YOUR SPINE OUT--!
K-KILL...
CHT
AAAH...

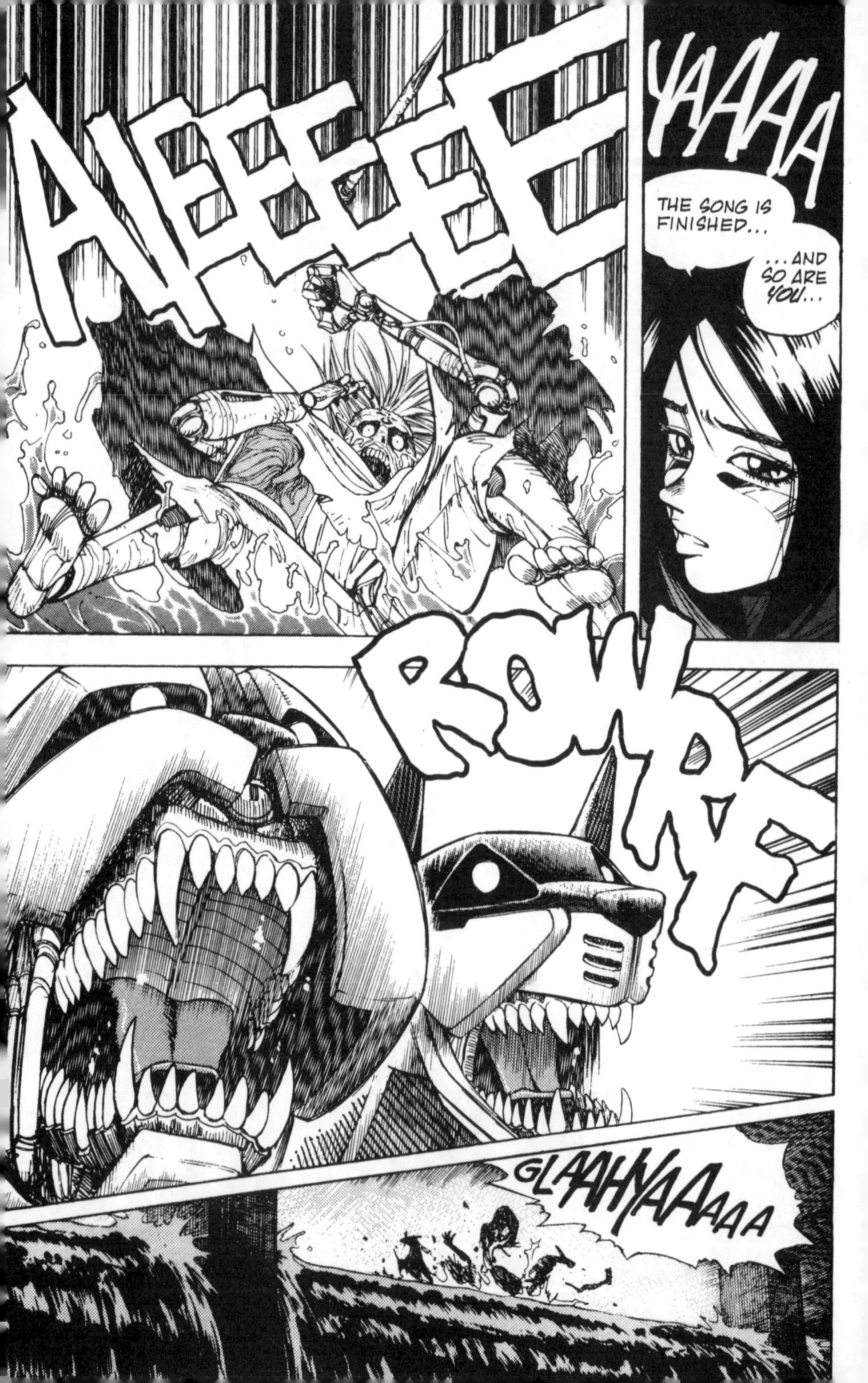
AIEEEEEE
YAAAAA
THE SONG IS FINISHED...
...AND SO ARE YOU...
BOWRF
GLAAHYAAAAAA

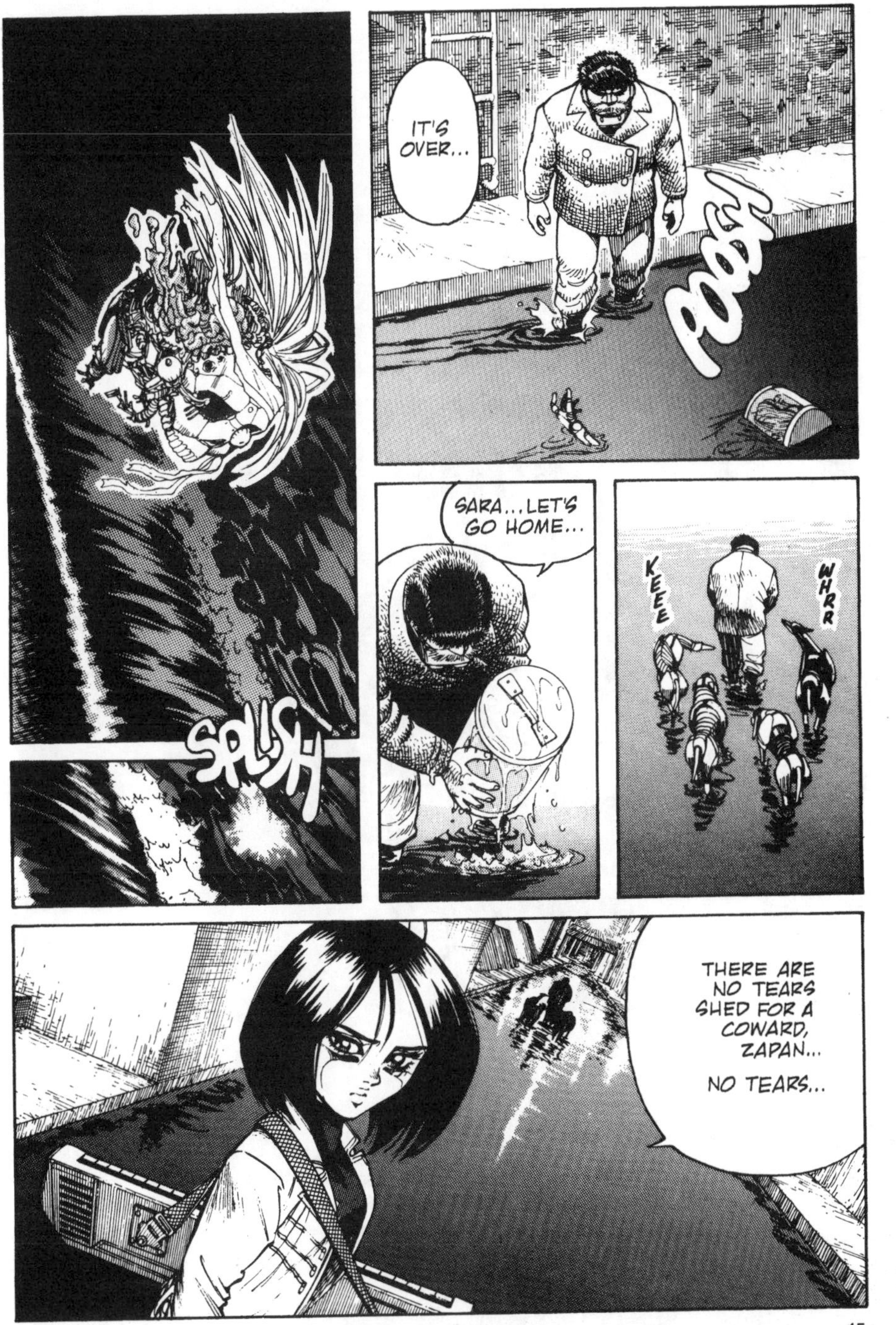
SPLISH
IT'S OVER...
POOSH
SARA... LET'S GO HOME...
KEEE
WHRR
THERE ARE NO TEARS SHED FOR A COWARD, ZAPAN...
NO TEARS...

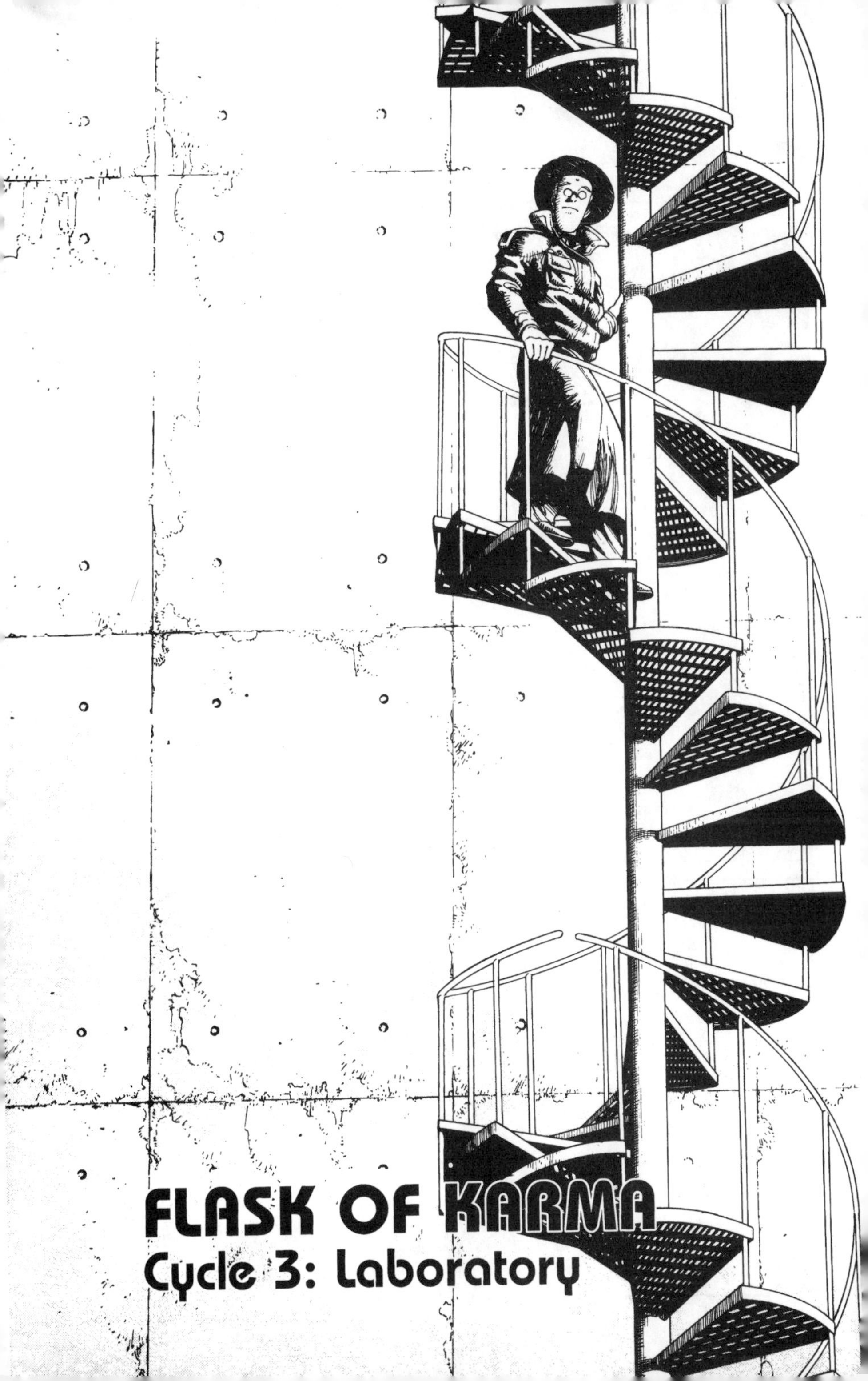
FLASK OF KARMA
Cycle 3: Laboratory

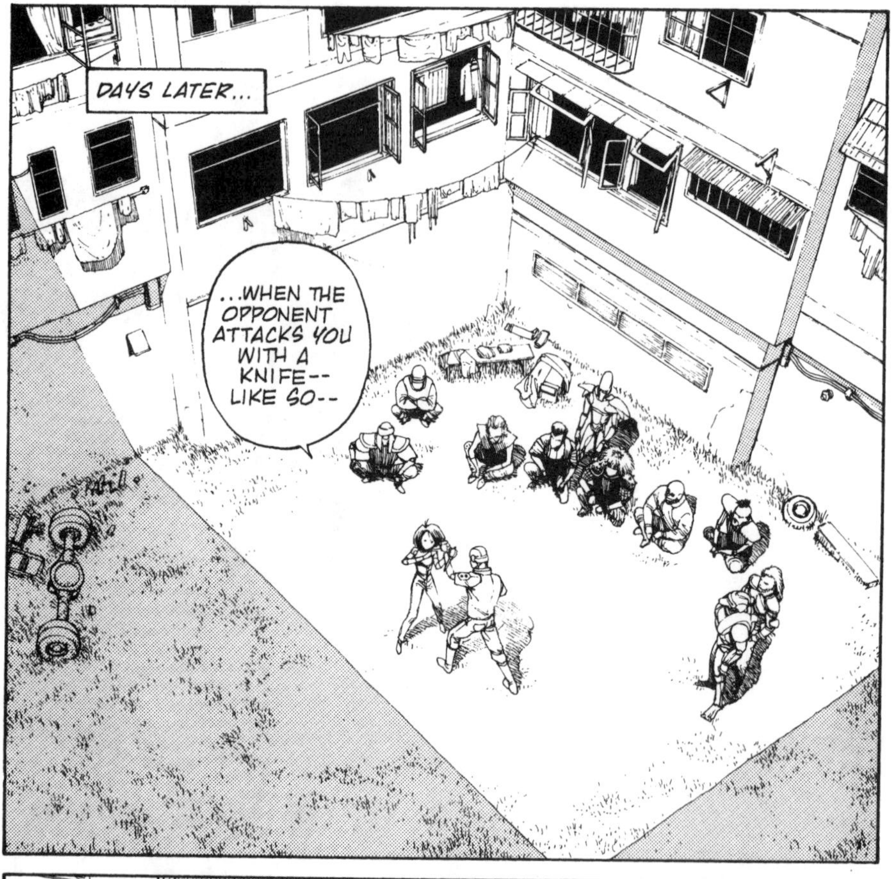
DAYS LATER...
...WHEN THE OPPONENT ATTACKS YOU WITH A KNIFE--LIKE SO--

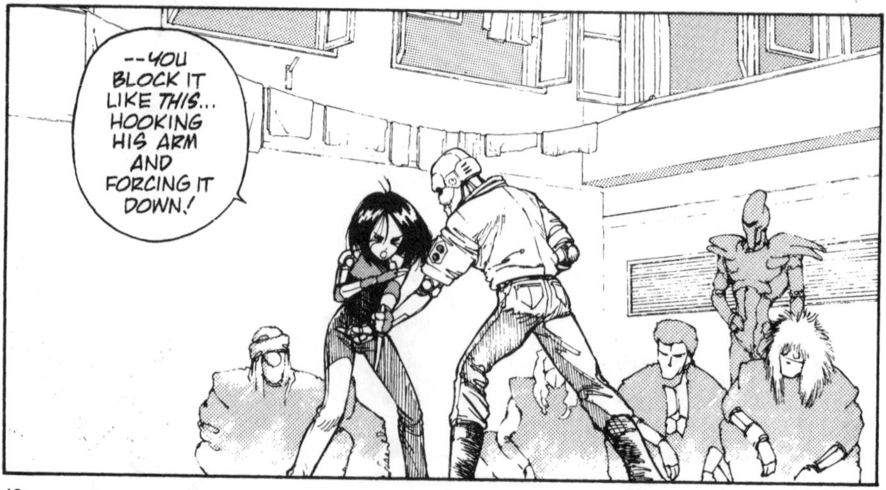
--YOU BLOCK IT LIKE THIS... HOOKING HIS ARM AND FORCING IT DOWN!

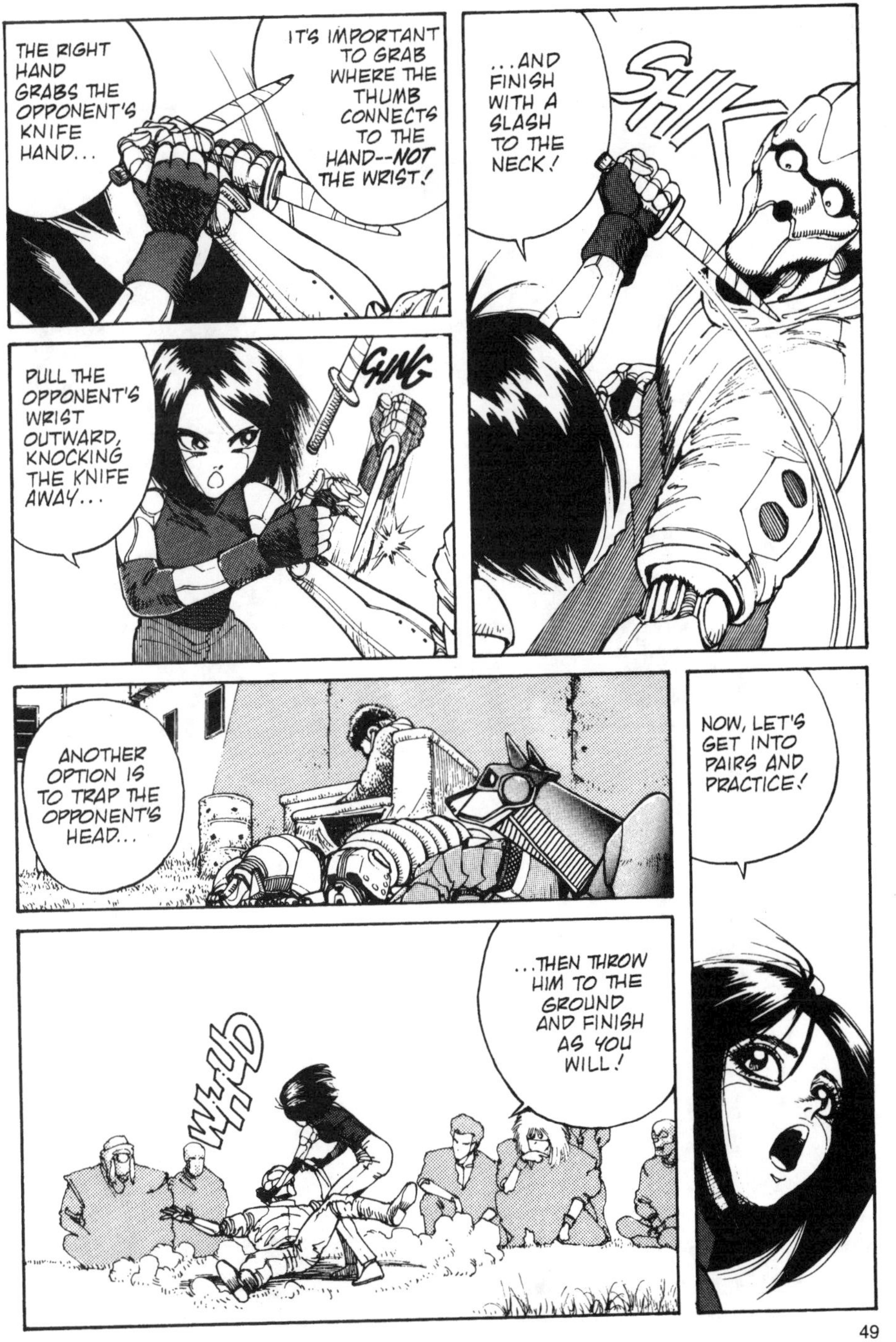
THE RIGHT HAND GRABS THE OPPONENT'S KNIFE HAND...
IT'S IMPORTANT TO GRAB WHERE THE THUMB CONNECTS TO THE HAND--NOT THE WRIST!
PULL THE OPPONENT'S WRIST OUTWARD, KNOCKING THE KNIFE AWAY...
GING
...AND FINISH WITH A SLASH TO THE NECK!
SHK
ANOTHER OPTION IS TO TRAP THE OPPONENT'S HEAD...
...THEN THROW HIM TO THE GROUND AND FINISH AS YOU WILL!
WHUD
NOW, LET'S GET INTO PAIRS AND PRACTICE!

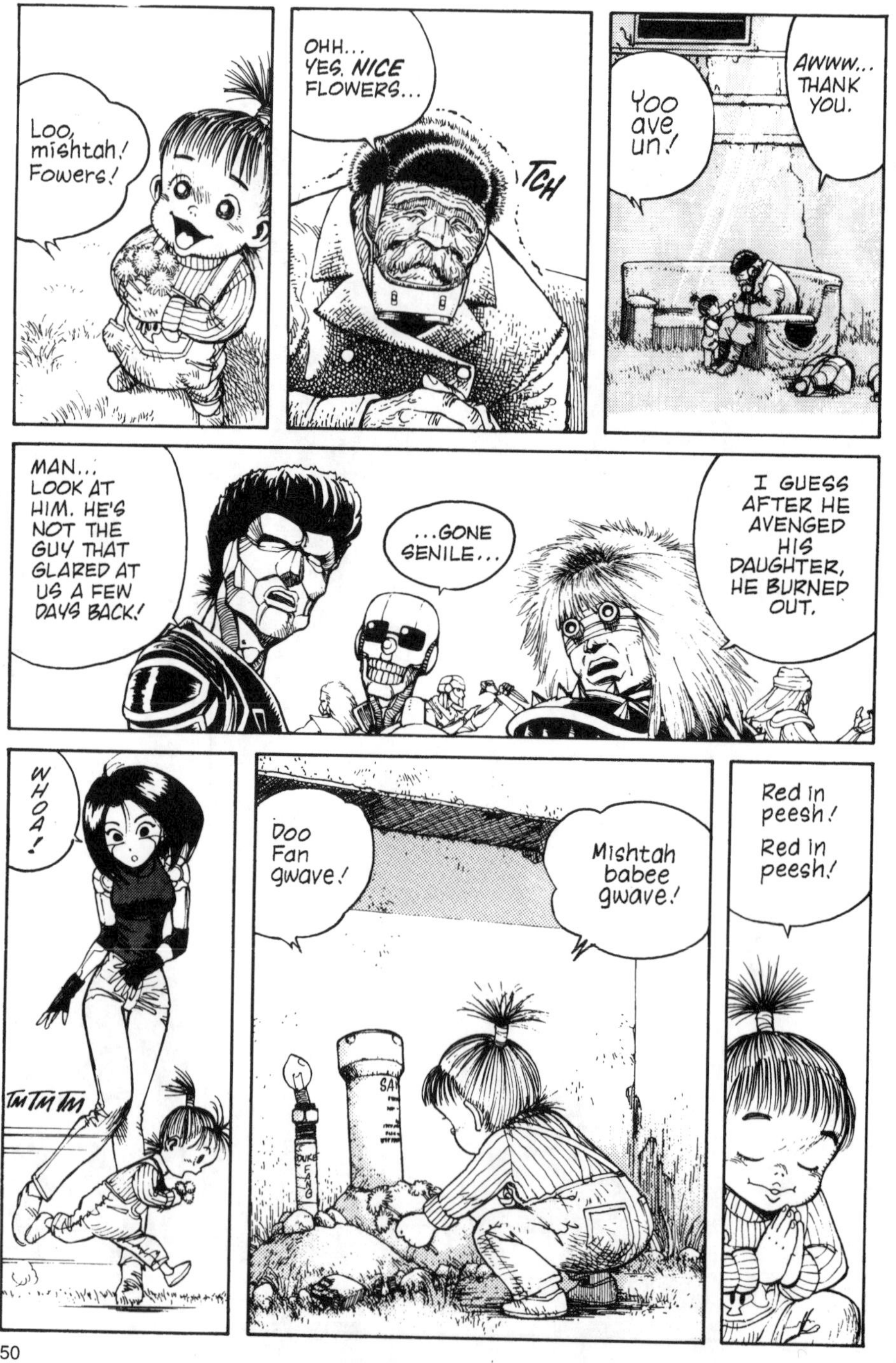
Loo, mishtah! Fowers!
OHH... YES, NICE FLOWERS...
TCH
Yoo ave un!
AWWW... THANK YOU.
MAN... LOOK AT HIM. HE'S NOT THE GUY THAT GLARED AT US A FEW DAYS BACK!
...GONE SENILE...
I GUESS AFTER HE AVENGED HIS DAUGHTER, HE BURNED OUT.
WHOA!
TM TM TM
Doo Fan gwave!
Mishtah babee gwave!
DUKE FANG
Red in peesh!
Red in peesh!

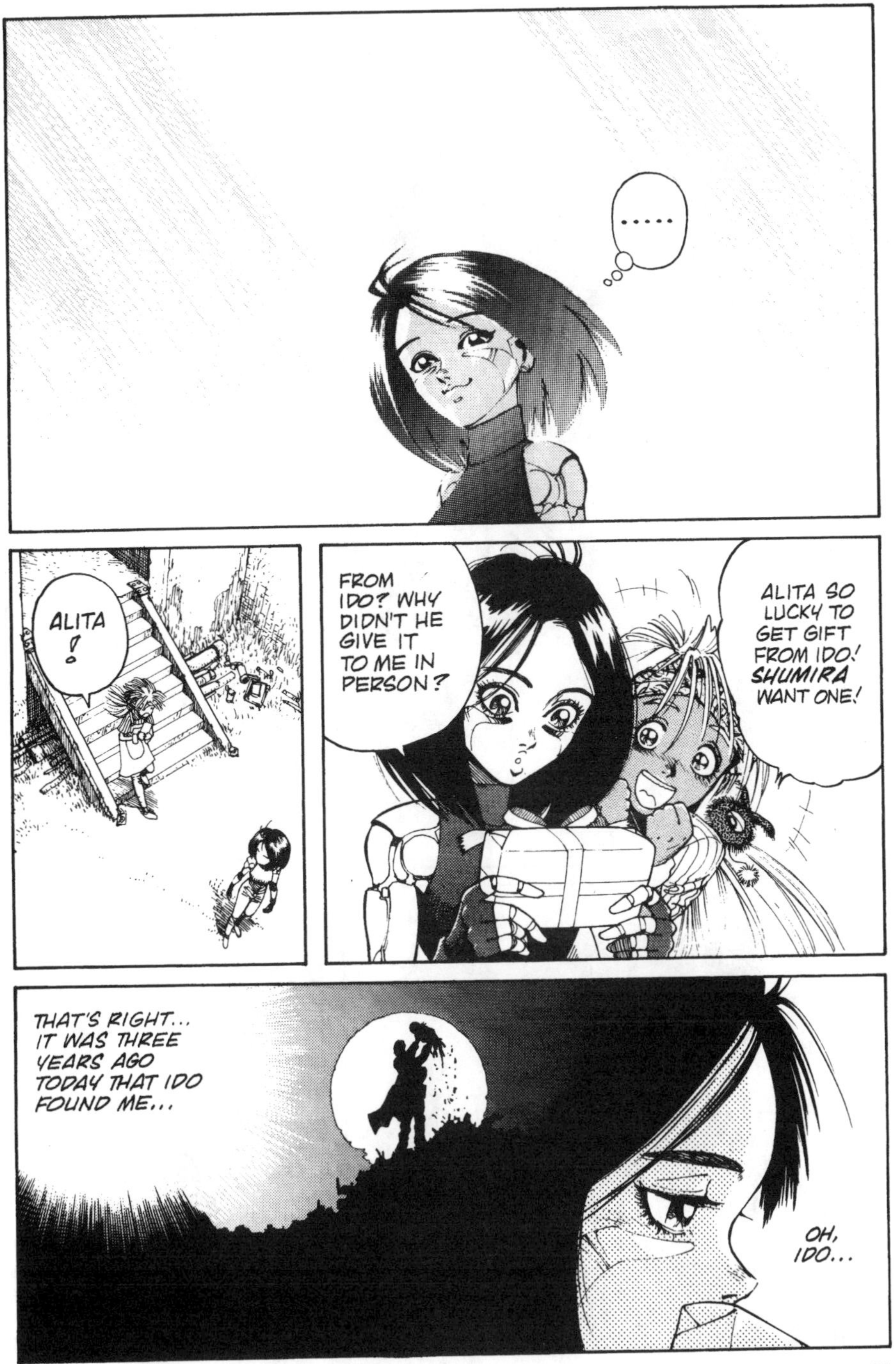

......
ALITA!
FROM IDO? WHY DIDN'T HE GIVE IT TO ME IN PERSON?
ALITA SO LUCKY TO GET GIFT FROM IDO! SHUMIRA WANT ONE!
THAT'S RIGHT... IT WAS THREE YEARS AGO TODAY THAT IDO FOUND ME...
OH, IDO...

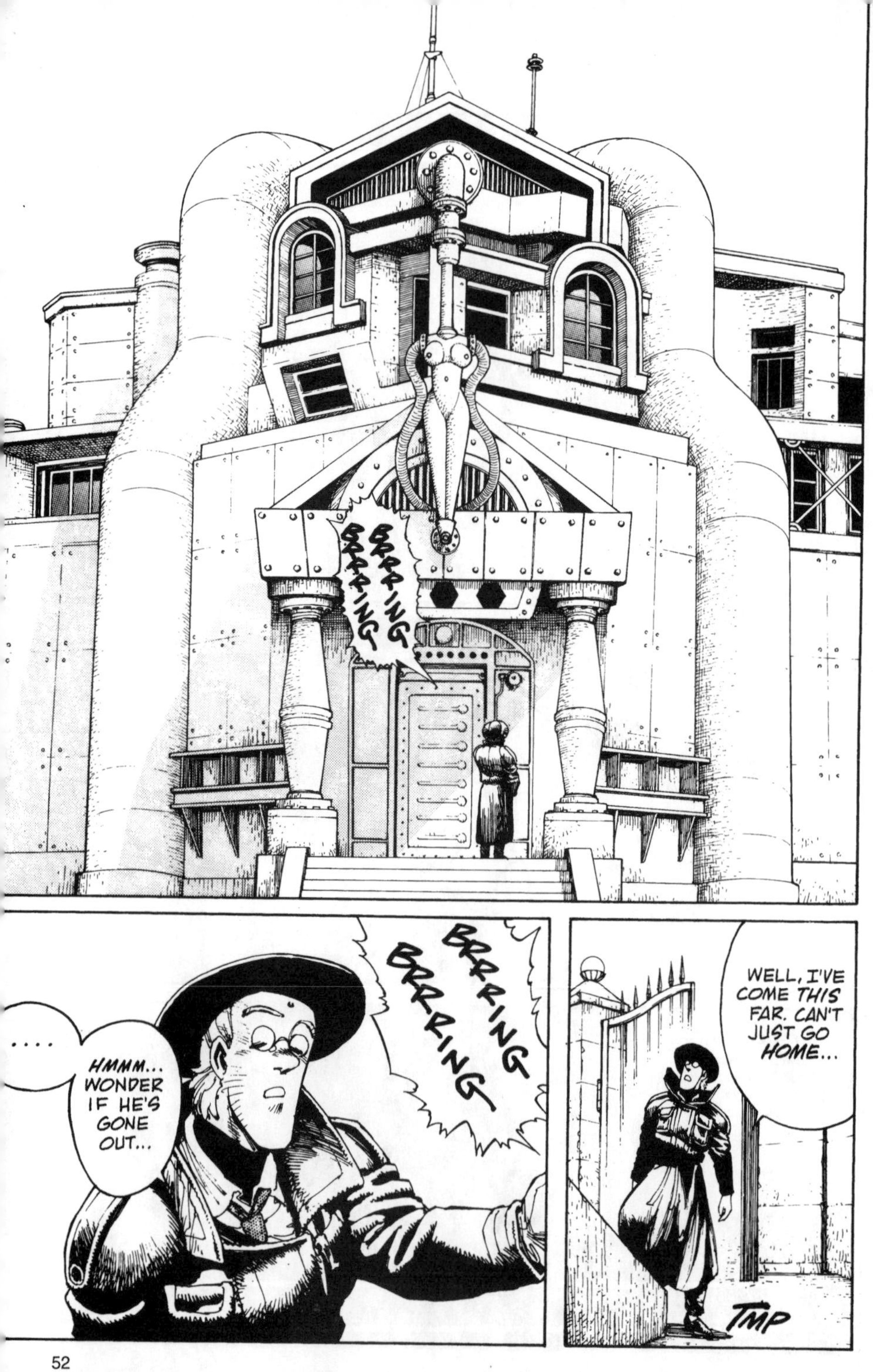

BRRRING BRRRING
....
HMMM... WONDER IF HE'S GONE OUT...
BRRRING BRRRING
WELL, I'VE COME THIS FAR. CAN'T JUST GO HOME...
TMP

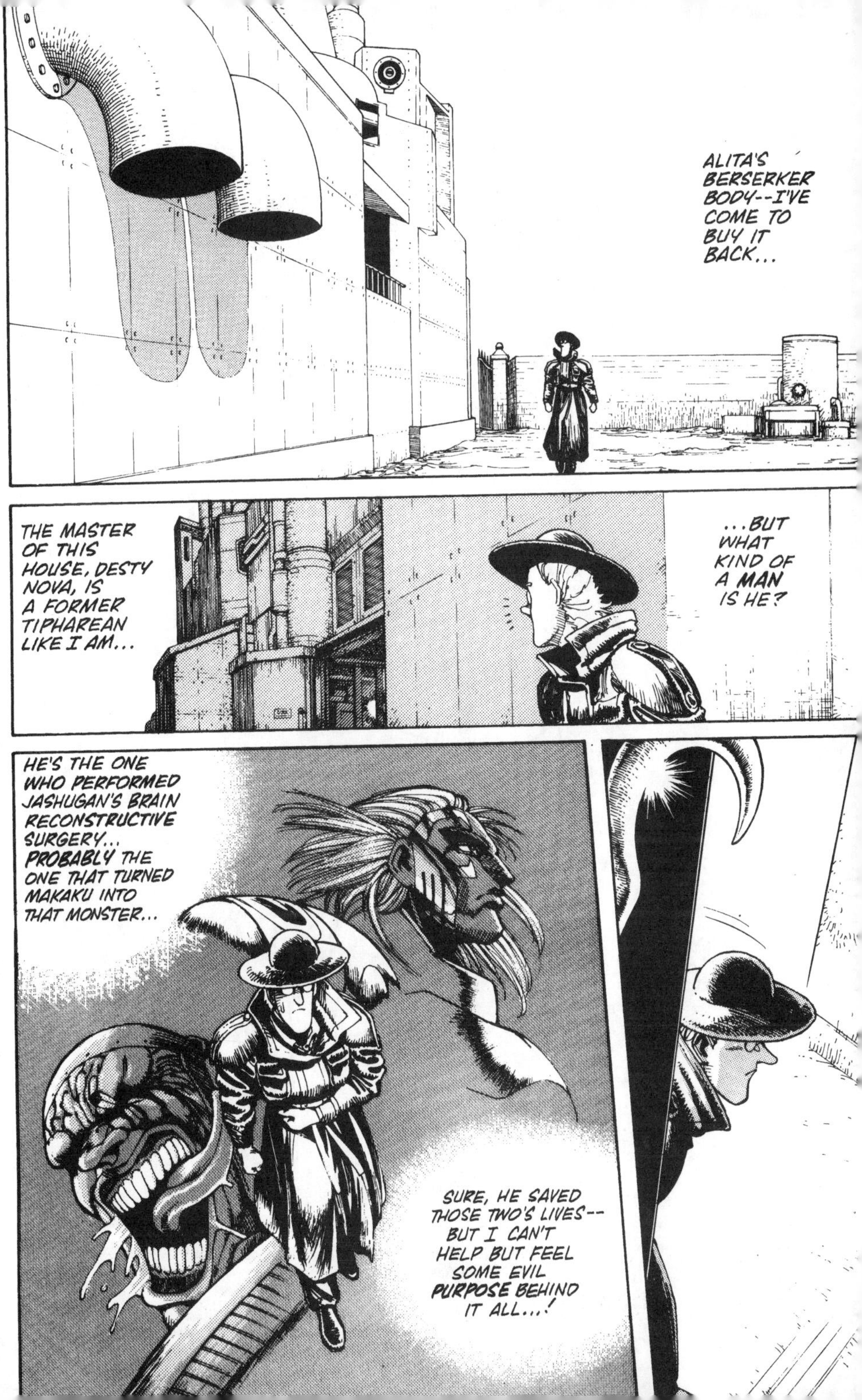
ALITA'S BERSERKER BODY--I'VE COME TO BUY IT BACK...
THE MASTER OF THIS HOUSE, DESTY NOVA, IS A FORMER TIPHAREAN LIKE I AM...
...BUT WHAT KIND OF A MAN IS HE?
HE'S THE ONE WHO PERFORMED JASHUGAN'S BRAIN RECONSTRUCTIVE SURGERY... PROBABLY THE ONE THAT TURNED MAKAKU INTO THAT MONSTER...
SURE, HE SAVED THOSE TWO'S LIVES--BUT I CAN'T HELP BUT FEEL SOME EVIL PURPOSE BEHIND IT ALL...!

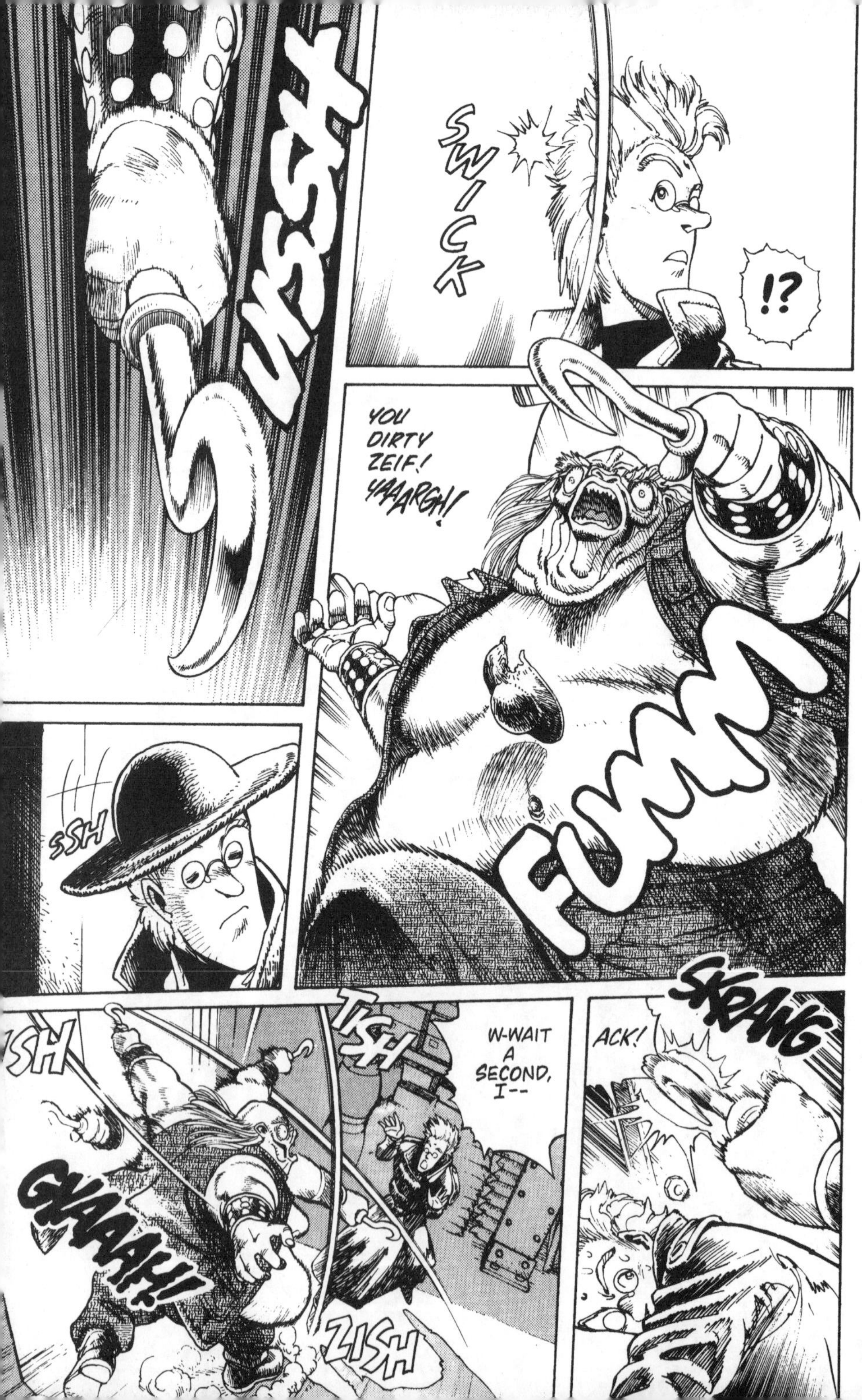

SWICK
!?
YOU DIRTY ZEIF! YAAARGH!
FUMM
SSH
TISH
GWAAAH!
ZISH
W-WAIT A SECOND, I--
SKRANG
ACK!

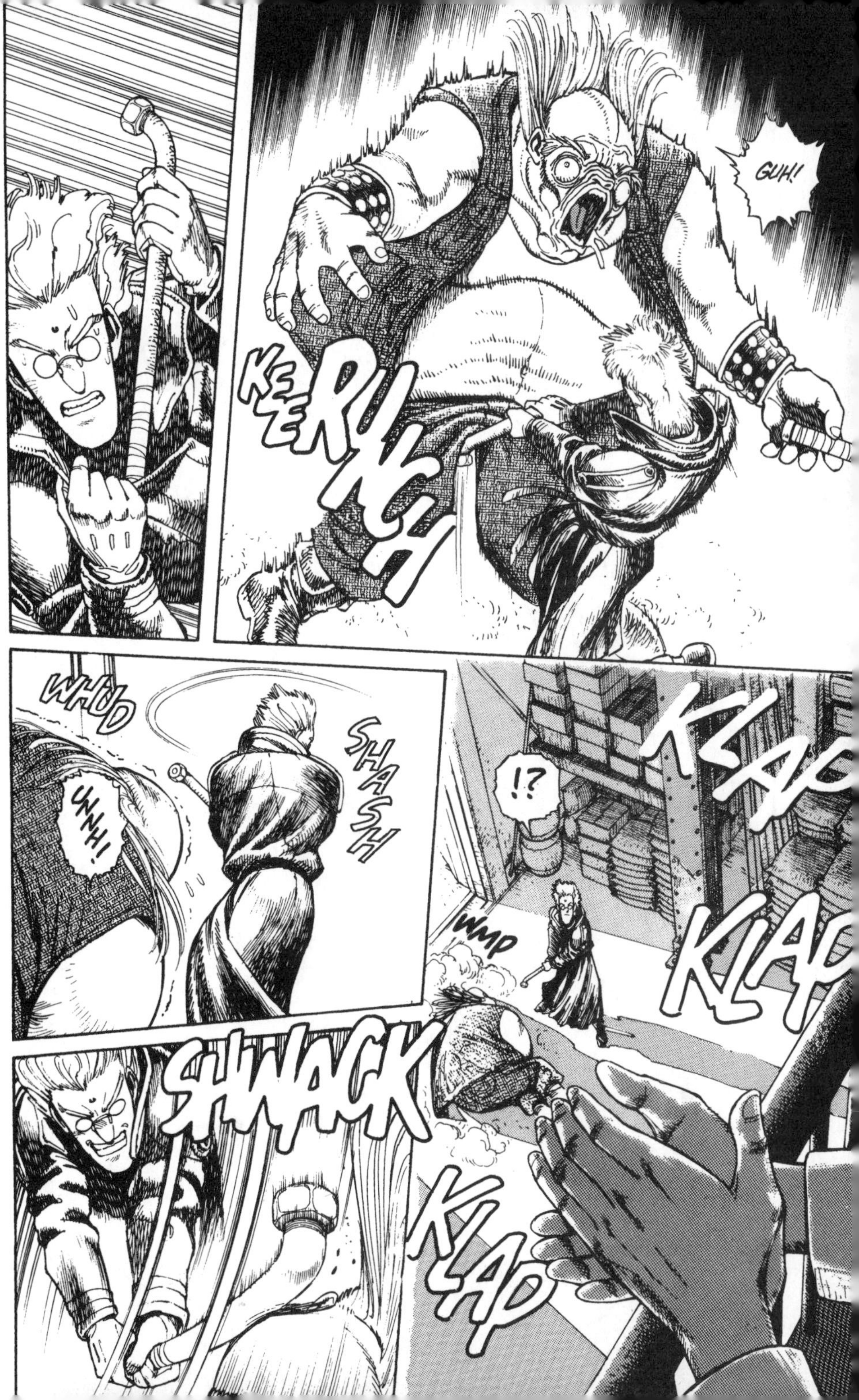
KERRUNCH
GUH!
WHUD
UNNH!
SHASH
!?
KLAP
KLAP
WMP
SHWACK
KLAP

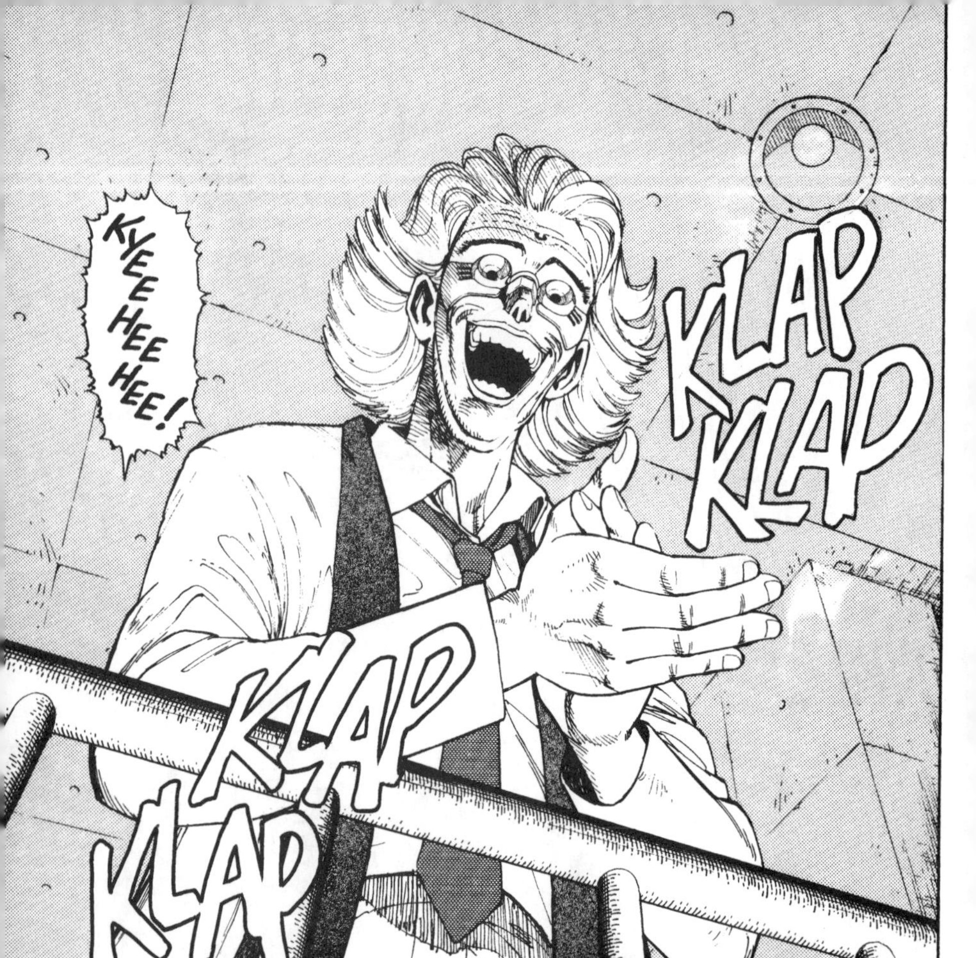
KYEEE HEE HEE!
KLAP KLAP
KLAP KLAP

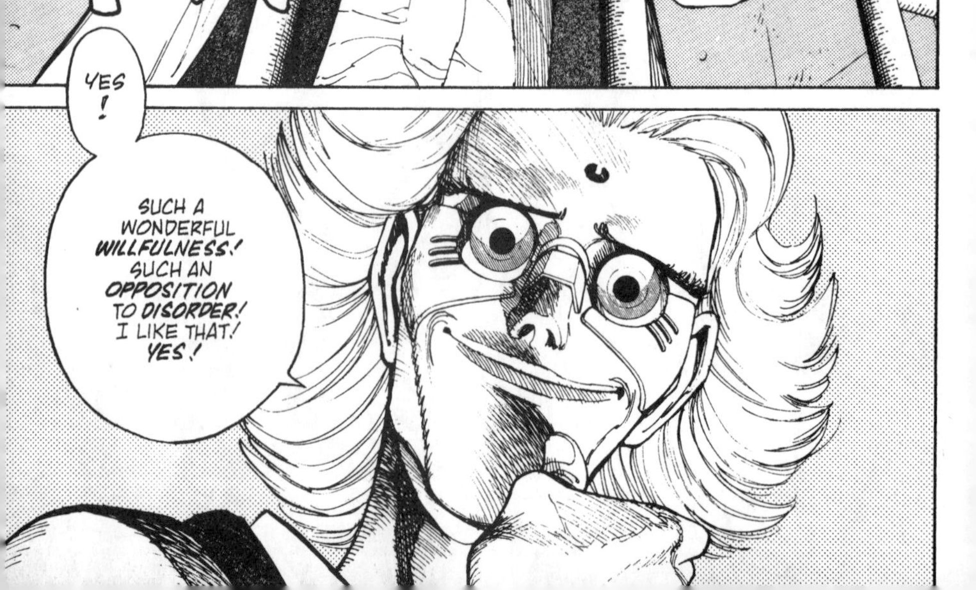
YES!
SUCH A WONDERFUL WILLFULNESS! SUCH AN OPPOSITION TO DISORDER! I LIKE THAT! YES!

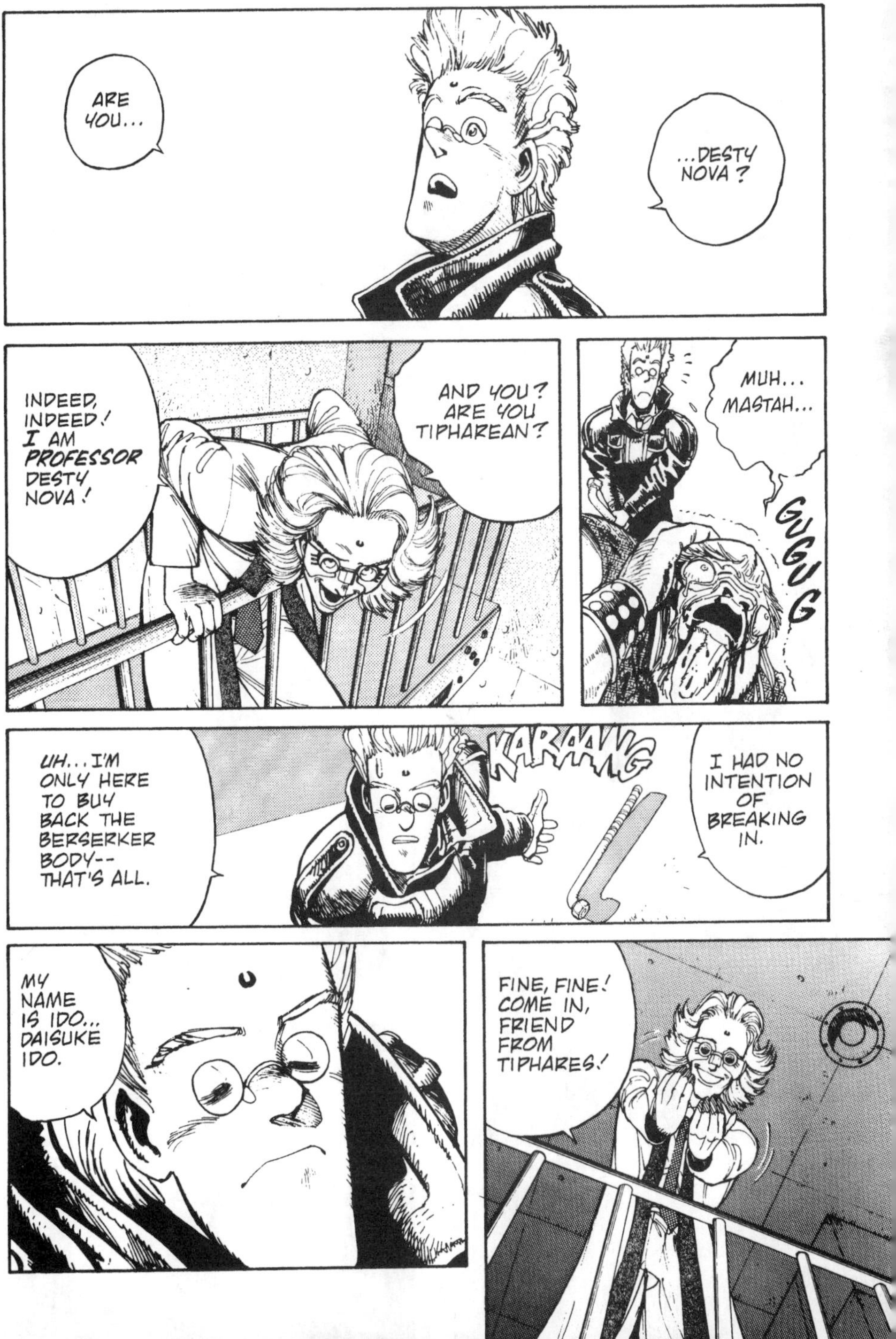
ARE YOU...
...DESTY NOVA?
INDEED, INDEED! I AM *PROFESSOR* DESTY NOVA!
AND YOU? ARE YOU TIPHAREAN?
MUH... MASTAH...
GUGUGG
UH... I'M ONLY HERE TO BUY BACK THE BERSERKER BODY-- THAT'S ALL.
KARAAANG
I HAD NO INTENTION OF BREAKING IN.
MY NAME IS IDO... DAISUKE IDO.
FINE, FINE! COME IN, FRIEND FROM TIPHARES!

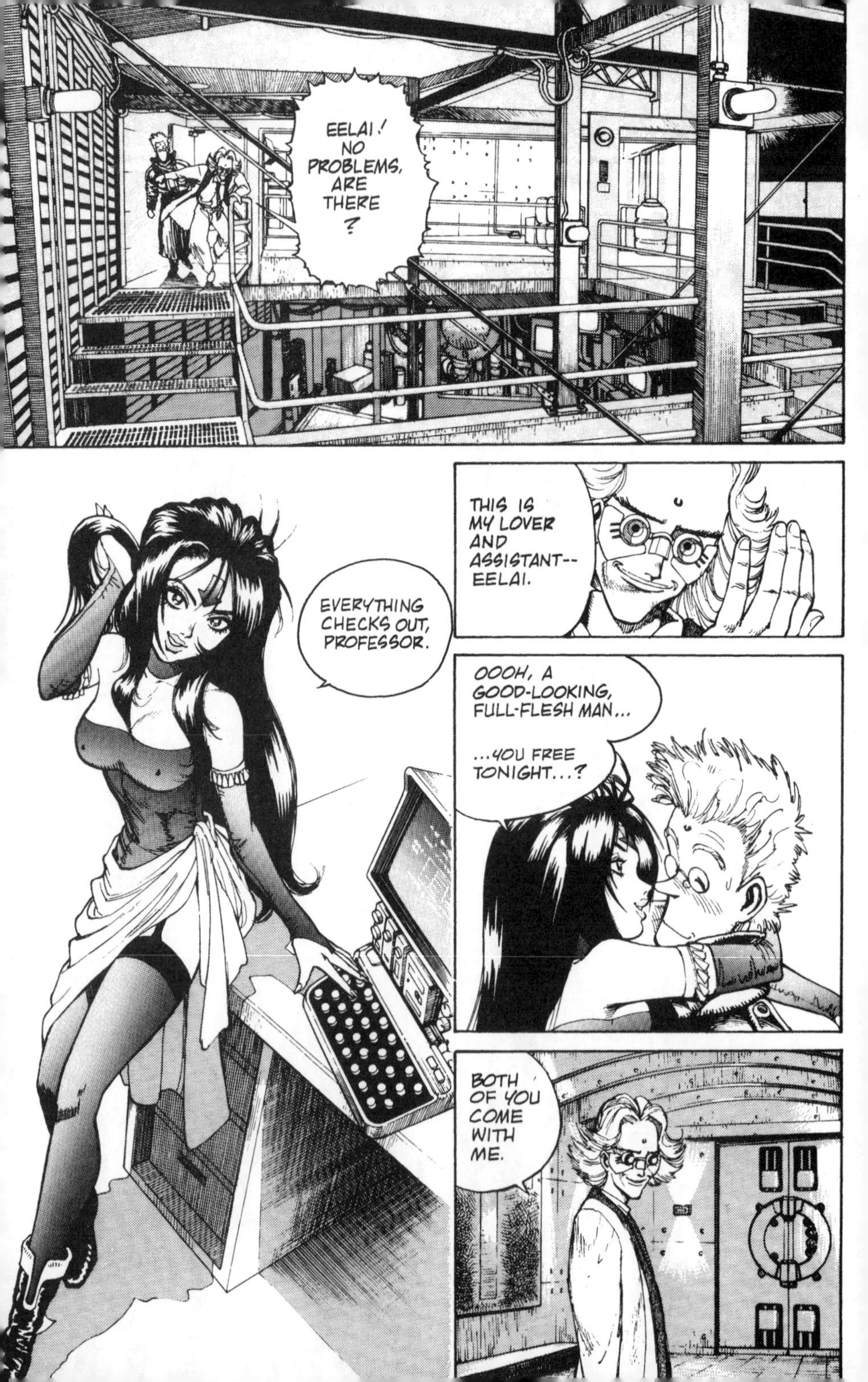
EELAI! NO PROBLEMS, ARE THERE?
EVERYTHING CHECKS OUT, PROFESSOR.
THIS IS MY LOVER AND ASSISTANT--EELAI.
OOOH, A GOOD-LOOKING, FULL-FLESH MAN...
...YOU FREE TONIGHT...?
BOTH OF YOU COME WITH ME.

WOOOO

SAAAAA

WH-WHAT IS THIS!?

KYEEHEEHEE! SURPRISED? THESE ARE ALL *FAILURES*, ACTUALLY...

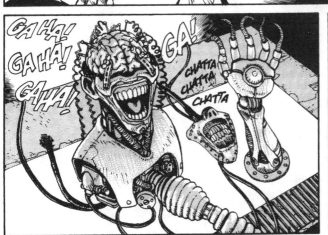

GAHA! GAHA! GAHA!

GA!

CHATTA CHATTA CHATTA

IT'S INSANE...

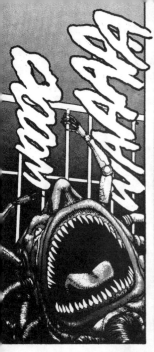

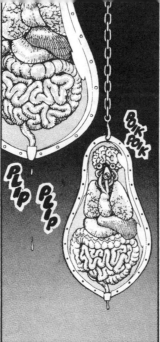

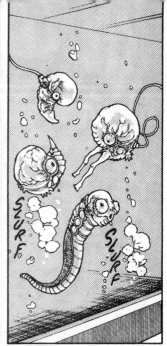

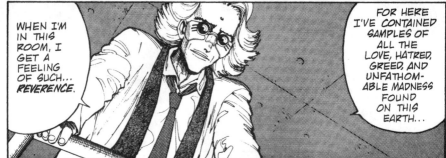

PLIP
PLIP
POIK POIK
SLURF
SLURF
WHEN I'M IN THIS ROOM, I GET A FEELING OF SUCH... REVERENCE.
FOR HERE I'VE CONTAINED SAMPLES OF ALL THE LOVE, HATRED, GREED, AND UNFATHOMABLE MADNESS FOUND ON THIS EARTH...
WHAT IS THIS?! WHAT IS THE TRUE PURPOSE OF YOUR RESEARCH, PROFESSOR NOVA!?

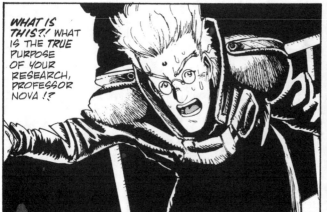

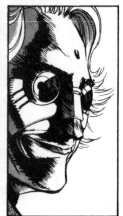

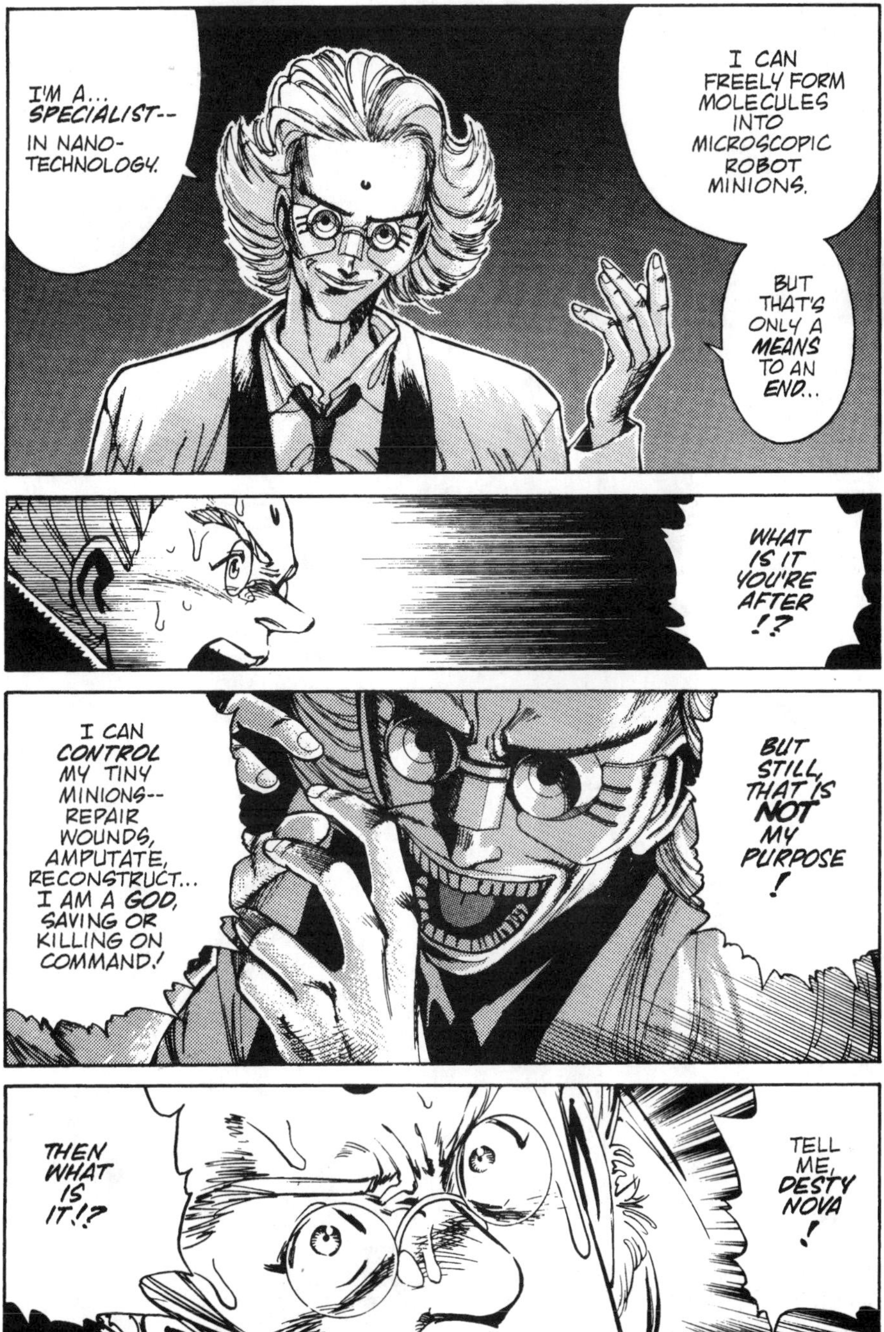
I'M A... SPECIALIST-- IN NANO-TECHNOLOGY.
I CAN FREELY FORM MOLECULES INTO MICROSCOPIC ROBOT MINIONS.
BUT THAT'S ONLY A MEANS TO AN END...
WHAT IS IT YOU'RE AFTER!?
I CAN CONTROL MY TINY MINIONS-- REPAIR WOUNDS, AMPUTATE, RECONSTRUCT... I AM A GOD, SAVING OR KILLING ON COMMAND!
BUT STILL, THAT IS NOT MY PURPOSE!
THEN WHAT IS IT!?
TELL ME, DESTY NOVA!

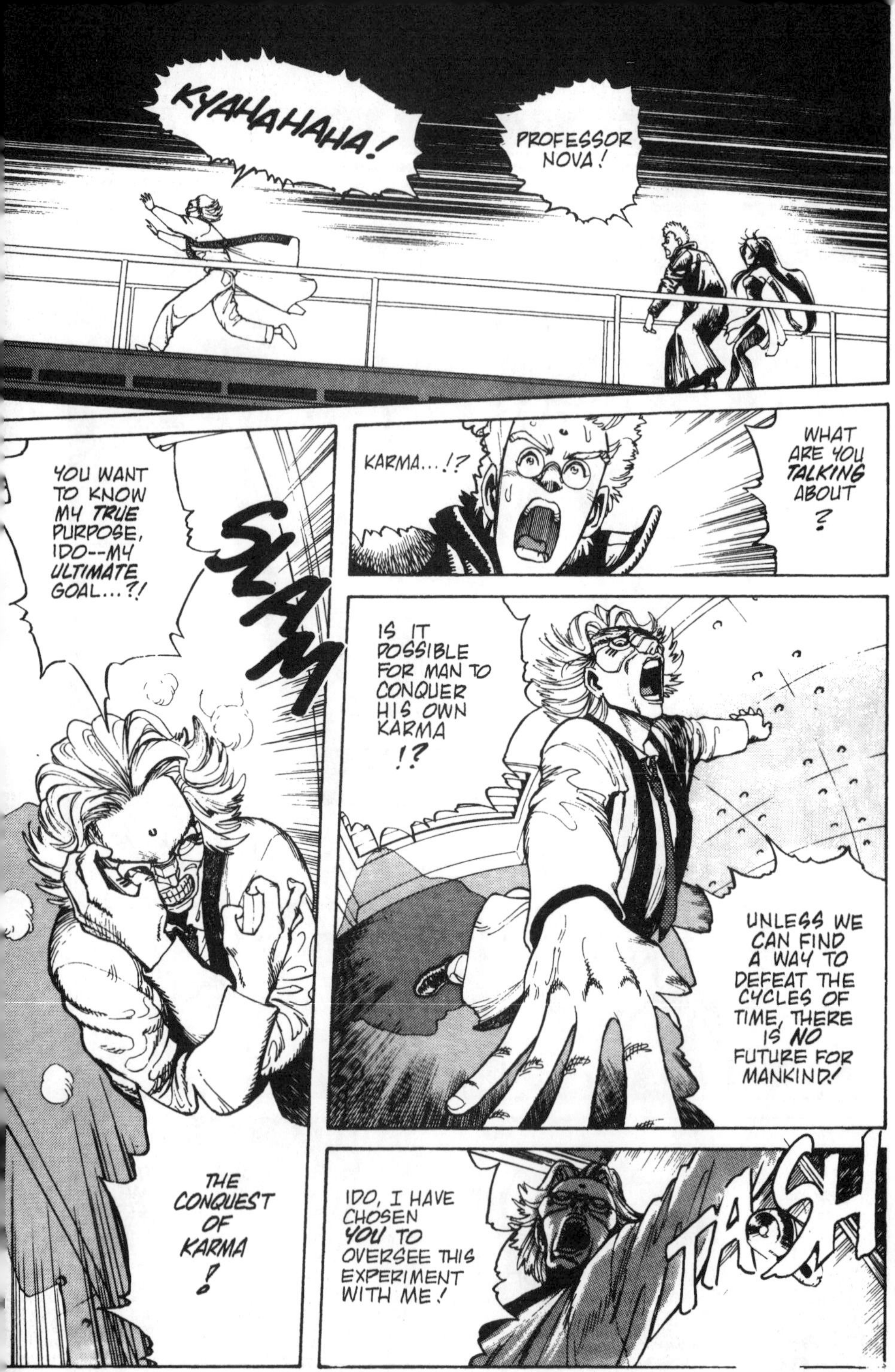

KYAHAHAHA!
PROFESSOR NOVA!
YOU WANT TO KNOW MY TRUE PURPOSE, IDO--MY ULTIMATE GOAL...?!
SLAM
THE CONQUEST OF KARMA!
KARMA...!?
WHAT ARE YOU TALKING ABOUT?
IS IT POSSIBLE FOR MAN TO CONQUER HIS OWN KARMA!?
UNLESS WE CAN FIND A WAY TO DEFEAT THE CYCLES OF TIME, THERE IS NO FUTURE FOR MANKIND!
IDO, I HAVE CHOSEN YOU TO OVERSEE THIS EXPERIMENT WITH ME!
TASH

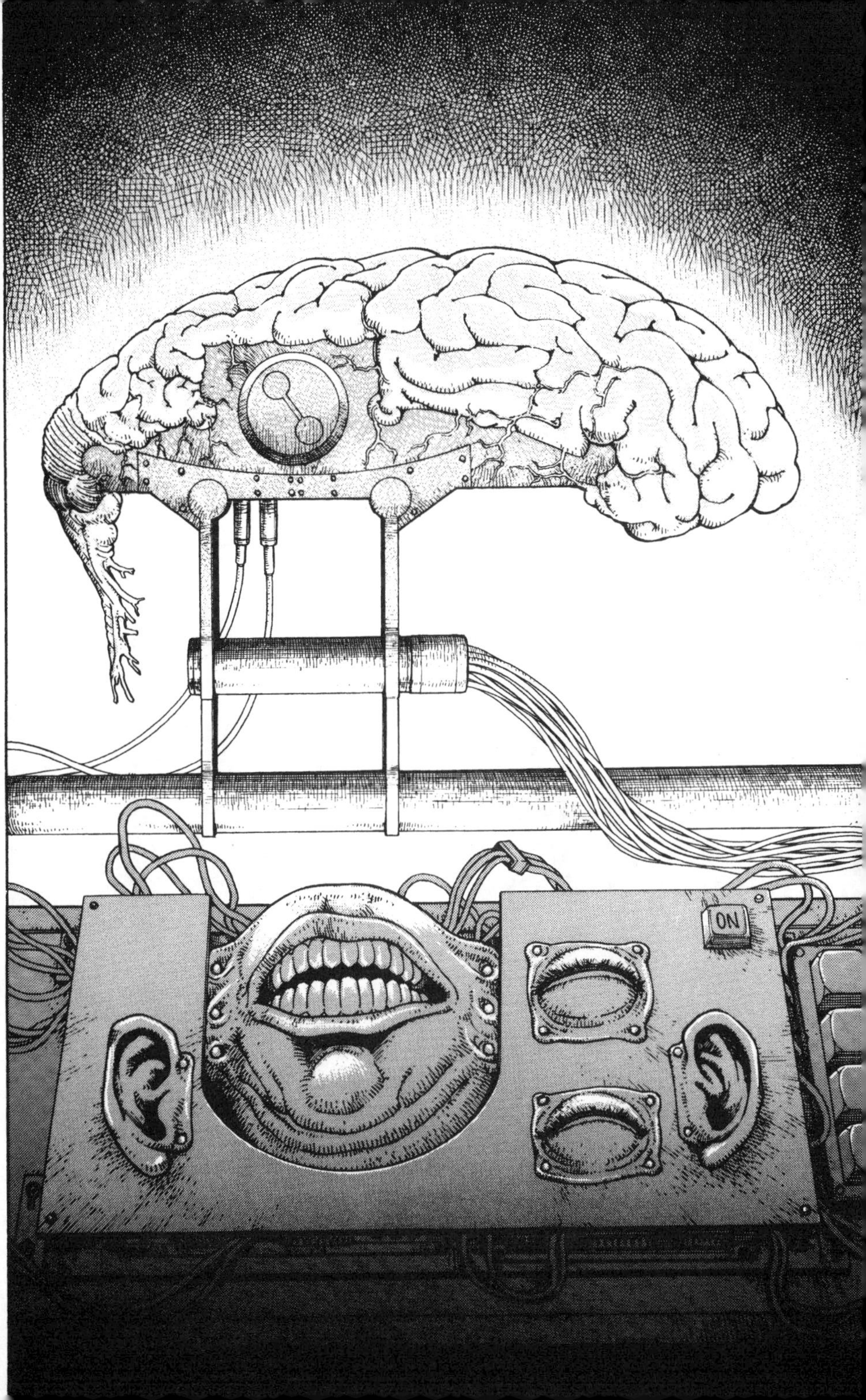
ON

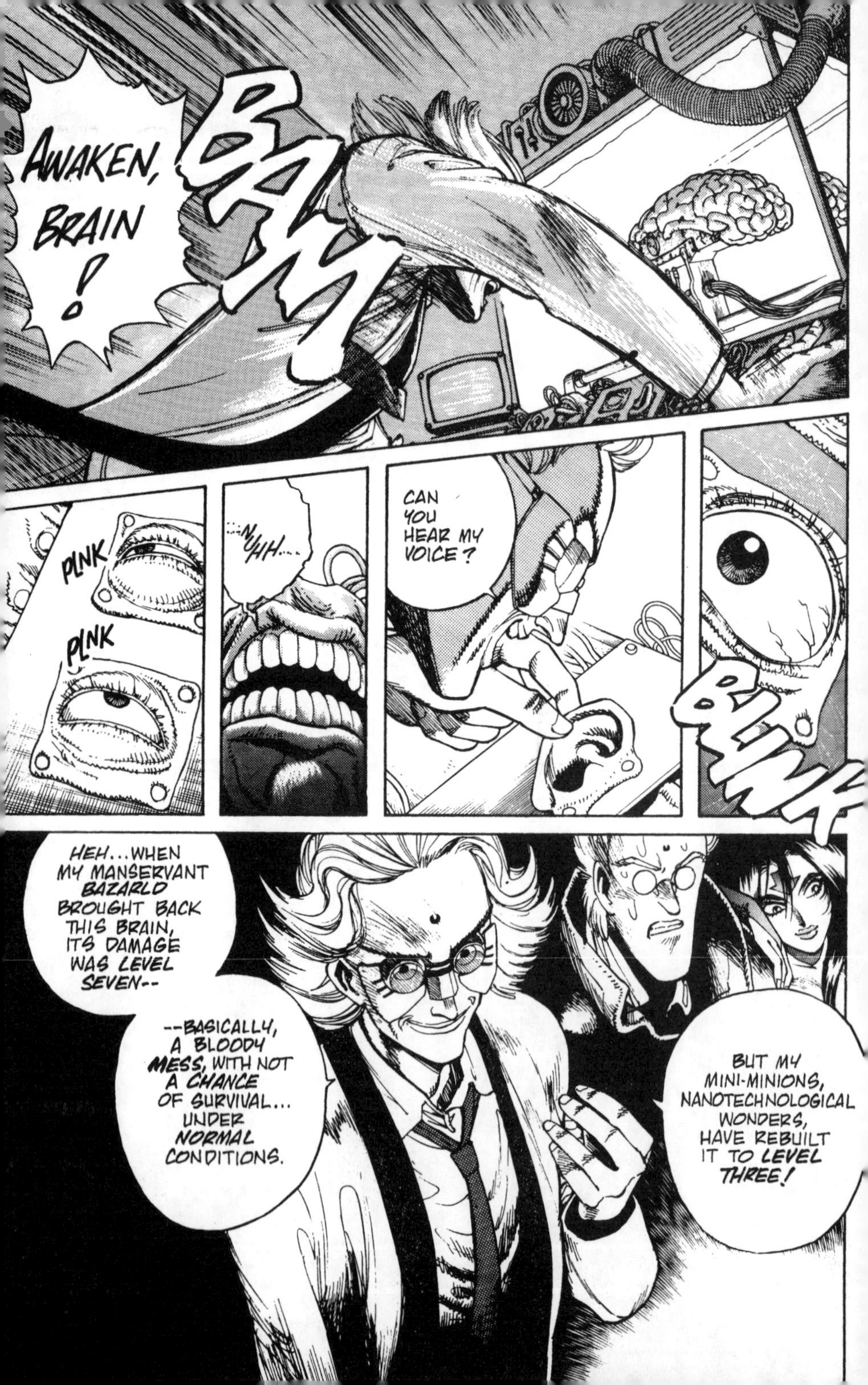
AWAKEN, BRAIN!
BAM
PLNK
PLNK
...NUHH....
CAN YOU HEAR MY VOICE?
BLINK
HEH...WHEN MY MANSERVANT BAZARLO BROUGHT BACK THIS BRAIN, ITS DAMAGE WAS LEVEL SEVEN--
--BASICALLY, A BLOODY MESS, WITH NOT A CHANCE OF SURVIVAL... UNDER NORMAL CONDITIONS.
BUT MY MINI-MINIONS, NANOTECHNOLOGICAL WONDERS, HAVE REBUILT IT TO LEVEL THREE!

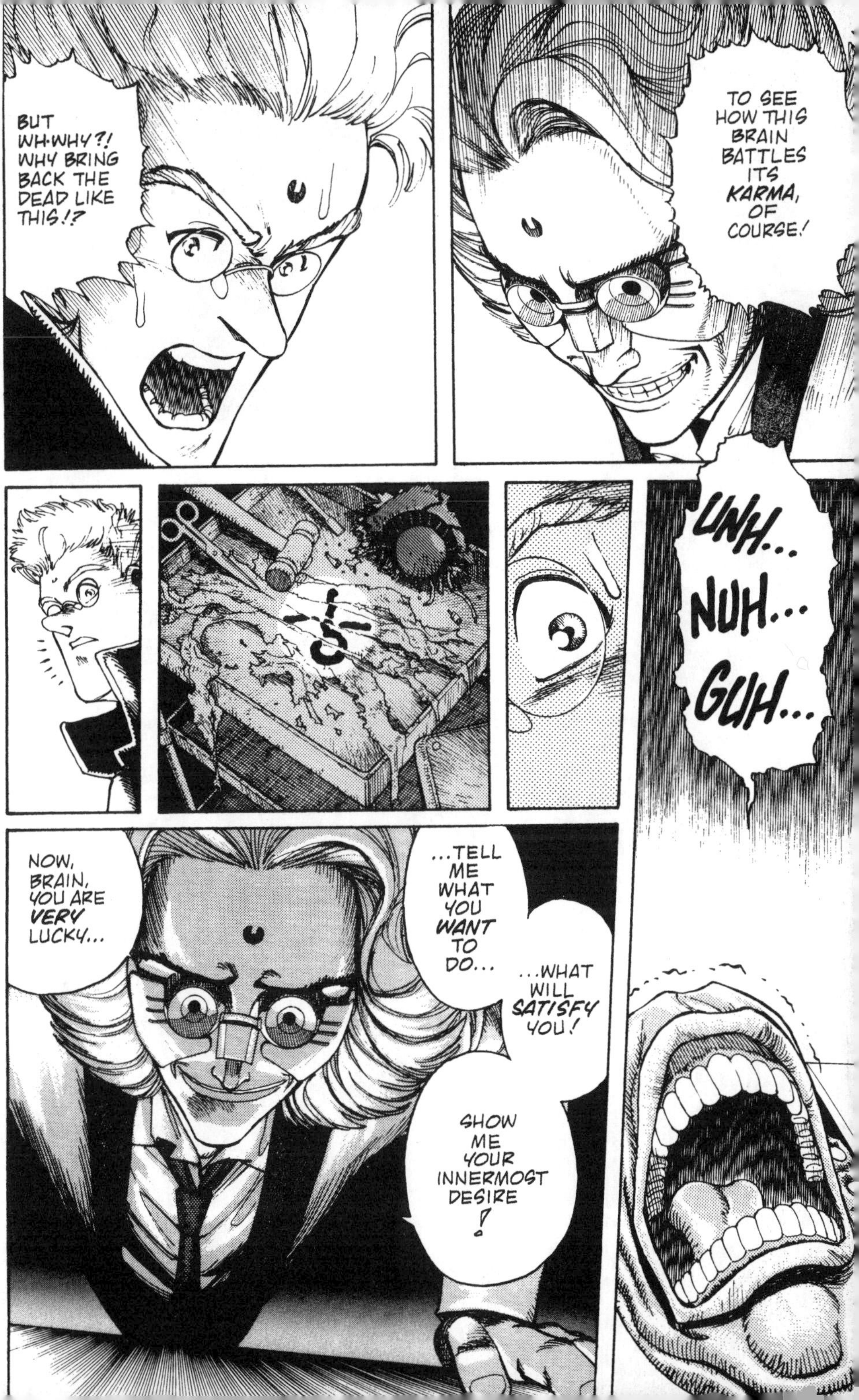

BUT WH-WHY?! WHY BRING BACK THE DEAD LIKE THIS!?
TO SEE HOW THIS BRAIN BATTLES ITS KARMA, OF COURSE!
UNH... NUH... GUH...
NOW, BRAIN, YOU ARE VERY LUCKY...
...TELL ME WHAT YOU WANT TO DO...
...WHAT WILL SATISFY YOU!
SHOW ME YOUR INNERMOST DESIRE!

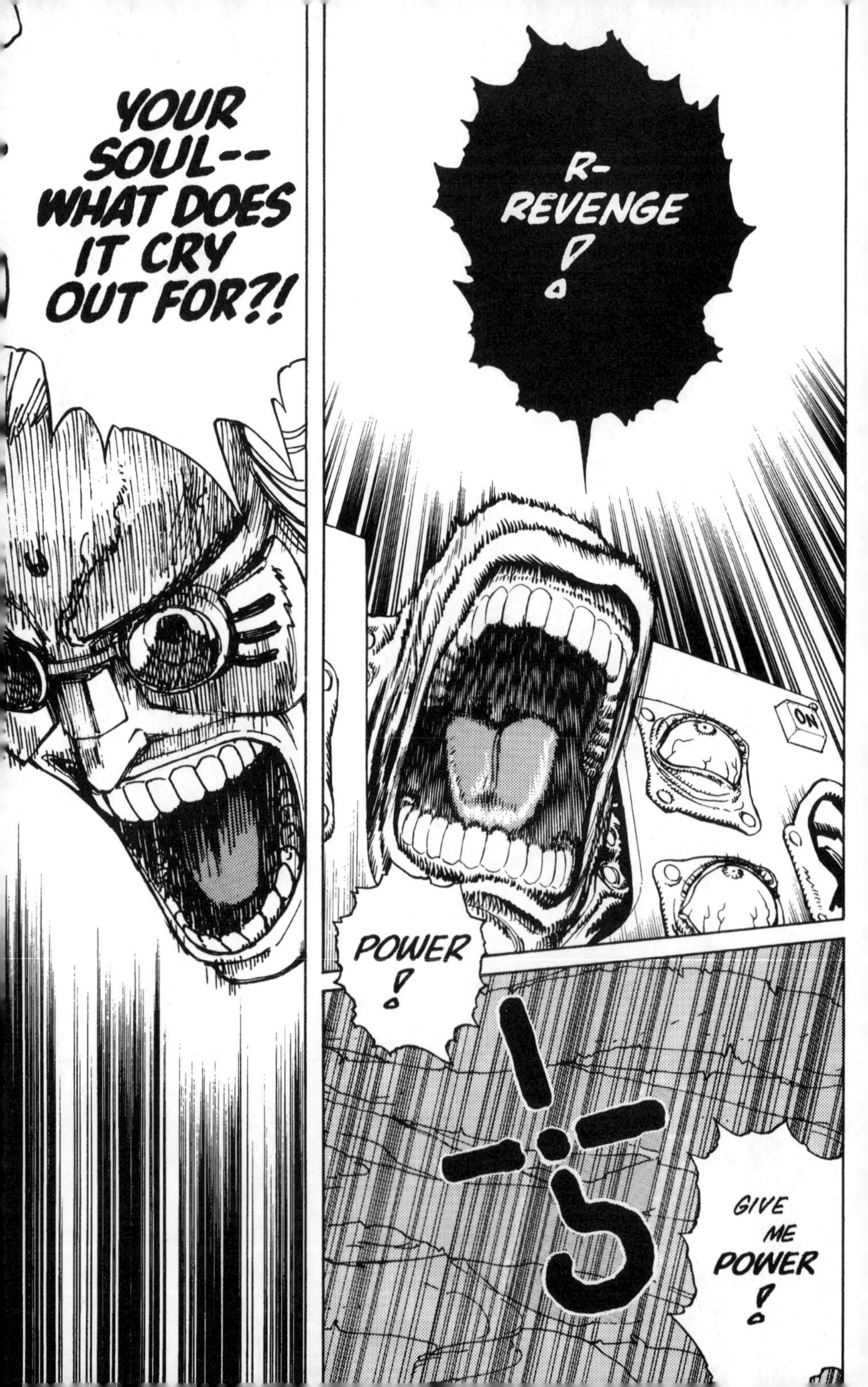
YOUR SOUL-- WHAT DOES IT CRY OUT FOR?!
R- REVENGE!
POWER!
GIVE ME POWER!

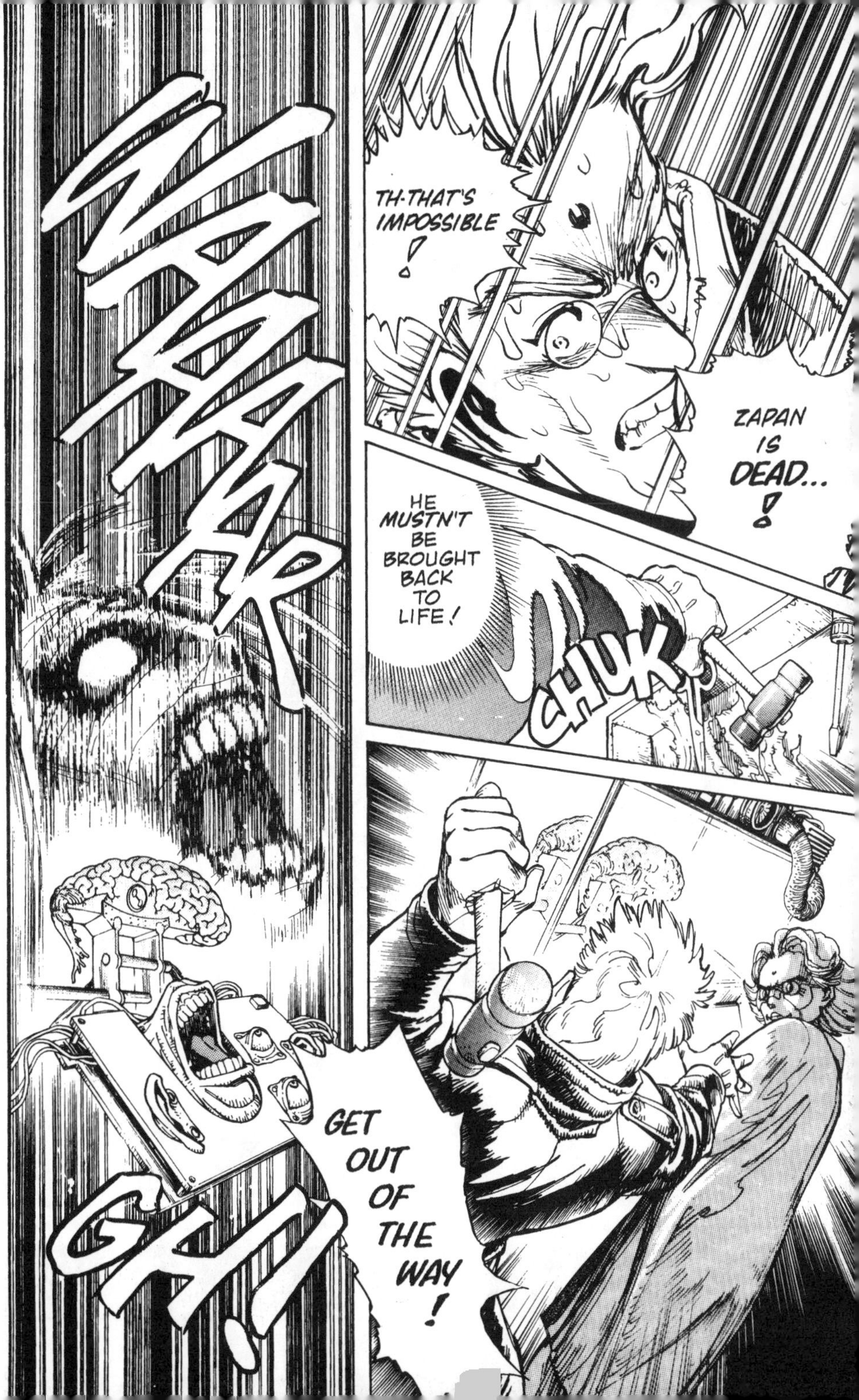
GA!
TH-THAT'S IMPOSSIBLE!
ZAPAN IS DEAD...!
HE MUSTN'T BE BROUGHT BACK TO LIFE!
CHUK
GET OUT OF THE WAY!

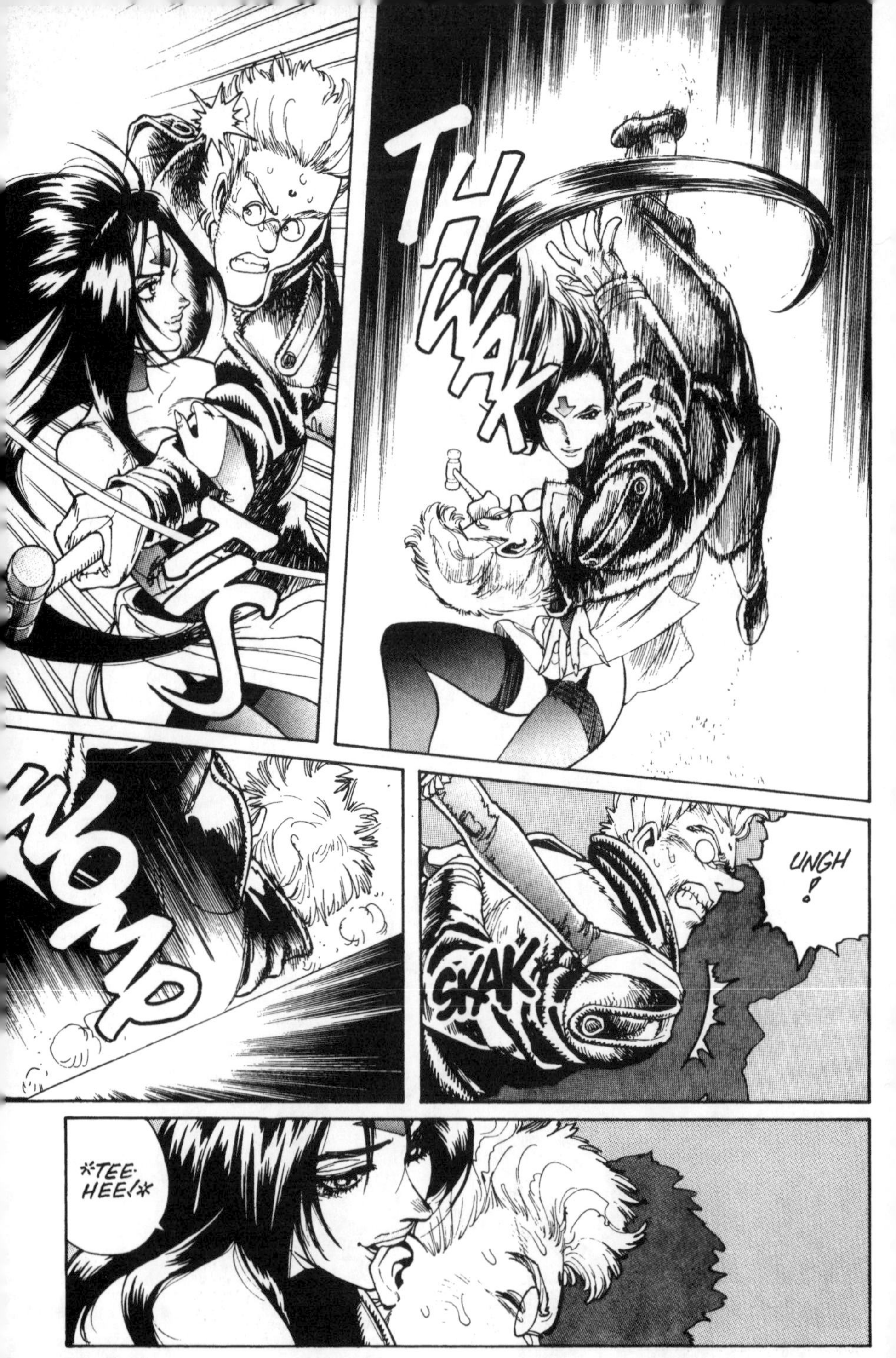
THWAK
WOMP
SKAK
UNGH!
TEE-HEE!

GYAAAAH!

WELL, THAT WAS A SURPRISE...!

CAN IT BE THAT YOU *KNOW* THIS BRAIN?

ERRRG... TH·THAT MAN-- HE'S A BRUTAL MURDERER! KILL IT!

NOW, NOW...I CAN'T DO *THAT*.

HE IS, AFTER ALL, MY *PATIENT*.

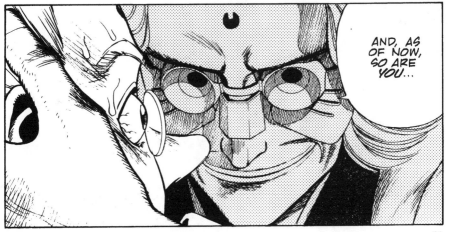

AND, AS OF NOW, SO ARE *YOU*...

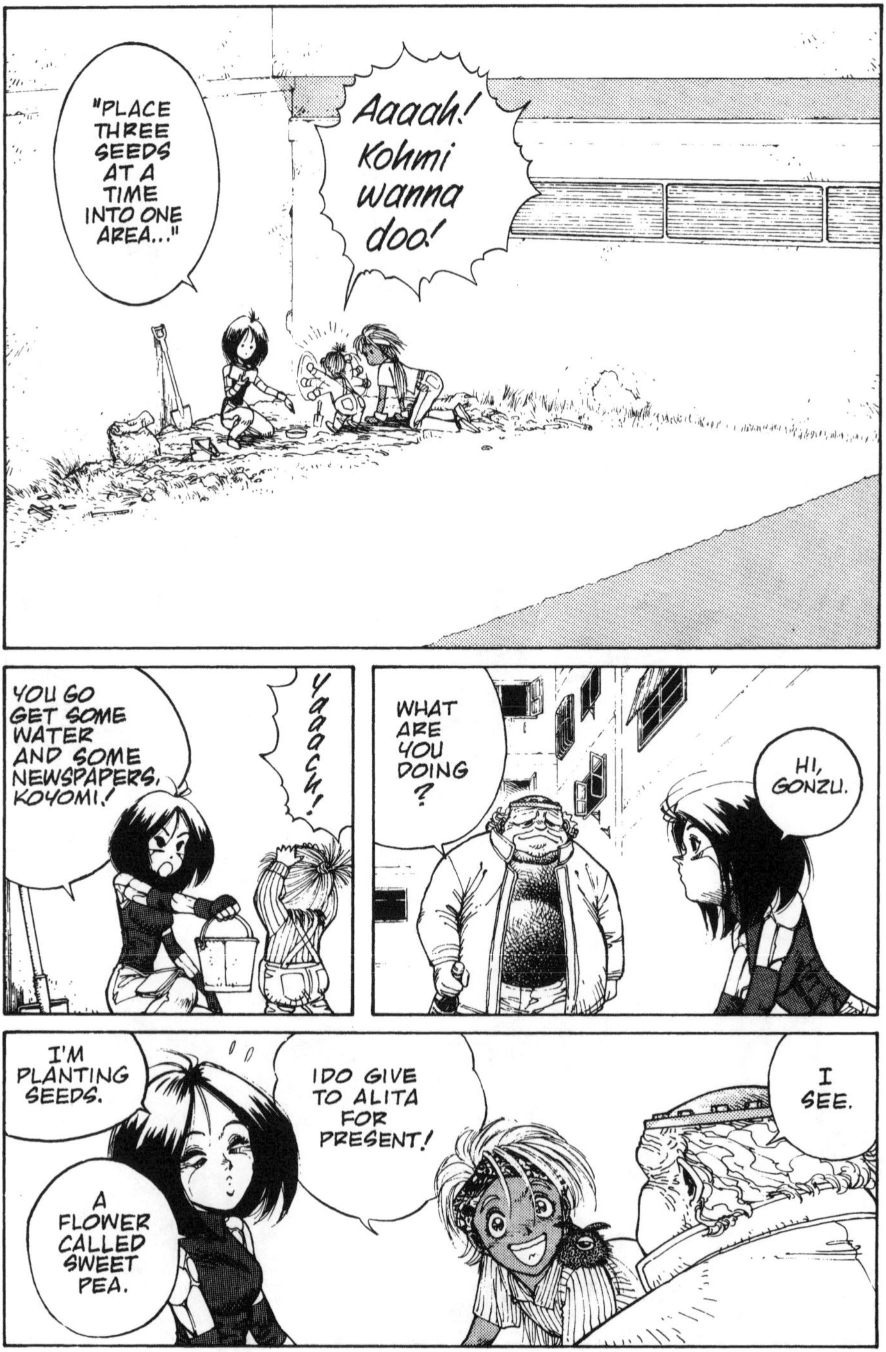
"PLACE THREE SEEDS AT A TIME INTO ONE AREA..."
Aaaah! Kohmi wanna doo!
YOU GO GET SOME WATER AND SOME NEWSPAPERS, KOYOMI!
Yaaach!
WHAT ARE YOU DOING?
HI, GONZU.
I'M PLANTING SEEDS.
A FLOWER CALLED SWEET PEA.
IDO GIVE TO ALITA FOR PRESENT!
I SEE.

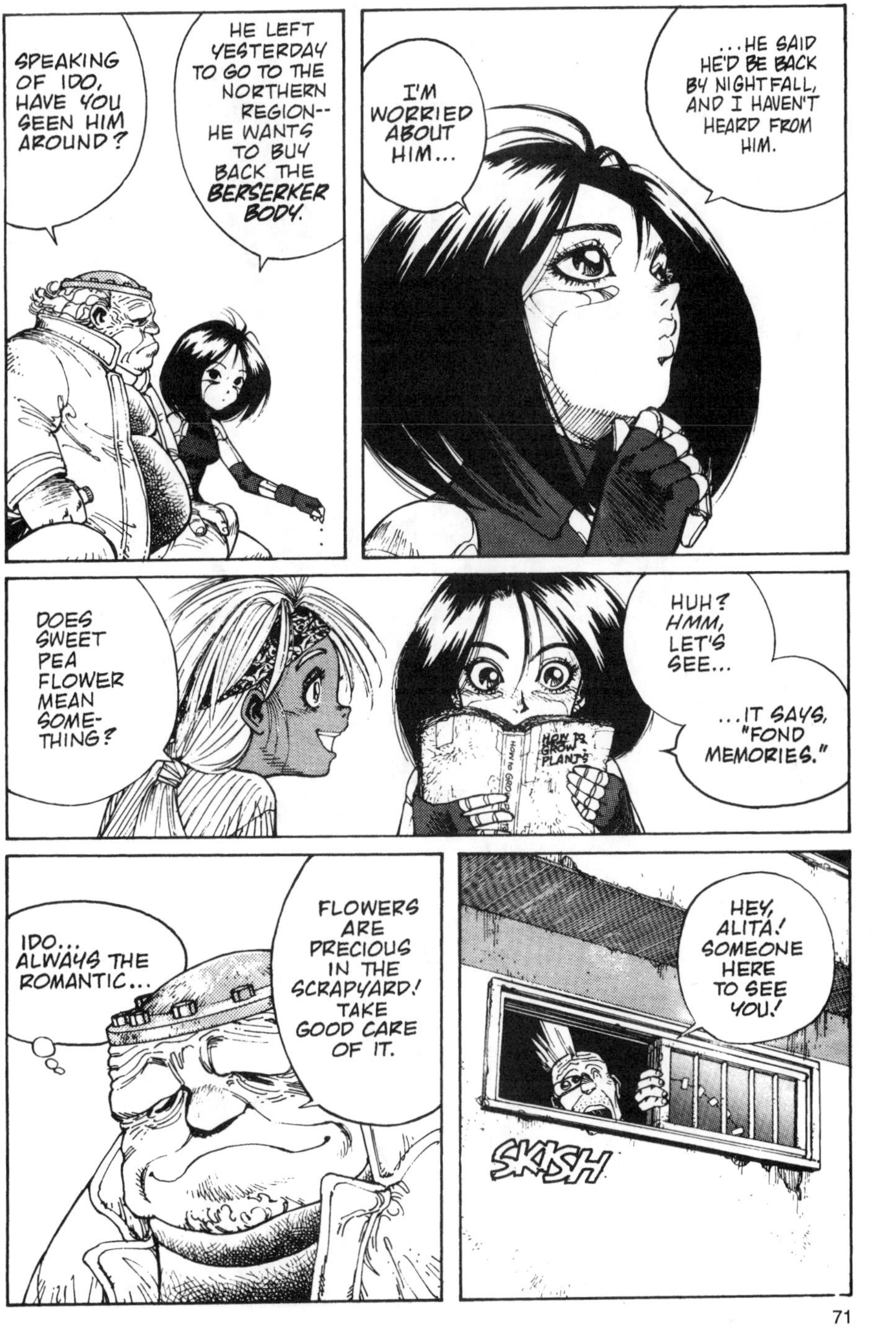
SPEAKING OF IDO, HAVE YOU SEEN HIM AROUND?
HE LEFT YESTERDAY TO GO TO THE NORTHERN REGION-- HE WANTS TO BUY BACK THE BERSERKER BODY.
I'M WORRIED ABOUT HIM...
...HE SAID HE'D BE BACK BY NIGHTFALL, AND I HAVEN'T HEARD FROM HIM.
DOES SWEET PEA FLOWER MEAN SOME-THING?
HUH? HMM, LET'S SEE...
...IT SAYS, "FOND MEMORIES."
IDO... ALWAYS THE ROMANTIC...
FLOWERS ARE PRECIOUS IN THE SCRAPYARD! TAKE GOOD CARE OF IT.
HEY, ALITA! SOMEONE HERE TO SEE YOU!
SKISH

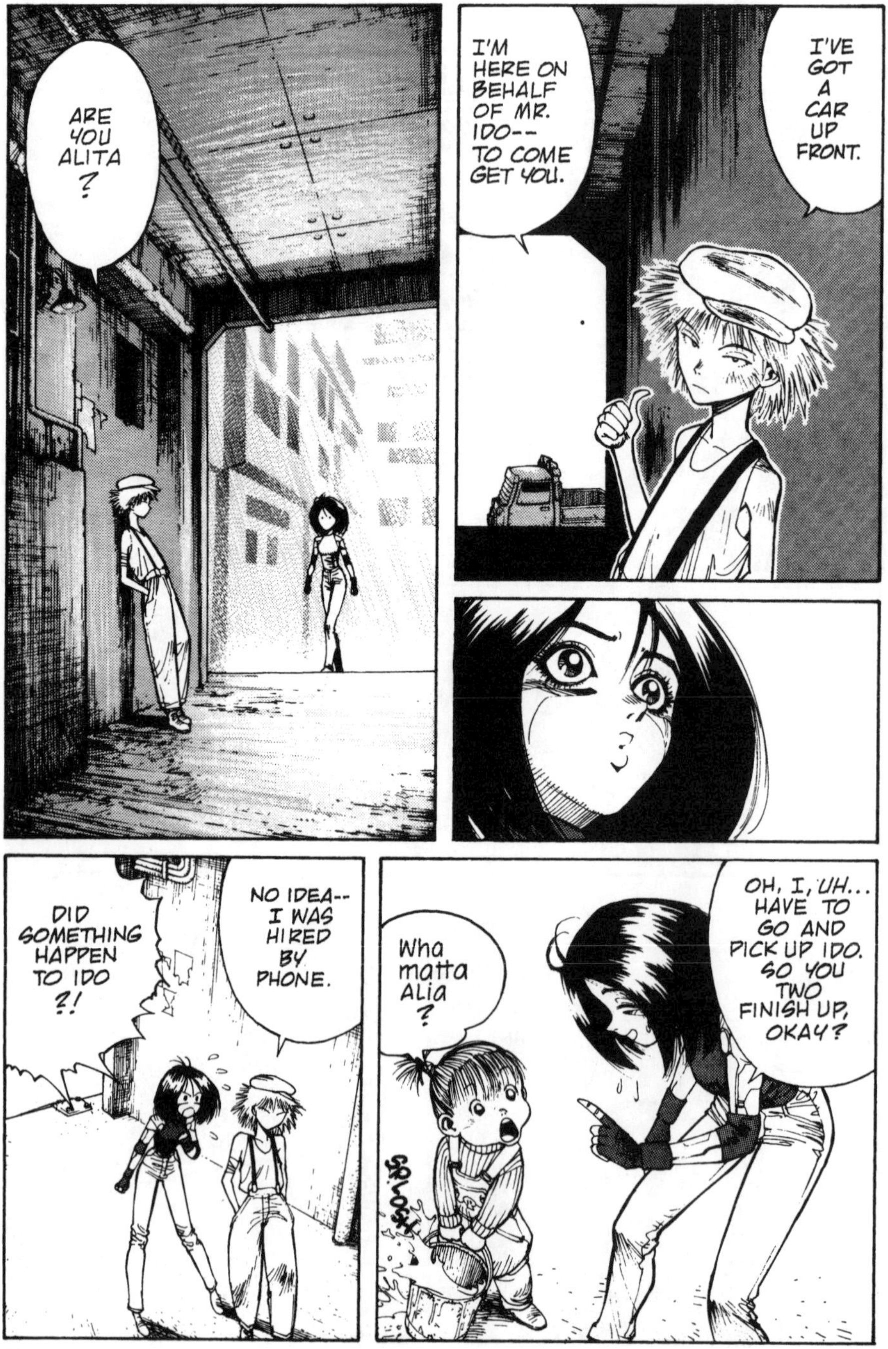
ARE YOU ALITA?
I'M HERE ON BEHALF OF MR. IDO-- TO COME GET YOU.
I'VE GOT A CAR UP FRONT.
DID SOMETHING HAPPEN TO IDO?!
NO IDEA-- I WAS HIRED BY PHONE.
Wha matta Alia?
OH, I, UH... HAVE TO GO AND PICK UP IDO. SO YOU TWO FINISH UP, OKAY?

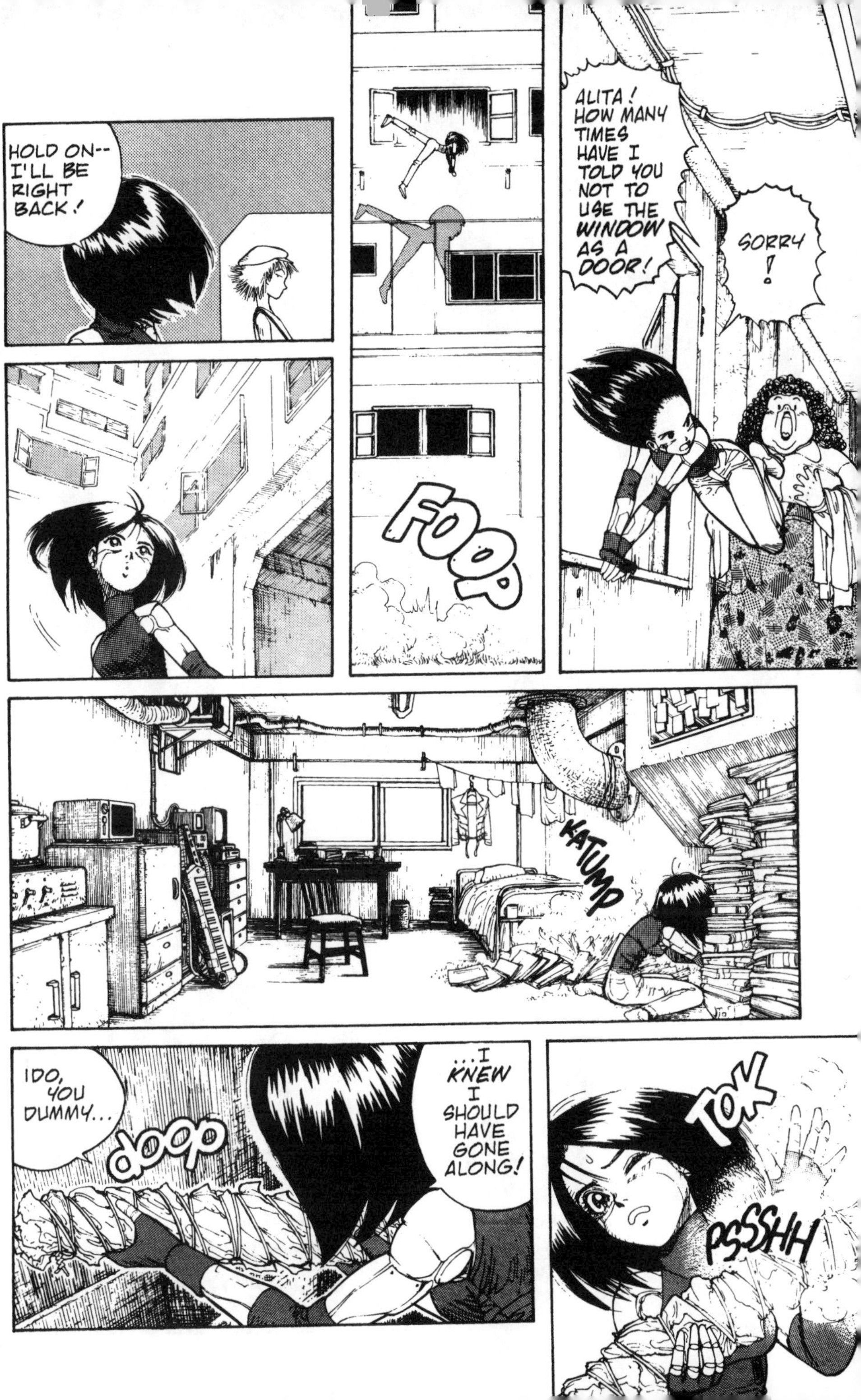
HOLD ON--
I'LL BE
RIGHT
BACK!
FOOP
ALITA! HOW MANY TIMES HAVE I TOLD YOU NOT TO USE THE WINDOW AS A DOOR!
SORRY!
KATUMP
IDO, YOU DUMMY...
doop
...I KNEW I SHOULD HAVE GONE ALONG!
TOK
PSSSHH

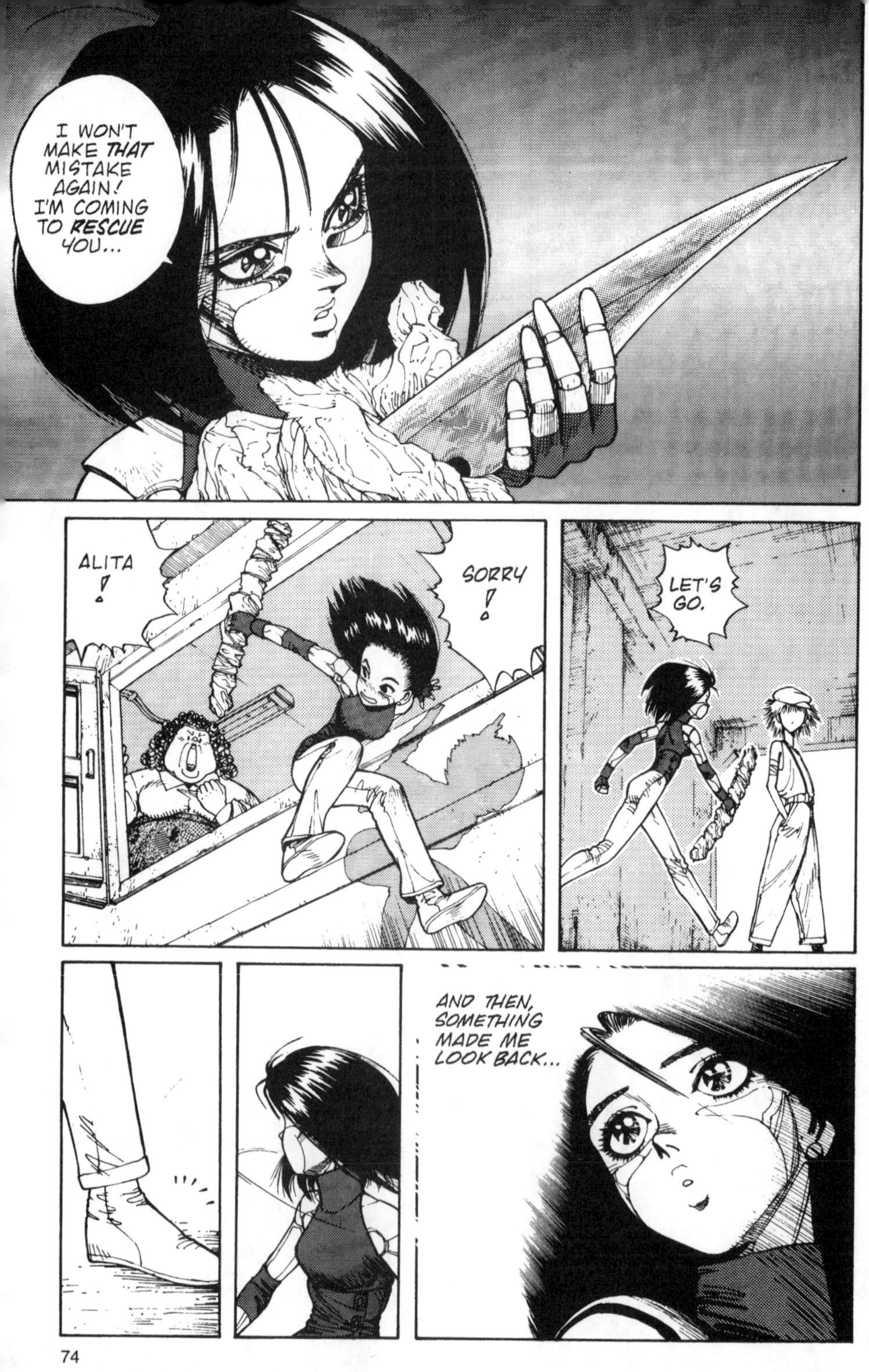
I WON'T MAKE THAT MISTAKE AGAIN! I'M COMING TO RESCUE YOU...
ALITA!
SORRY!
LET'S GO.
AND THEN, SOMETHING MADE ME LOOK BACK...

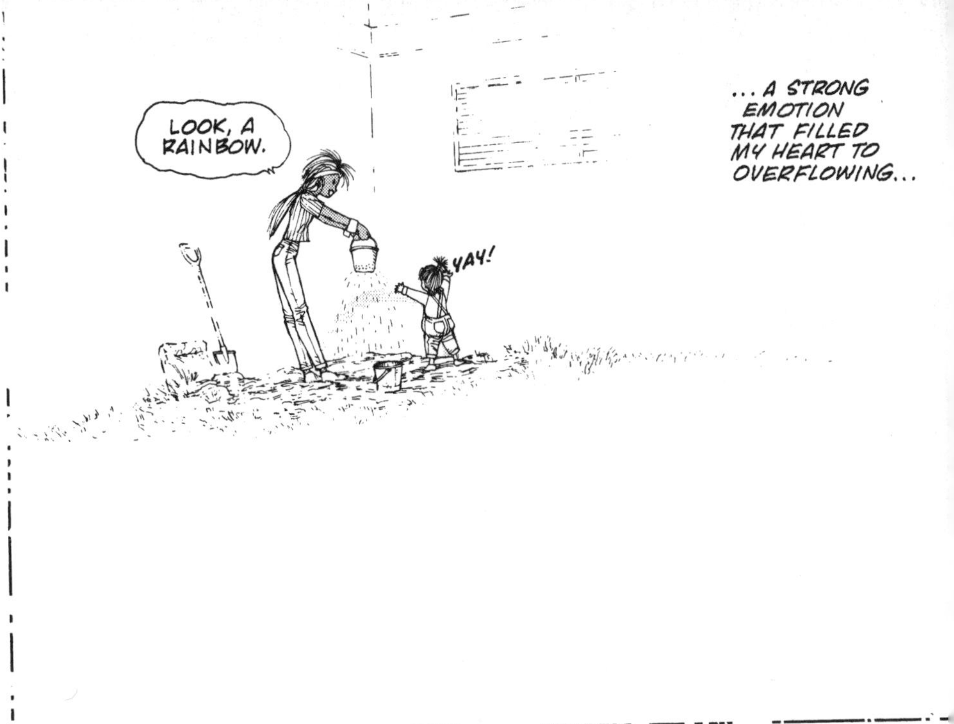
LOOK, A RAINBOW.
... A STRONG EMOTION THAT FILLED MY HEART TO OVERFLOWING...
YAY!

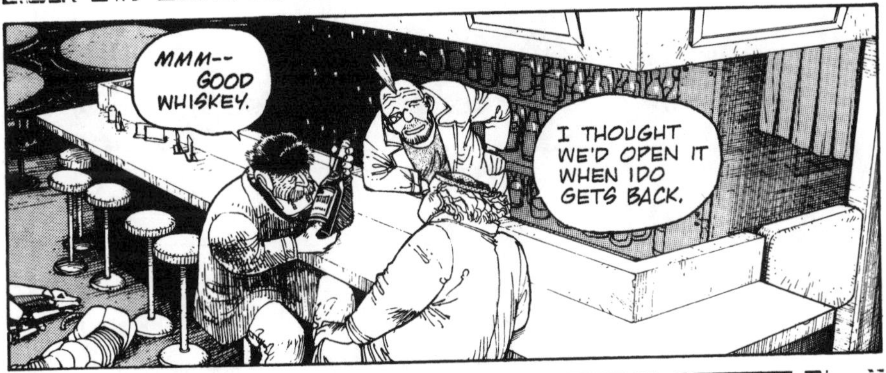
MMM-- GOOD WHISKEY.
I THOUGHT WE'D OPEN IT WHEN IDO GETS BACK.

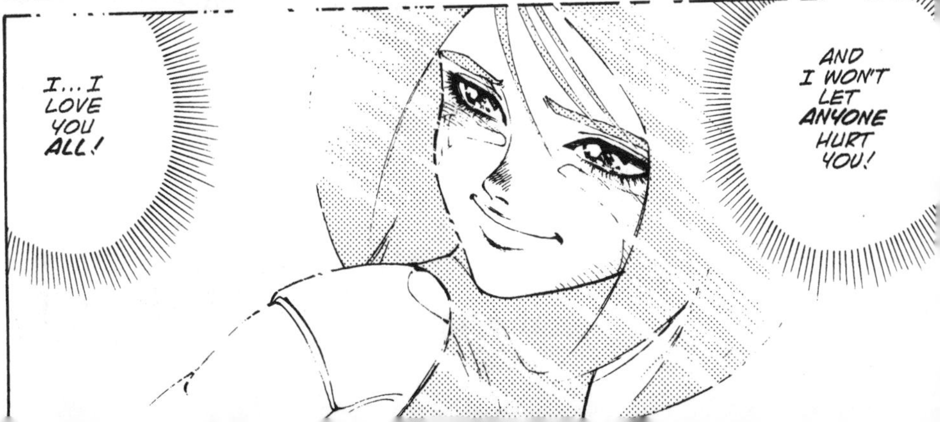
I... I LOVE YOU ALL!
AND I WON'T LET ANYONE HURT YOU!

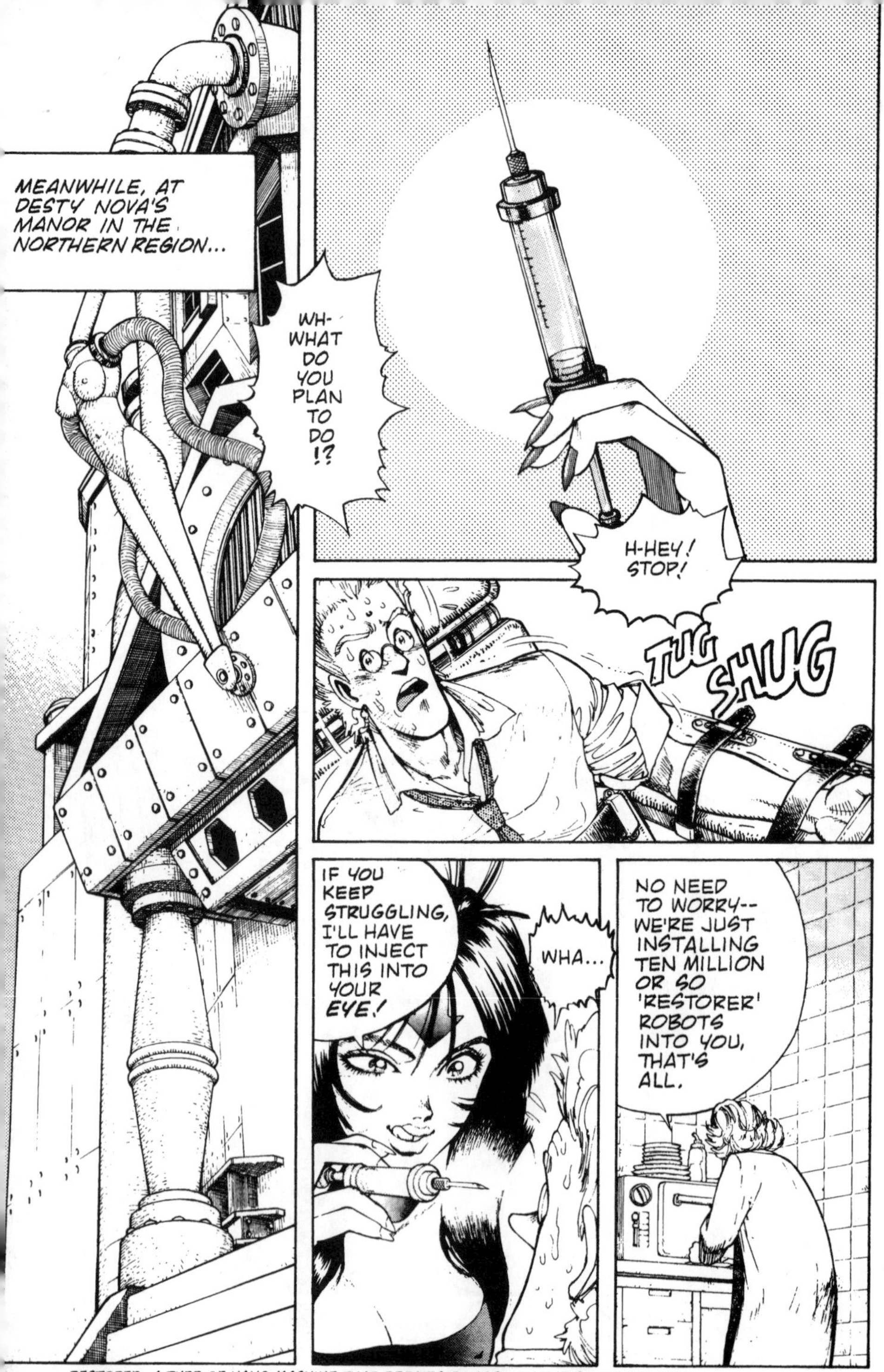

MEANWHILE, AT DESTY NOVA'S MANOR IN THE NORTHERN REGION...
WH-WHAT DO YOU PLAN TO DO!?
H-HEY! STOP!
TUG
SHUG
IF YOU KEEP STRUGGLING, I'LL HAVE TO INJECT THIS INTO YOUR *EYE!*
WHA...
NO NEED TO WORRY--WE'RE JUST INSTALLING TEN MILLION OR SO 'RESTORER' ROBOTS INTO YOU, THAT'S ALL.

RESTORER: A TYPE OF NANO-MACHINE THAT REPAIRS DAMAGE ON THE CELLULAR LEVEL. INDIVIDUALS WITH THESE ROBOTS INSIDE THEM HEAL AT AN INCREDIBLE RATE.

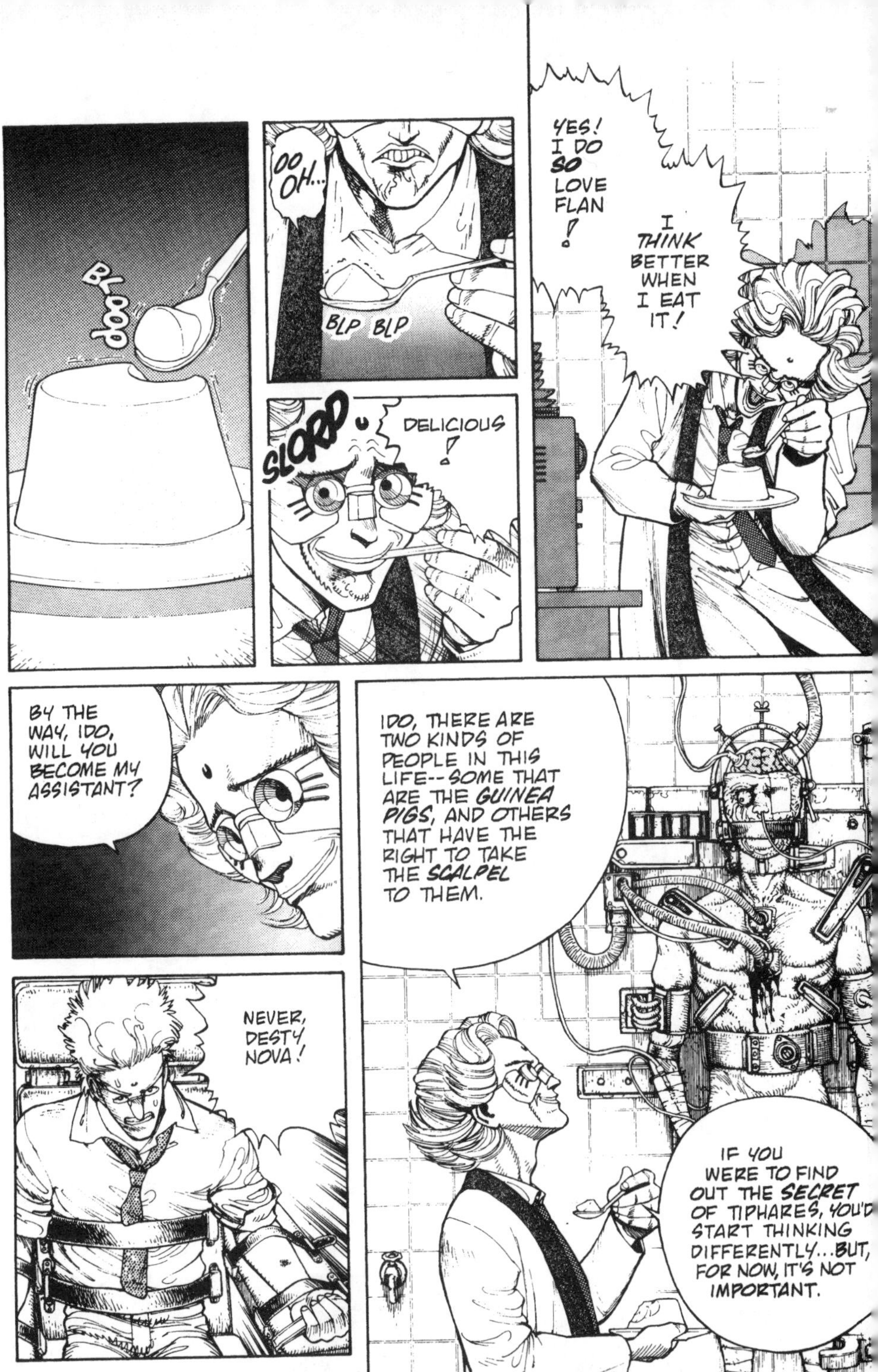
BLOOP
OO OH...
BLP BLP
SLORP
DELICIOUS!
YES! I DO SO LOVE FLAN!
I THINK BETTER WHEN I EAT IT!
BY THE WAY, IDO, WILL YOU BECOME MY ASSISTANT?
IDO, THERE ARE TWO KINDS OF PEOPLE IN THIS LIFE--SOME THAT ARE THE GUINEA PIGS, AND OTHERS THAT HAVE THE RIGHT TO TAKE THE SCALPEL TO THEM.
NEVER, DESTY NOVA!
IF YOU WERE TO FIND OUT THE SECRET OF TIPHARES, YOU'D START THINKING DIFFERENTLY...BUT, FOR NOW, IT'S NOT IMPORTANT.

ALL THAT MATTERS *TODAY* ARE THE DESIRES OF *THIS* BRAIN.

NUGH...

OH, BY THE WAY-- I'VE SUMMONED YOUR *ALITA*. SHE SHOULD BE HERE IN ABOUT AN HOUR.

I MUST FINISH THIS EXPERIMENT *BEFORE* SHE ARRIVES.

WHAT !?

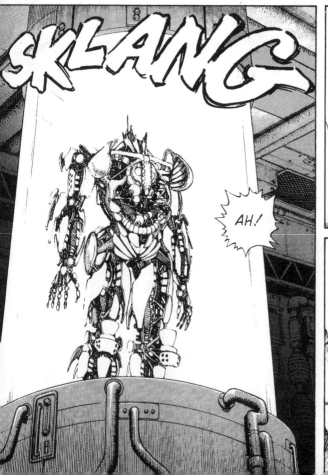

SKLANG

AH!

SO, YOU DO PLAN TO GIVE *ZAPAN* THE *BERSERKER* BODY!

SO ELEGANT... SO BEAUTIFUL...

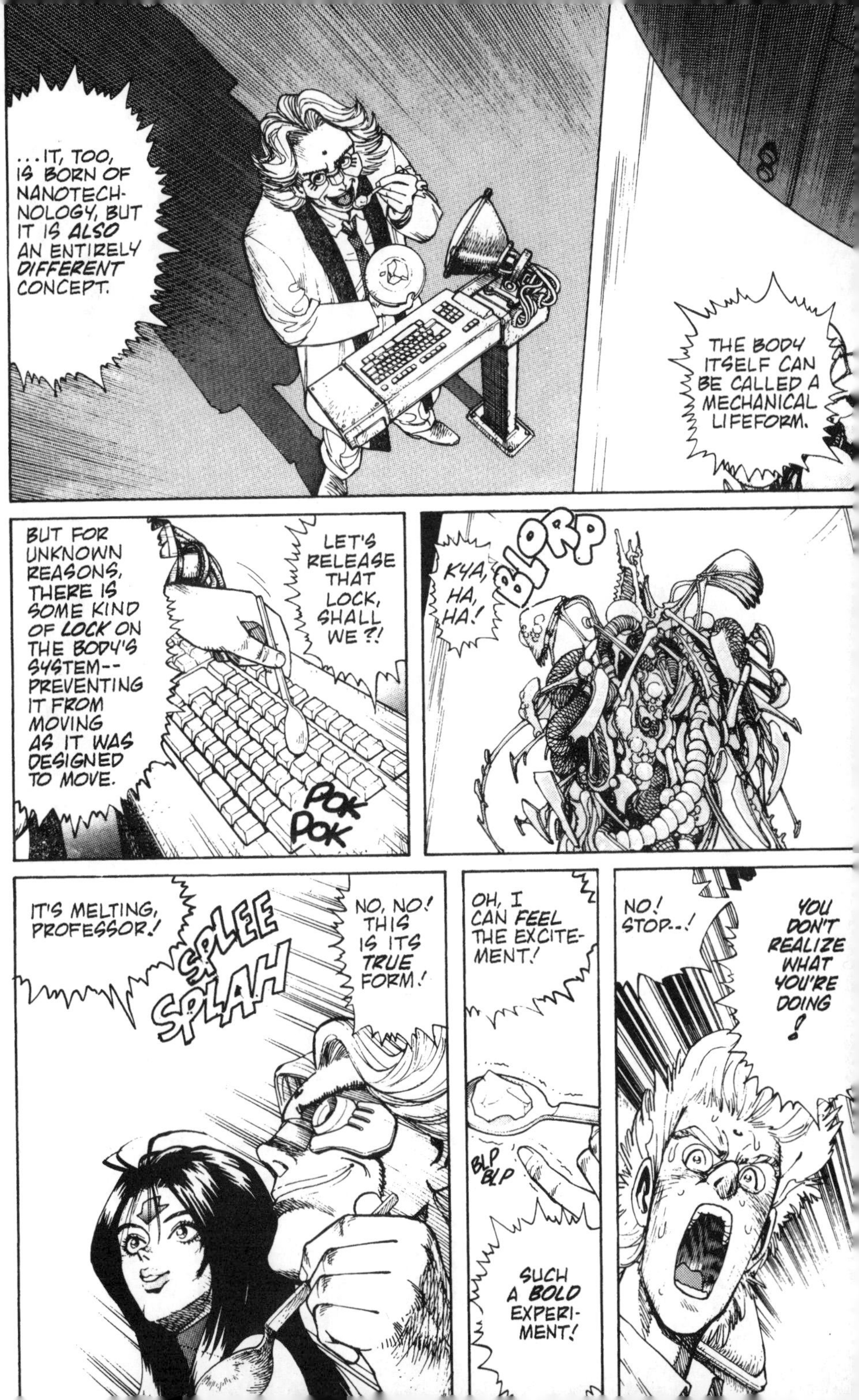
...IT, TOO, IS BORN OF NANOTECHNOLOGY, BUT IT IS ALSO AN ENTIRELY DIFFERENT CONCEPT.
THE BODY ITSELF CAN BE CALLED A MECHANICAL LIFEFORM.
BUT FOR UNKNOWN REASONS, THERE IS SOME KIND OF LOCK ON THE BODY'S SYSTEM--PREVENTING IT FROM MOVING AS IT WAS DESIGNED TO MOVE.
LET'S RELEASE THAT LOCK, SHALL WE?!
POK POK
KYA, HA, HA!
BLORP
IT'S MELTING, PROFESSOR!
SPLEE SPLAH
NO, NO! THIS IS ITS TRUE FORM!
OH, I CAN FEEL THE EXCITEMENT!
BLP BLP
SUCH A BOLD EXPERIMENT!
NO! STOP--!
YOU DON'T REALIZE WHAT YOU'RE DOING!

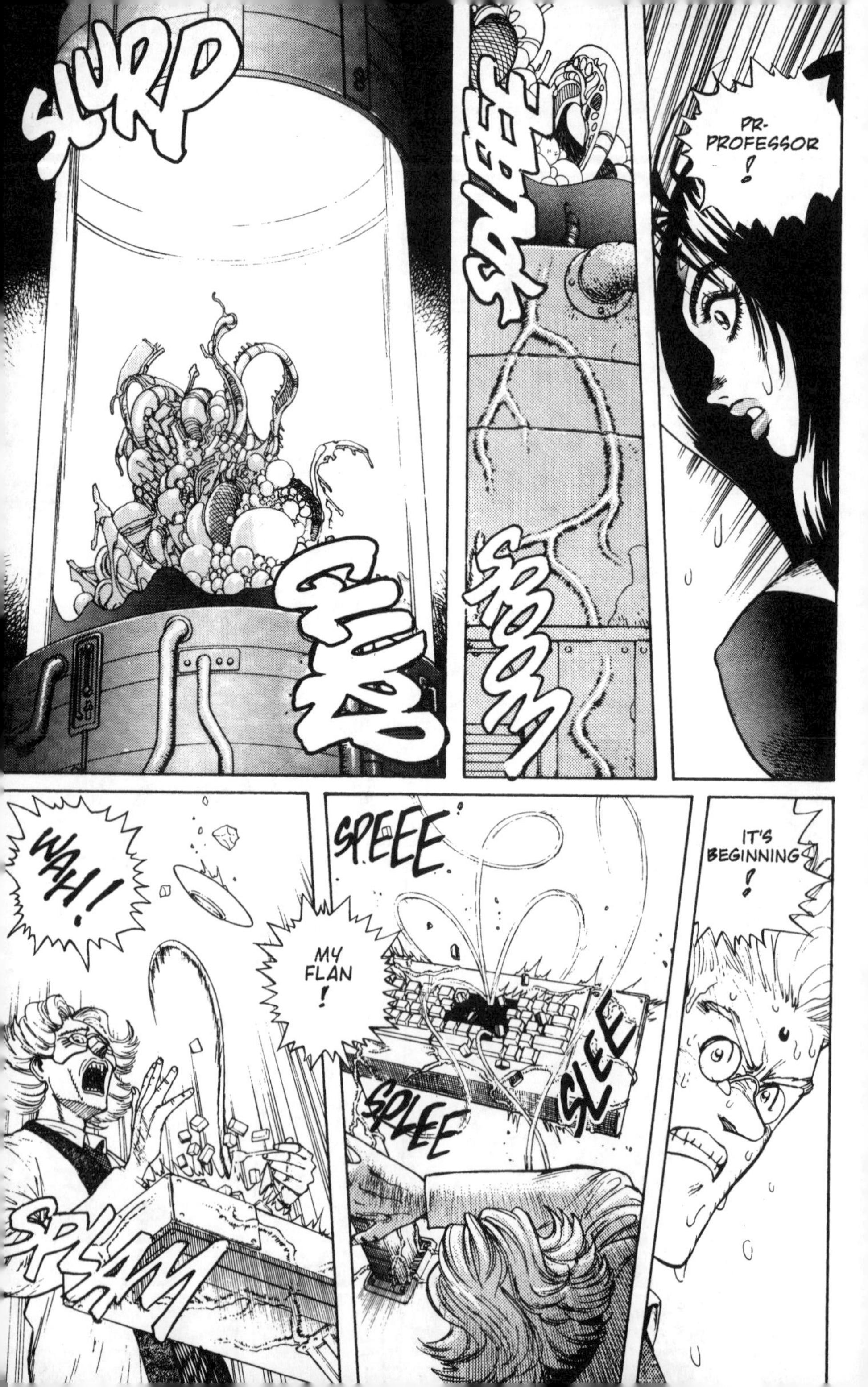
SLURP
GLUP
SPLEE
SPLOOSH
PR-
PROFESSOR!
WAH!
MY FLAN!
SPLAM
SPEEE
SPLEE
SLEE
IT'S BEGINNING!

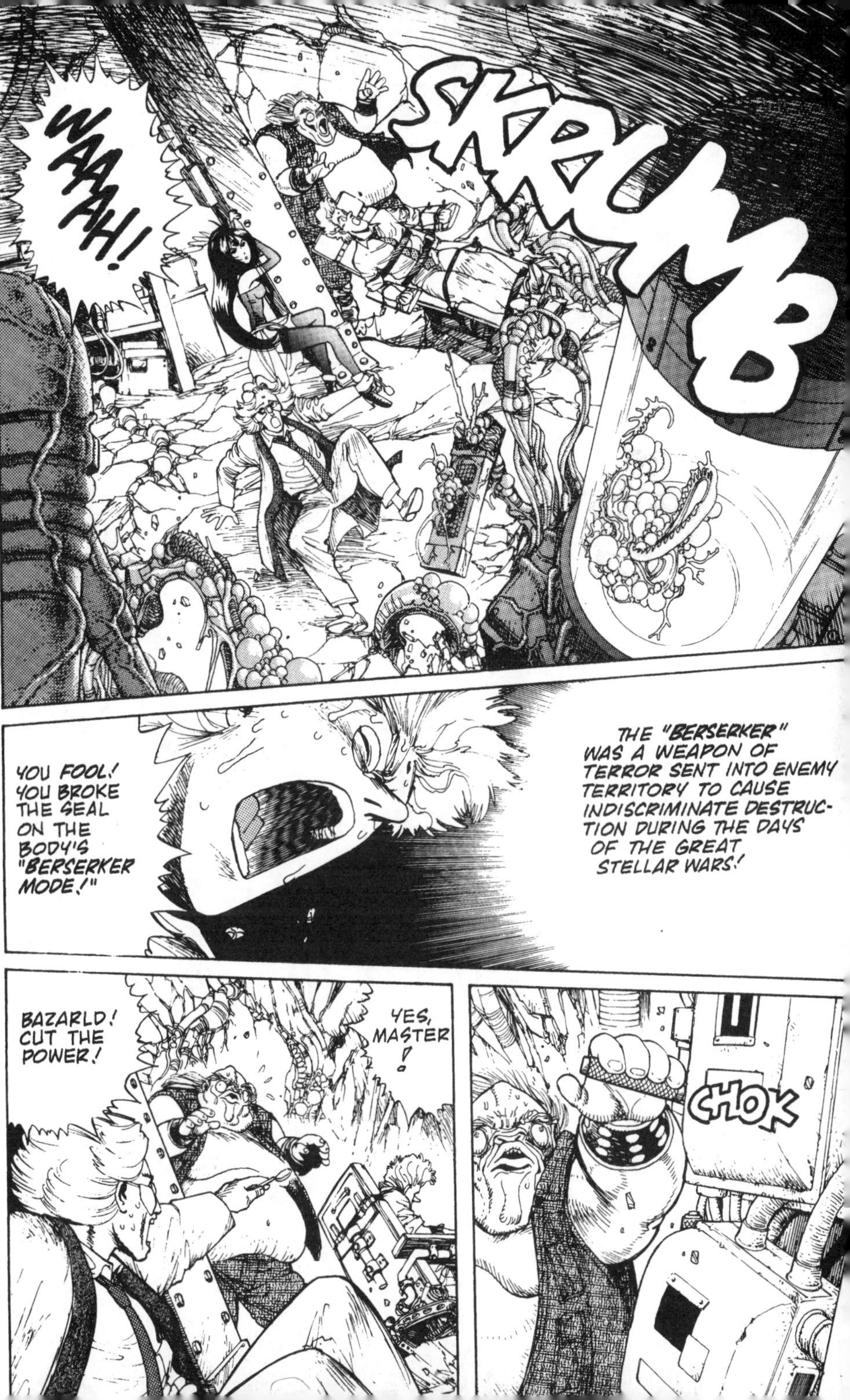
WAAAAH!
SKRUMB
YOU FOOL! YOU BROKE THE SEAL ON THE BODY'S "BERSERKER MODE!"
THE "BERSERKER" WAS A WEAPON OF TERROR SENT INTO ENEMY TERRITORY TO CAUSE INDISCRIMINATE DESTRUCTION DURING THE DAYS OF THE GREAT STELLAR WARS!
BAZARLD! CUT THE POWER!
YES, MASTER!
CHOK

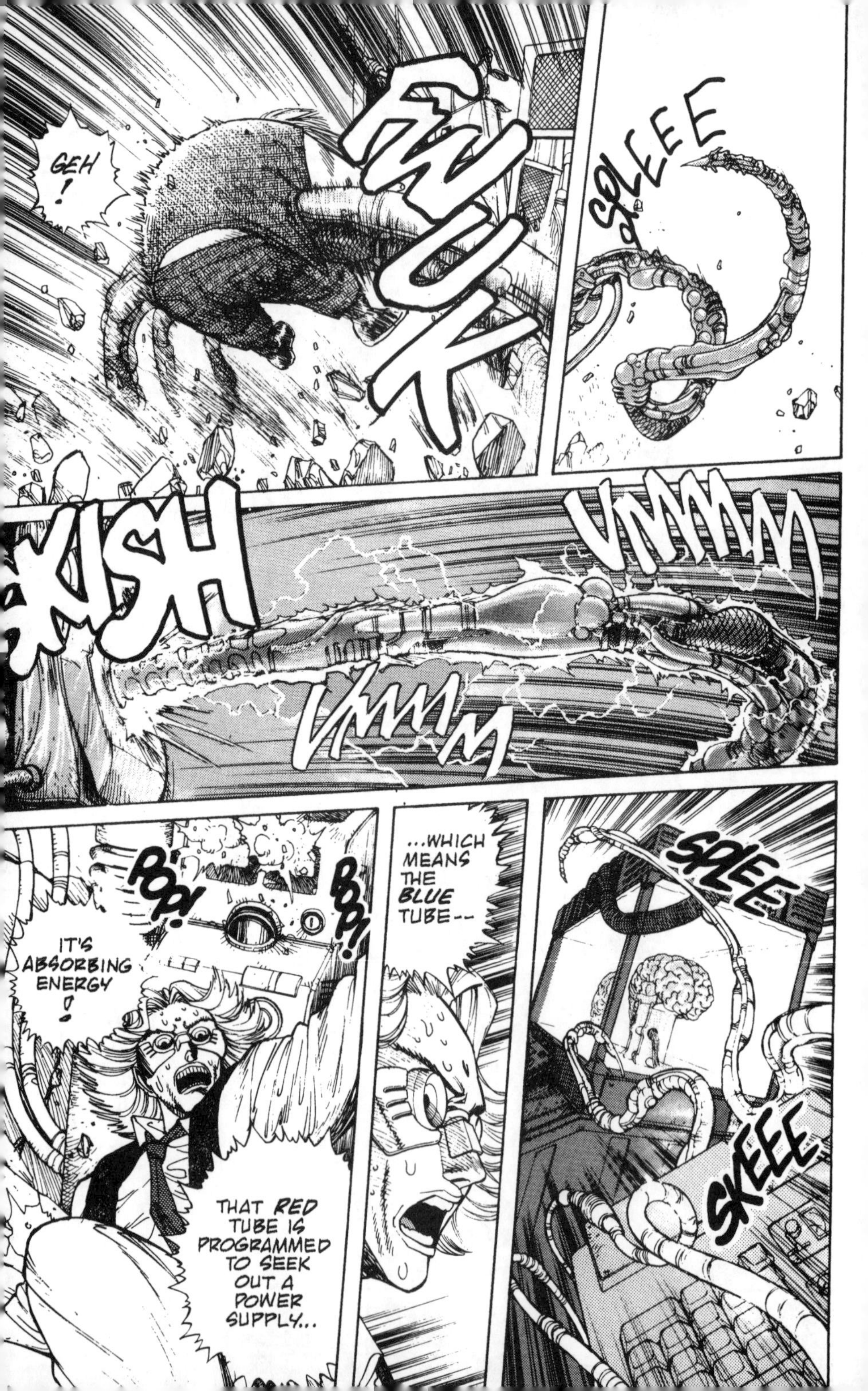
GEH!
CHUNK
SPLEEE
KRISH
VMMMM
VMMMM
POP!
POP!
IT'S ABSORBING ENERGY!
THAT RED TUBE IS PROGRAMMED TO SEEK OUT A POWER SUPPLY...
...WHICH MEANS THE BLUE TUBE--
SPLEEE
SKEEE

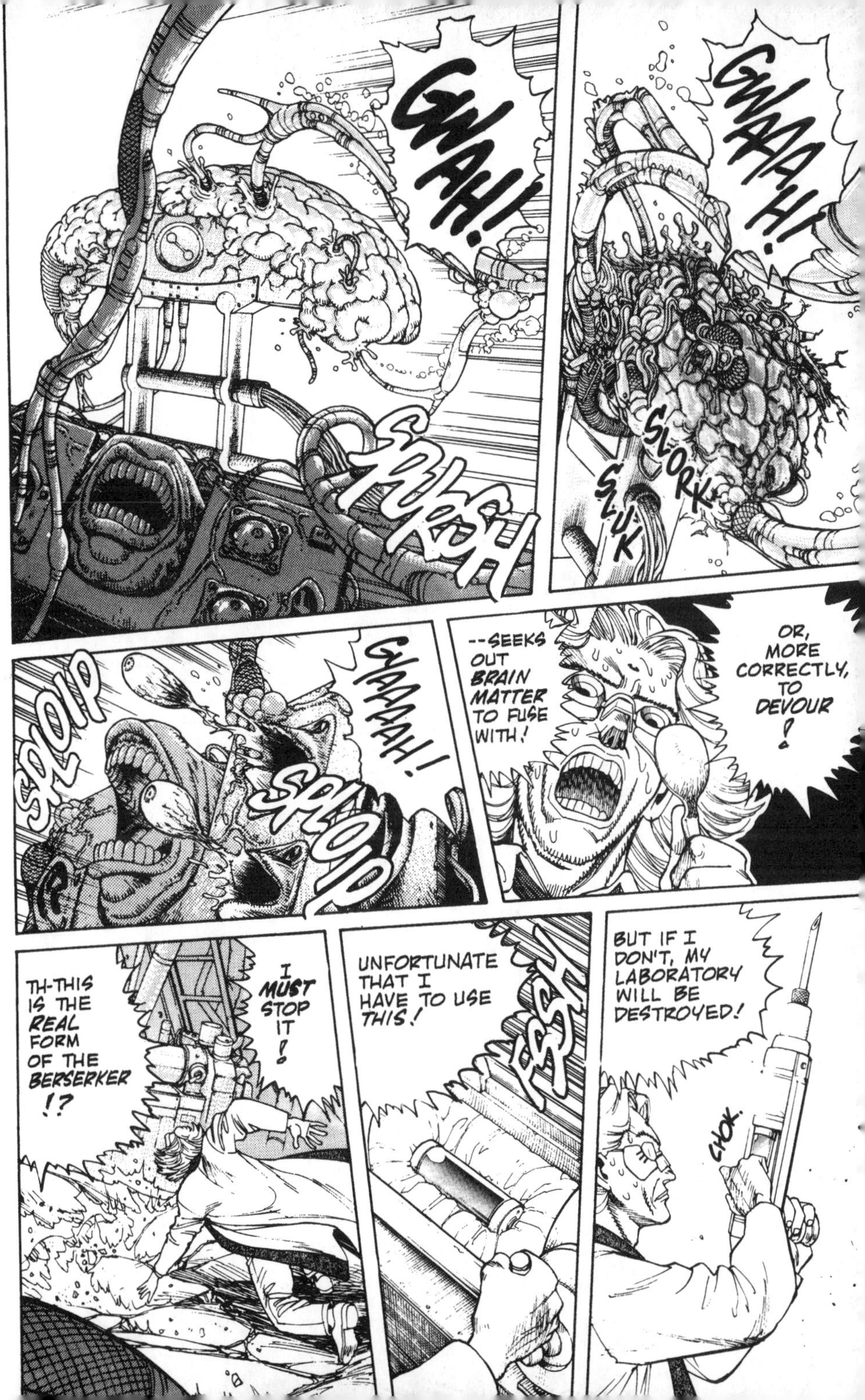
GWAH!!
SPLUSH
GWAAAH!!
SLORK
SLUK
SPLOIP
GWAAAAH!
SPLOIP
--SEEKS OUT BRAIN MATTER TO FUSE WITH!
OR, MORE CORRECTLY, TO DEVOUR!
TH-THIS IS THE REAL FORM OF THE BERSERKER!?
I MUST STOP IT!
UNFORTUNATE THAT I HAVE TO USE THIS!
BUT IF I DON'T, MY LABORATORY WILL BE DESTROYED!
CHOK

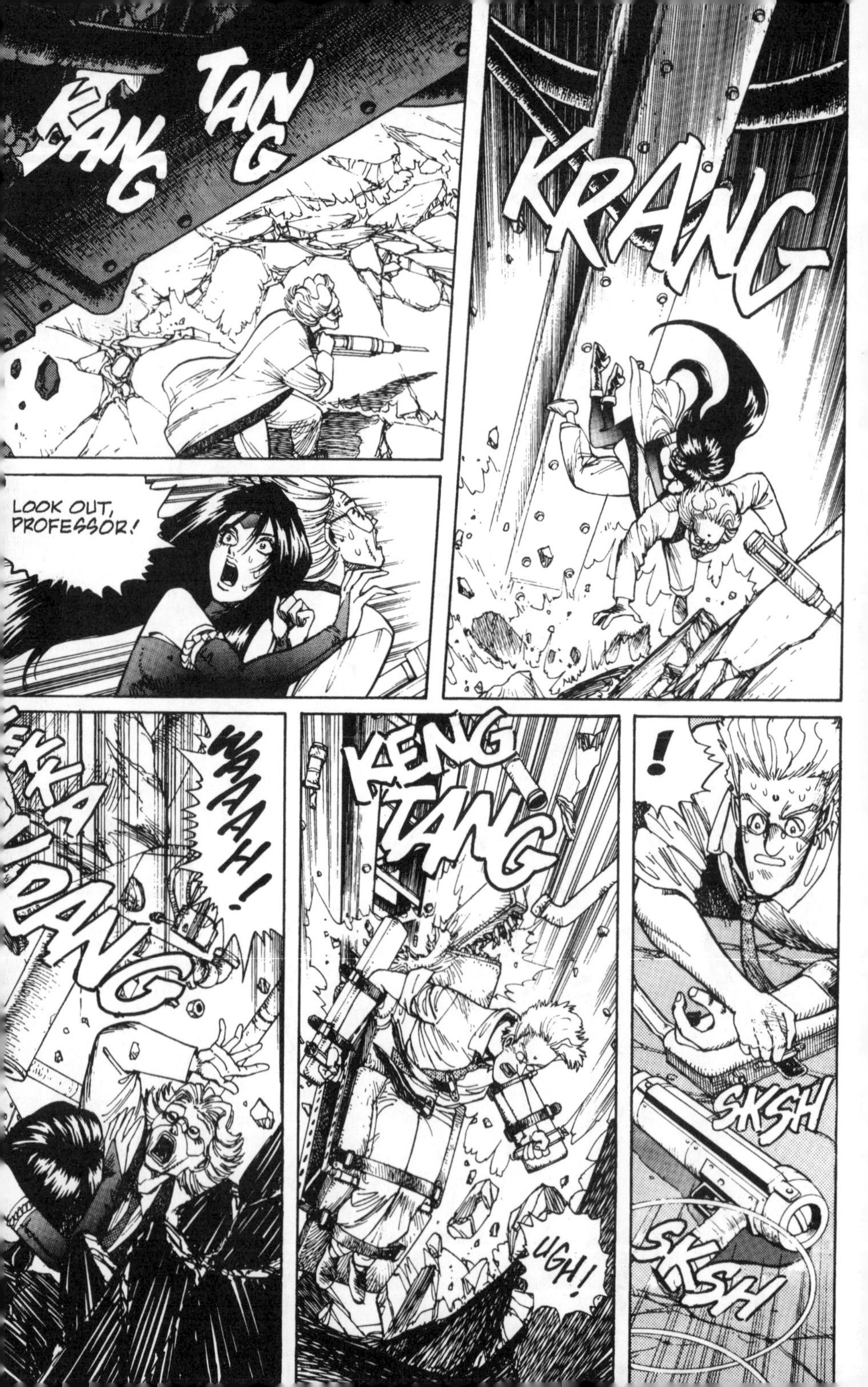
KRANG
TAN TANG
LOOK OUT, PROFESSOR!
KRANG
KA DANG
WAAAH!
KENG KANG
UGH!
!
SKSH
SKSH

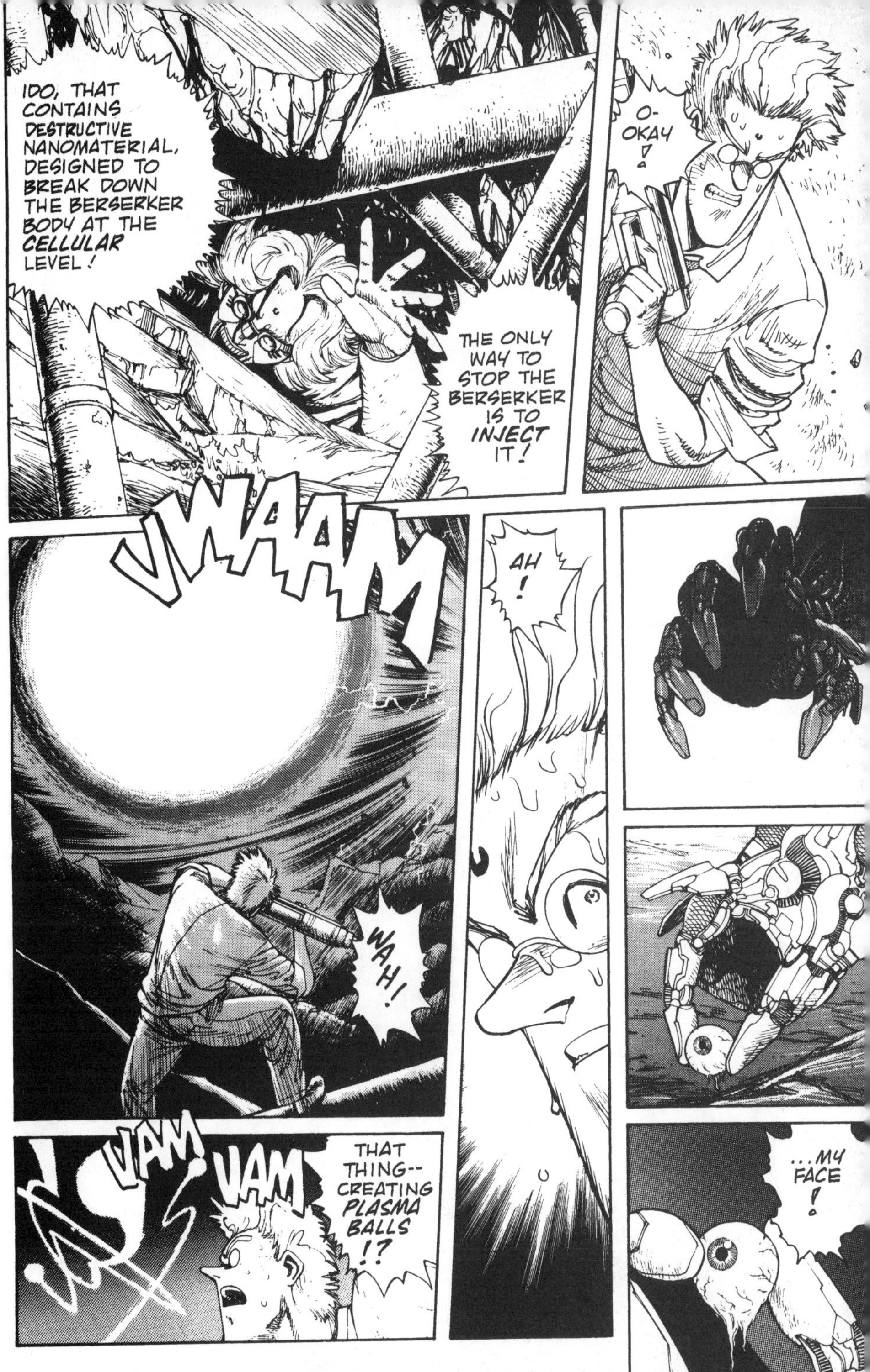
IDO, THAT CONTAINS DESTRUCTIVE NANOMATERIAL, DESIGNED TO BREAK DOWN THE BERSERKER BODY AT THE CELLULAR LEVEL!
THE ONLY WAY TO STOP THE BERSERKER IS TO INJECT IT!
O-OKAY!
VWAAM
WAH!
AH!
JAM JAM
THAT THING--CREATING PLASMA BALLS!?
...MY FACE!

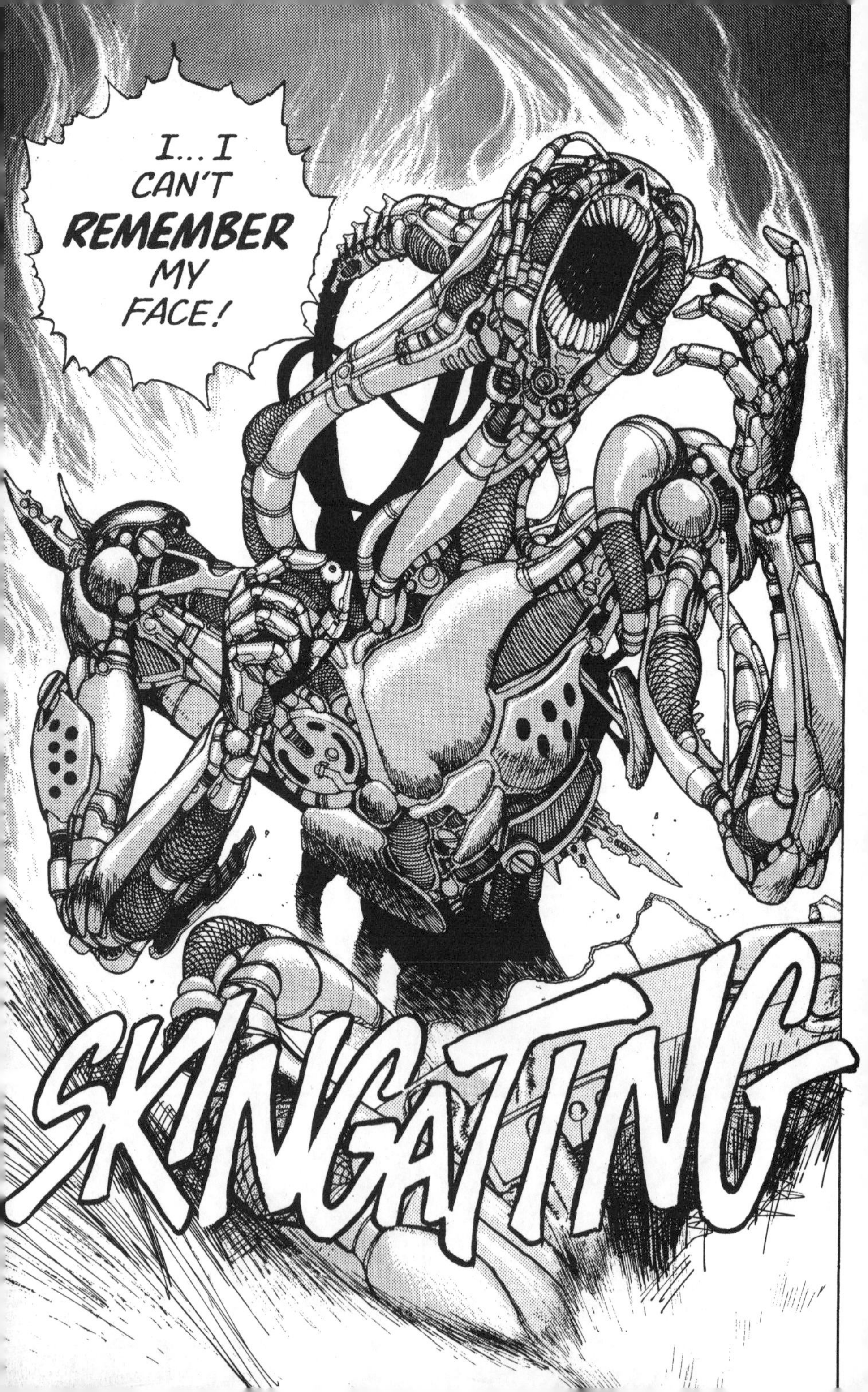
I... I CAN'T **REMEMBER** MY FACE!
SKNGATING

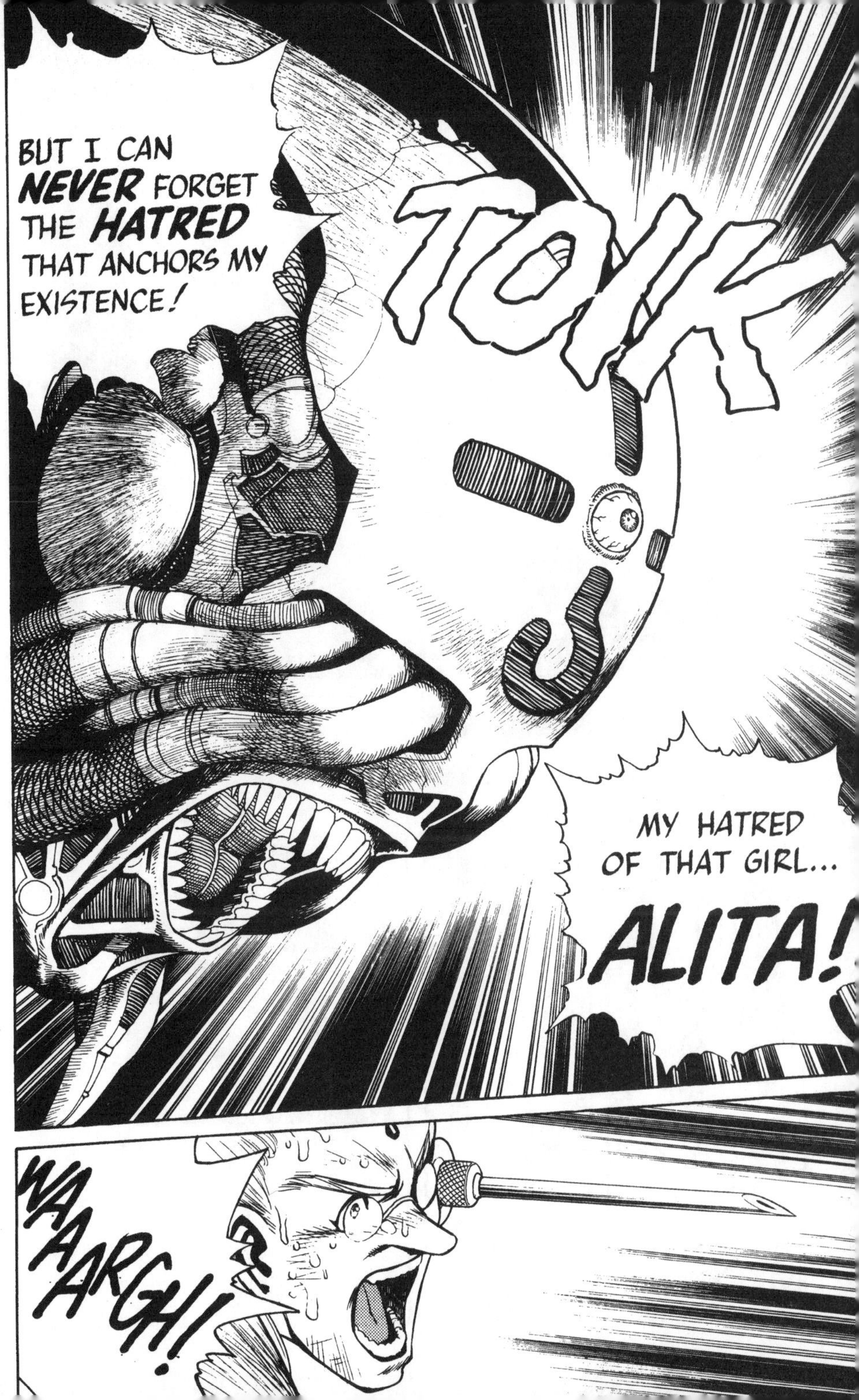
BUT I CAN **NEVER** FORGET THE **HATRED** THAT ANCHORS MY EXISTENCE!
TOIK
MY HATRED OF THAT GIRL...
ALITA!
WAAARGH!

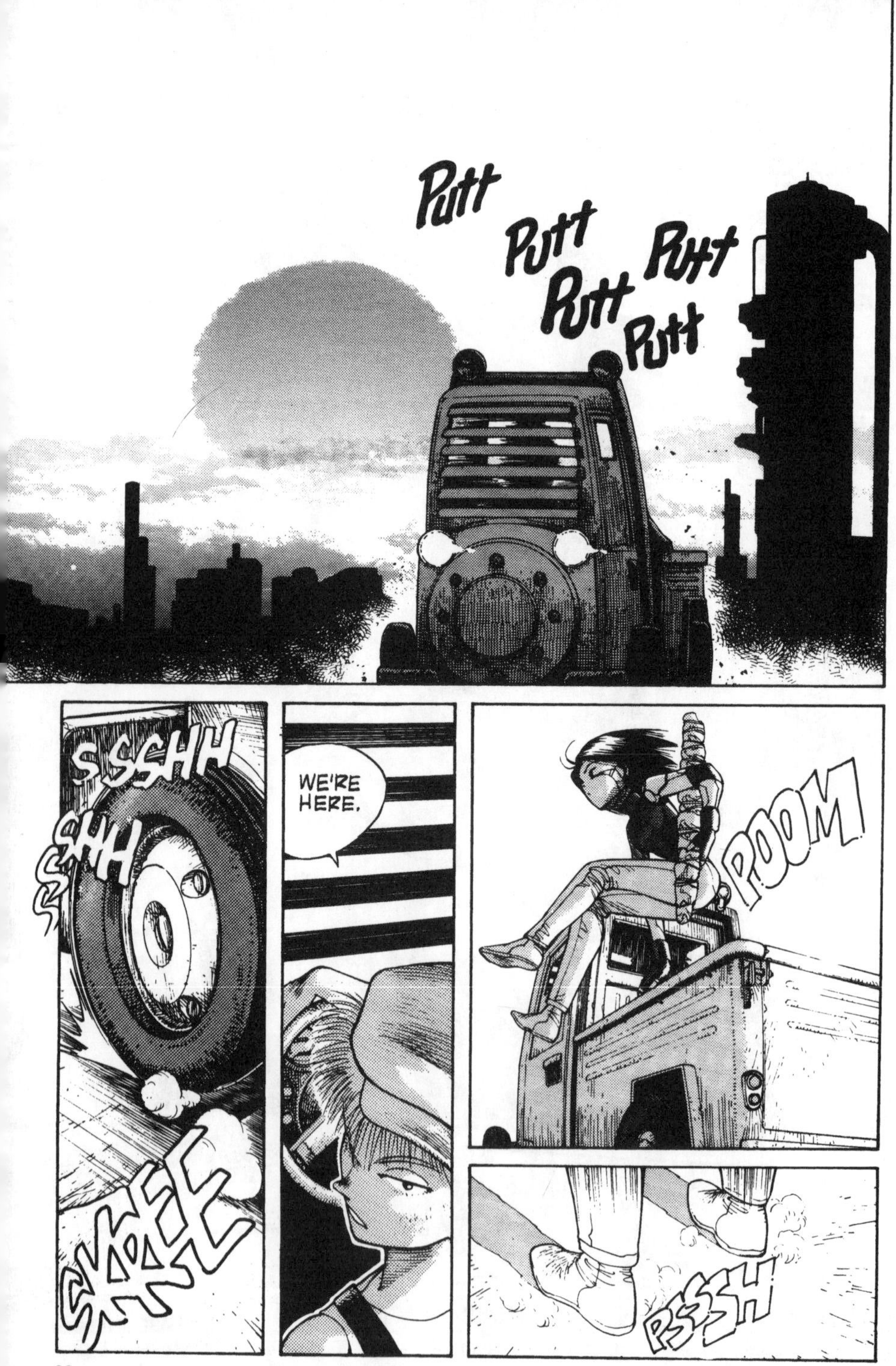

PUTT
PUTT
PUTT
PUTT
PUTT
S SSHH
SSHH
SKREE
WE'RE HERE.
POOM
PSSSH

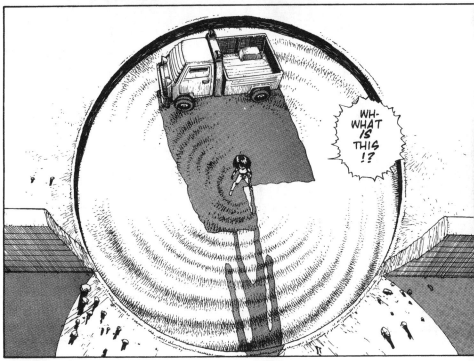

WH-
WHAT
IS
THIS
!?

THE
SURFACE
HAS BEEN
MELTED--
TURNED TO
GLASS...

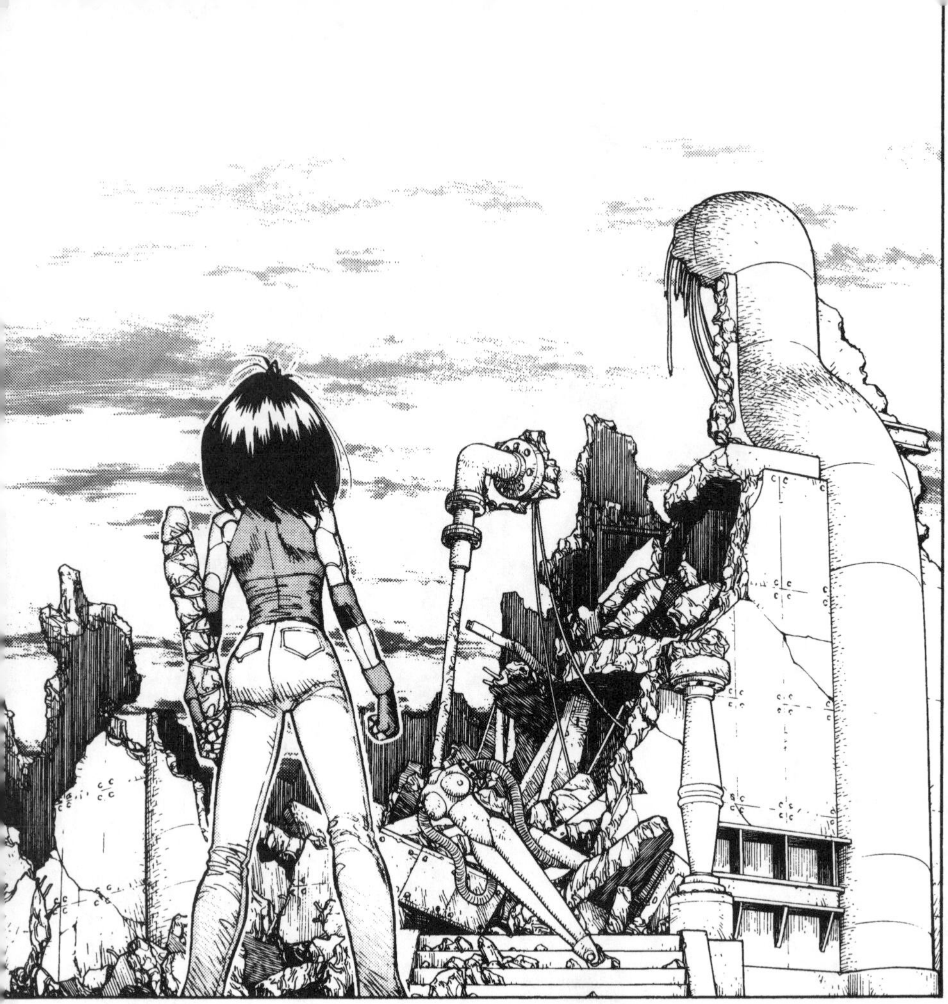

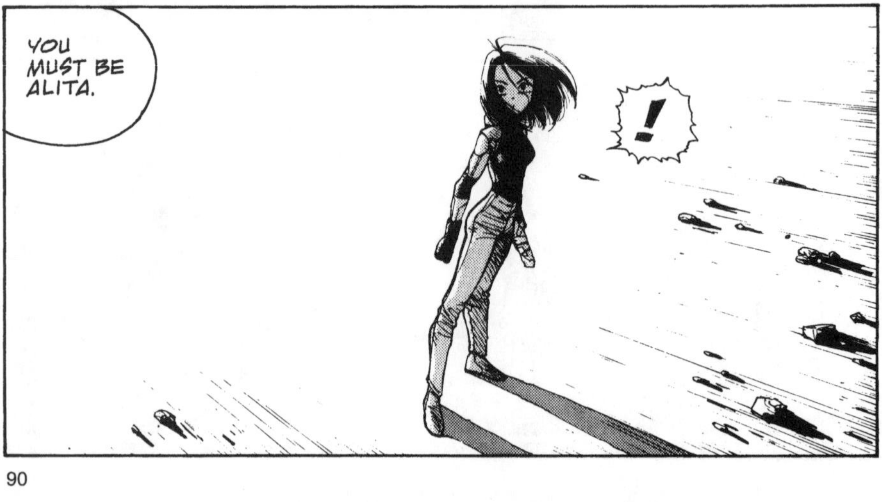
YOU MUST BE ALITA.
!

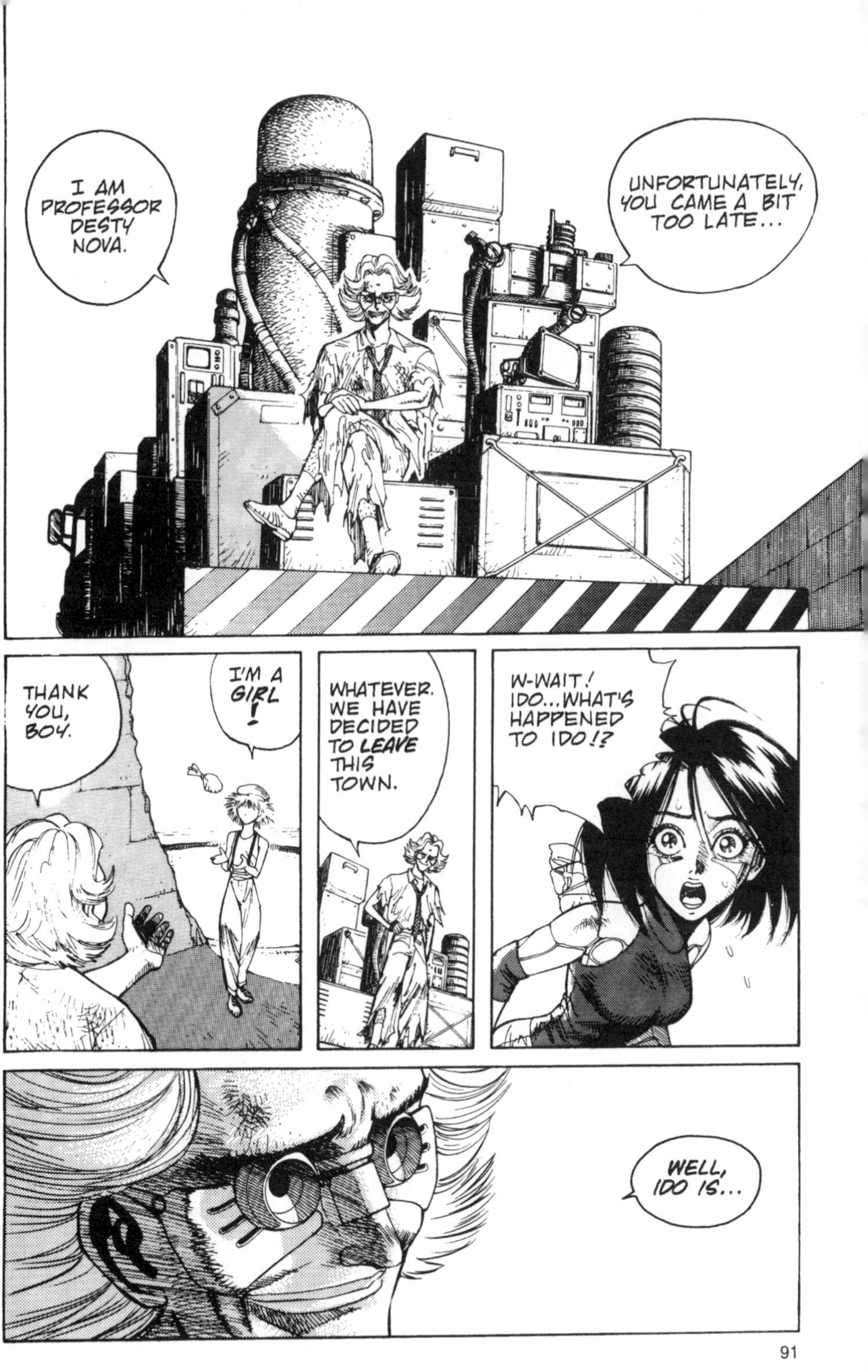
I AM PROFESSOR DESTY NOVA.
UNFORTUNATELY, YOU CAME A BIT TOO LATE...
THANK YOU, BOY.
I'M A GIRL!
WHATEVER. WE HAVE DECIDED TO LEAVE THIS TOWN.
W-WAIT! IDO...WHAT'S HAPPENED TO IDO!?
WELL, IDO IS...

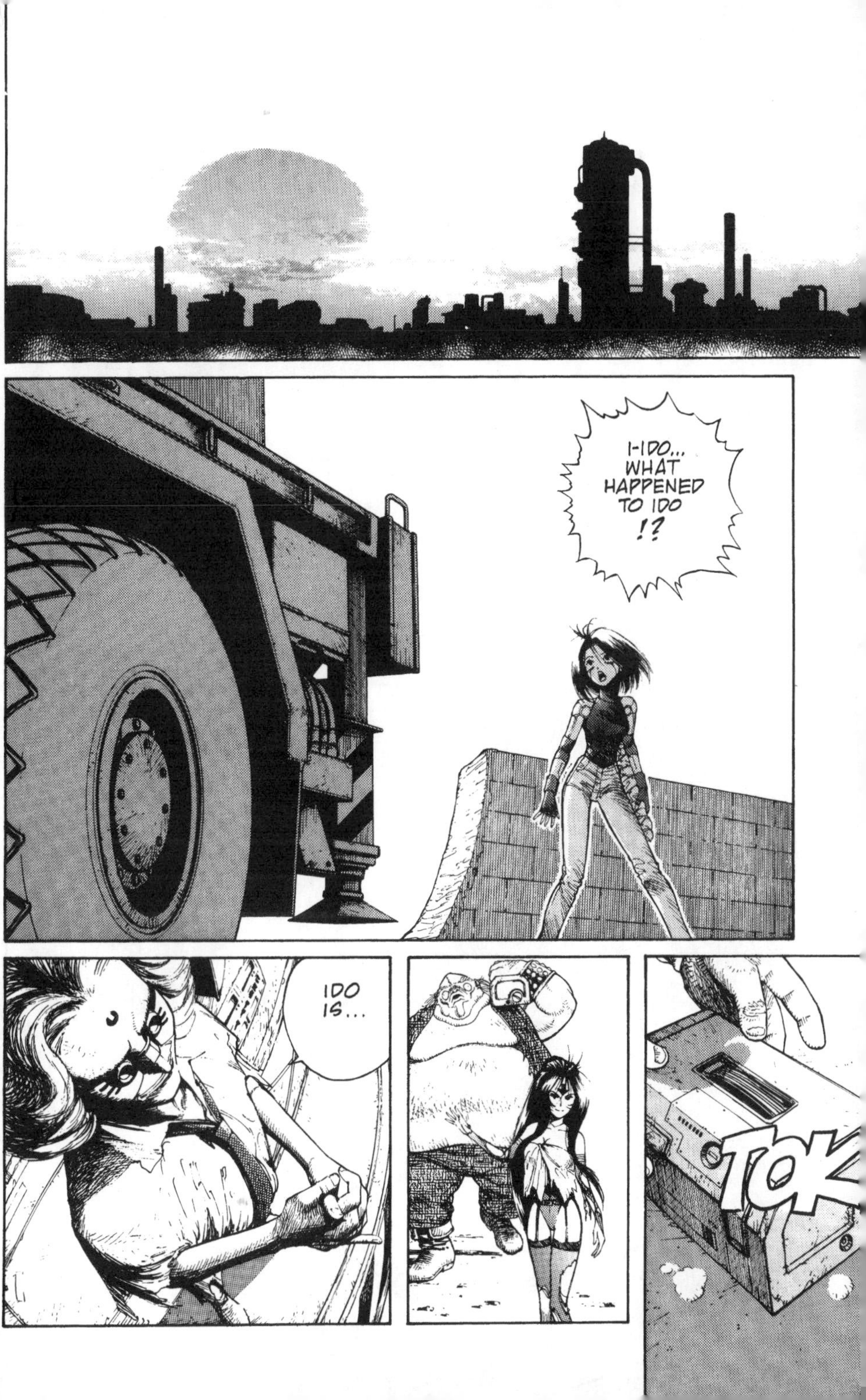
I-IDO... WHAT HAPPENED TO IDO !?
IDO IS...
TOK

COLLAPSE
Cycle 4: Reality Crumbles

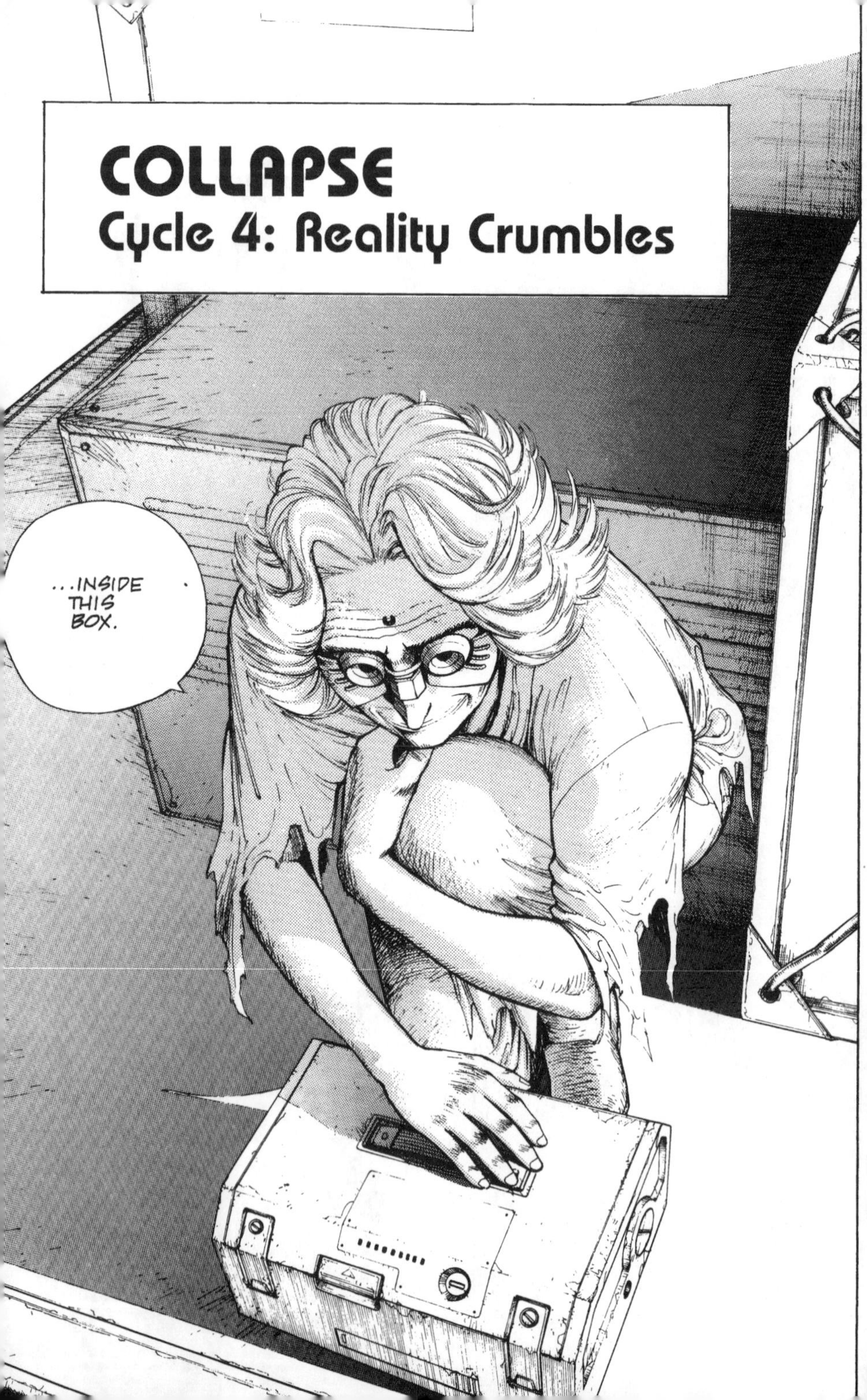
...INSIDE THIS BOX.

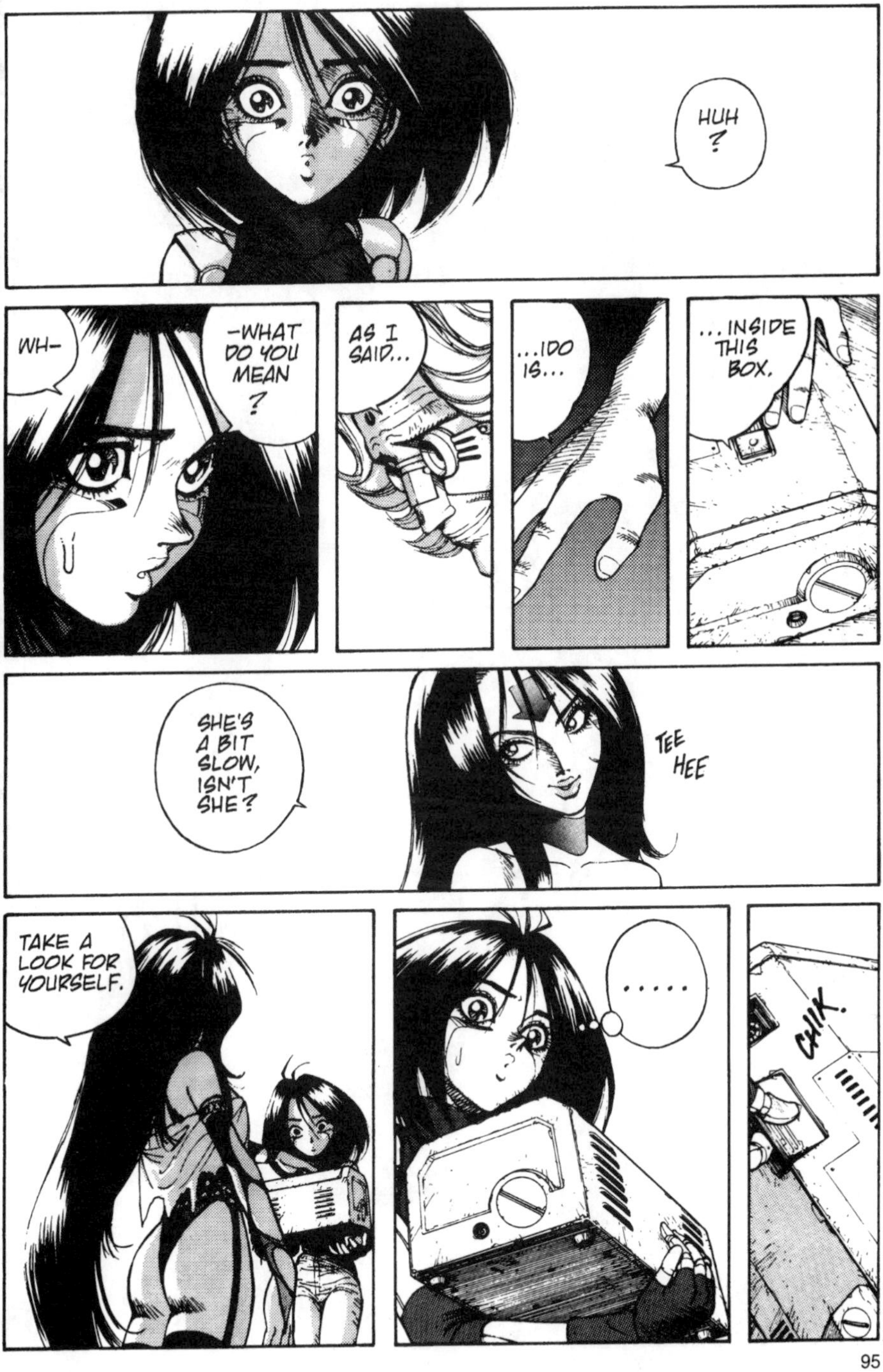
HUH ?
WH-
-WHAT DO YOU MEAN ?
AS I SAID...
...IDO IS...
...INSIDE THIS BOX.
SHE'S A BIT SLOW, ISN'T SHE?
TEE HEE
TAKE A LOOK FOR YOURSELF.
.....
CHIK.

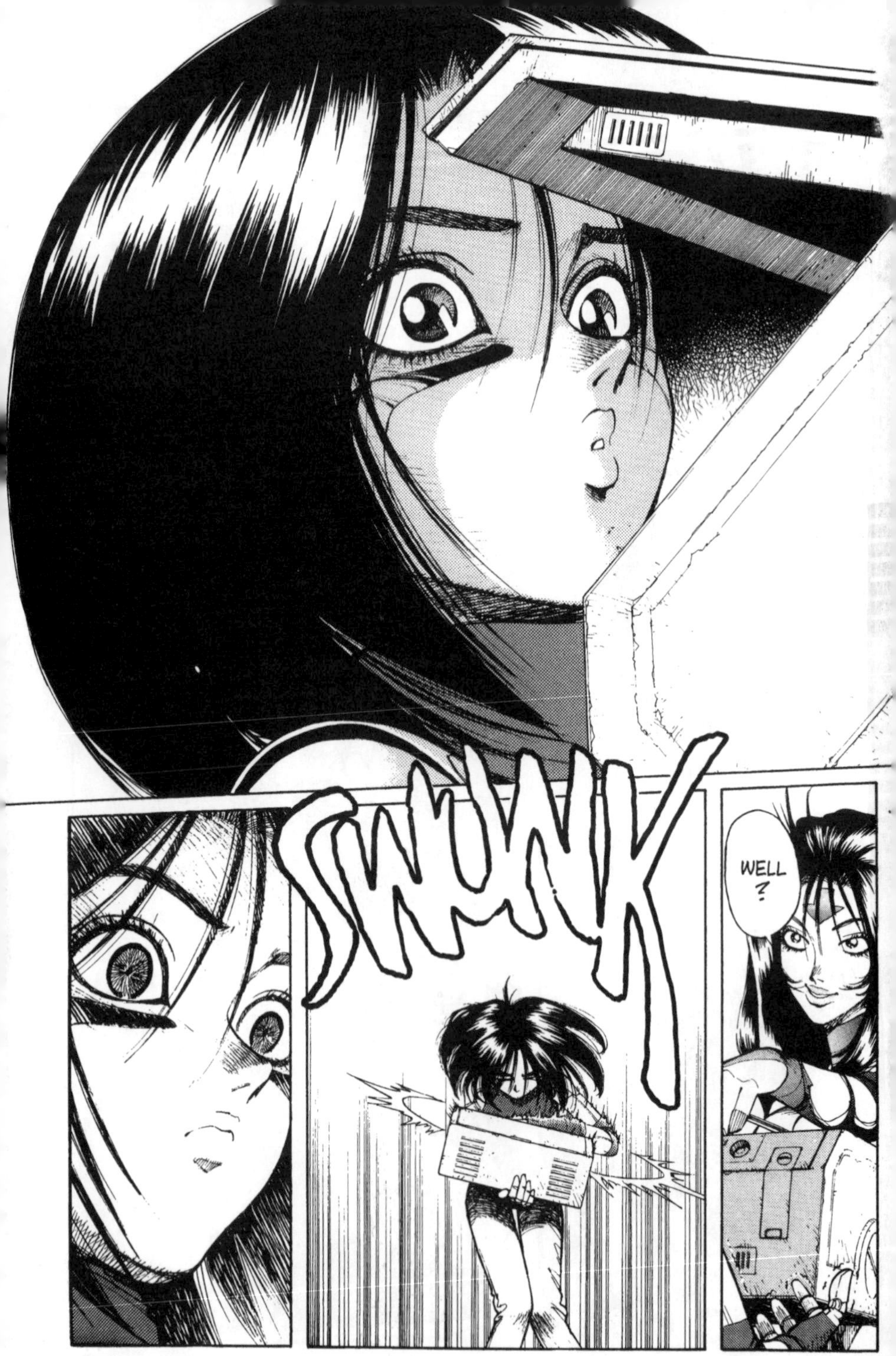
SHUNK
WELL?

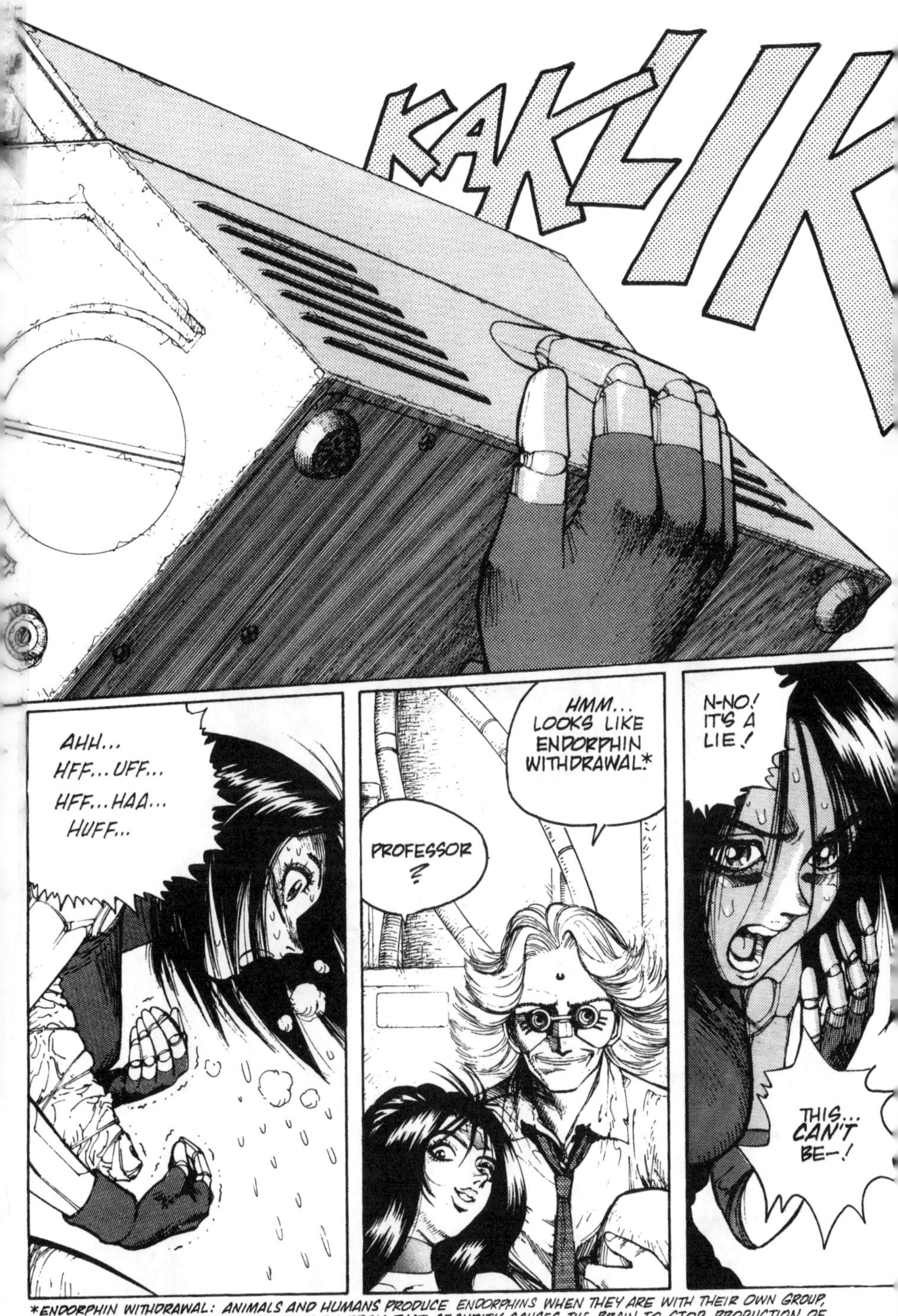
KAKLIIK
AHH... HFF...UFF... HFF...HAA... HUFF...
PROFESSOR ?
HMM... LOOKS LIKE ENDORPHIN WITHDRAWAL.*
N-NO! IT'S A LIE!
THIS... CAN'T BE--!

*ENDORPHIN WITHDRAWAL: ANIMALS AND HUMANS PRODUCE ENDORPHINS WHEN THEY ARE WITH THEIR OWN GROUP, FEELING SECURE AND HAPPY. SEPARATION FROM THAT SECURITY CAUSES THE BRAIN TO STOP PRODUCTION OF ENDORPHINS, CAUSING SYMPTOMS SIMILAR TO DRUG WITHDRAWAL.

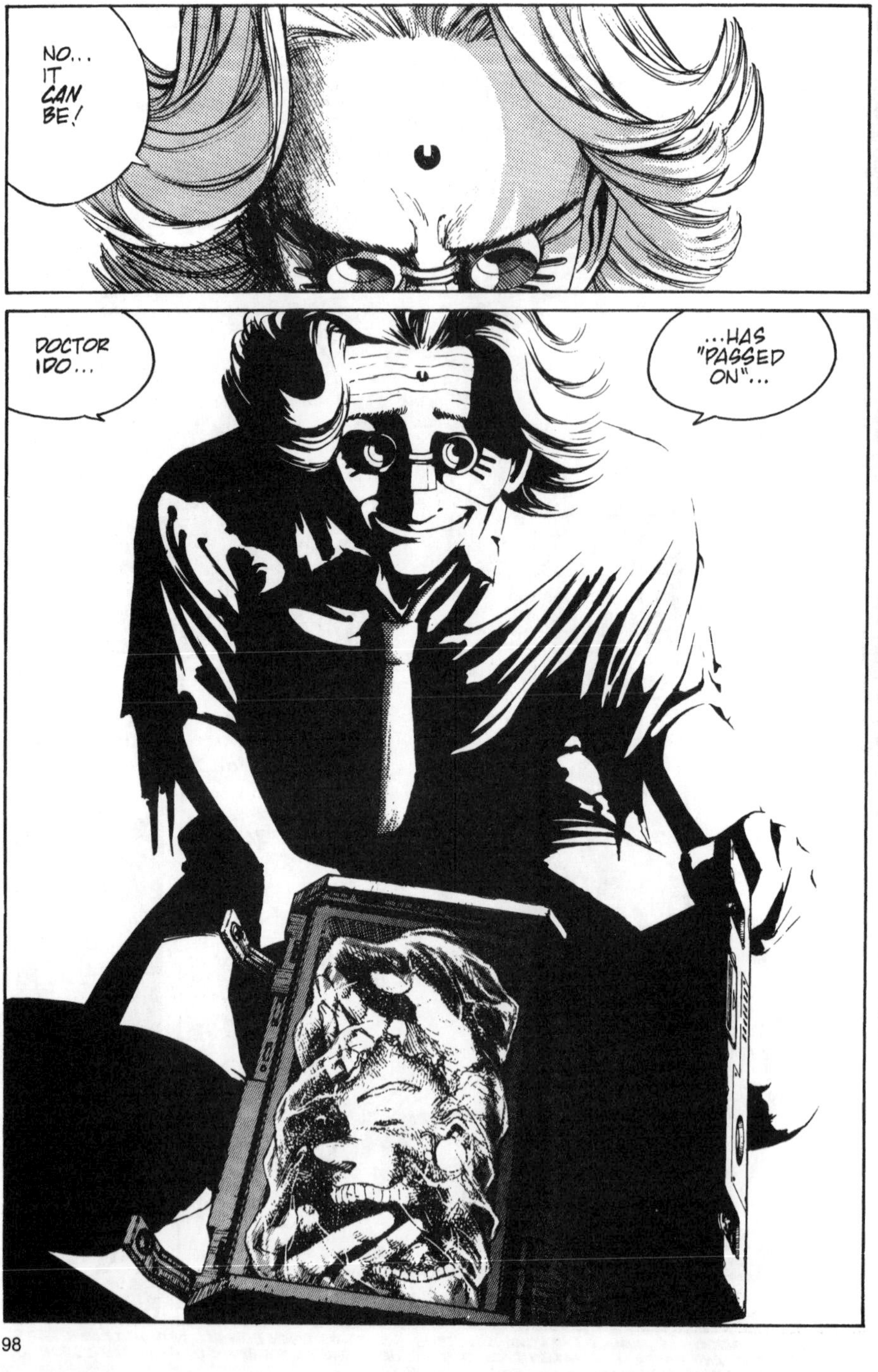
NO... IT CAN BE!
DOCTOR IDO...
...HAS "PASSED ON"...

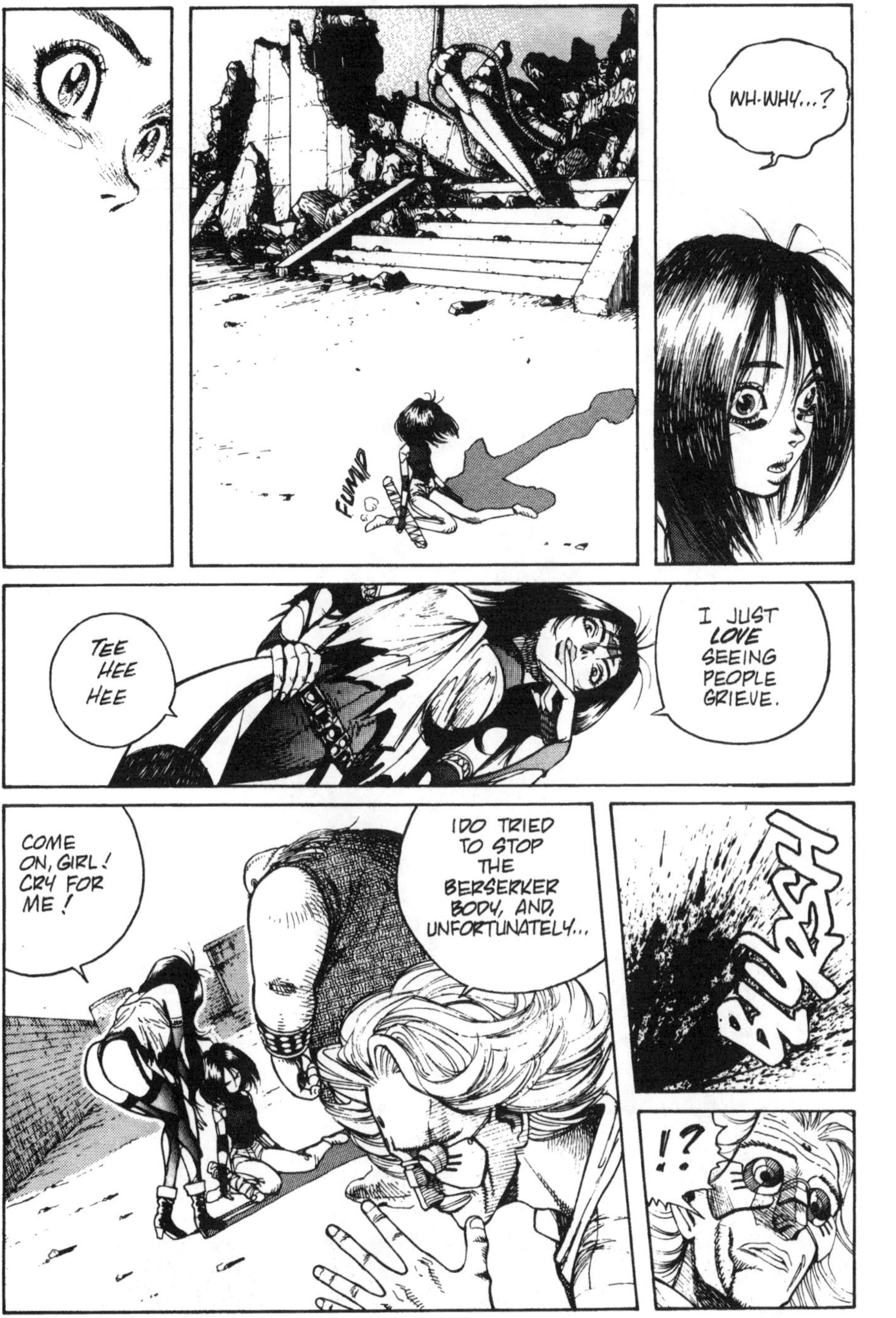
FUMP
WH-WHY...?
TEE HEE HEE
I JUST LOVE SEEING PEOPLE GRIEVE.
COME ON, GIRL! CRY FOR ME!
IDO TRIED TO STOP THE BERSERKER BODY, AND, UNFORTUNATELY...
BLURCH
!?

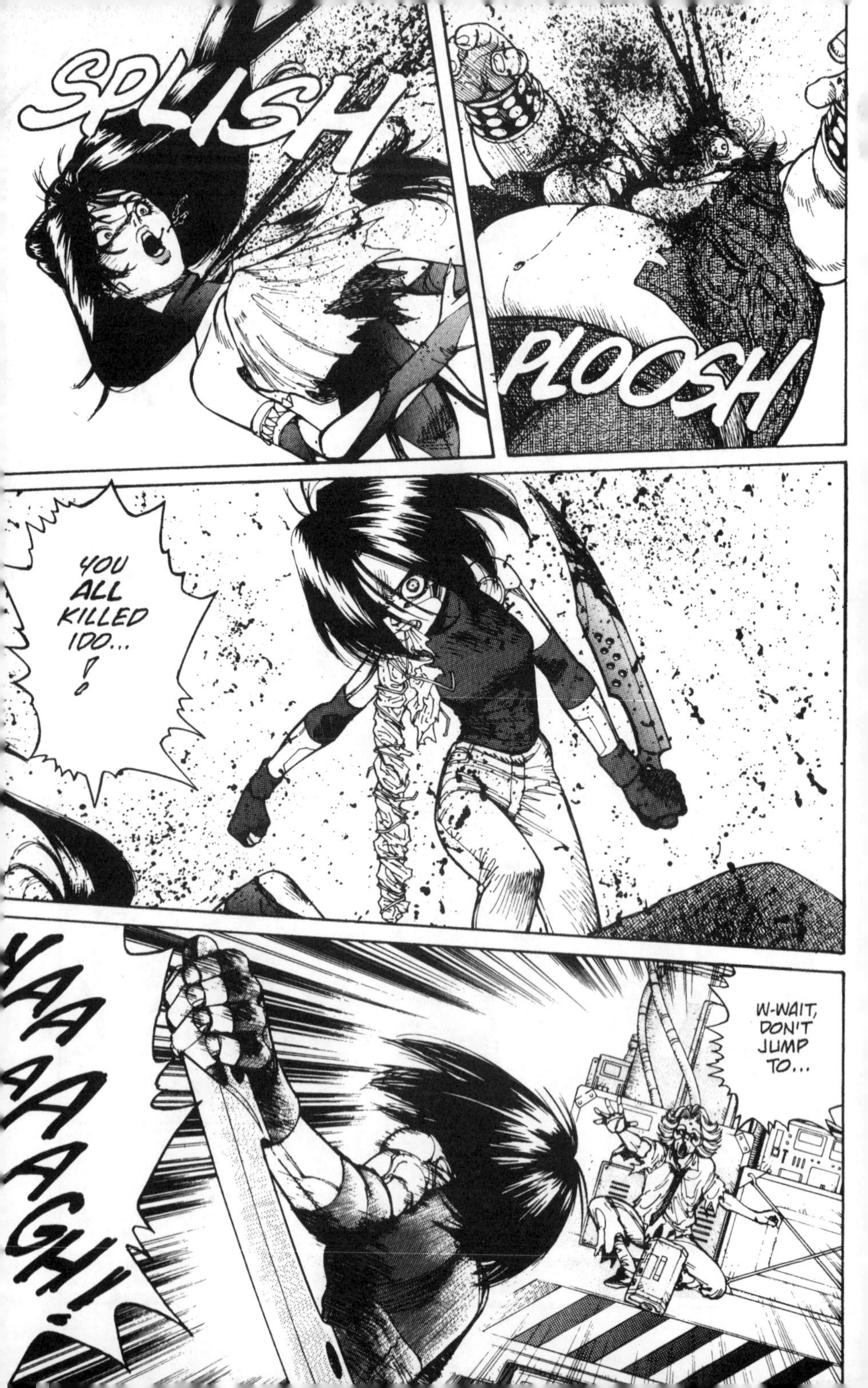
SPLISH
PLOOSH
YOU ALL KILLED IDO...!
YAAAAAAGH!!
W-WAIT, DON'T JUMP TO...

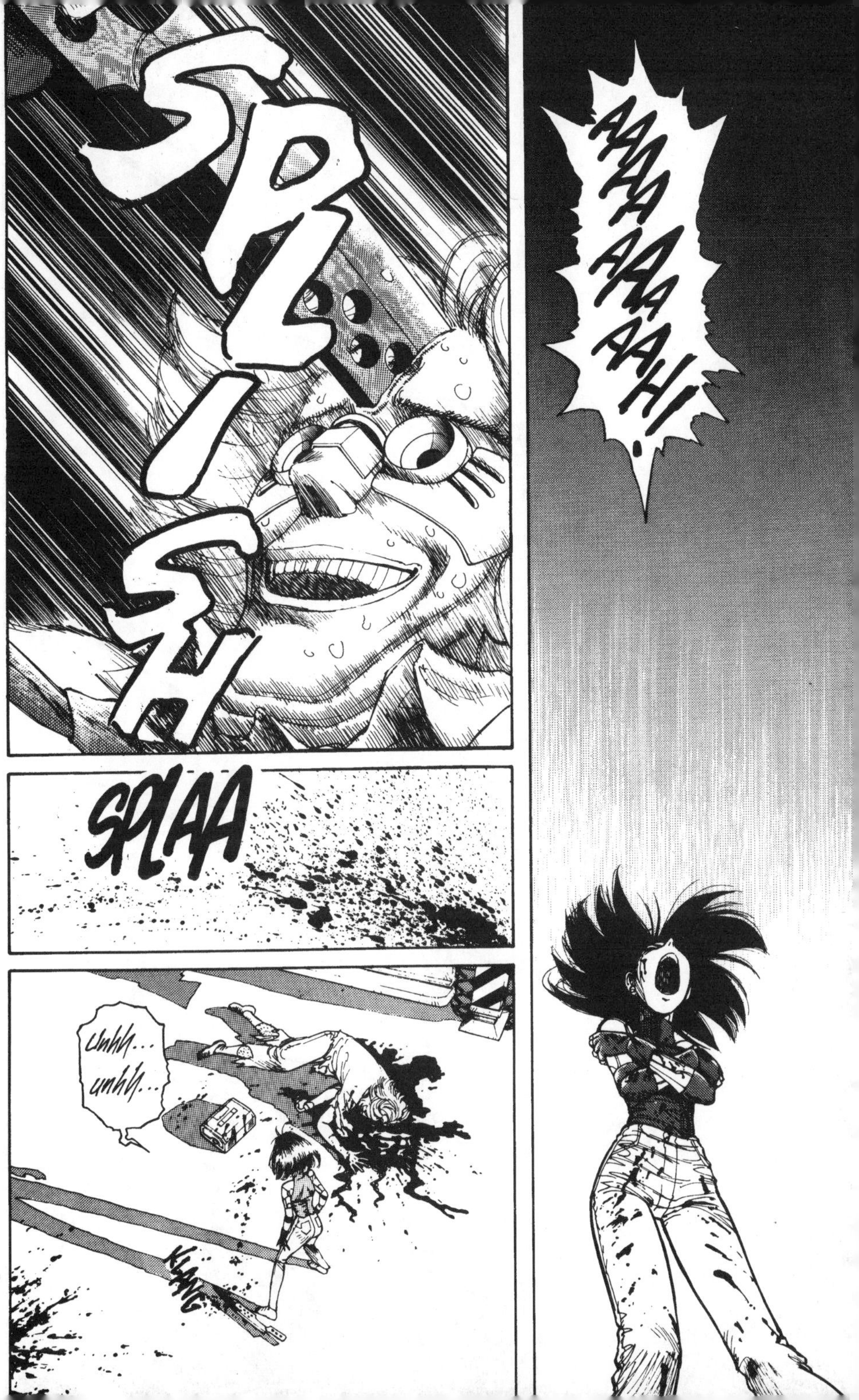
SPLISH
SPLAA
unhh...
unhh...
KLANG
AAAAAAAAAAAH!!

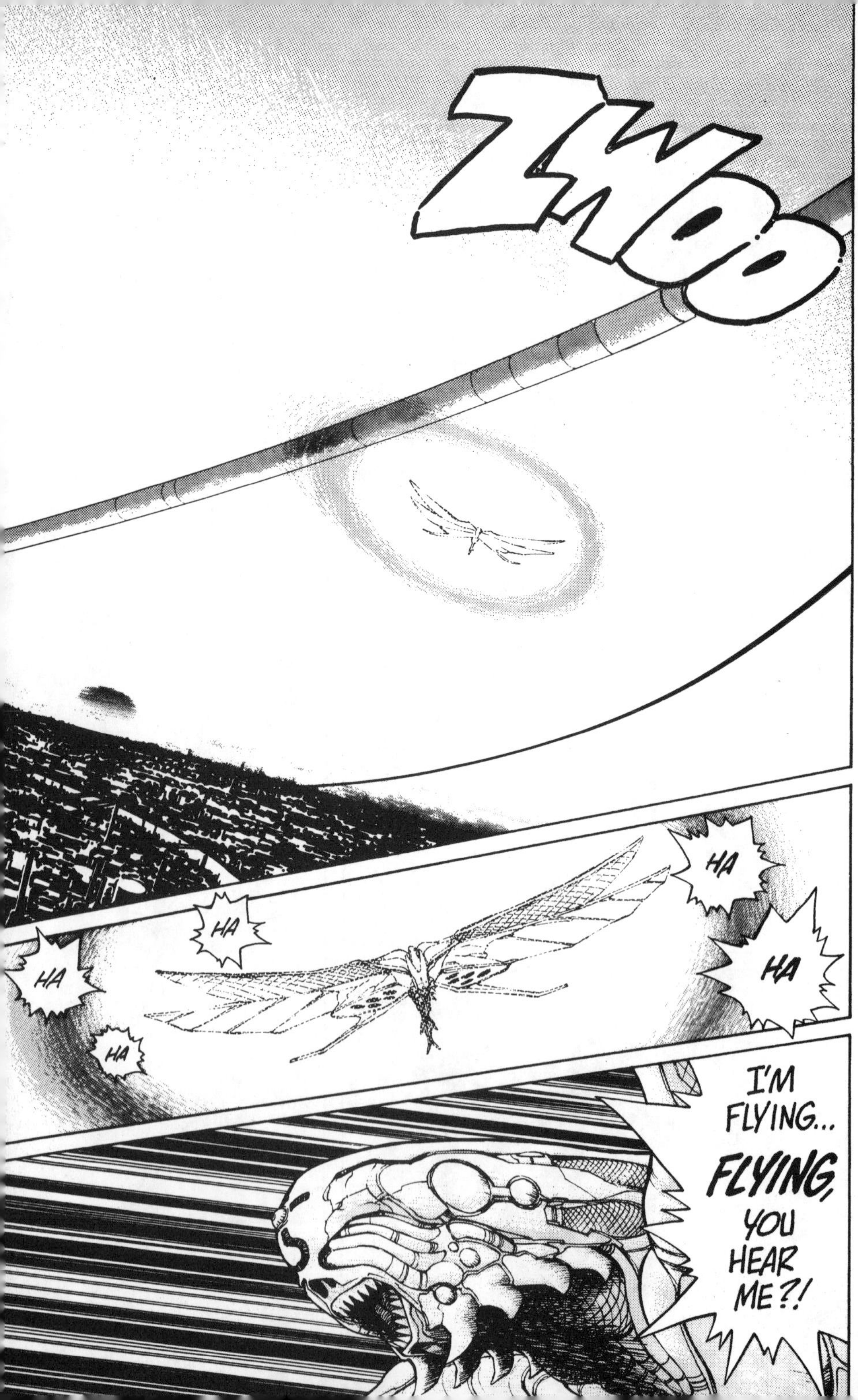
ZWOO
HA
HA
HA
HA
HA
I'M FLYING... FLYING, YOU HEAR ME?!

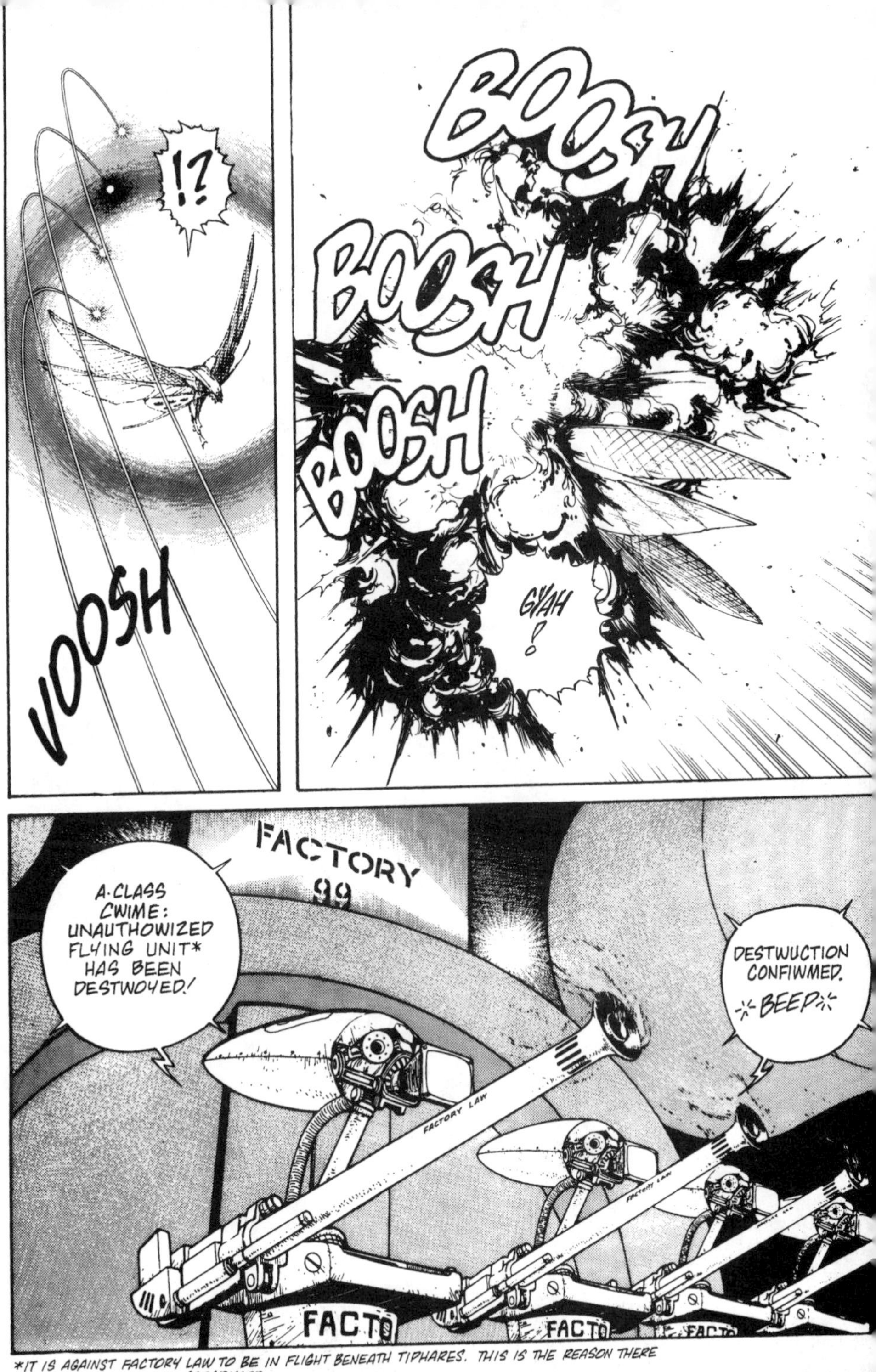
!?
VOOSH
BOOSH
BOOSH
BOOSH
GYAH!
FACTORY 99
A·CLASS CWIME: UNAUTHOWIZED FLYING UNIT* HAS BEEN DESTWOYED!
DESTWUCTION CONFIWMED.
BEEP
FACTORY LAW
FACTO
FACTO

*IT IS AGAINST FACTORY LAW TO BE IN FLIGHT BENEATH TIPHARES. THIS IS THE REASON THERE ARE NO BIRDS IN THE SCRAPYARD.

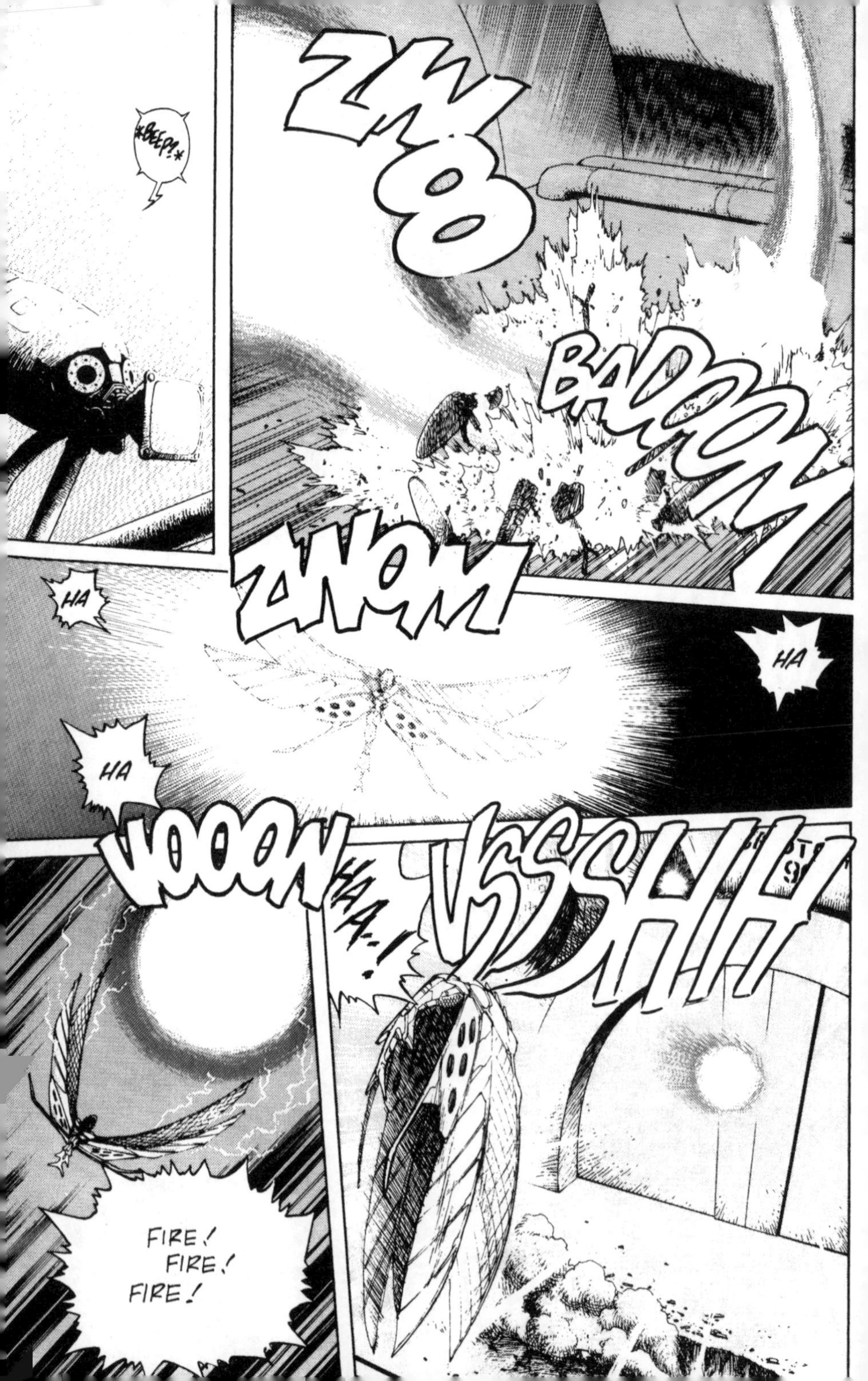
BEEP!
BADOOM
ZWOM
HA
HA
HA
VOOON
HAA-!
VSSHH
FIRE!
FIRE!
FIRE!

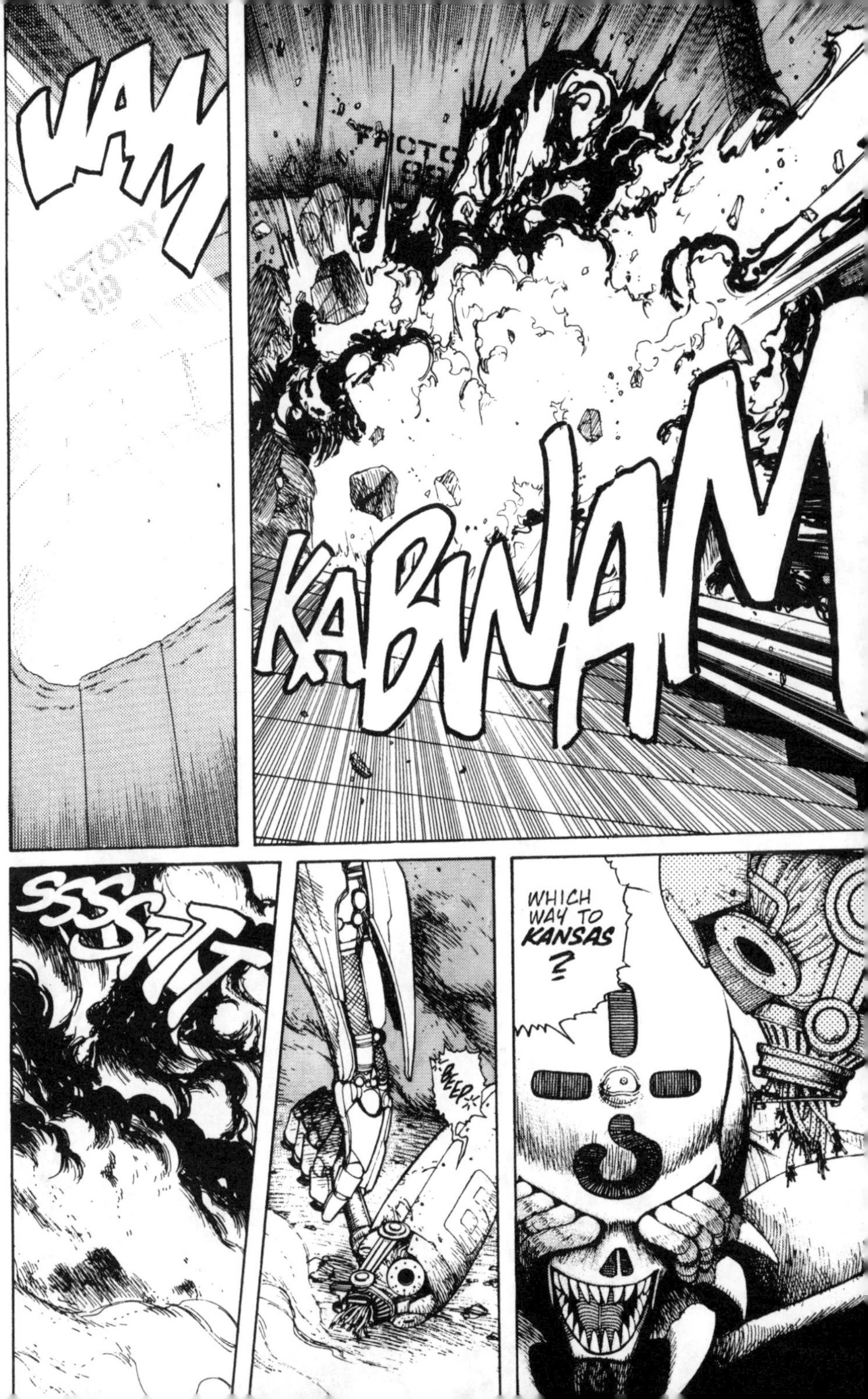
WAM
KABWAM
SSSSTT
BEEP
WHICH WAY TO KANSAS ?

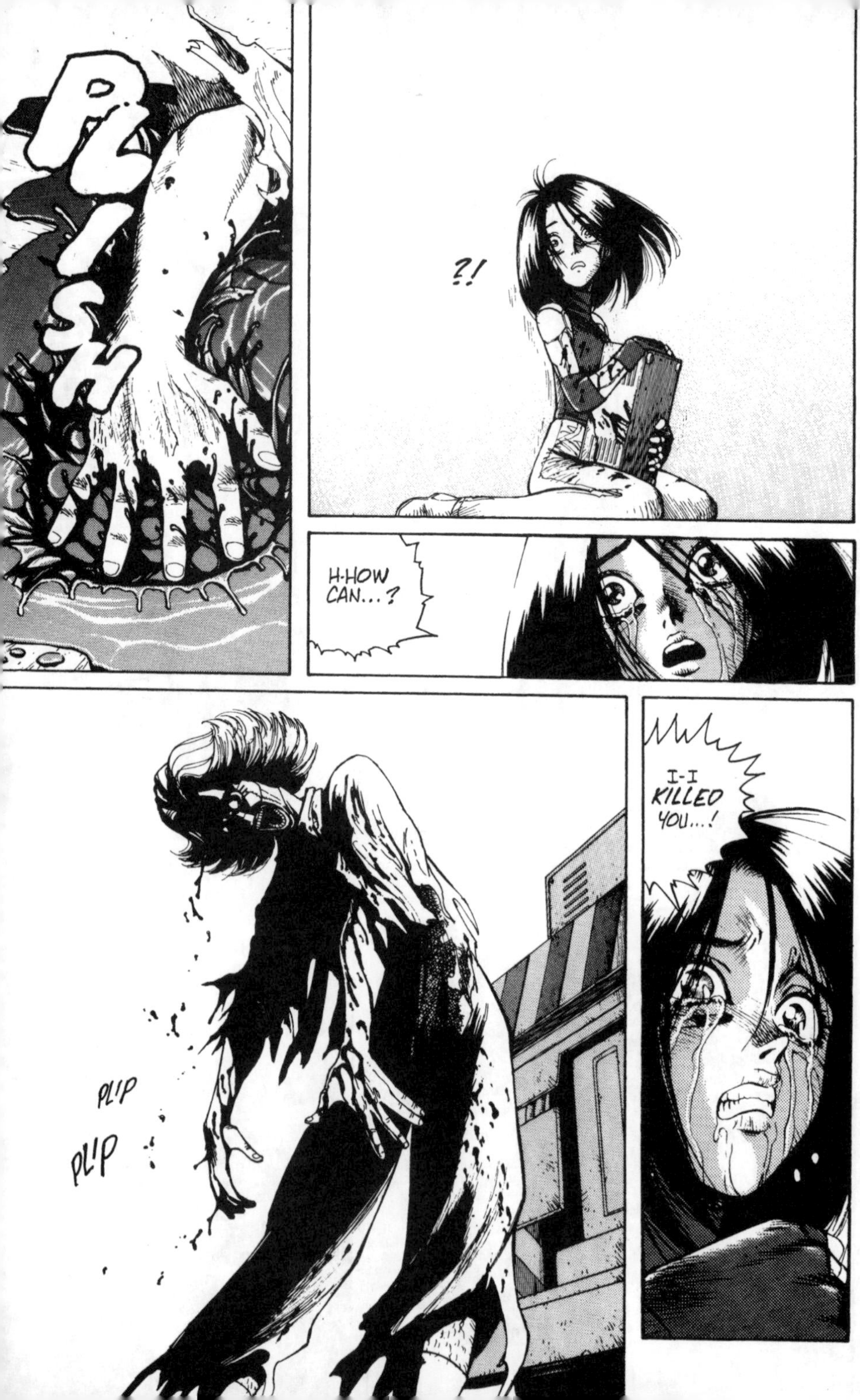
PLISH
?!
H-HOW CAN...?
PLIP
PLIP
I-I KILLED YOU...!

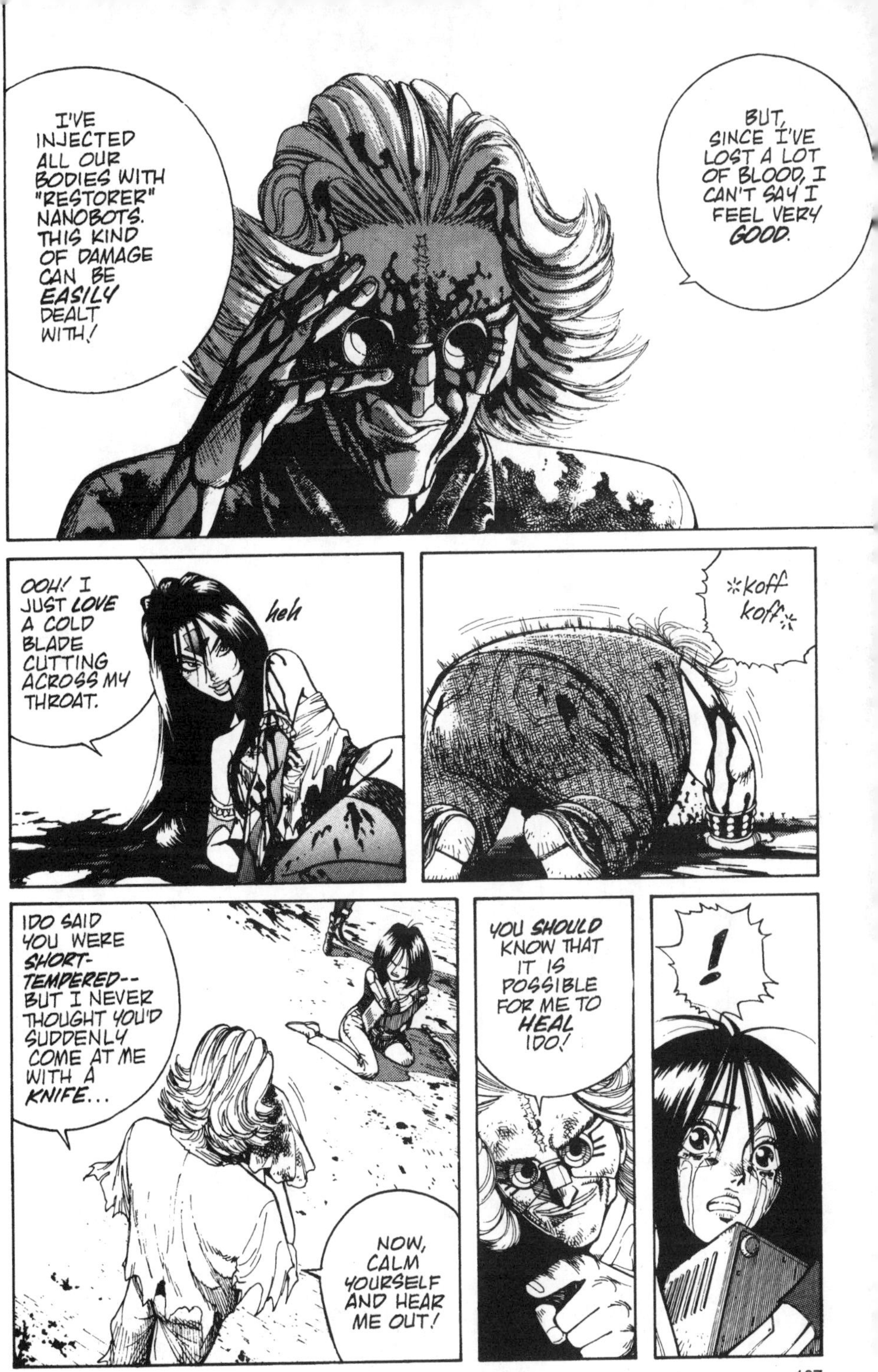
I'VE INJECTED ALL OUR BODIES WITH "RESTORER" NANOBOTS. THIS KIND OF DAMAGE CAN BE EASILY DEALT WITH!
BUT, SINCE I'VE LOST A LOT OF BLOOD, I CAN'T SAY I FEEL VERY GOOD.
OOH! I JUST LOVE A COLD BLADE CUTTING ACROSS MY THROAT.
heh
koff koff
IDO SAID YOU WERE SHORT-TEMPERED-- BUT I NEVER THOUGHT YOU'D SUDDENLY COME AT ME WITH A KNIFE...
NOW, CALM YOURSELF AND HEAR ME OUT!
YOU SHOULD KNOW THAT IT IS POSSIBLE FOR ME TO HEAL IDO!
!

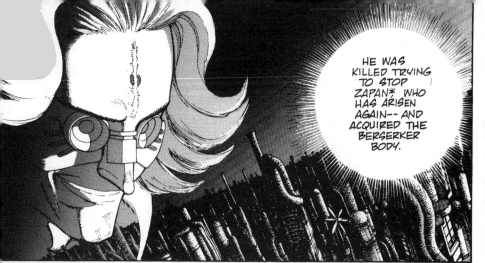

HE WAS KILLED TRYING TO STOP ZAPAN* WHO HAS ARISEN AGAIN-- AND ACQUIRED THE BERSERKER BODY.

FOOOM

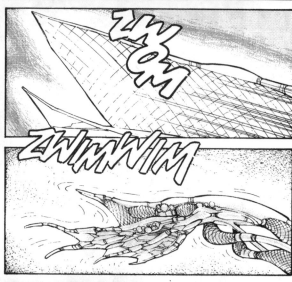

ZWOM

ZWIMWIM

YAAAH!

* ZAPAN: ACCORDING TO 16TH CENTURY DEMONOLOGISTS, THE FOUR REGIONS OF HELL WERE RULED BY SEVEN KINGS/OVERLORDS, INCLUDING ZAPAN, BAAL, ASMODEUS, BELIAL, AND OTHERS.

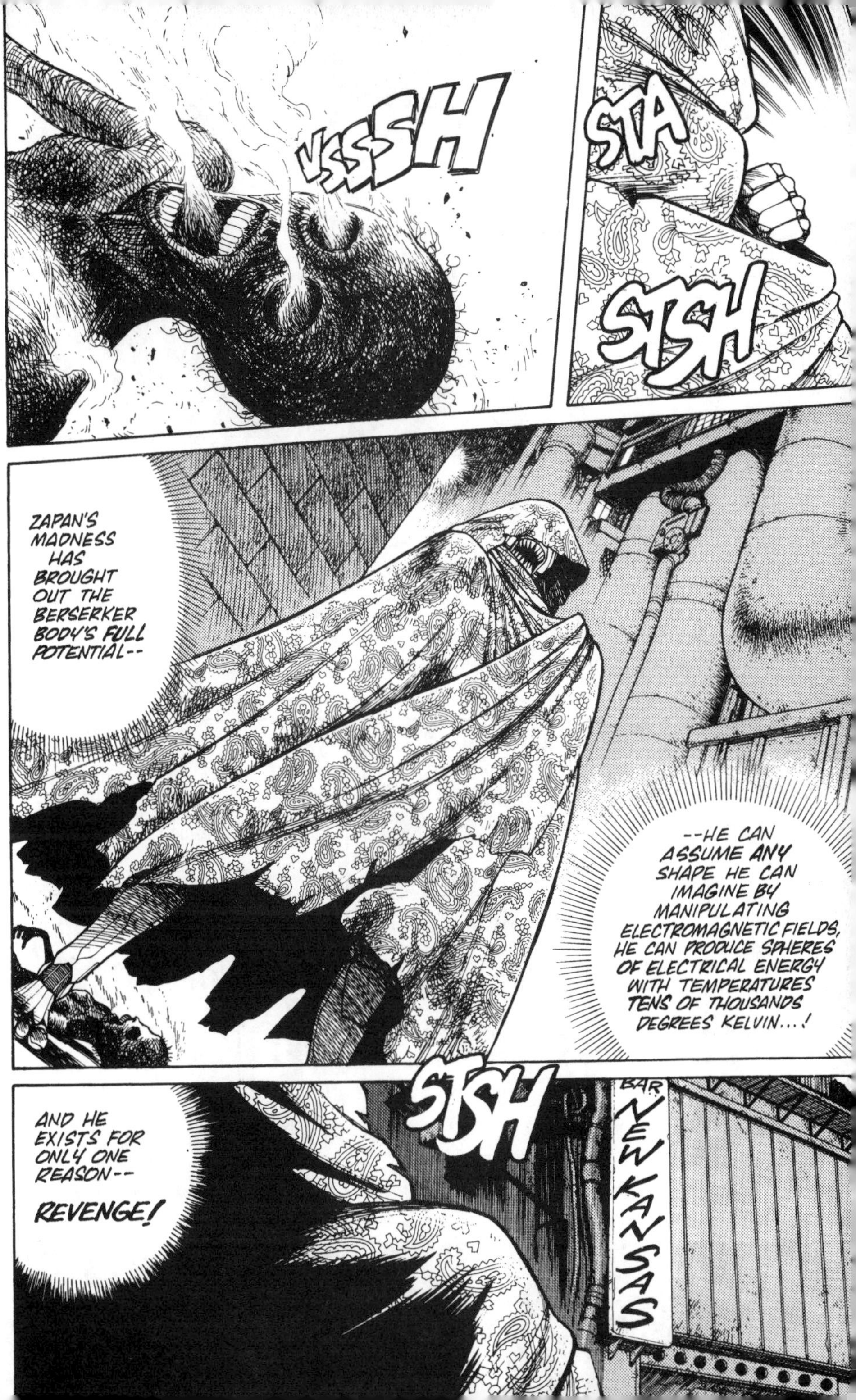
VSSSH
STA
STISH
ZAPAN'S MADNESS HAS BROUGHT OUT THE BERSERKER BODY'S FULL POTENTIAL--
--HE CAN ASSUME ANY SHAPE HE CAN IMAGINE BY MANIPULATING ELECTROMAGNETIC FIELDS, HE CAN PRODUCE SPHERES OF ELECTRICAL ENERGY WITH TEMPERATURES TENS OF THOUSANDS DEGREES KELVIN...!
STISH
AND HE EXISTS FOR ONLY ONE REASON--
REVENGE!
BAR NEW KANSAS

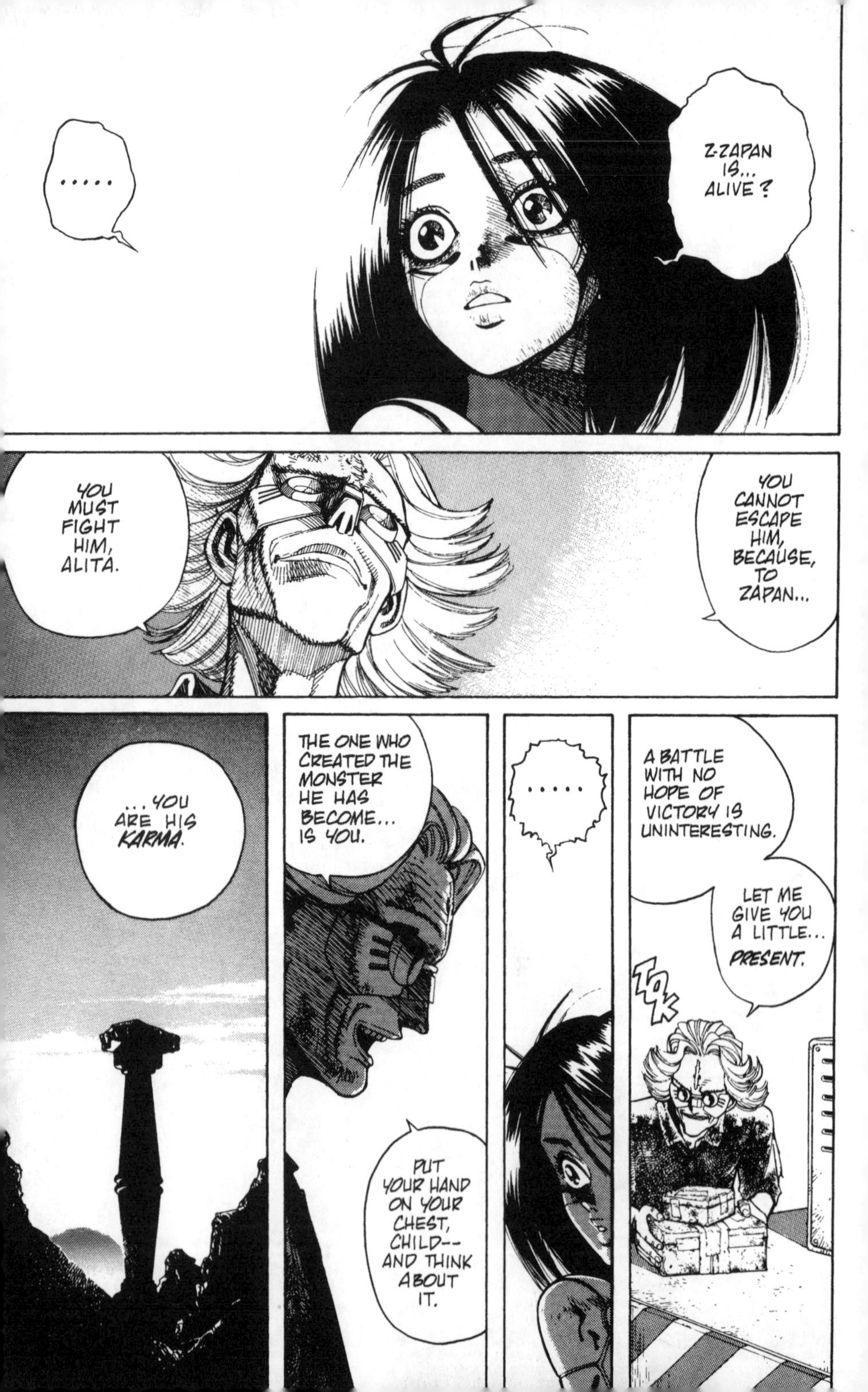
.....
Z-ZAPAN IS... ALIVE?
YOU MUST FIGHT HIM, ALITA.
YOU CANNOT ESCAPE HIM, BECAUSE, TO ZAPAN...
...YOU ARE HIS *KARMA*.
THE ONE WHO CREATED THE MONSTER HE HAS BECOME... IS YOU.
PUT YOUR HAND ON YOUR CHEST, CHILD-- AND THINK ABOUT IT.
.....
A BATTLE WITH NO HOPE OF VICTORY IS UNINTERESTING.
LET ME GIVE YOU A LITTLE... *PRESENT*.
TOK

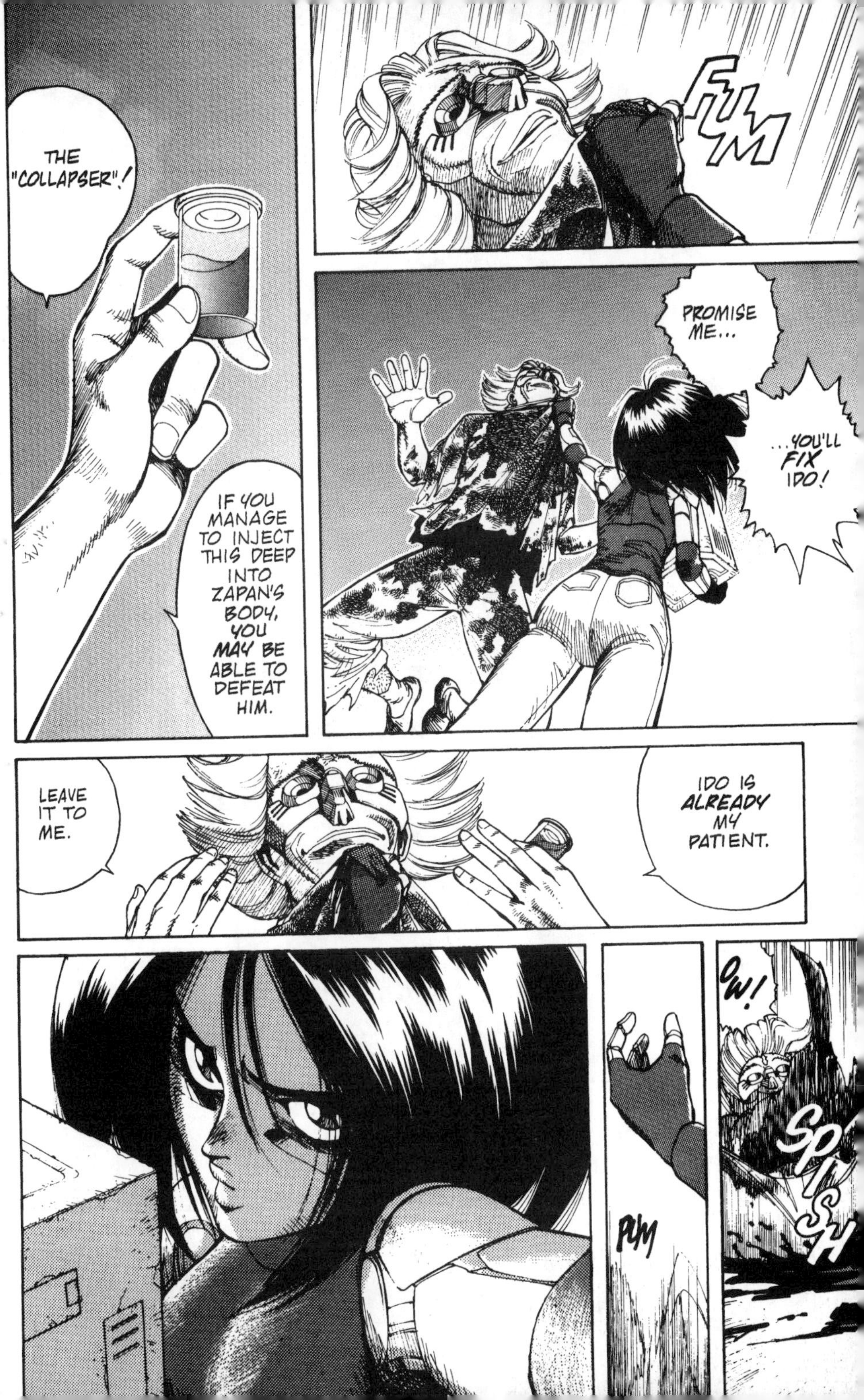
THE "COLLAPSER"!
IF YOU MANAGE TO INJECT THIS DEEP INTO ZAPAN'S BODY, YOU MAY BE ABLE TO DEFEAT HIM.
FUM
PROMISE ME...
...YOU'LL FIX IDO!
LEAVE IT TO ME.
IDO IS ALREADY MY PATIENT.
PUM
OW!
SPLISH

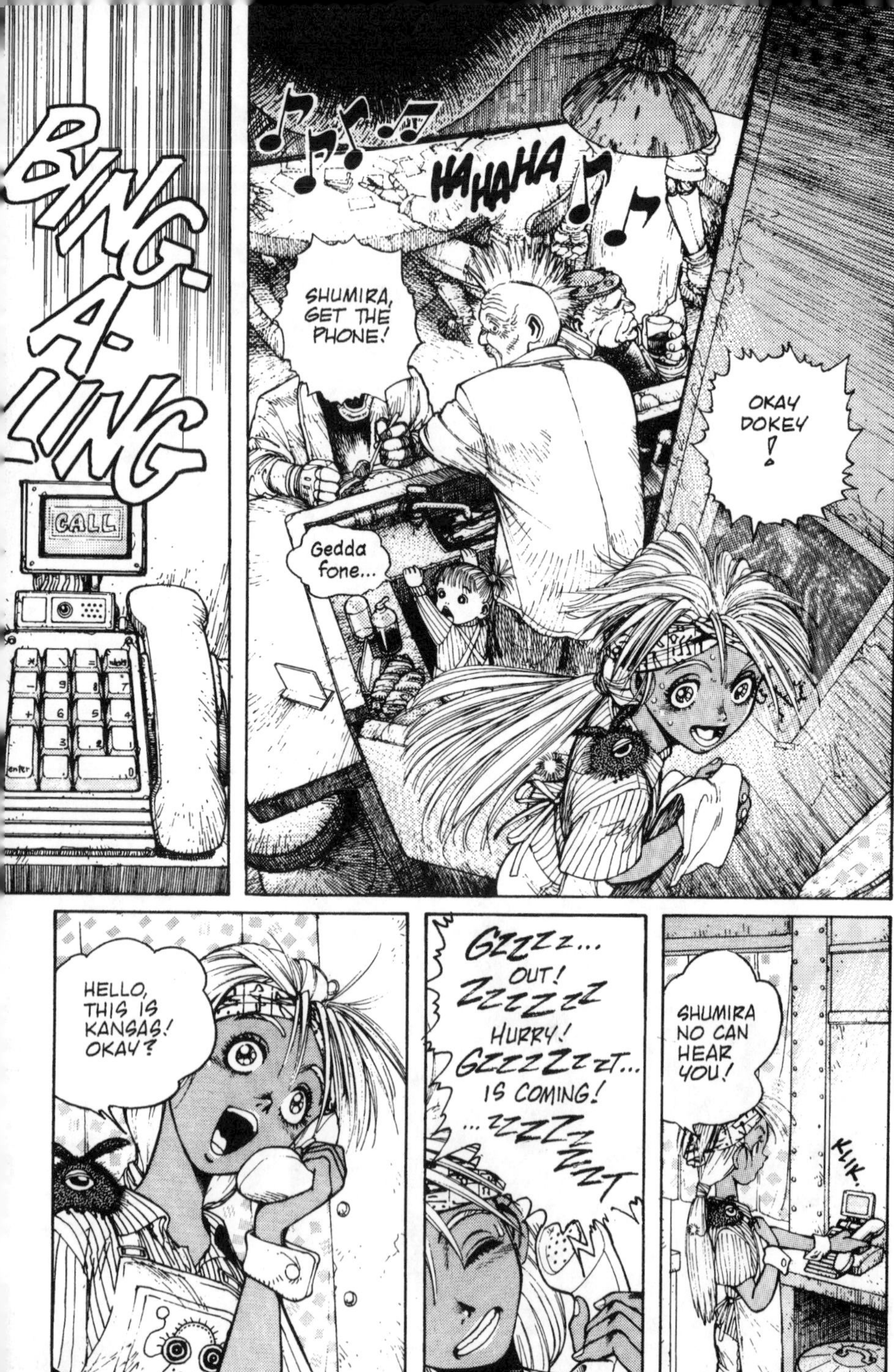
BING-A-LING
CALL
HAHAHA
SHUMIRA, GET THE PHONE!
Gedda fone...
OKAY DOKEY!
HELLO, THIS IS KANSAS! OKAY?
GZZZz... OUT! ZZZZZZZ HURRY! GZZZZzzT... IS COMING! ...ZZZZZZZT
SHUMIRA NO CAN HEAR YOU!
KLIK.

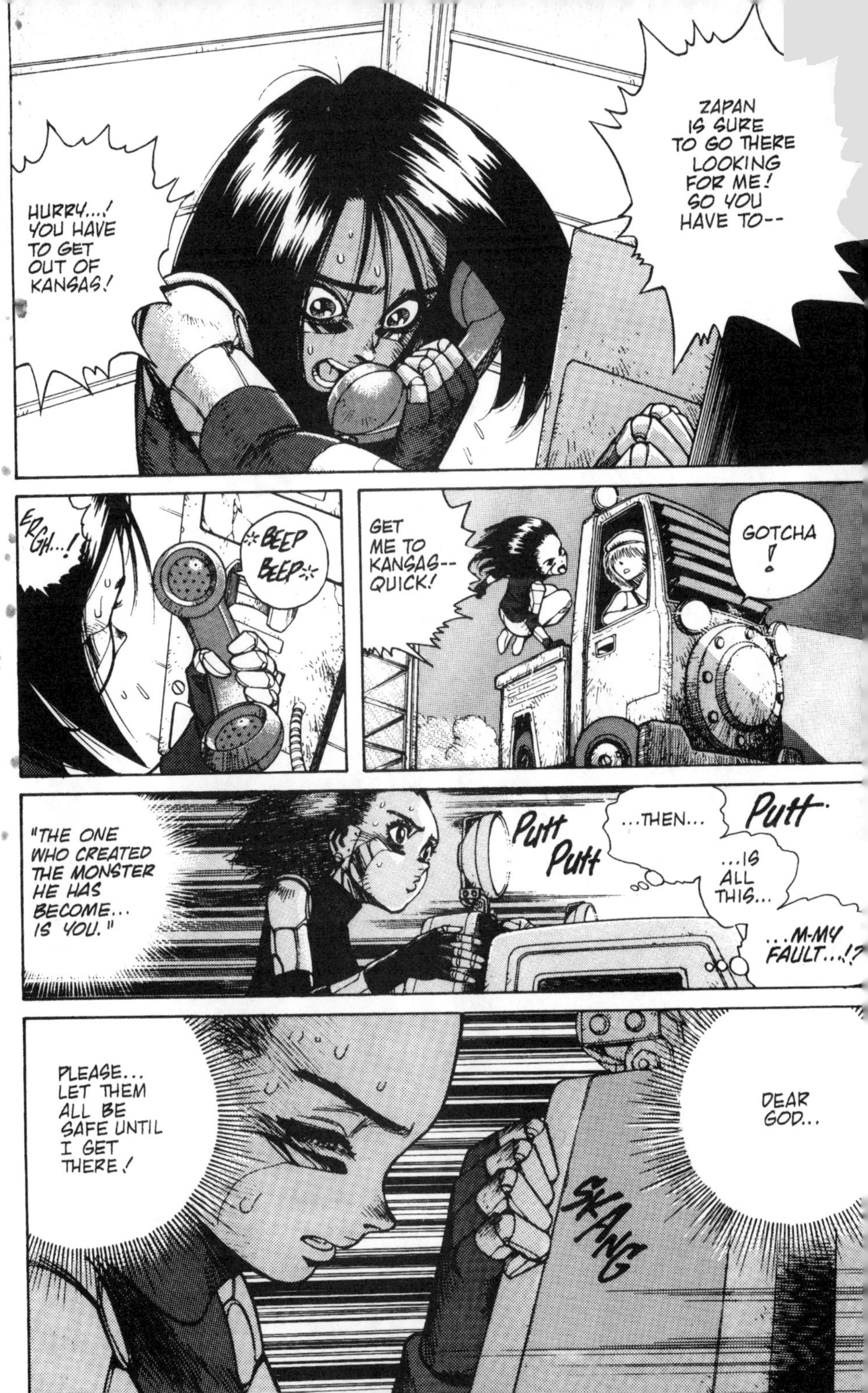
HURRY...! YOU HAVE TO GET OUT OF KANSAS!
ZAPAN IS SURE TO GO THERE LOOKING FOR ME! SO YOU HAVE TO--
ERGH...!
BEEP BEEP
GET ME TO KANSAS-- QUICK!
GOTCHA!
"THE ONE WHO CREATED THE MONSTER HE HAS BECOME... IS YOU."
Putt Putt
...THEN...
Putt
...IS ALL THIS...
...M-MY FAULT...!?
PLEASE... LET THEM ALL BE SAFE UNTIL I GET THERE!
DEAR GOD...
SKANG

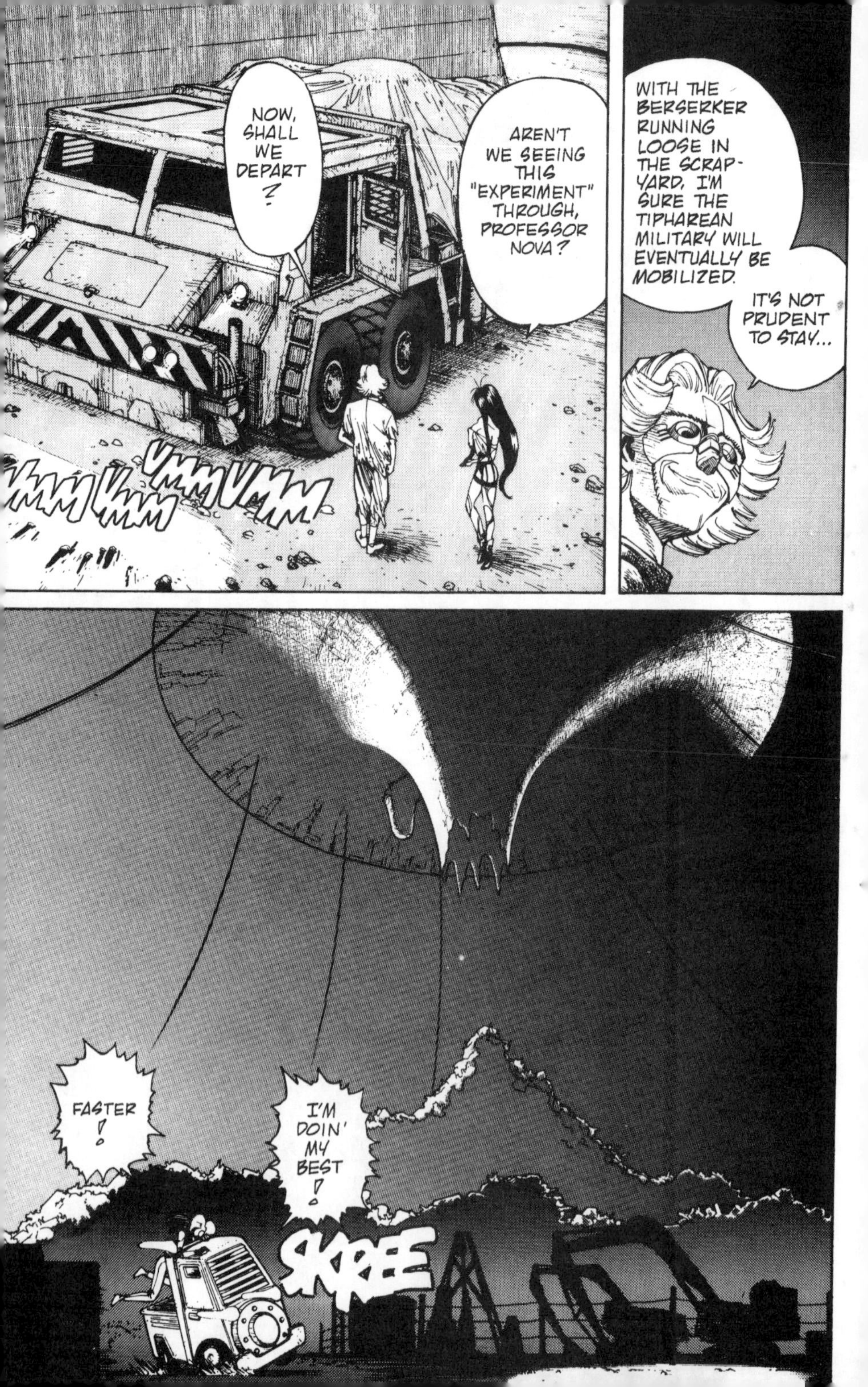
NOW, SHALL WE DEPART?
AREN'T WE SEEING THIS "EXPERIMENT" THROUGH, PROFESSOR NOVA?
VMM VMM VMM VMM
WITH THE BERSERKER RUNNING LOOSE IN THE SCRAP-YARD, I'M SURE THE TIPHAREAN MILITARY WILL EVENTUALLY BE MOBILIZED.
IT'S NOT PRUDENT TO STAY...
FASTER!
I'M DOIN' MY BEST!
SKREE

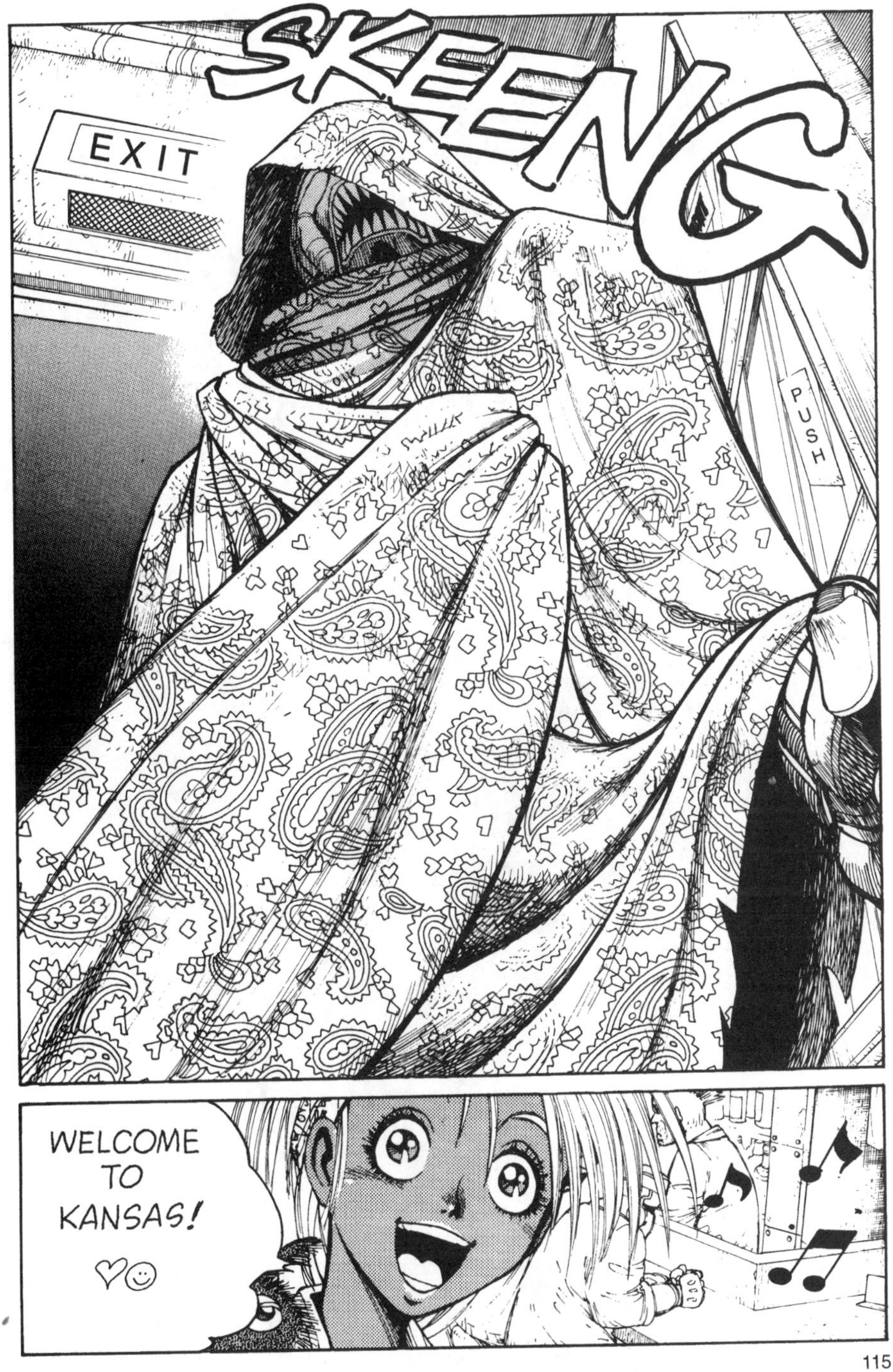
SKEENG
EXIT
PUSH
WELCOME TO KANSAS! ♡☺

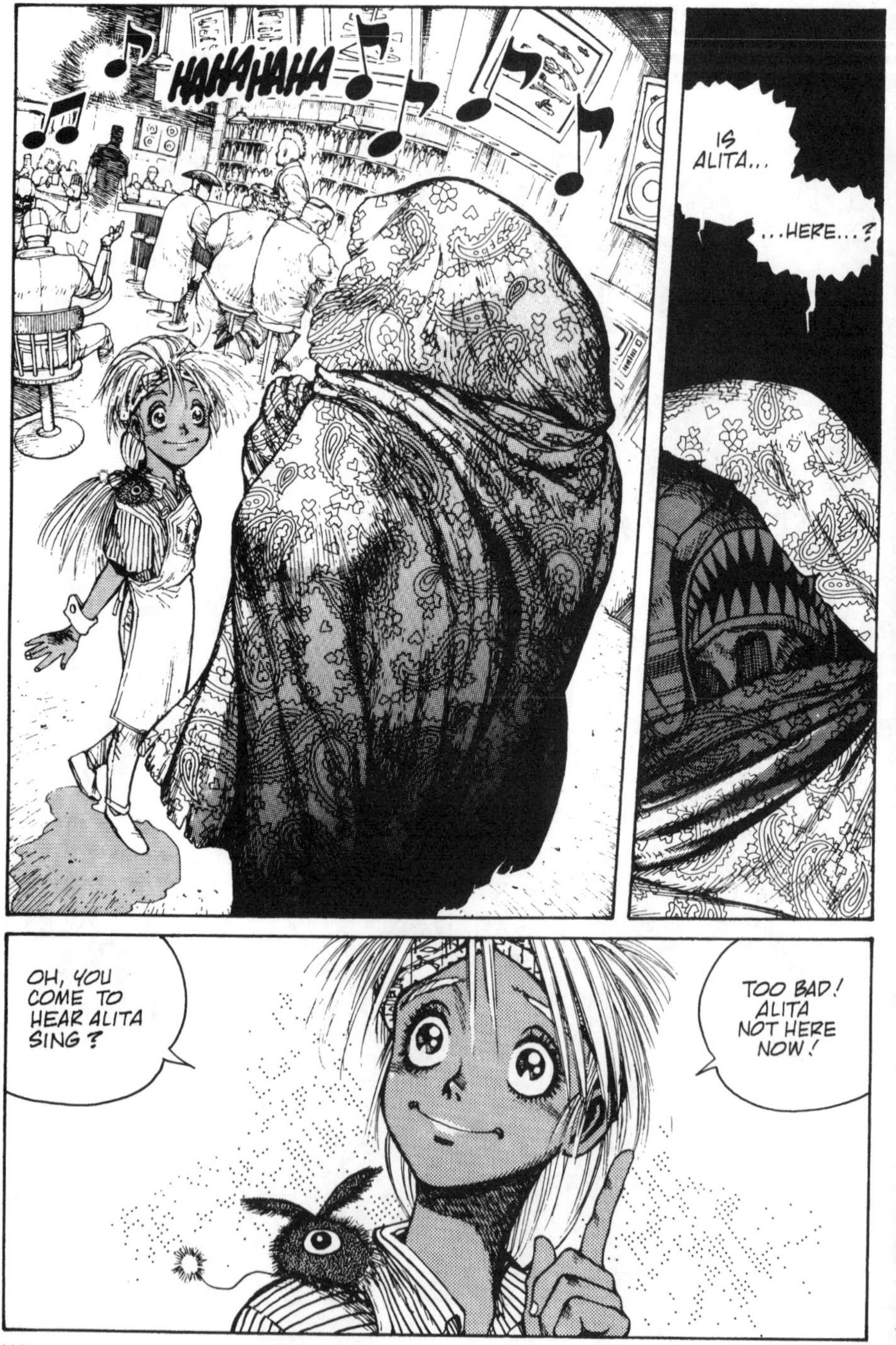
HAHAHAHA
IS ALITA...
...HERE...?
OH, YOU COME TO HEAR ALITA SING?
TOO BAD! ALITA NOT HERE NOW!

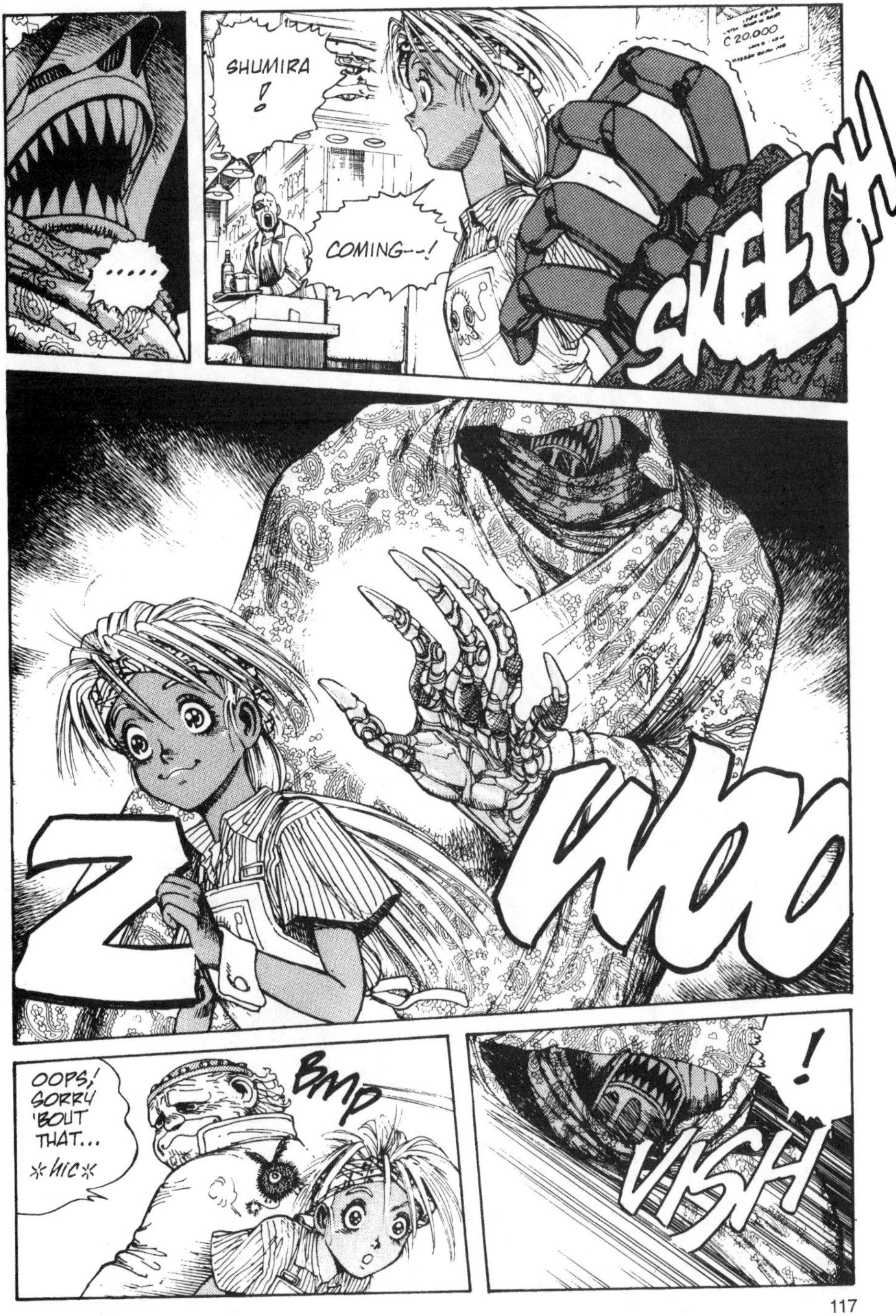

.....
SHUMIRA !
COMING--!
C20,000
SKEECH
ZWOO
OOPS! SORRY 'BOUT THAT... *HIC*
BMP
!
VISH

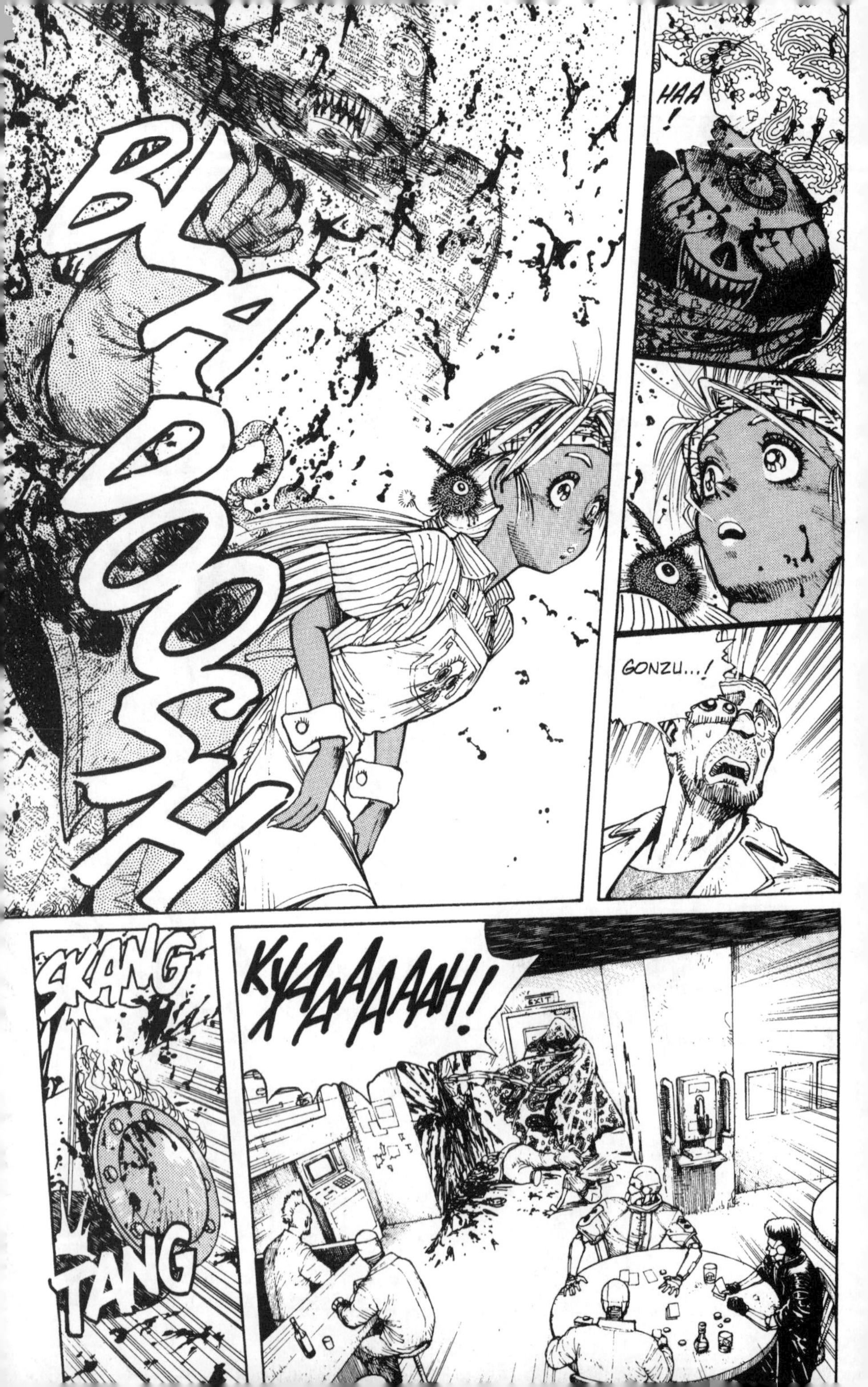
BLAOOOOOM
HAA!
GONZU...!
SKANG
TANG
KYAAAAAAAH!
EXIT

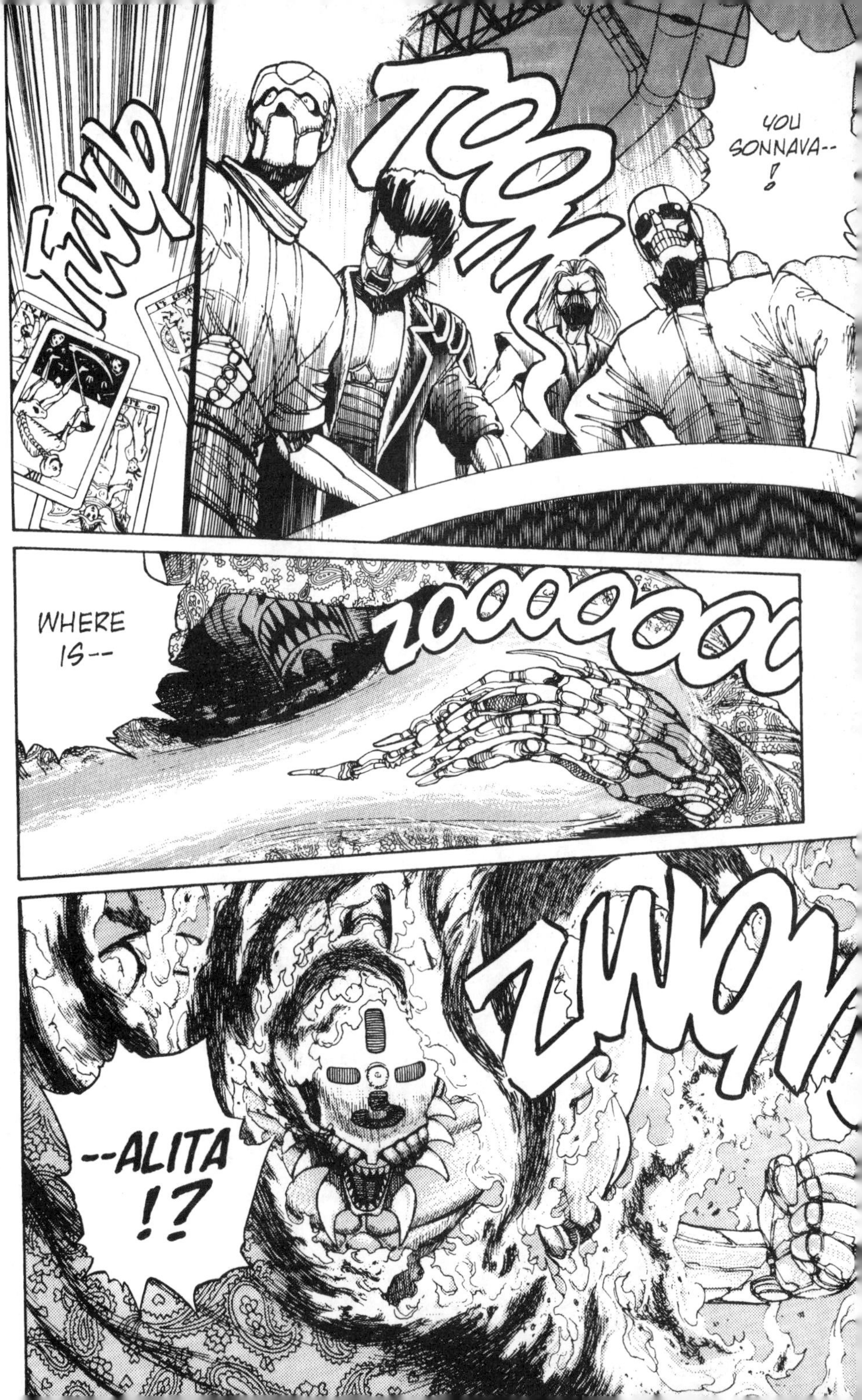
THWIP
TOOM
YOU SONNAVA-- !
WHERE IS--
ZOOOOOO
ZWOM
--ALITA !?

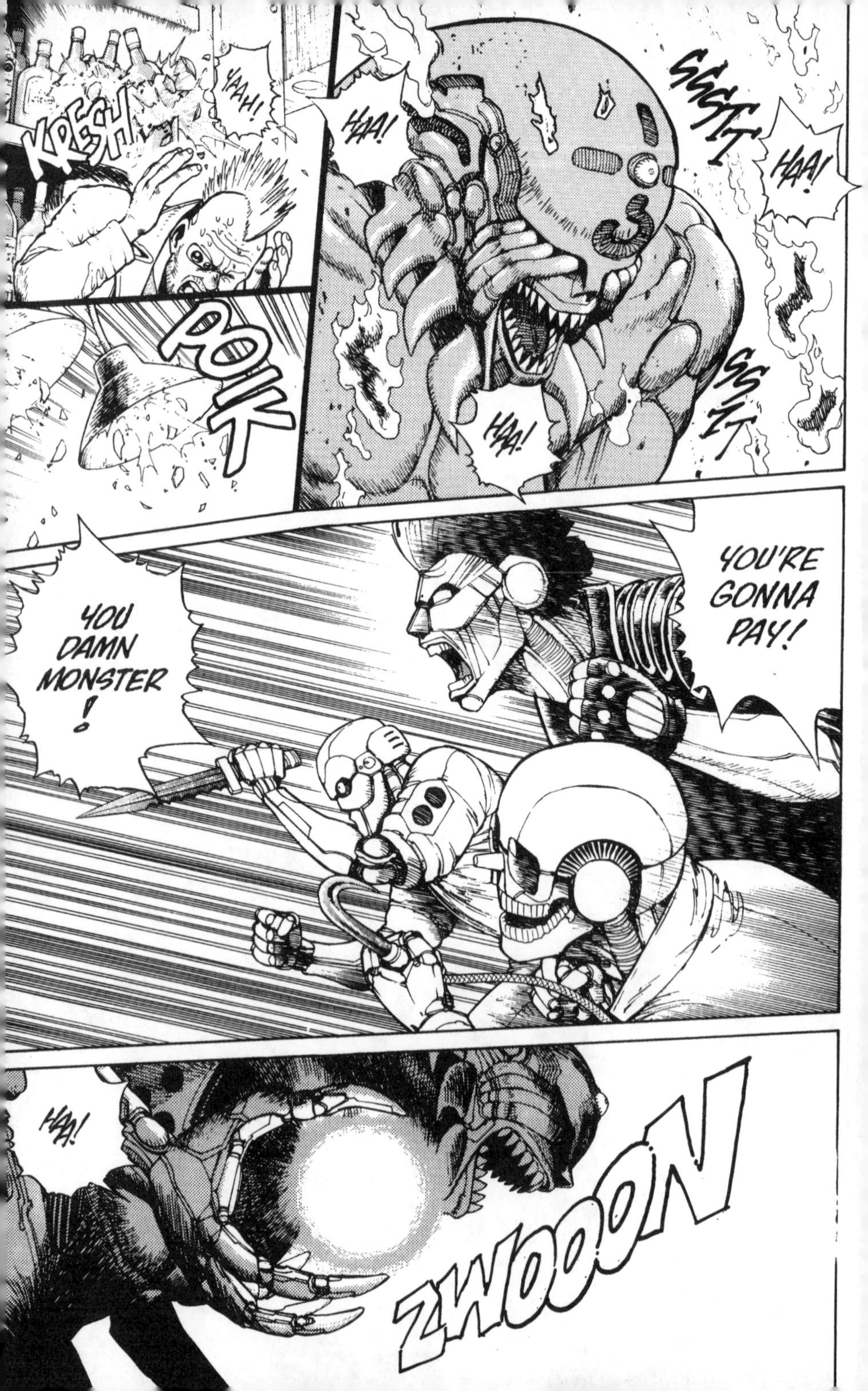
YAAH!
KRESH
POIK
HAA!
SSSST
HAA!
HAA!
SSSZZT
YOU DAMN MONSTER!
YOU'RE GONNA PAY!
HAA!
ZWOOOON

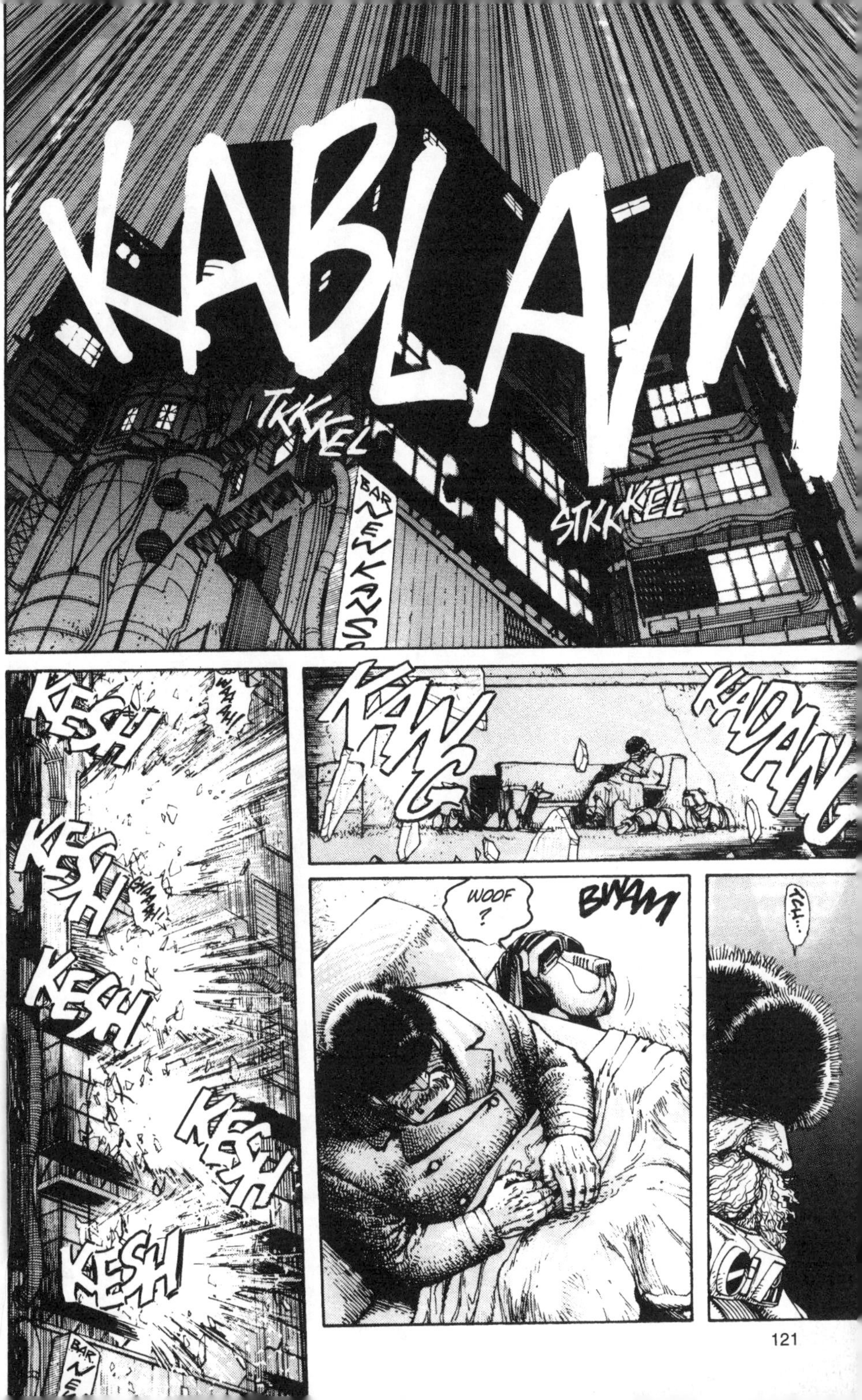
KABLAM
TKKKEL
BAR NEW KANSA
STKKKEL
KESH
KESH KESH
KESH
KESH
KESH
BAR NE
KAWANG
KADANG
WOOF ?
BWAM
TCH...

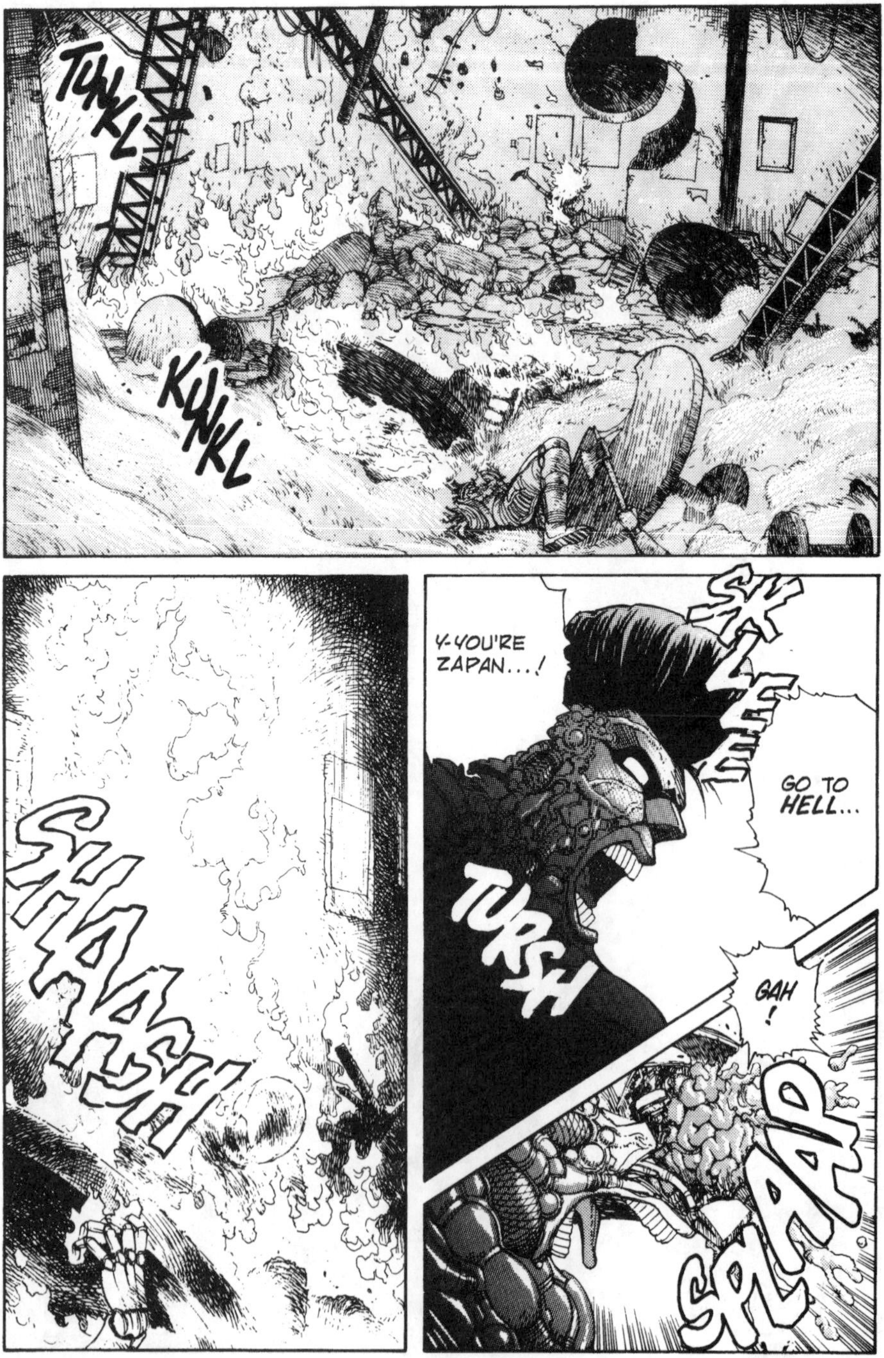
TUNKL
KUNKL
SHAASH
Y-YOU'RE ZAPAN...!
SKLEEE
GO TO HELL...
TURSH
GAH!
SPLAP

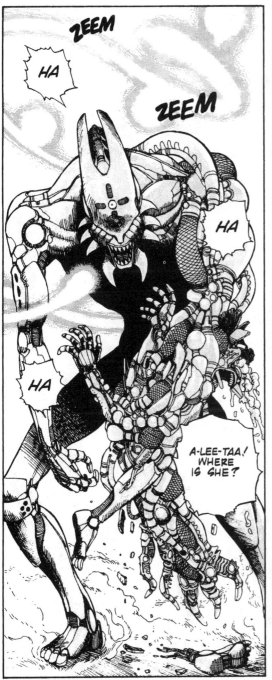

ZEEM

HA

ZEEM

HA

HA

A-LEE-TAA! WHERE IS SHE?

OH...

OH...

CHT CHT CHT

UNHHHH...

SPAK

WHERE'S ALITA...?

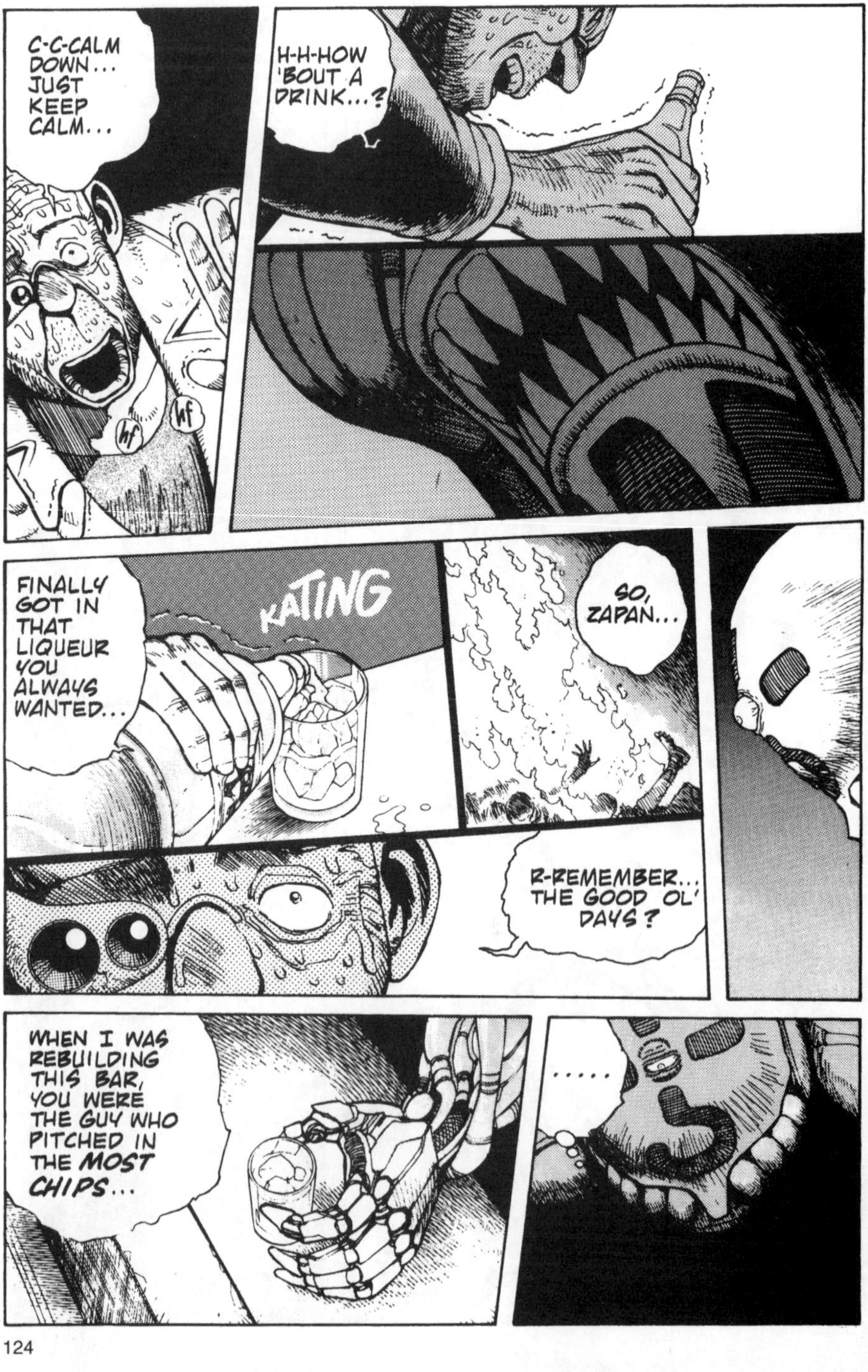

C-C-CALM DOWN... JUST KEEP CALM...
hf
hf
H-H-HOW 'BOUT A DRINK...?
FINALLY GOT IN THAT LIQUEUR YOU ALWAYS WANTED...
KATING
SO, ZAPAN...
R-REMEMBER... THE GOOD OL' DAYS?
WHEN I WAS REBUILDING THIS BAR, YOU WERE THE GUY WHO PITCHED IN THE ***MOST CHIPS***...
.....

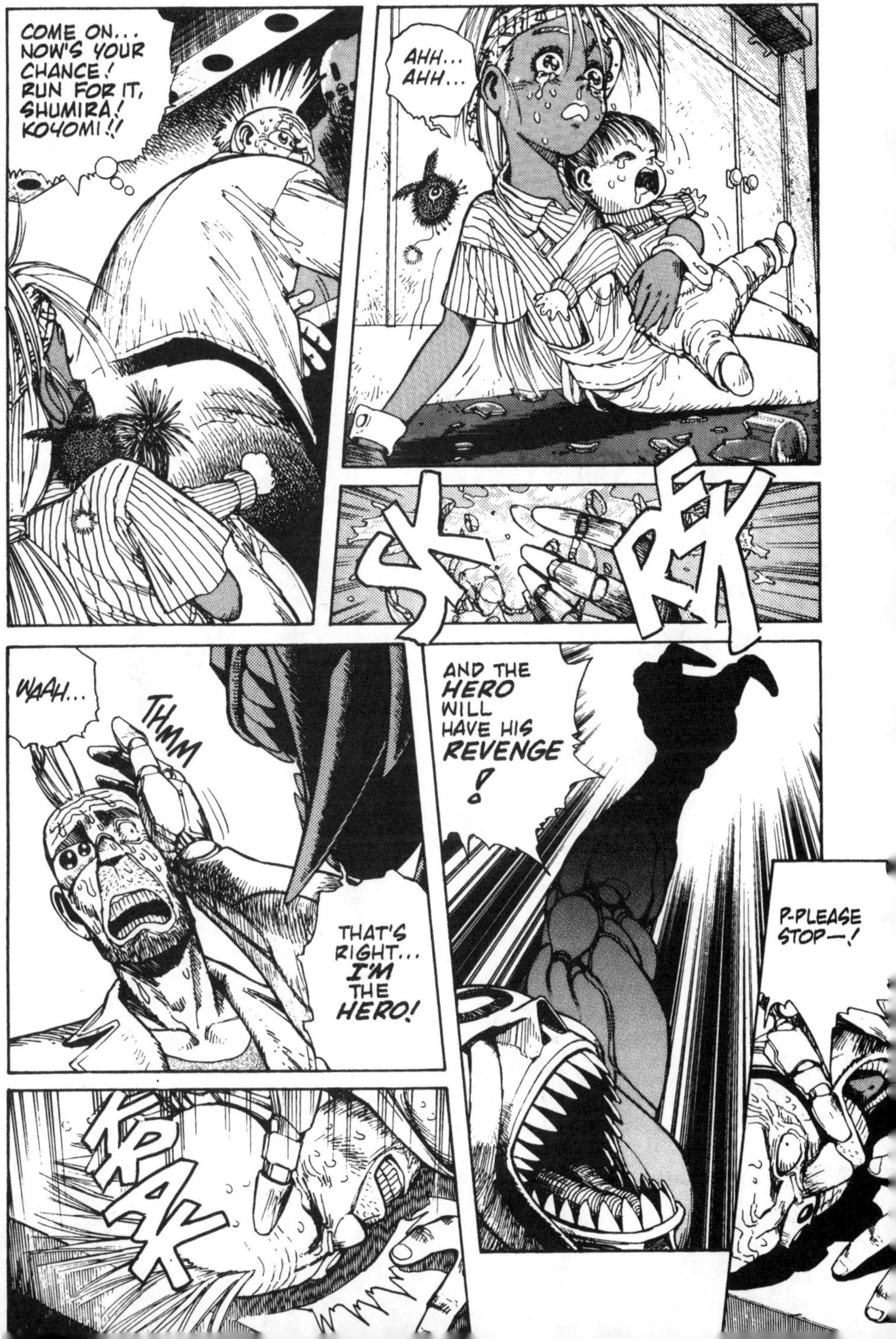
COME ON... NOW'S YOUR CHANCE! RUN FOR IT, SHUMIRA! KOYOMI!!
AHH... AHH...
SKREK
WAAH...
THMM
THAT'S RIGHT... I'M THE HERO!
AND THE HERO WILL HAVE HIS REVENGE!
P-PLEASE STOP—!
KRAK

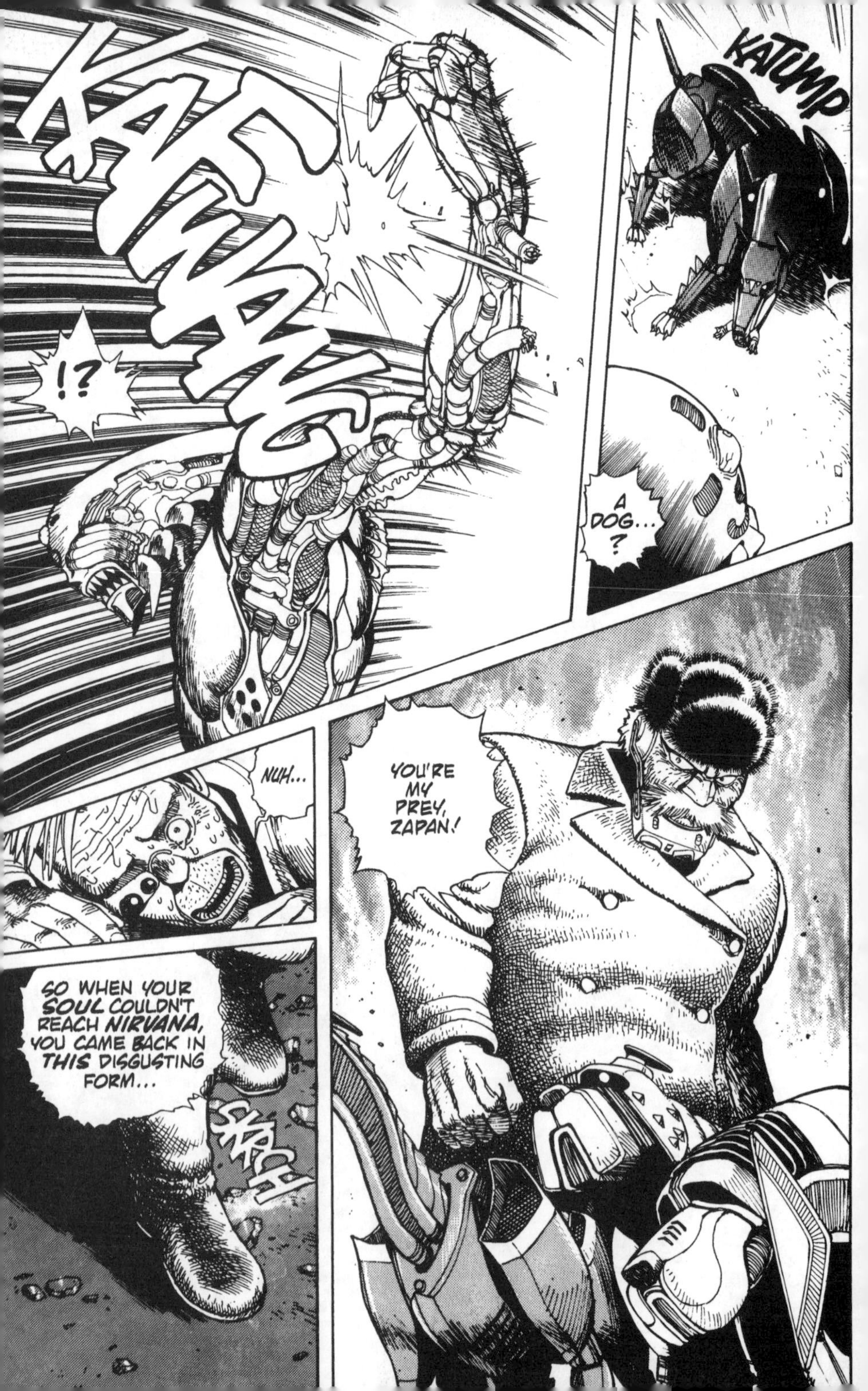
KATWANG
!?
KATUMP
A DOG...?
NUH...
YOU'RE MY PREY, ZAPAN!
SO WHEN YOUR SOUL COULDN'T REACH NIRVANA, YOU CAME BACK IN THIS DISGUSTING FORM...
SKRCH

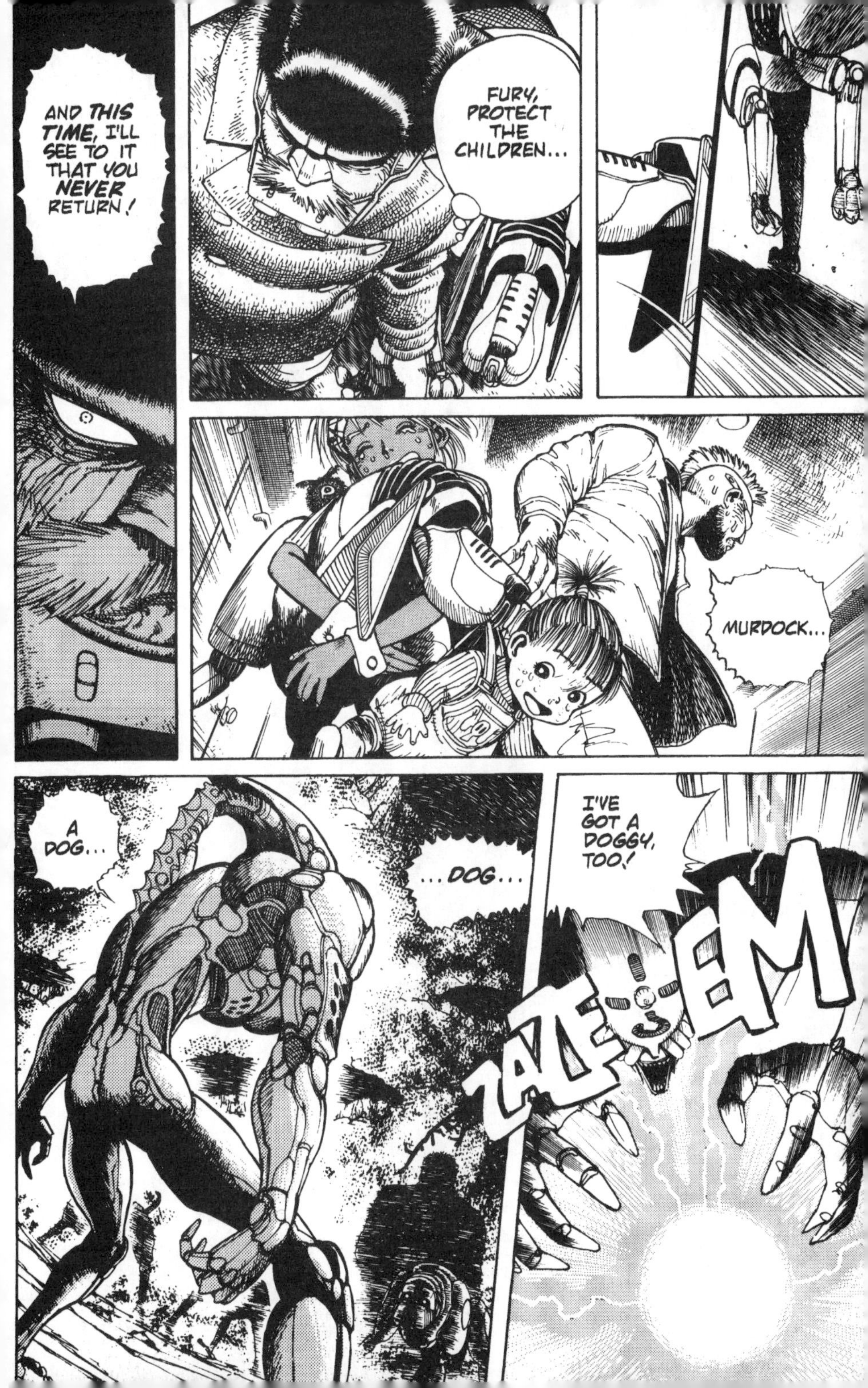

AND THIS TIME, I'LL SEE TO IT THAT YOU NEVER RETURN!
FURY, PROTECT THE CHILDREN...
MURDOCK...
A DOG...
...DOG...
I'VE GOT A DOGGY, TOO!
ZAZE EM

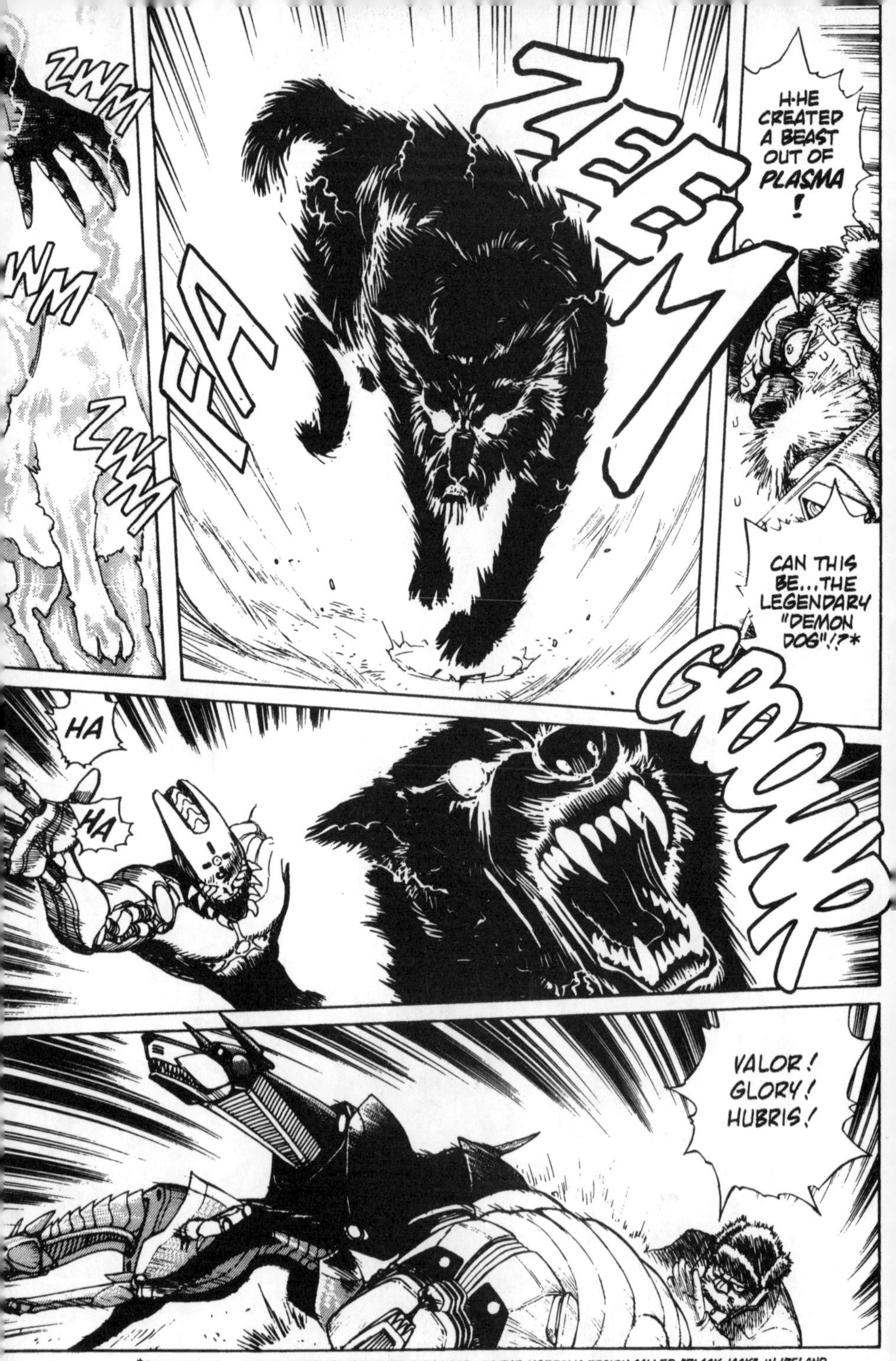
ZWM
WM
ZWM
ZEEM
H-HE CREATED A BEAST OUT OF PLASMA!
CAN THIS BE...THE LEGENDARY "DEMON DOG"!?*
HA
HA
VALOR! GLORY! HUBRIS!

*"DEMON DOG": A SUPERNATURAL BEAST OF BRITISH LORE. IN THE NORFOLK REGION CALLED "BLACK JACK," IN IRELAND "POOKA," AND IN SOMMERSET "GUARD DOG." THEY PREY ON HUMANS, DISAPPEARING IN A THUNDERBOLT WHICH SMELLS OF SULFUR.

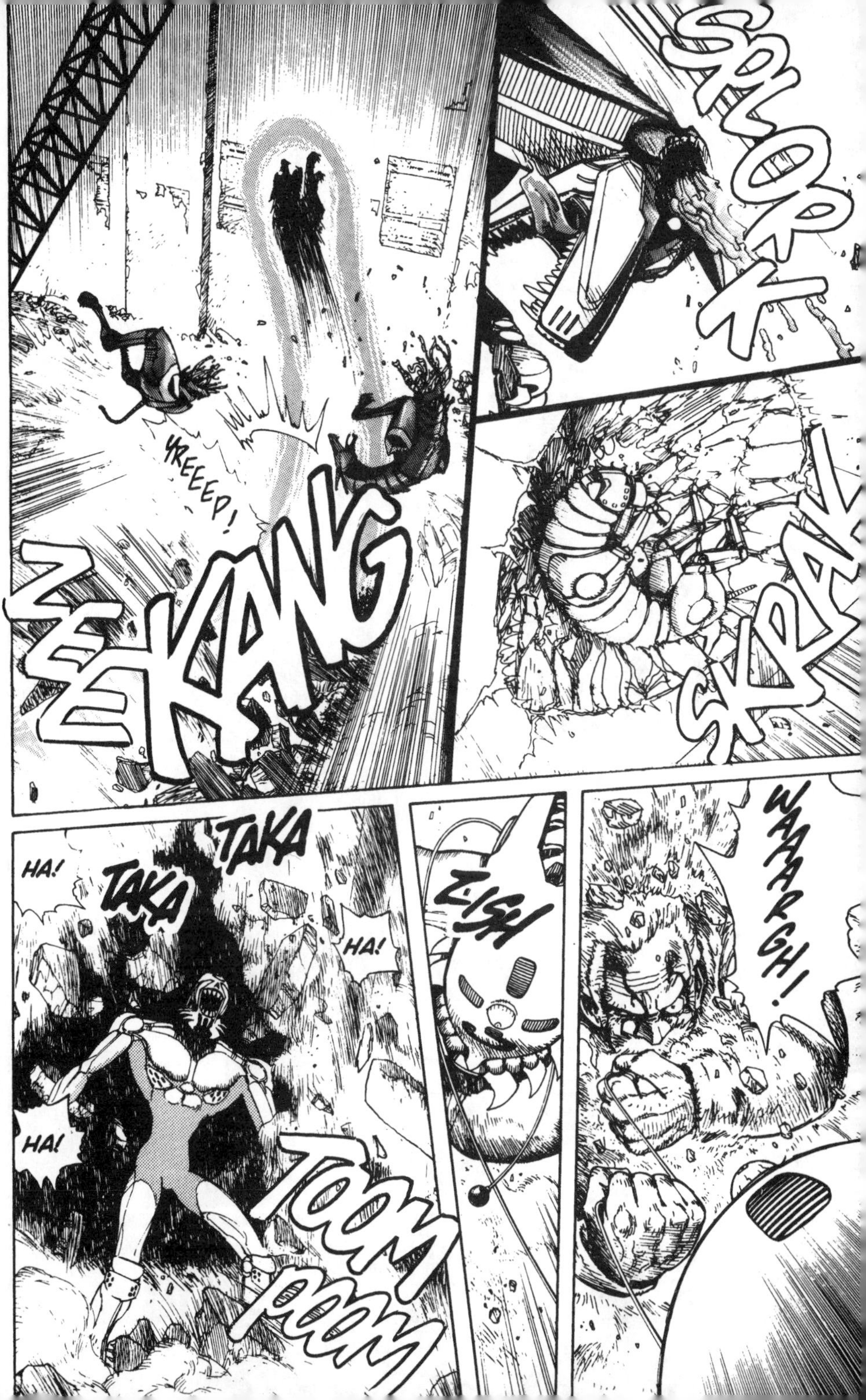
YREEEEP!
ZEKANG
SPLORK
SKRA
HA!
TAKA
TAKA
HA!
HA!
TOOM
POOM
Z-ISH
WAAARGH!

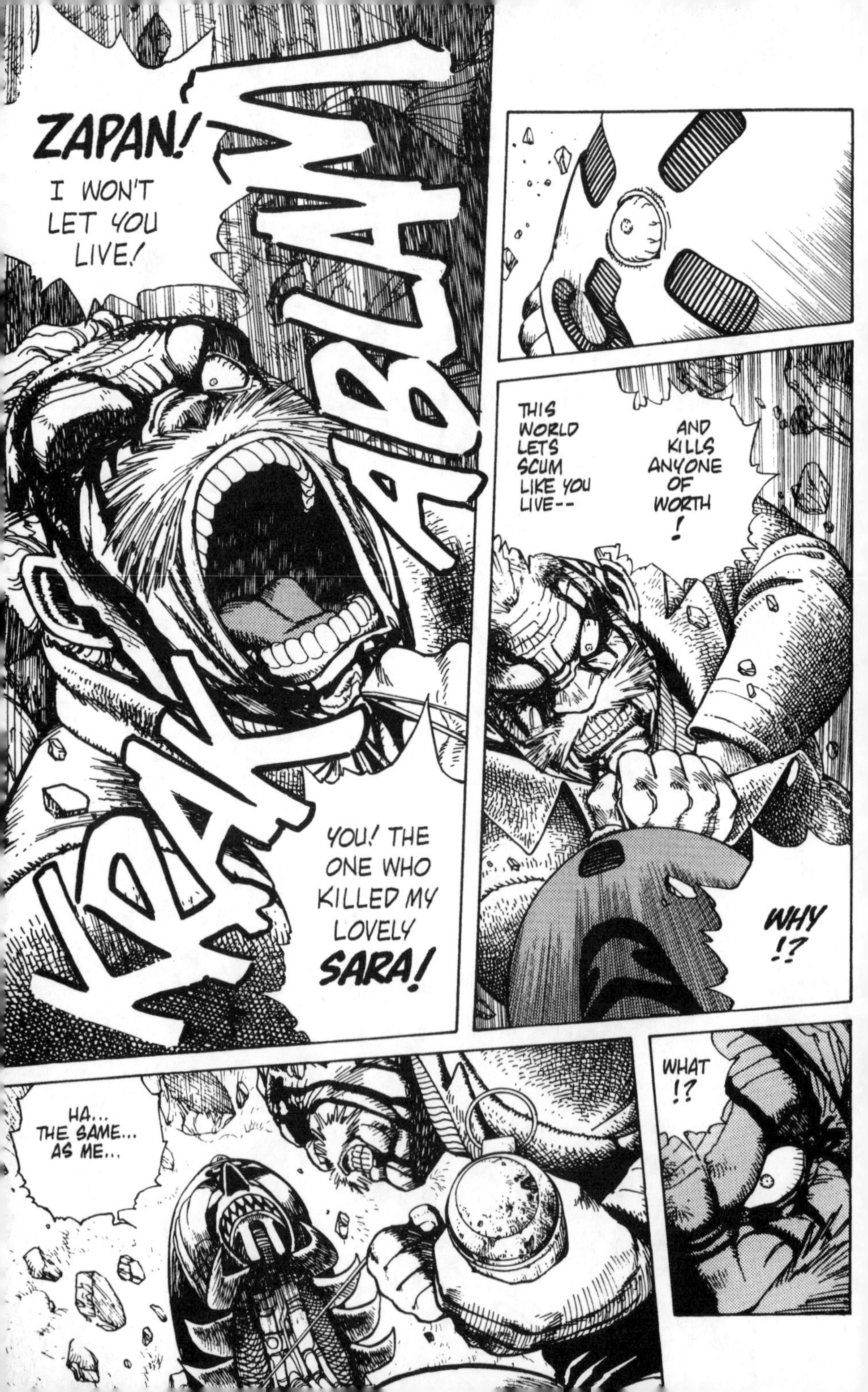
ZAPAN!
I WON'T LET YOU LIVE!
KRABLAM
YOU! THE ONE WHO KILLED MY LOVELY SARA!
THIS WORLD LETS SCUM LIKE YOU LIVE--
AND KILLS ANYONE OF WORTH!
WHY!?
HA... THE SAME... AS ME...
WHAT!?

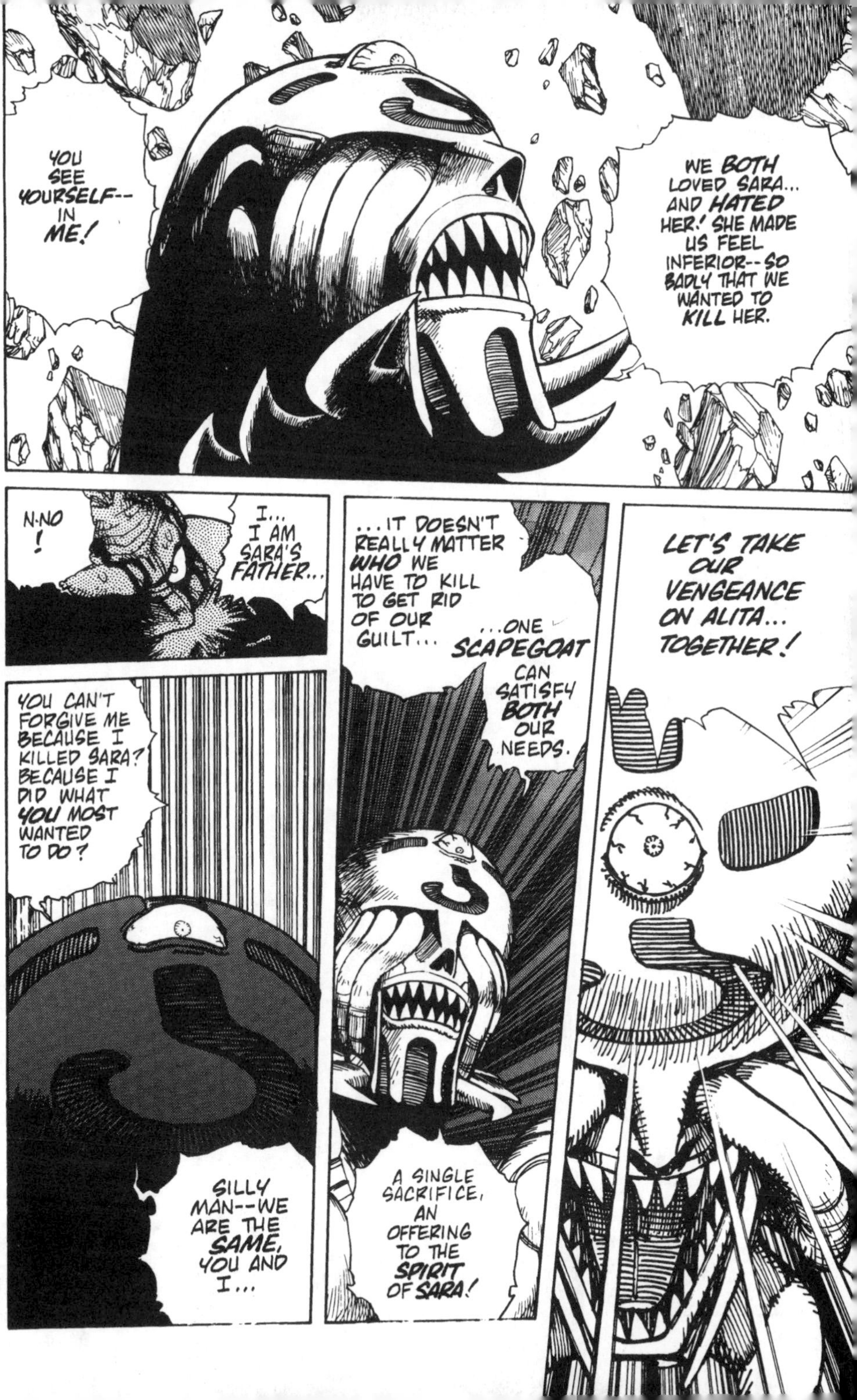
YOU SEE YOURSELF-- IN ME!
WE BOTH LOVED SARA... AND HATED HER! SHE MADE US FEEL INFERIOR--SO BADLY THAT WE WANTED TO KILL HER.
N-NO!
I... I AM SARA'S FATHER...
YOU CAN'T FORGIVE ME BECAUSE I KILLED SARA? BECAUSE I DID WHAT YOU MOST WANTED TO DO?
SILLY MAN--WE ARE THE SAME, YOU AND I...
...IT DOESN'T REALLY MATTER WHO WE HAVE TO KILL TO GET RID OF OUR GUILT...
...ONE SCAPEGOAT CAN SATISFY BOTH OUR NEEDS.
A SINGLE SACRIFICE, AN OFFERING TO THE SPIRIT OF SARA!
LET'S TAKE OUR VENGEANCE ON ALITA... TOGETHER!

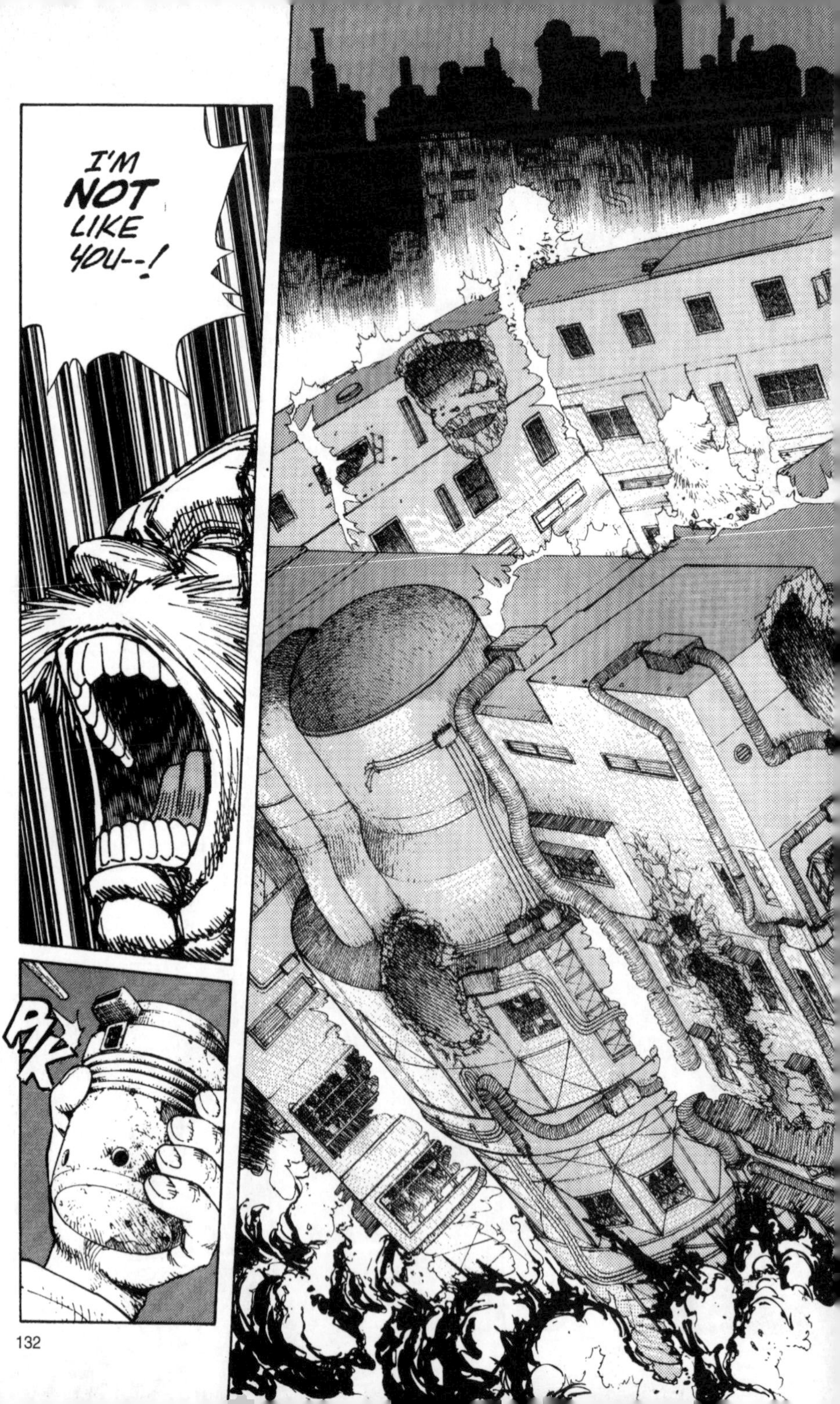
I'M NOT LIKE YOU--!
PAK

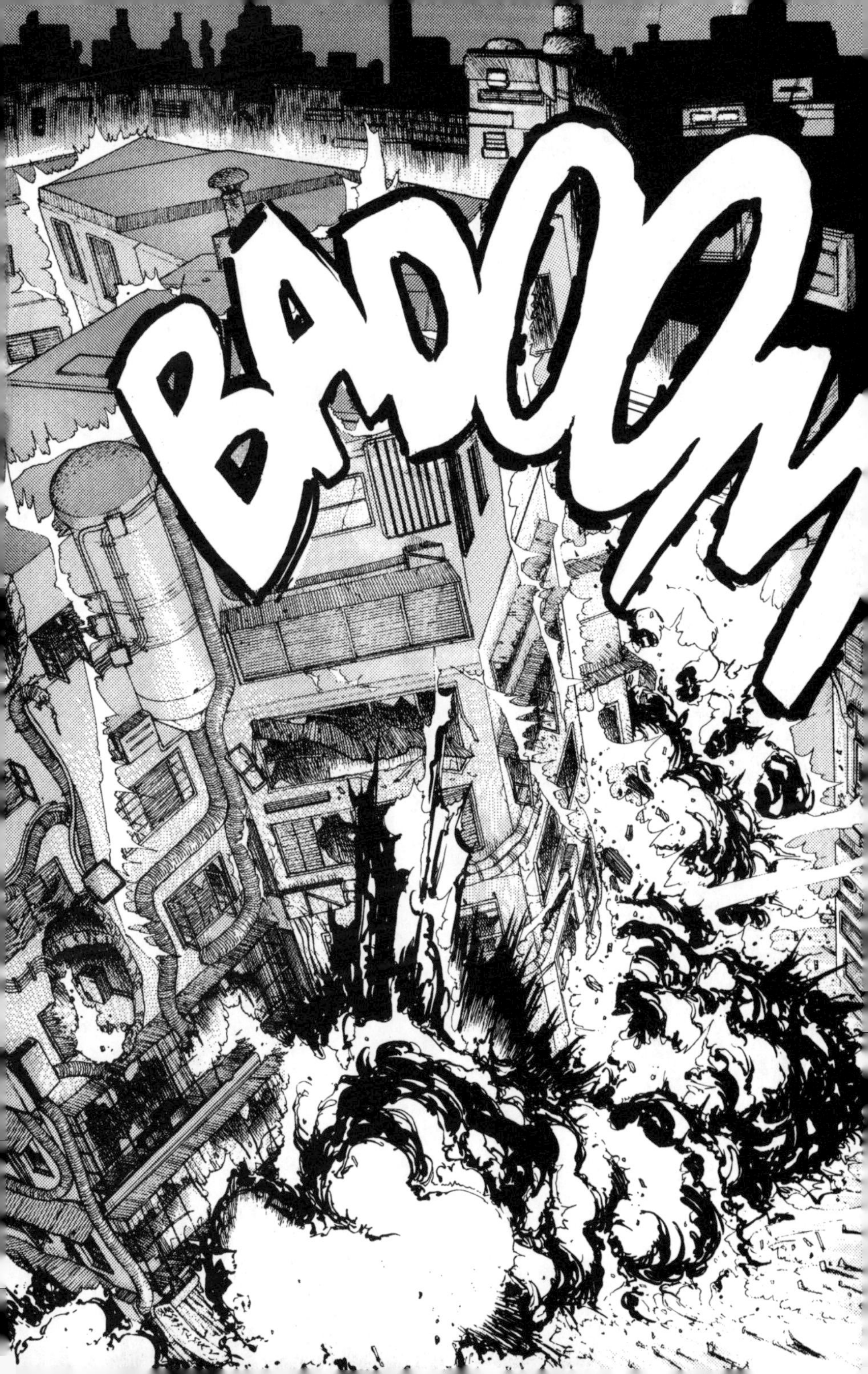
BADOOM

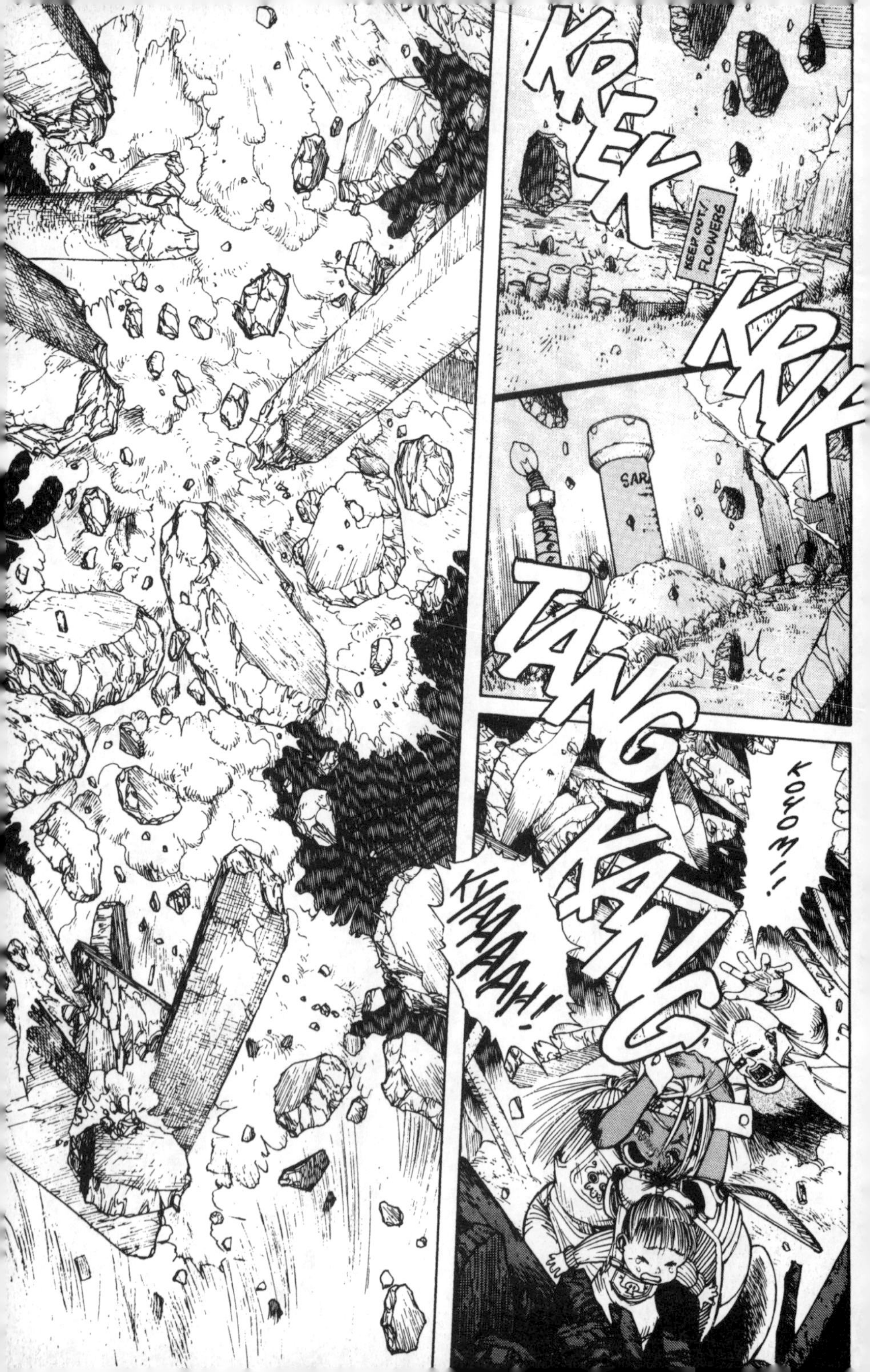
KREEK
KEEP OUT/ FLOWERS
KRIK
SARA
TANG
KANG
KOYOMI!!
KYAAAAAH!!

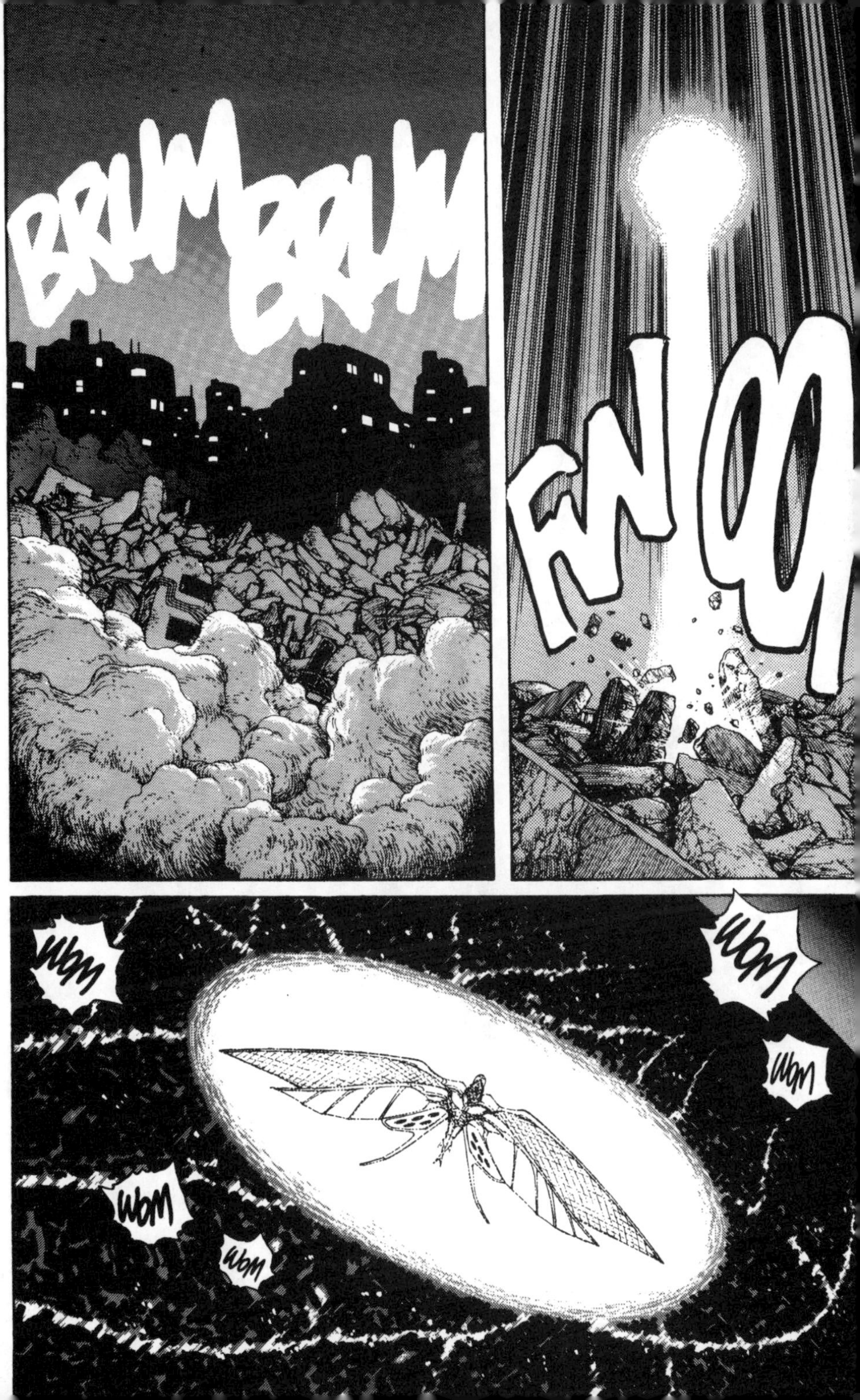
BRUM BRUM
FWOO
WOM
WOM
WOM
WOM
WOM

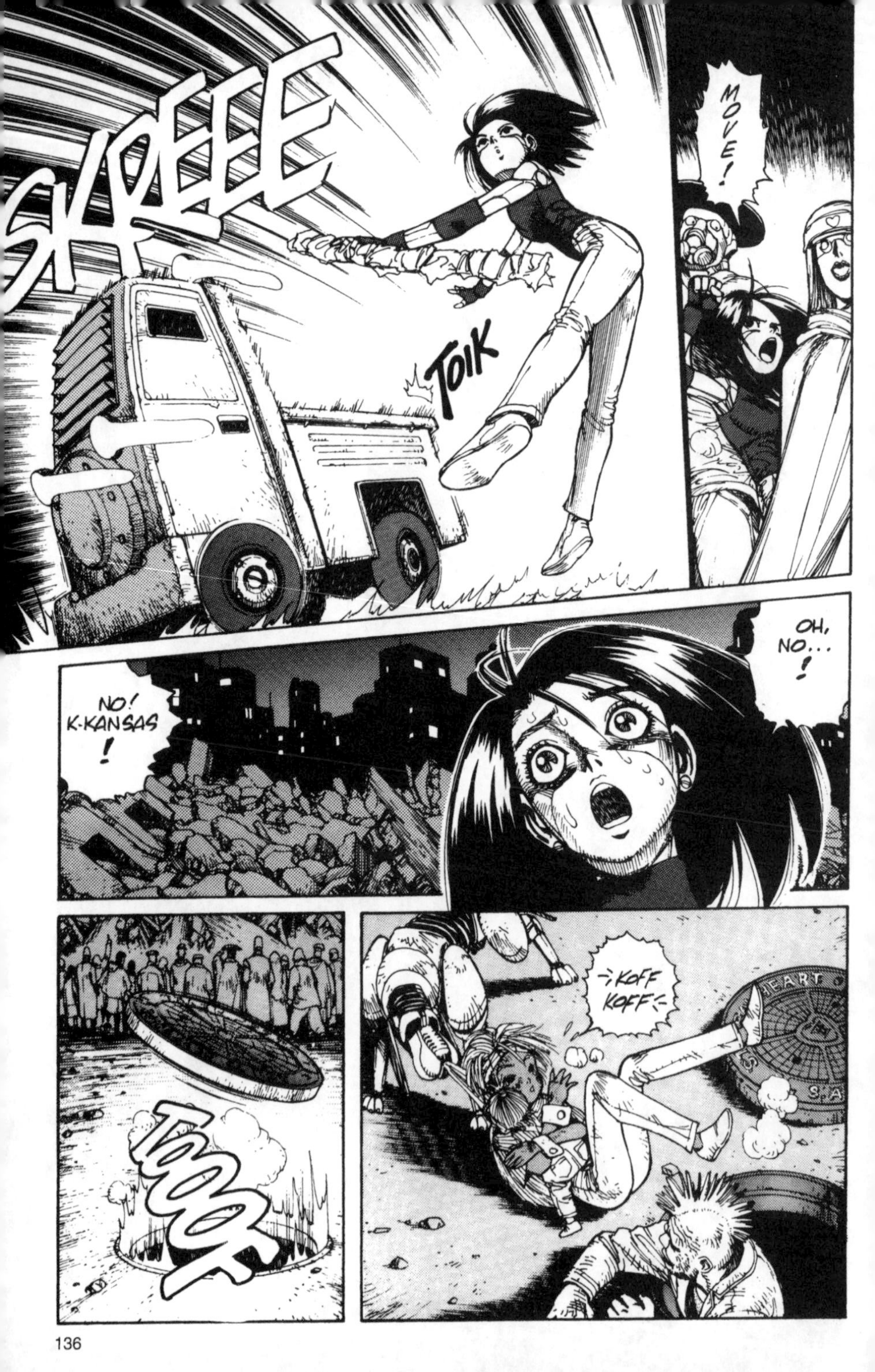
SKREEE
TOIK
MOVE!
NO! K-KANSAS!
OH, NO...!
TOOOF
KOFF KOFF

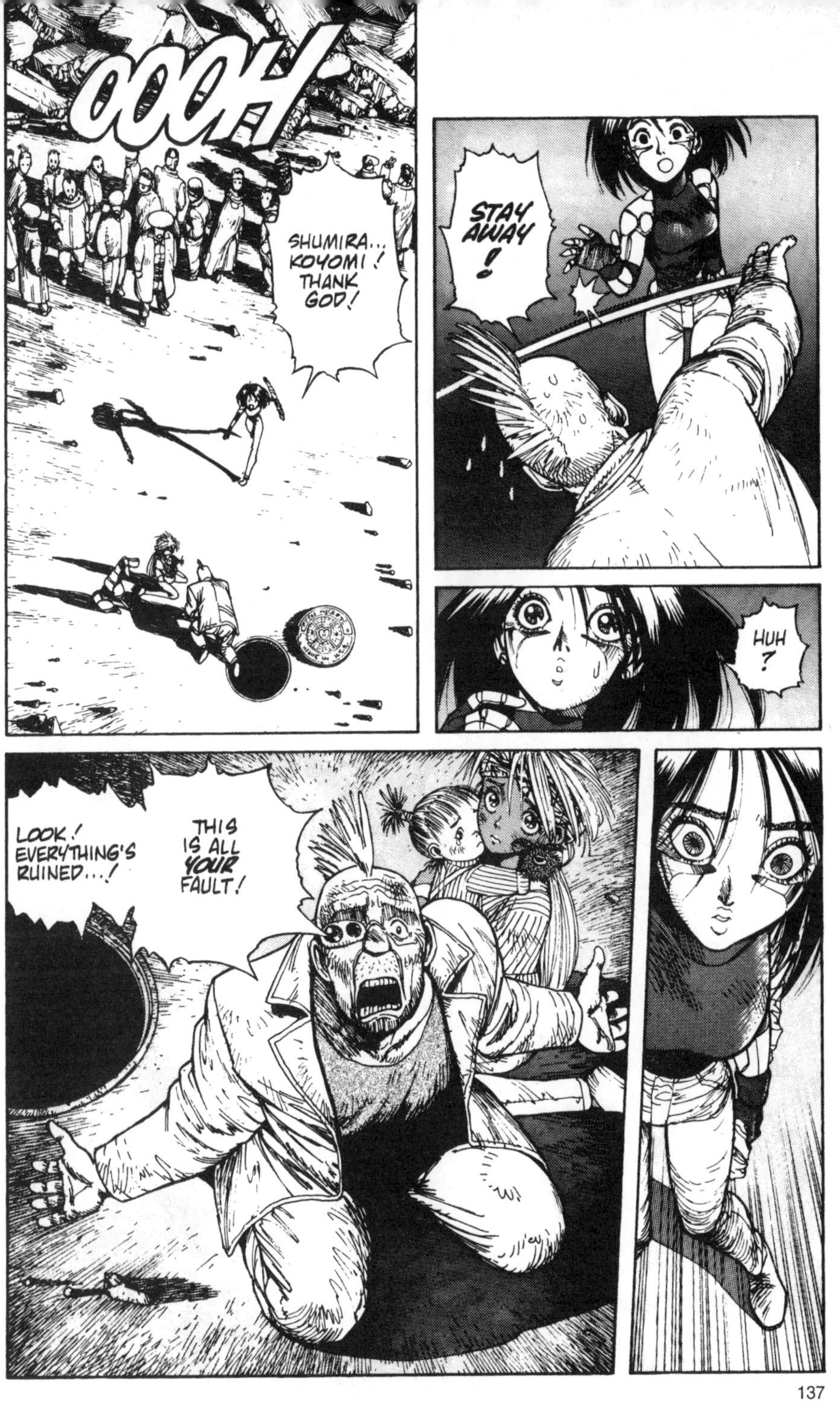
OOOH
SHUMIRA... KOYOMI! THANK GOD!
STAY AWAY!
HUH?
LOOK! EVERYTHING'S RUINED...!
THIS IS ALL YOUR FAULT!

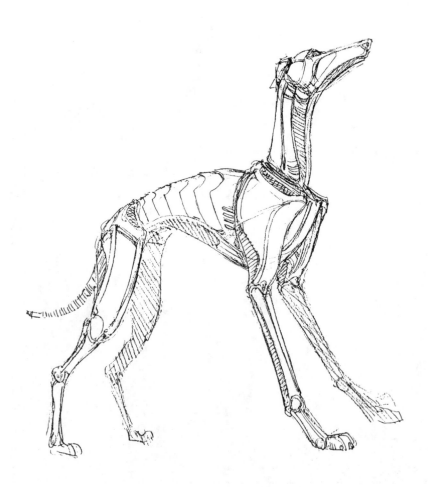

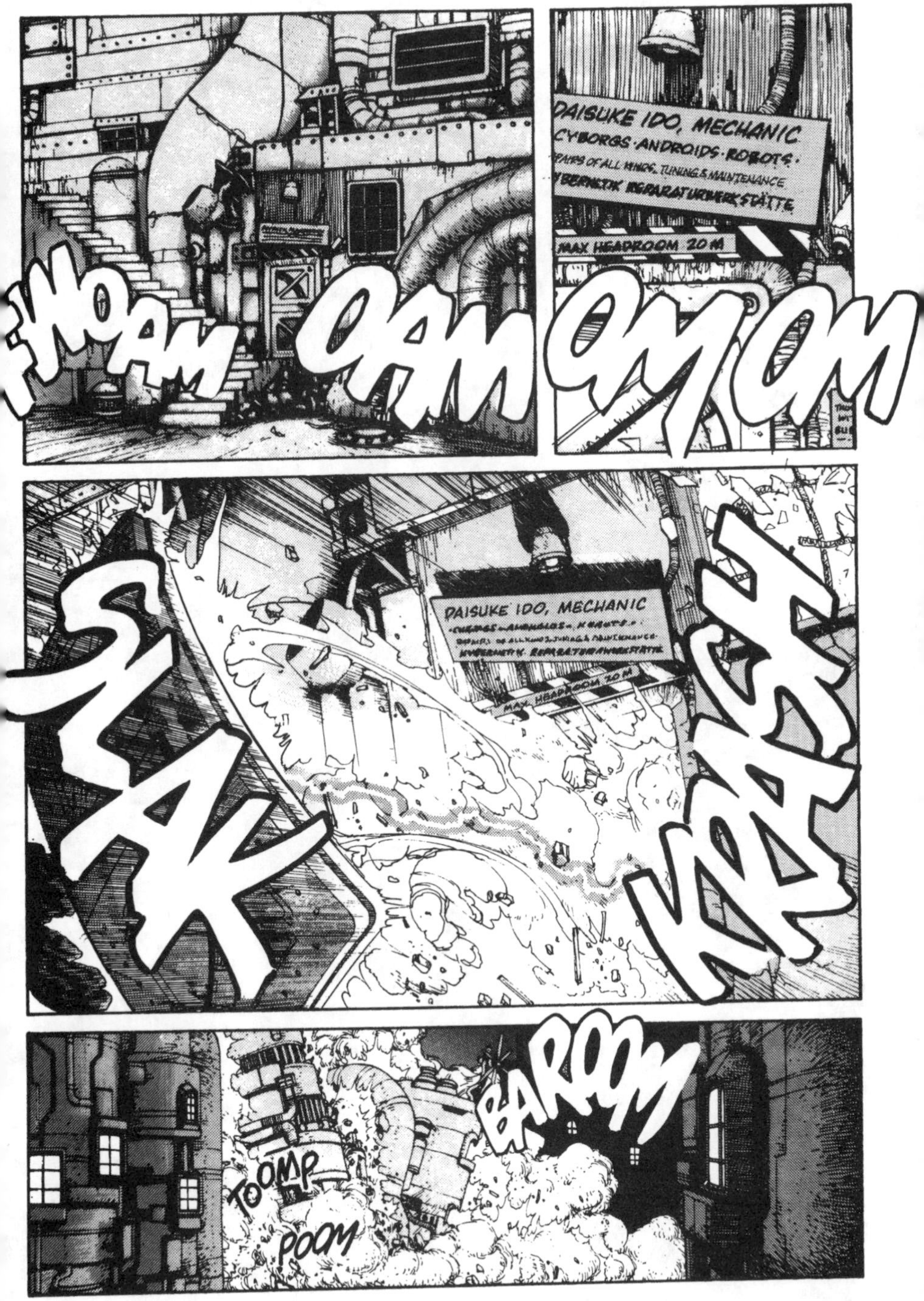

DAISUKE IDO, MECHANIC
CYBORGS · ANDROIDS · ROBOTS ·
PAIRS OF ALL KINDS, TUNING & MAINTENANCE
YBERNETIK REPARATURWERKSTÄTTE
MAX HEADROOM 2.0 M
HOAM OAMOMOM
SMAK
DAISUKE IDO, MECHANIC
MAX HEADROOM 2.0 M
KRASH
BAROOM
TOOMP
POOM

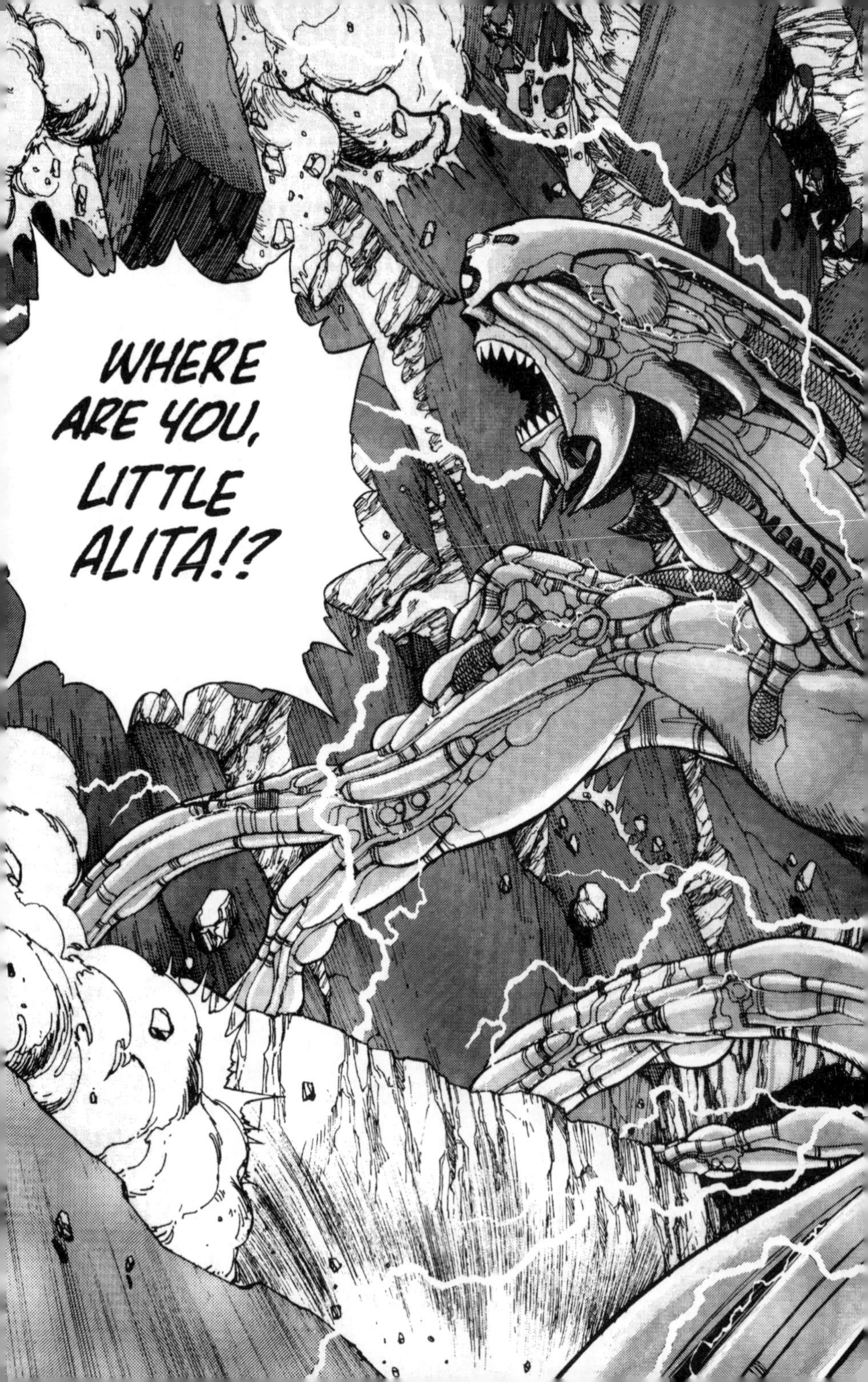
WHERE ARE YOU, LITTLE ALITA!?

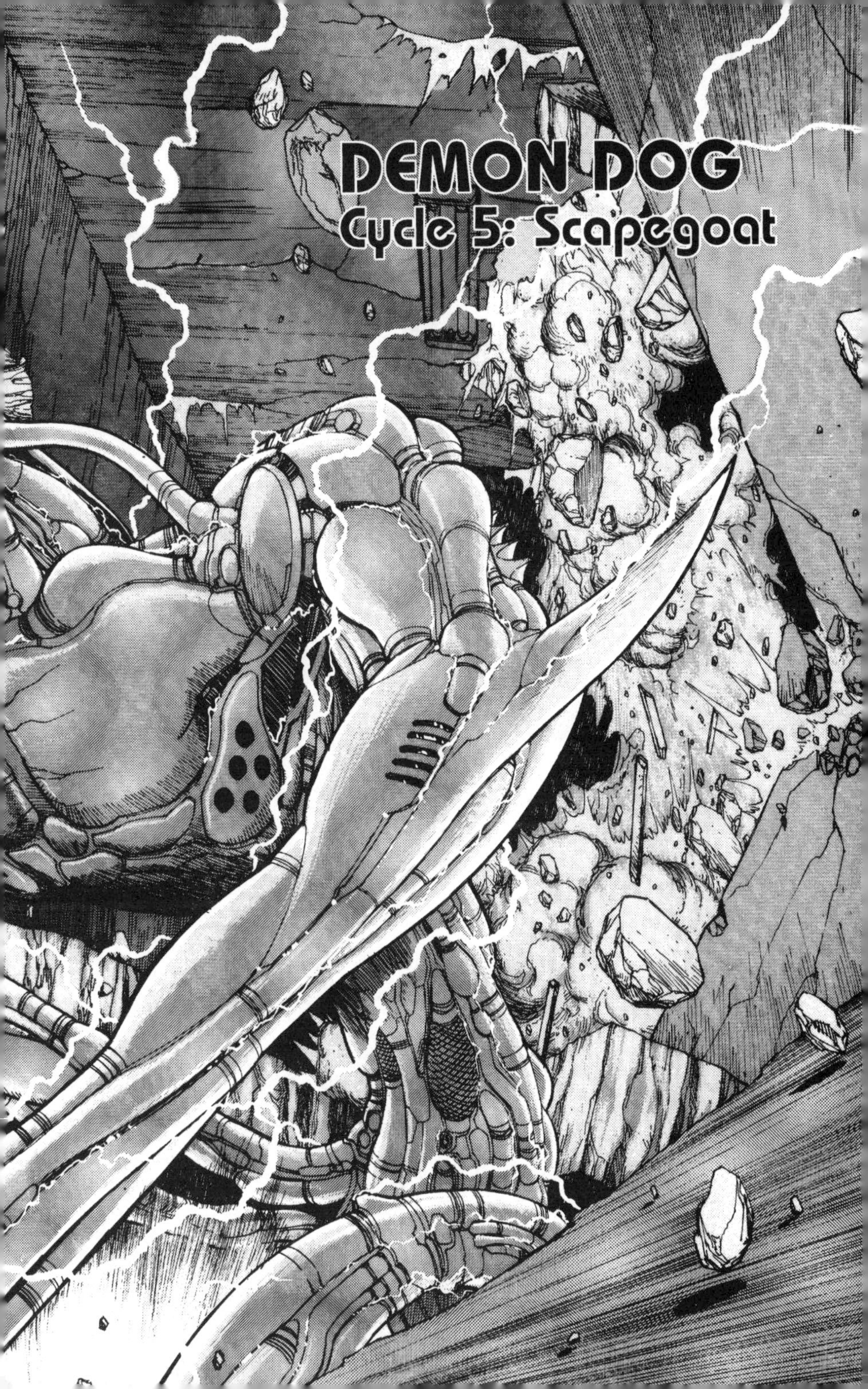
DEMON DOG
Cycle 5: Scapegoat

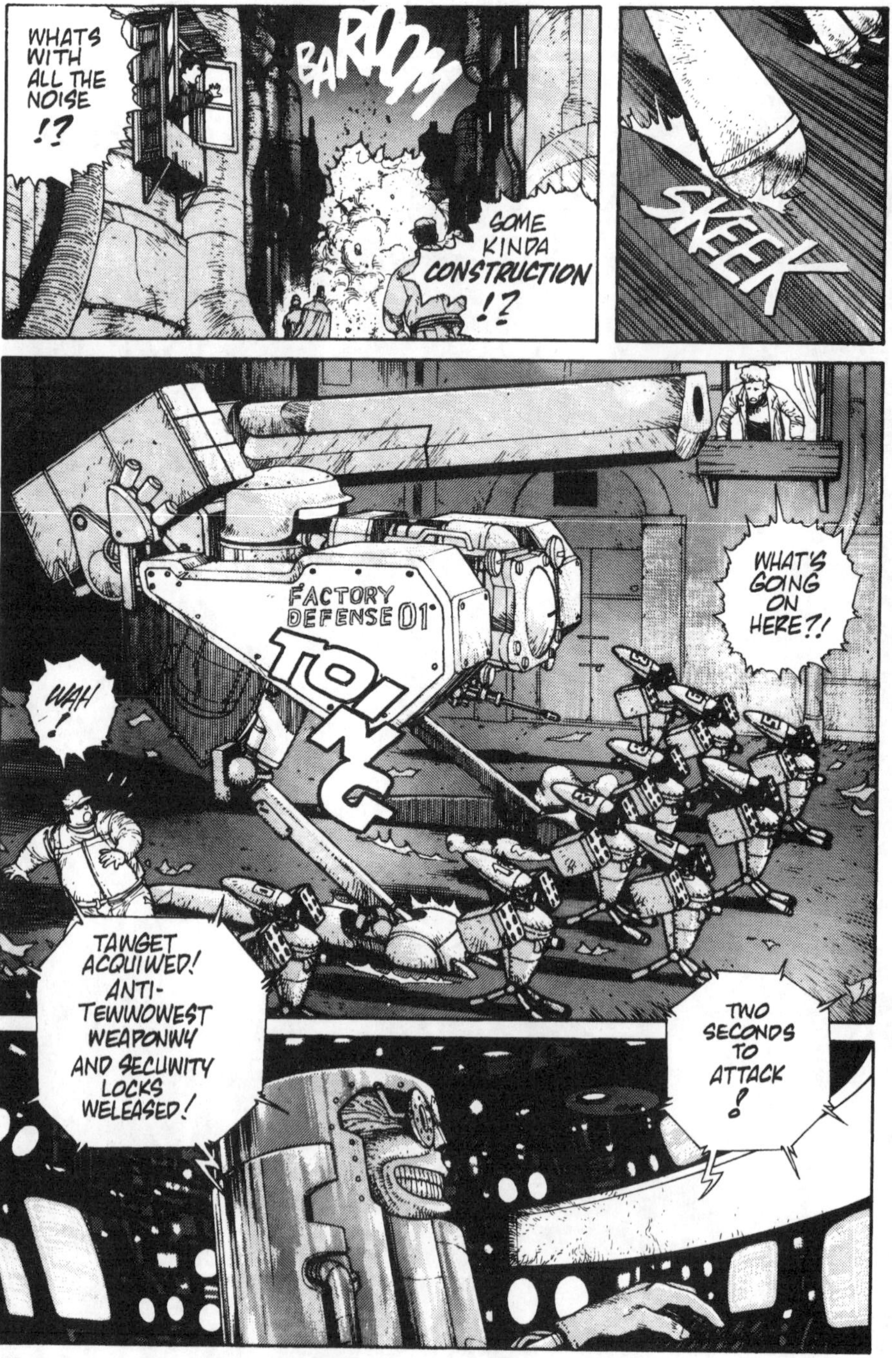
WHATS WITH ALL THE NOISE !?
BAROOM
SOME KINDA CONSTRUCTION !?
SKEEK
FACTORY DEFENSE 01
TOING
WHAT'S GOING ON HERE?!
WAH!
TAWGET ACQUIWED! ANTI-TEWWOWEST WEAPONWY AND SECUWITY LOCKS WELEASED!
TWO SECONDS TO ATTACK!

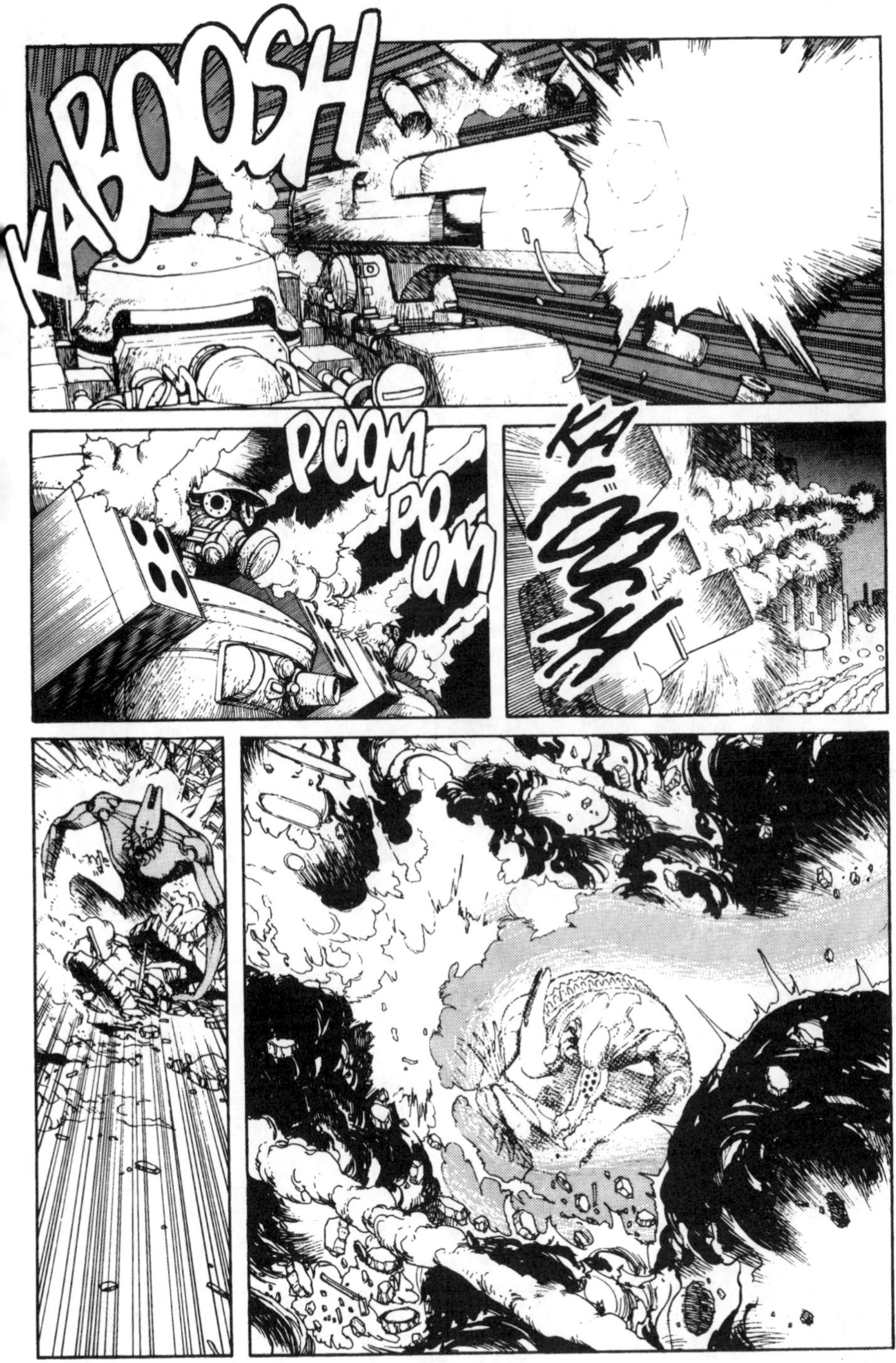
KABOOSH
POOM POOM
KA FOOSH

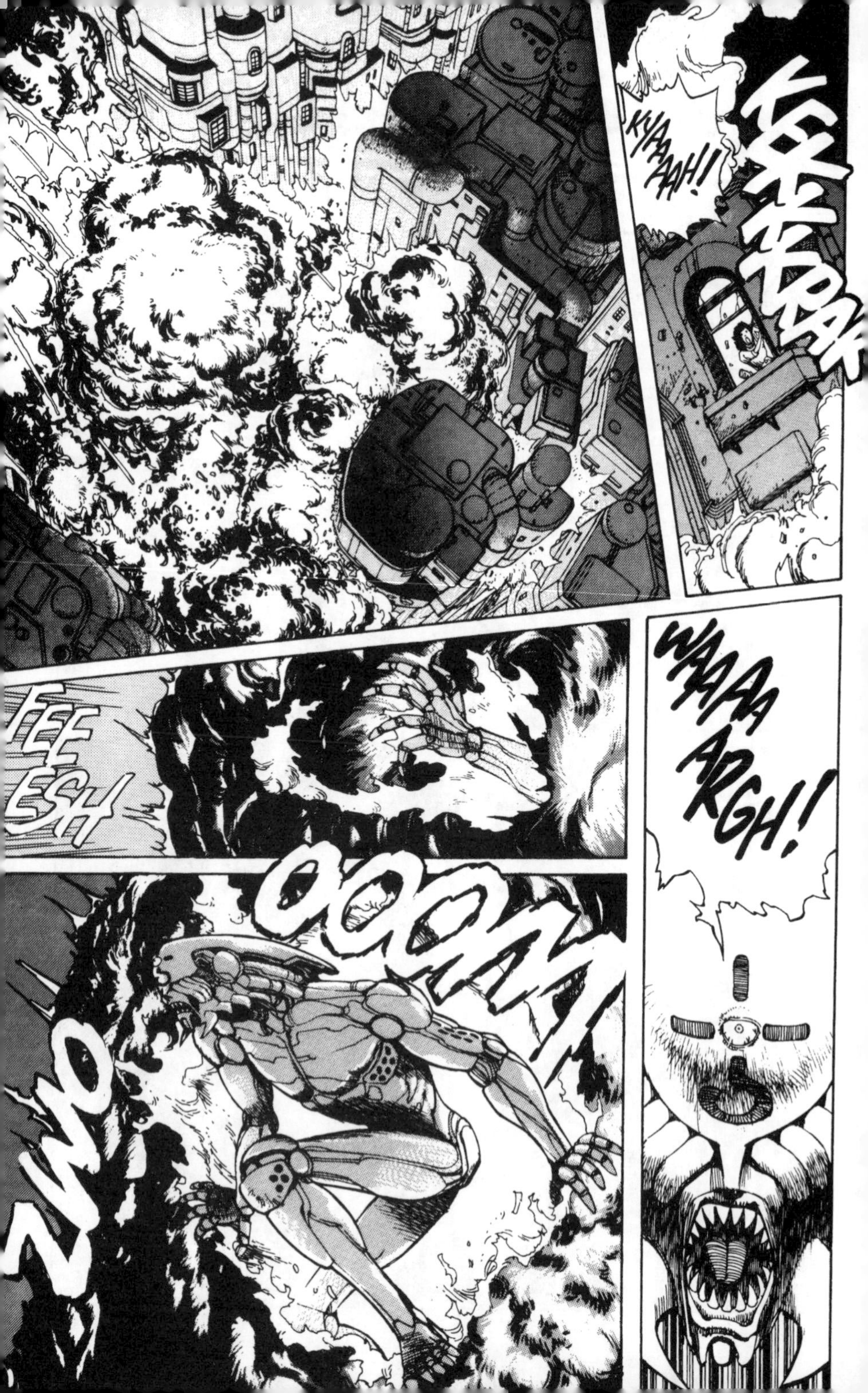
KYAAAAH!!
KKKRAK
FEE
ESH
ZWO
OOOM
WAAAAA
ARGH!

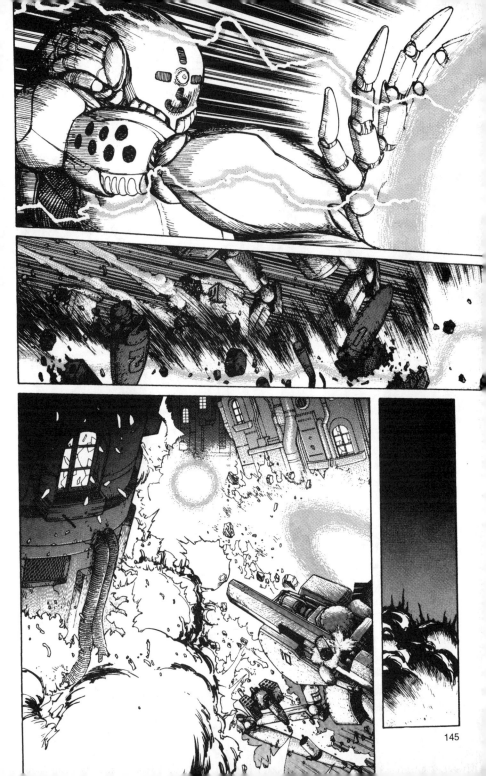

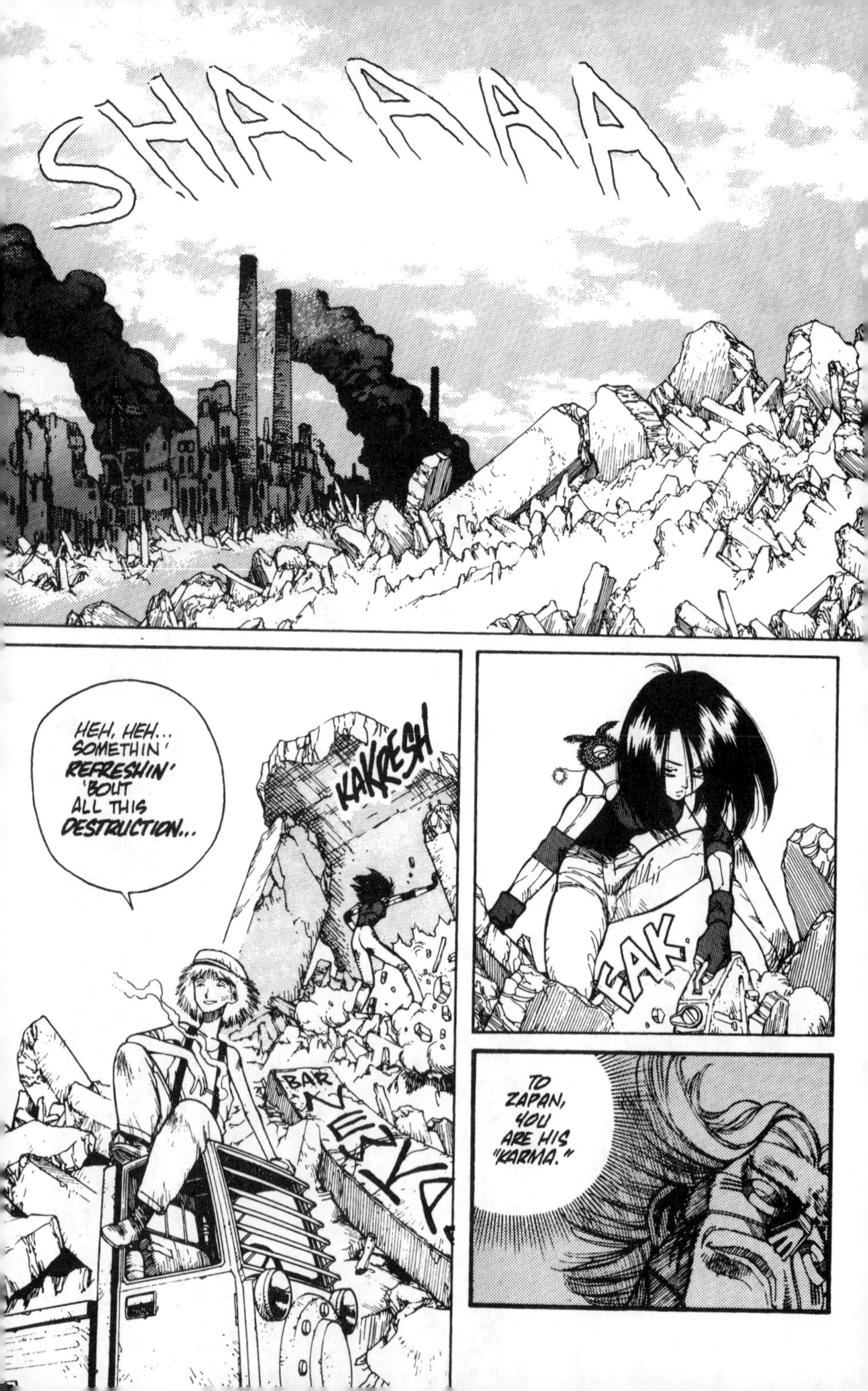
SHAAAAA
HEH, HEH... SOMETHIN' REFRESHIN' 'BOUT ALL THIS DESTRUCTION...
KAKRESH
BAR
FAK
TO ZAPAN, YOU ARE HIS "KARMA."

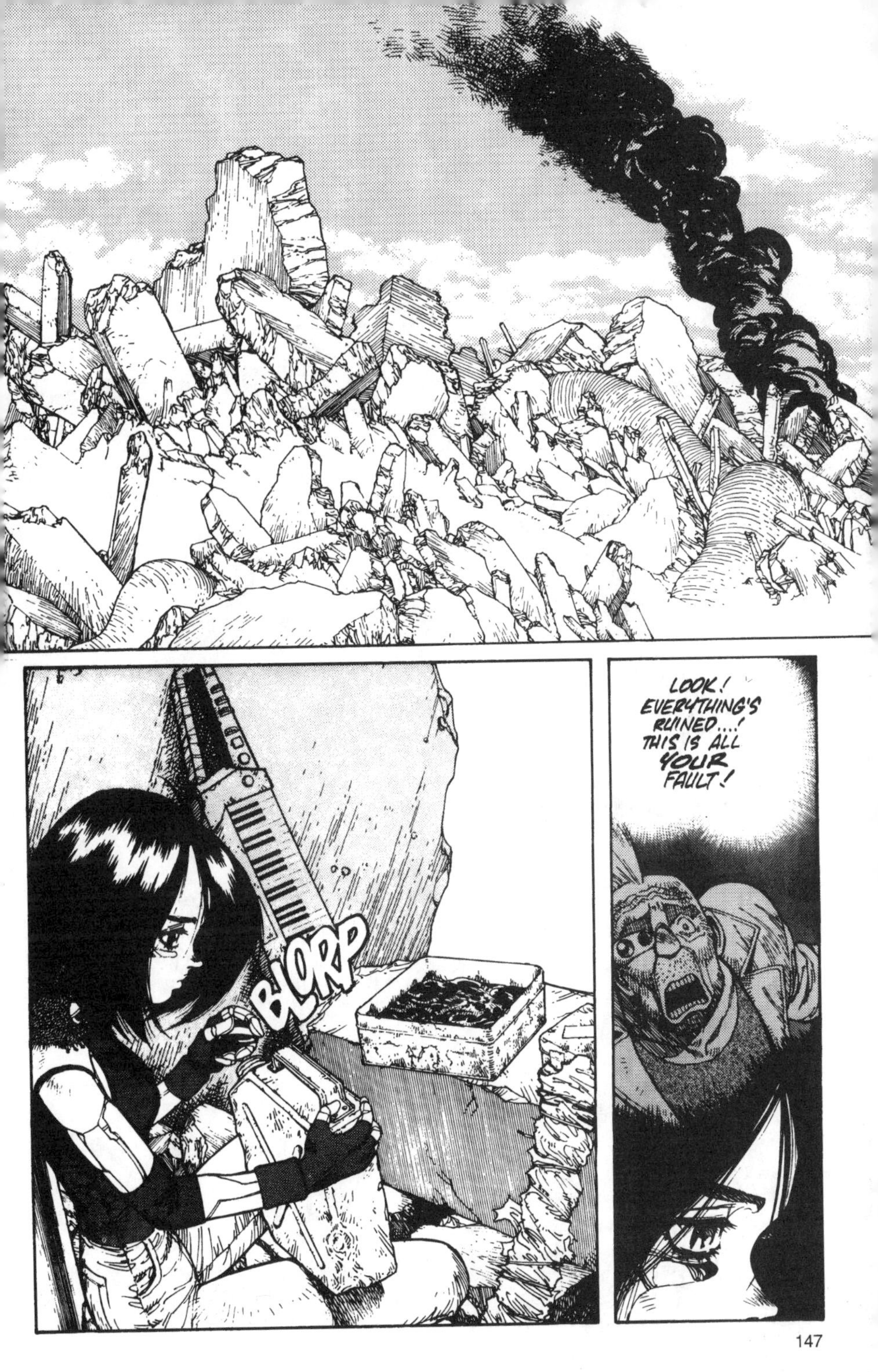
BLORP
LOOK! EVERYTHING'S RUINED...! THIS IS ALL YOUR FAULT!

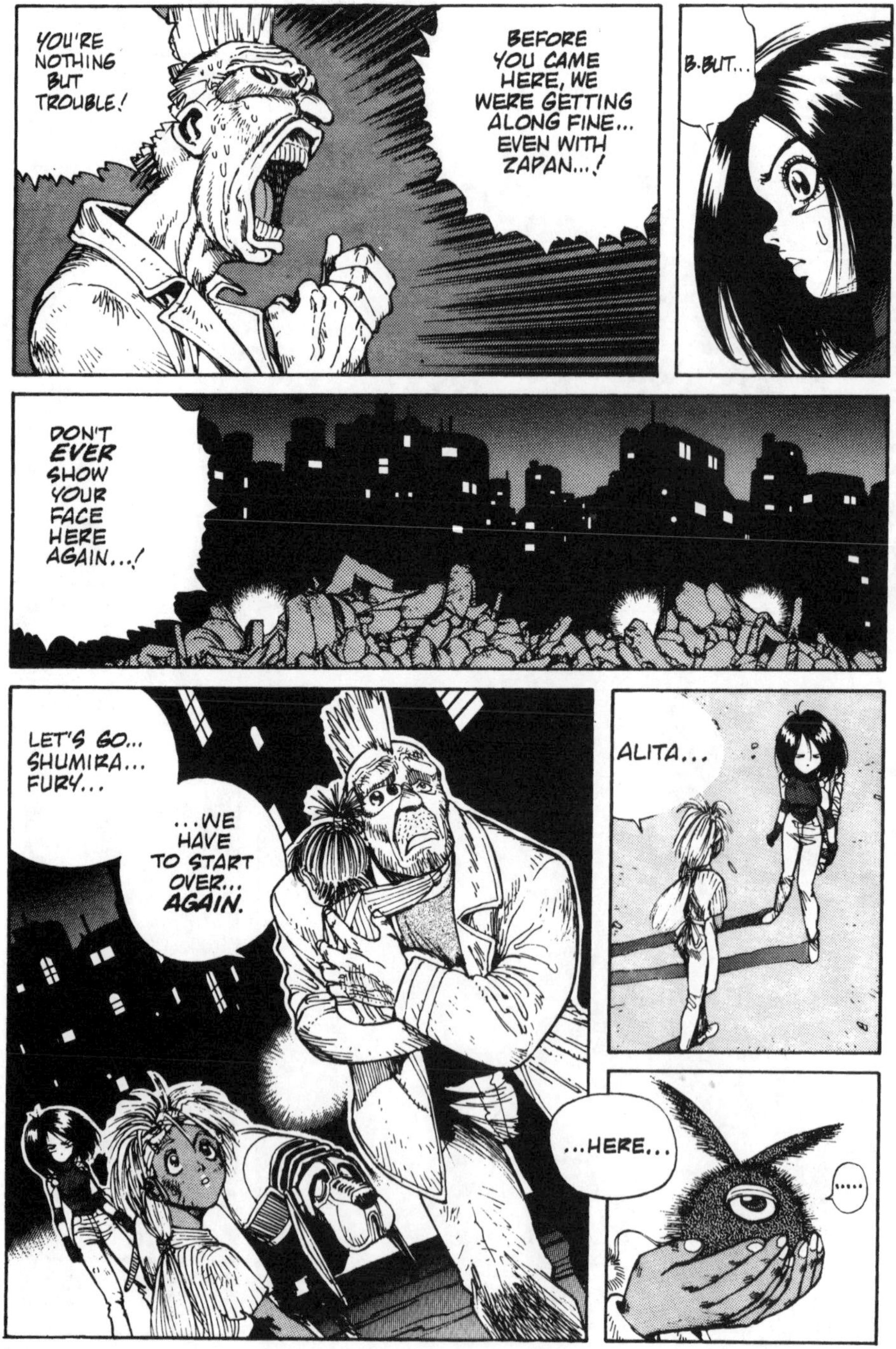
YOU'RE NOTHING BUT TROUBLE!
BEFORE YOU CAME HERE, WE WERE GETTING ALONG FINE... EVEN WITH ZAPAN...!
B.BUT...
DON'T EVER SHOW YOUR FACE HERE AGAIN...!
LET'S GO... SHUMIRA... FURY...
...WE HAVE TO START OVER... AGAIN.
ALITA...
...HERE...
.....

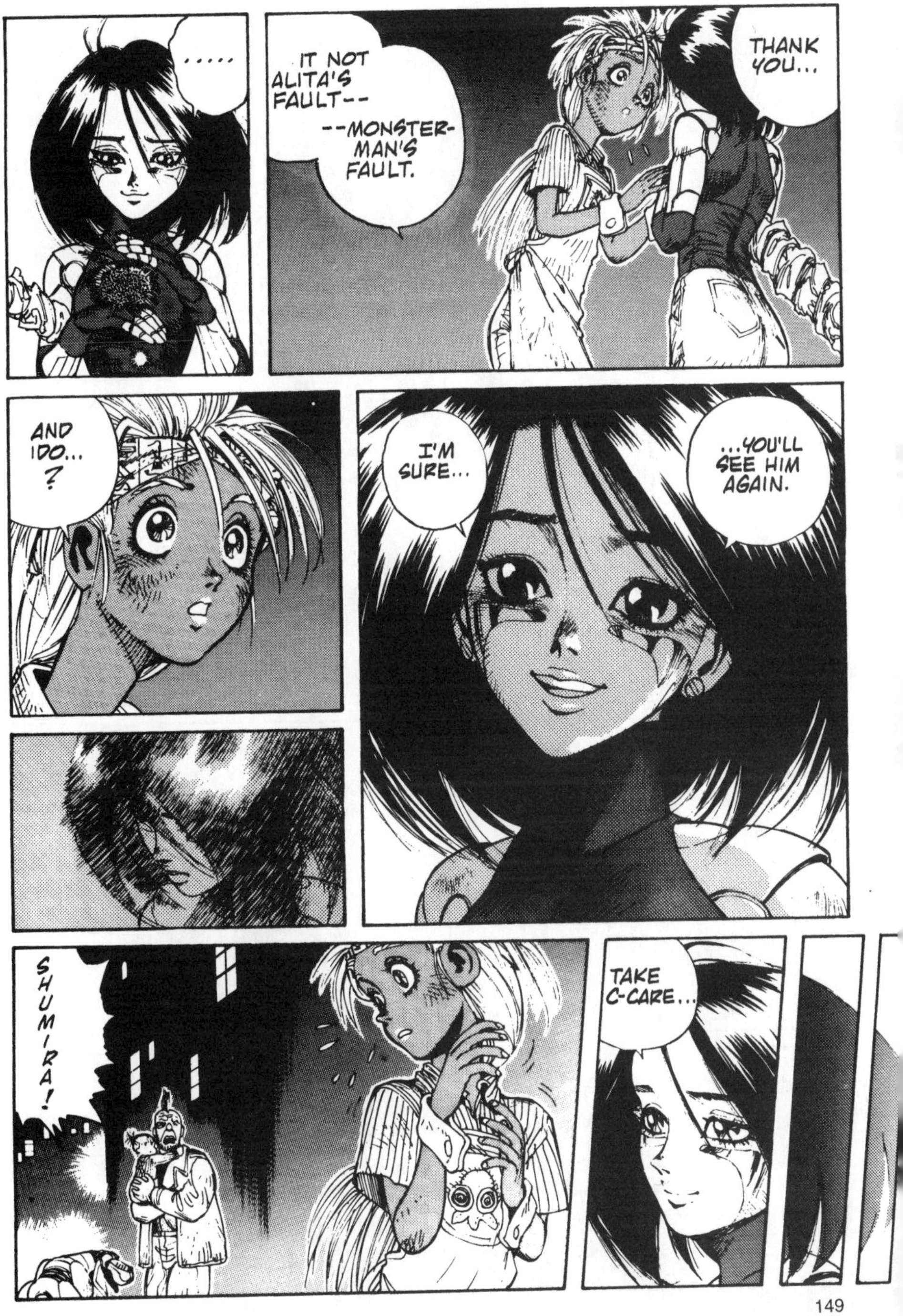
. . . . .
IT NOT ALITA'S FAULT--
--MONSTER-MAN'S FAULT.
THANK YOU...
AND IDO... ?
I'M SURE...
...YOU'LL SEE HIM AGAIN.
SHUMIRA!
TAKE C-CARE...

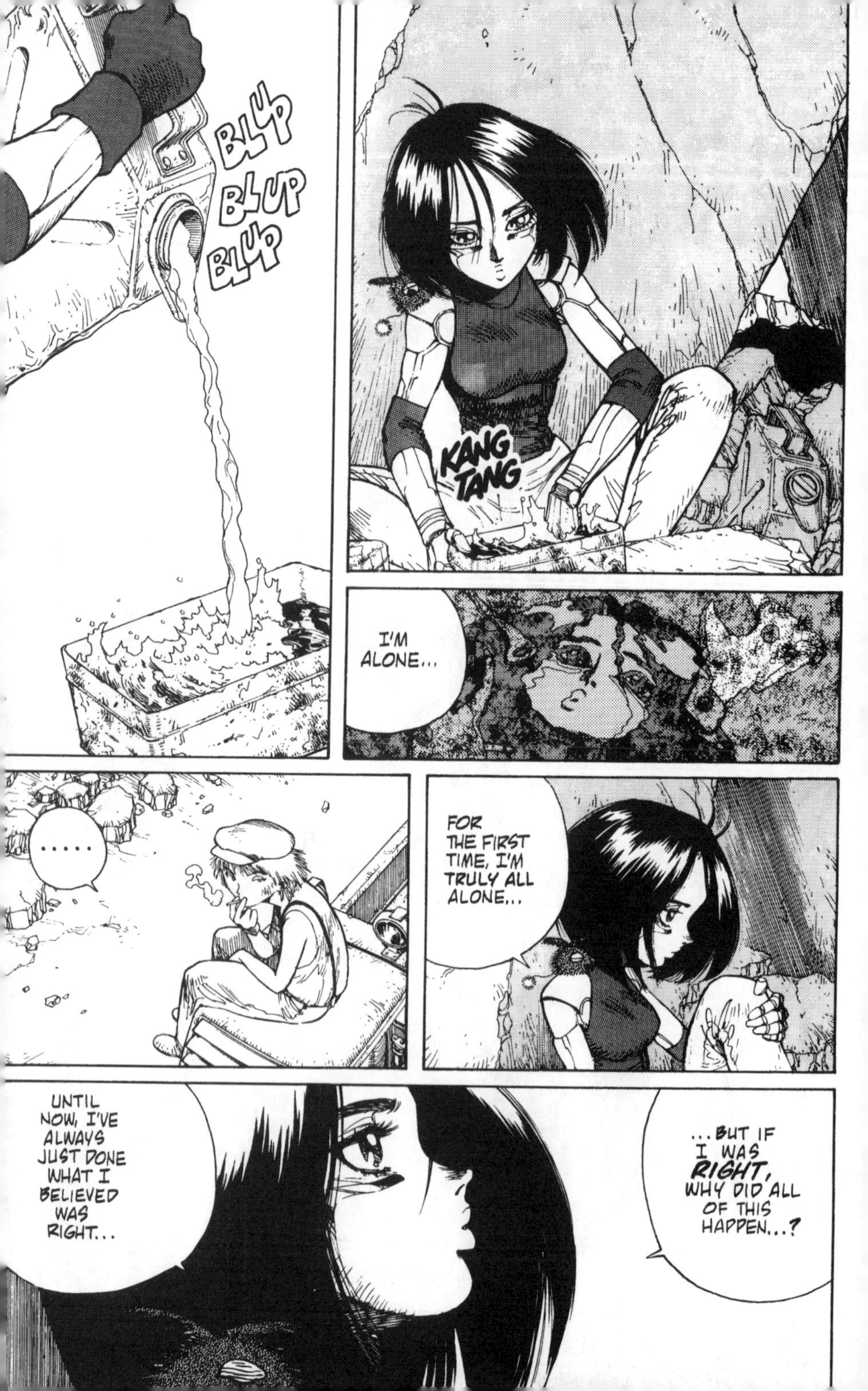
BLUP
BLUP
BLUP
KANG
TANG
I'M ALONE...
.....
FOR THE FIRST TIME, I'M TRULY ALL ALONE...
UNTIL NOW, I'VE ALWAYS JUST DONE WHAT I BELIEVED WAS RIGHT...
...BUT IF I WAS RIGHT, WHY DID ALL OF THIS HAPPEN...?

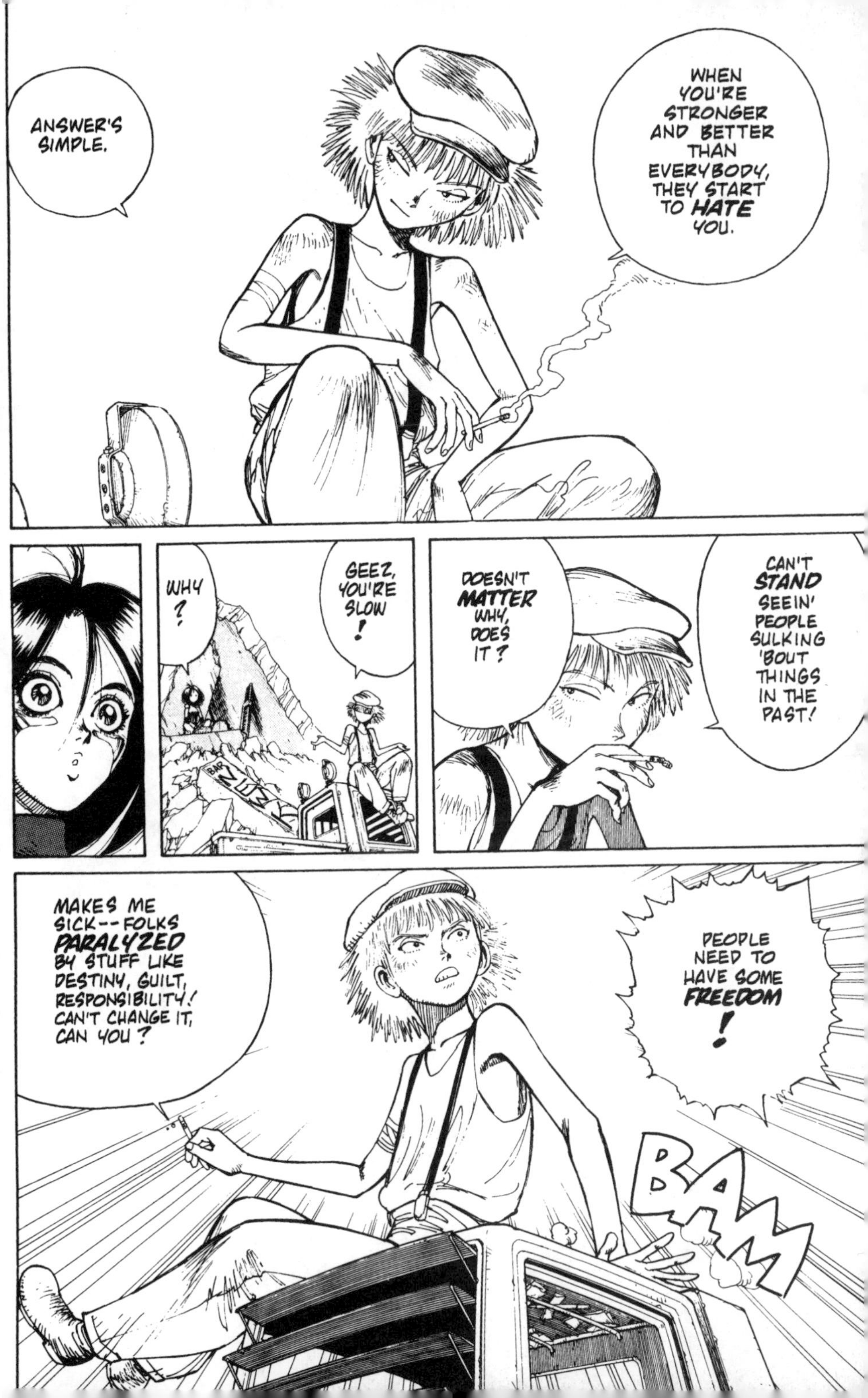
ANSWER'S SIMPLE.
WHEN YOU'RE STRONGER AND BETTER THAN EVERYBODY, THEY START TO HATE YOU.
WHY ?
GEEZ, YOU'RE SLOW !
DOESN'T MATTER WHY, DOES IT ?
CAN'T STAND SEEIN' PEOPLE SULKING 'BOUT THINGS IN THE PAST!
MAKES ME SICK--FOLKS PARALYZED BY STUFF LIKE DESTINY, GUILT, RESPONSIBILITY! CAN'T CHANGE IT, CAN YOU ?
PEOPLE NEED TO HAVE SOME FREEDOM !
BAM

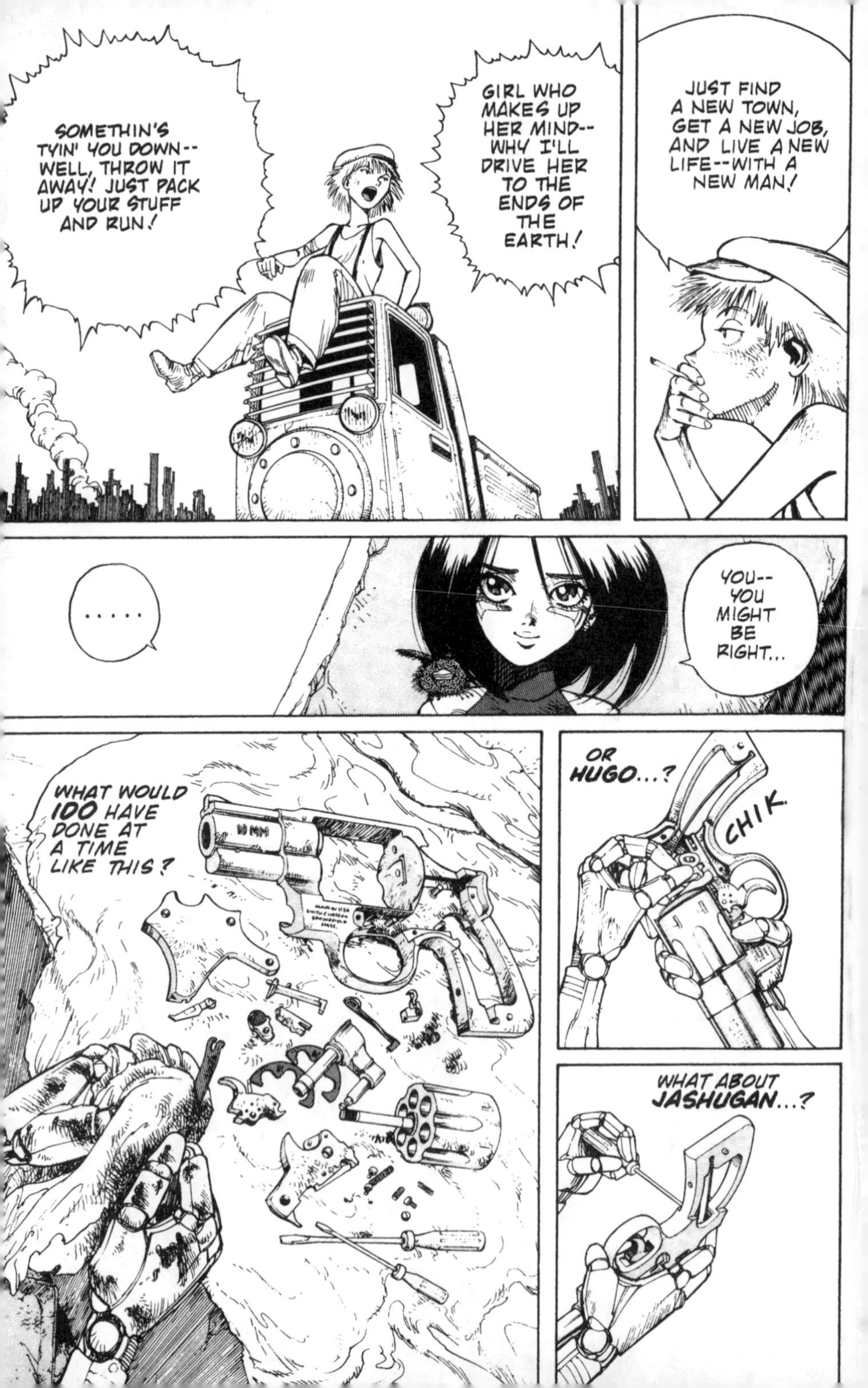
SOMETHIN'S TYIN' YOU DOWN-- WELL, THROW IT AWAY! JUST PACK UP YOUR STUFF AND RUN!
GIRL WHO MAKES UP HER MIND-- WHY I'LL DRIVE HER TO THE ENDS OF THE EARTH!
JUST FIND A NEW TOWN, GET A NEW JOB, AND LIVE A NEW LIFE--WITH A NEW MAN!
.....
YOU-- YOU MIGHT BE RIGHT...
WHAT WOULD IDO HAVE DONE AT A TIME LIKE THIS?
10 MM
OR HUGO...?
CHIK
WHAT ABOUT JASHUGAN...?

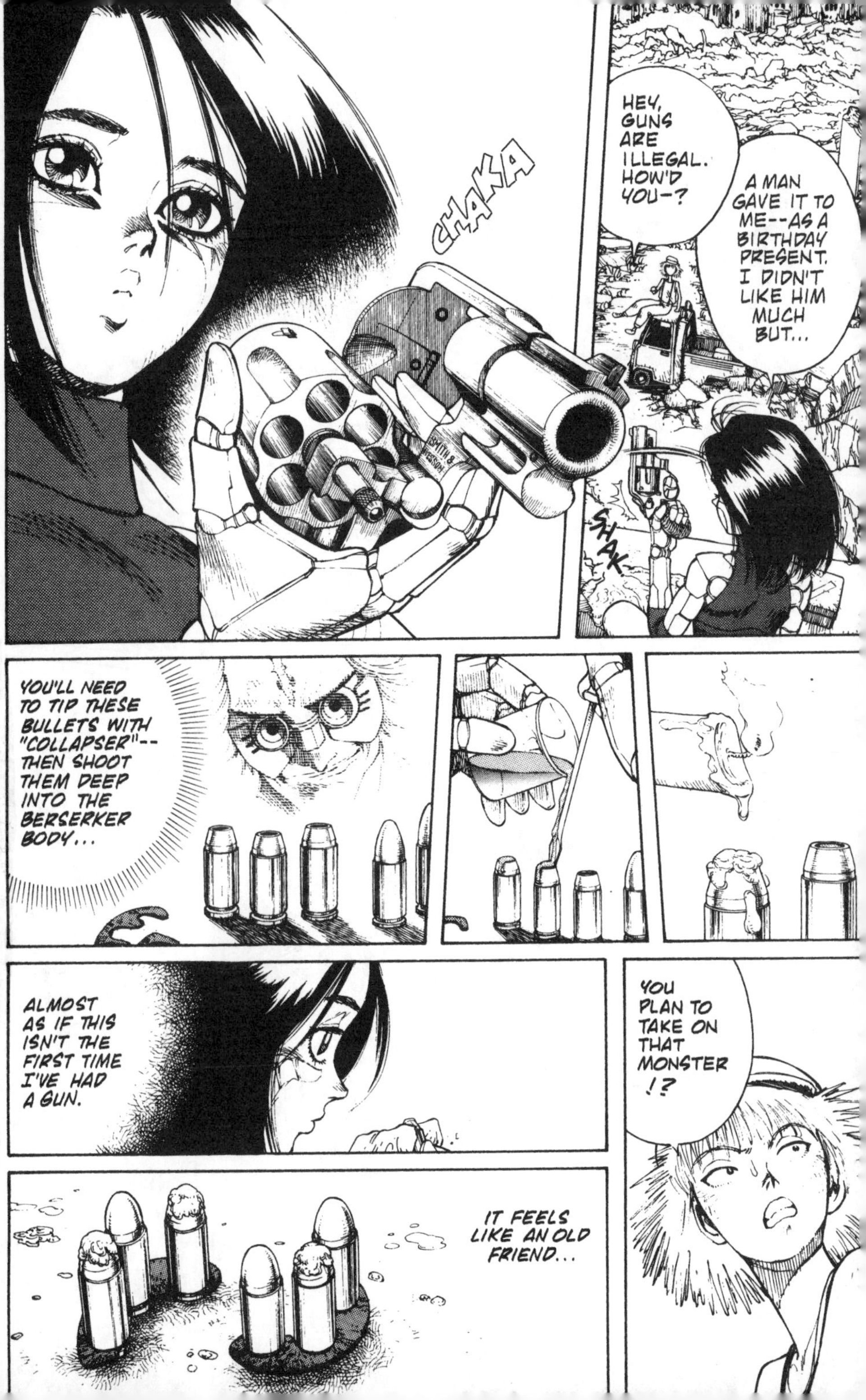
CHAKA
HEY, GUNS ARE ILLEGAL. HOW'D YOU-?
A MAN GAVE IT TO ME--AS A BIRTHDAY PRESENT. I DIDN'T LIKE HIM MUCH BUT...
SHAK
YOU'LL NEED TO TIP THESE BULLETS WITH "COLLAPSER"--THEN SHOOT THEM DEEP INTO THE BERSERKER BODY...
ALMOST AS IF THIS ISN'T THE FIRST TIME I'VE HAD A GUN.
YOU PLAN TO TAKE ON THAT MONSTER !?
IT FEELS LIKE AN OLD FRIEND...

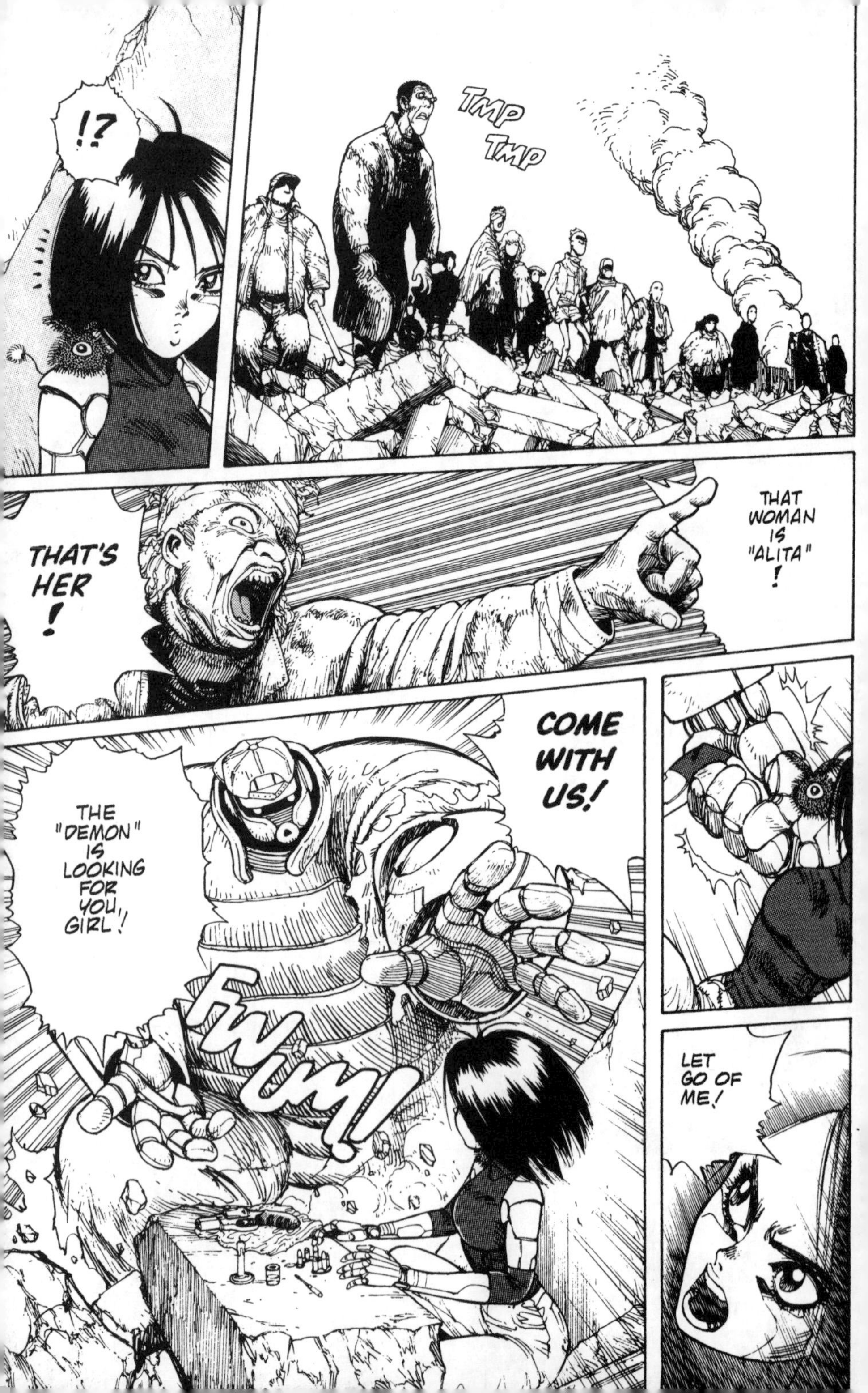
!?
TMP
TMP
THAT'S HER!
THAT WOMAN IS "ALITA"!
THE "DEMON" IS LOOKING FOR YOU, GIRL!
COME WITH US!
FWUM!
LET GO OF ME!

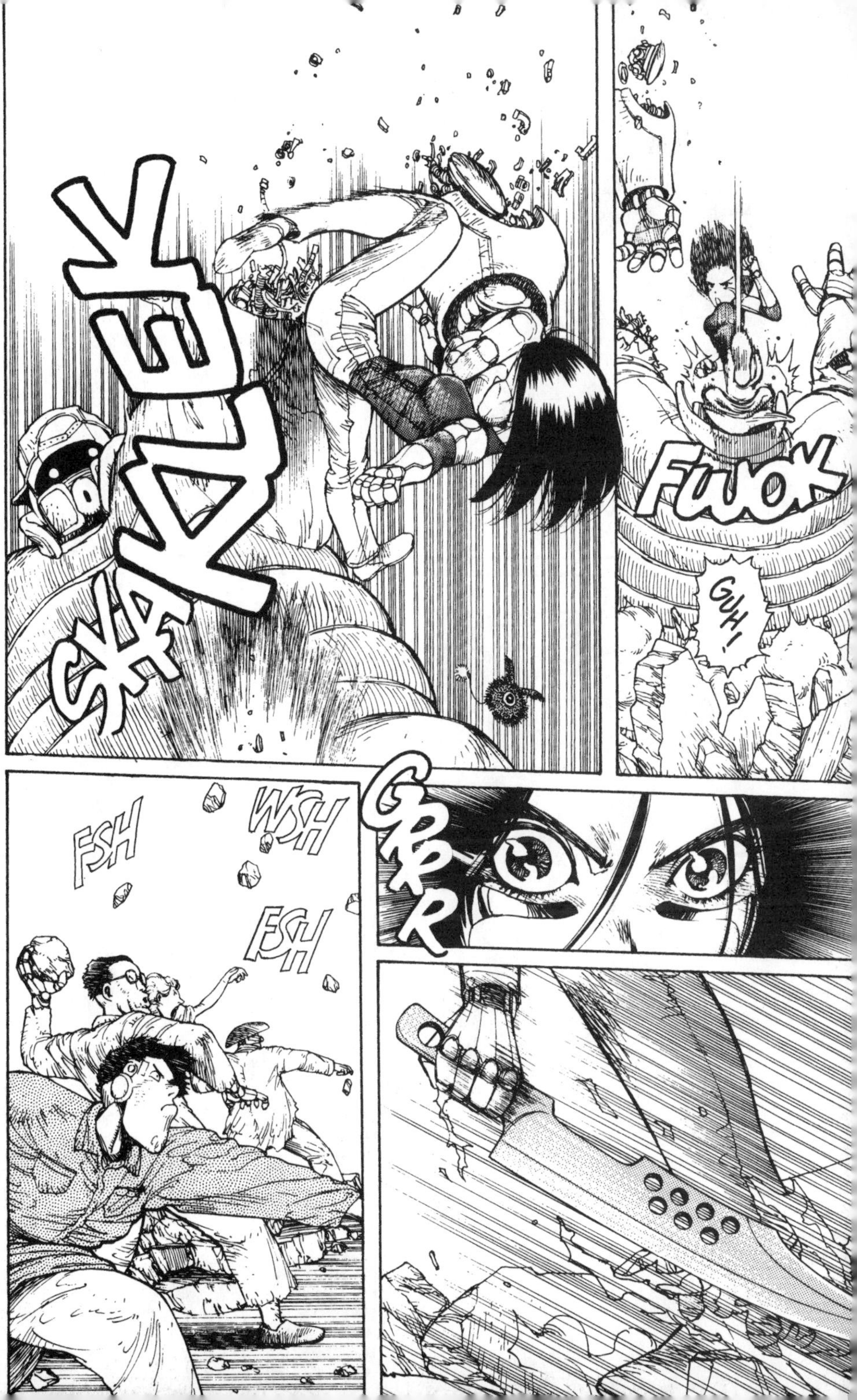
SKAEK
FWOK
GUH!
FSH
WSH
FSH
GRRR

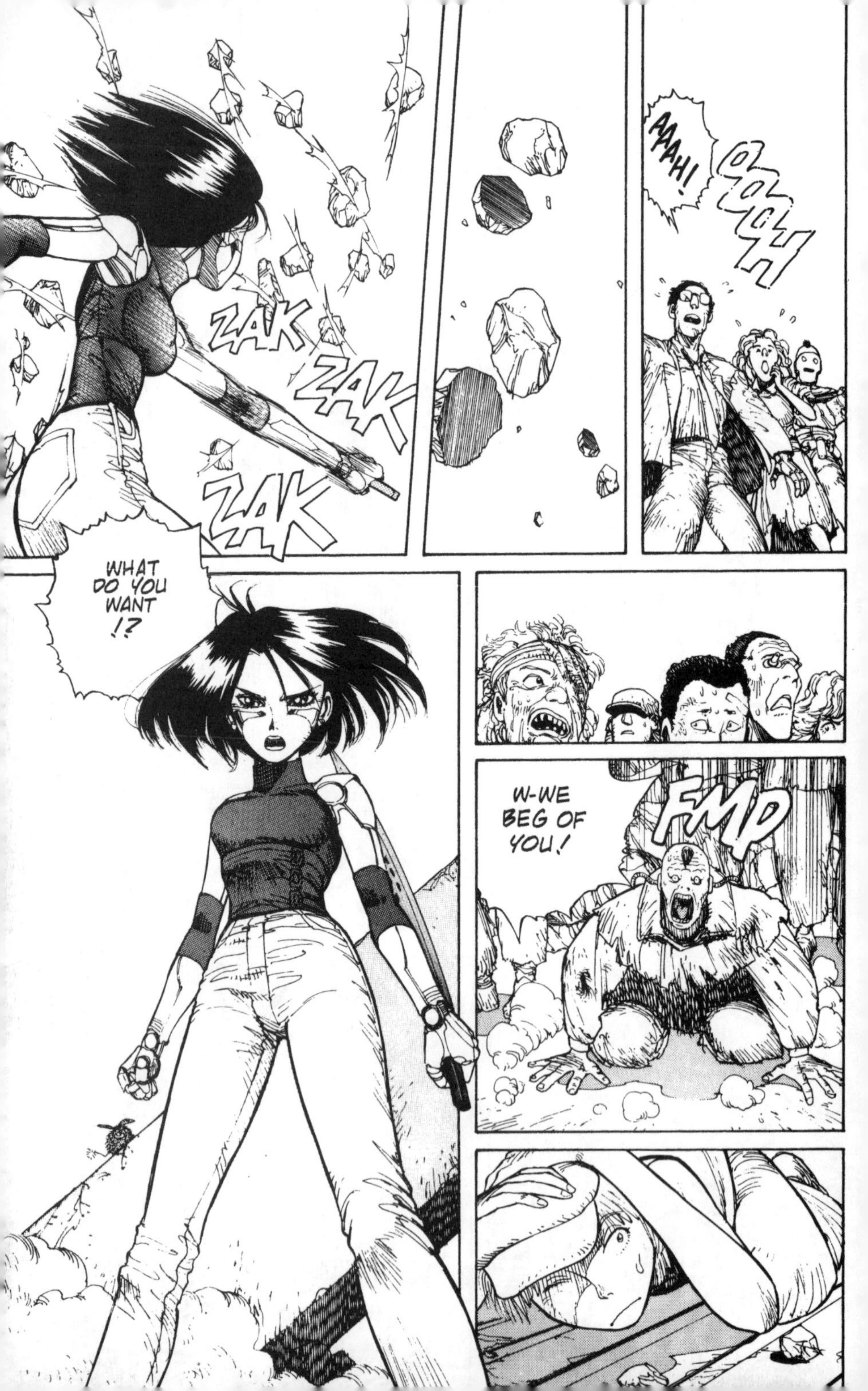
ZAK
ZAK
ZAK
AAAAH!
OOOOHH
WHAT DO YOU WANT !?
W-WE BEG OF YOU!
FMP

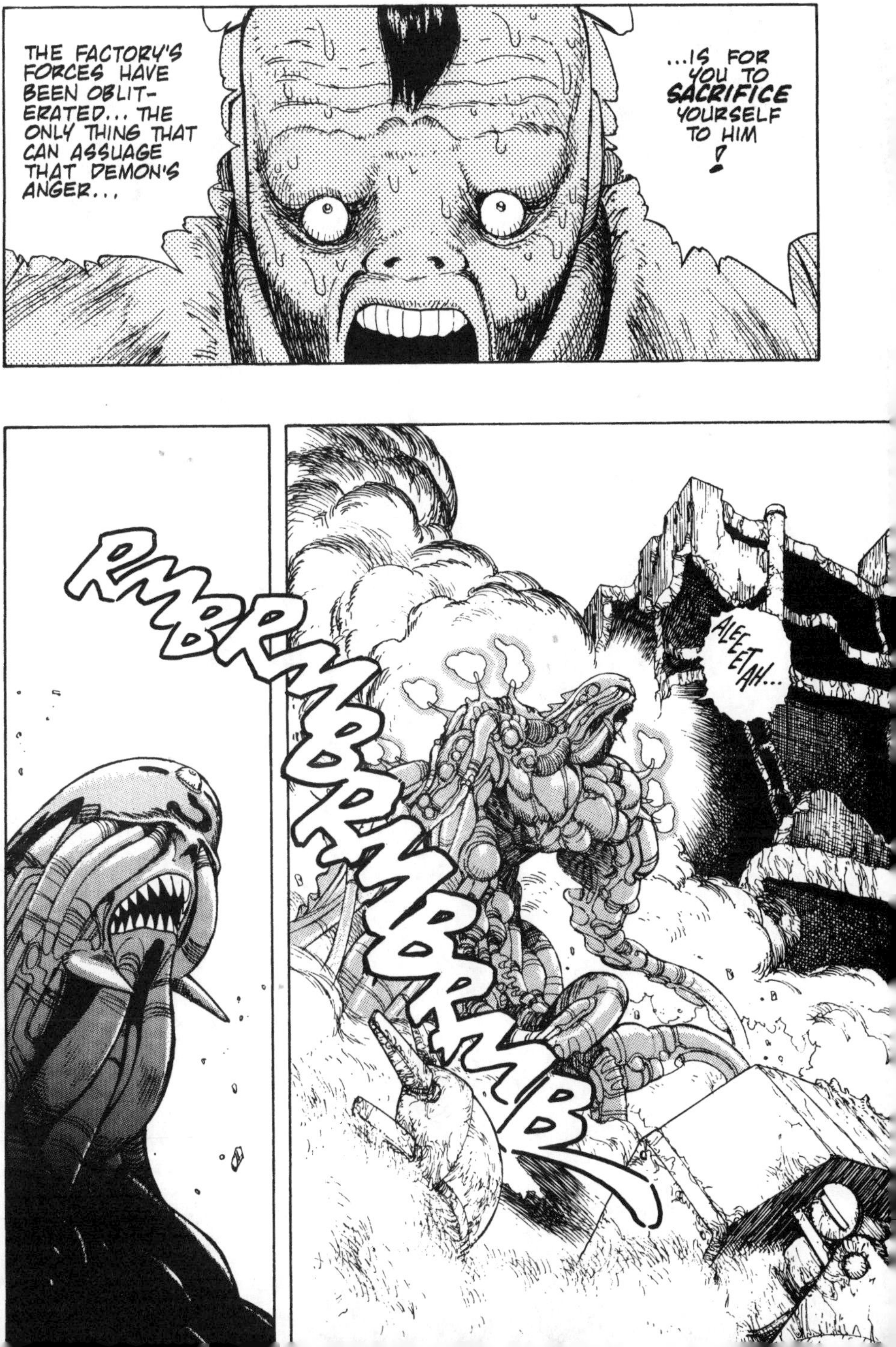
THE FACTORY'S FORCES HAVE BEEN OBLITERATED... THE ONLY THING THAT CAN ASSUAGE THAT DEMON'S ANGER...
...IS FOR YOU TO SACRIFICE YOURSELF TO HIM!
RMBRMBRMBRMBRMB!
ALEEETAH...

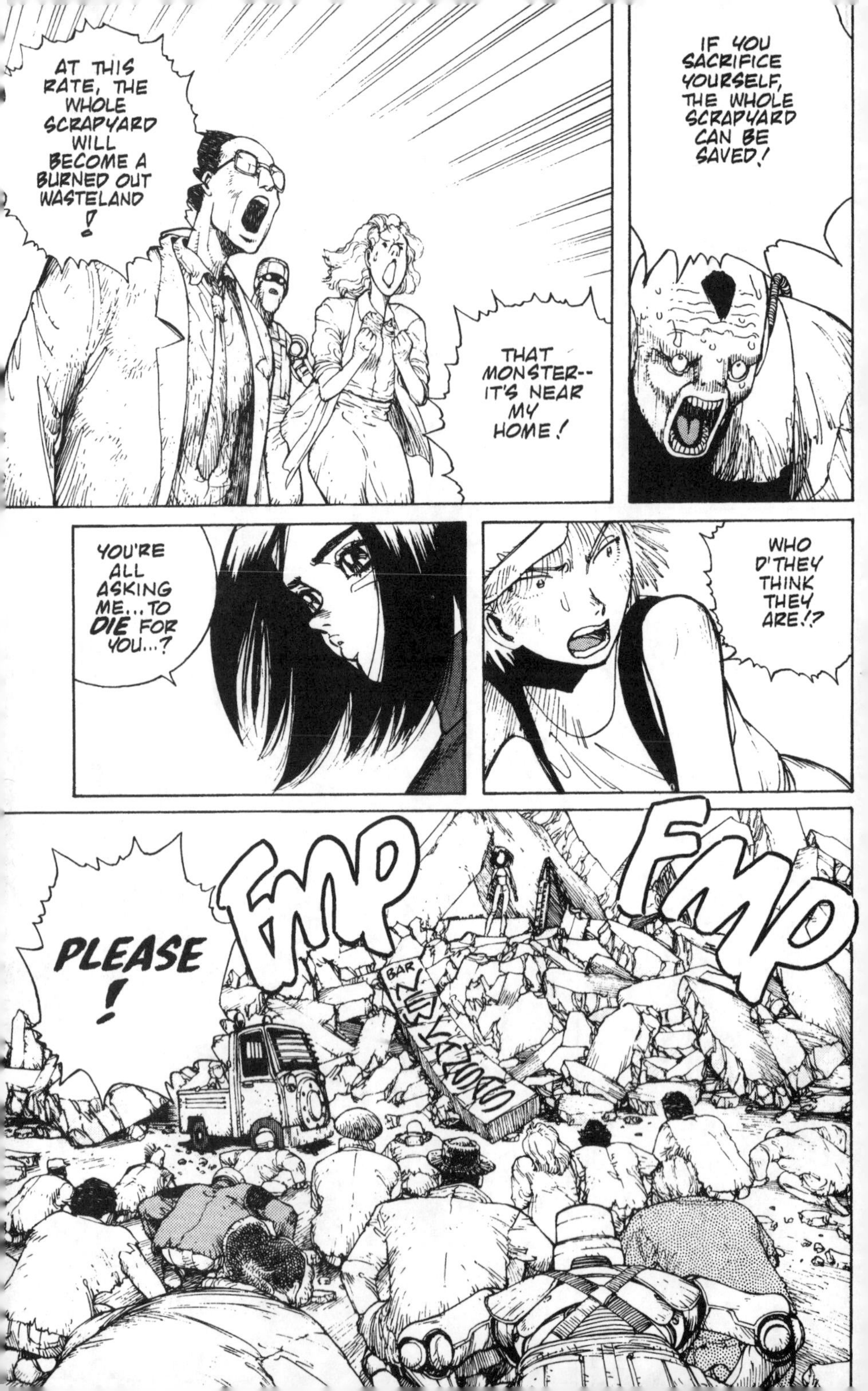
AT THIS RATE, THE WHOLE SCRAPYARD WILL BECOME A BURNED OUT WASTELAND!
THAT MONSTER-- IT'S NEAR MY HOME!
IF YOU SACRIFICE YOURSELF, THE WHOLE SCRAPYARD CAN BE SAVED!
YOU'RE ALL ASKING ME... TO DIE FOR YOU...?
WHO D'THEY THINK THEY ARE!?
PLEASE!
FMP
FMP
BAR

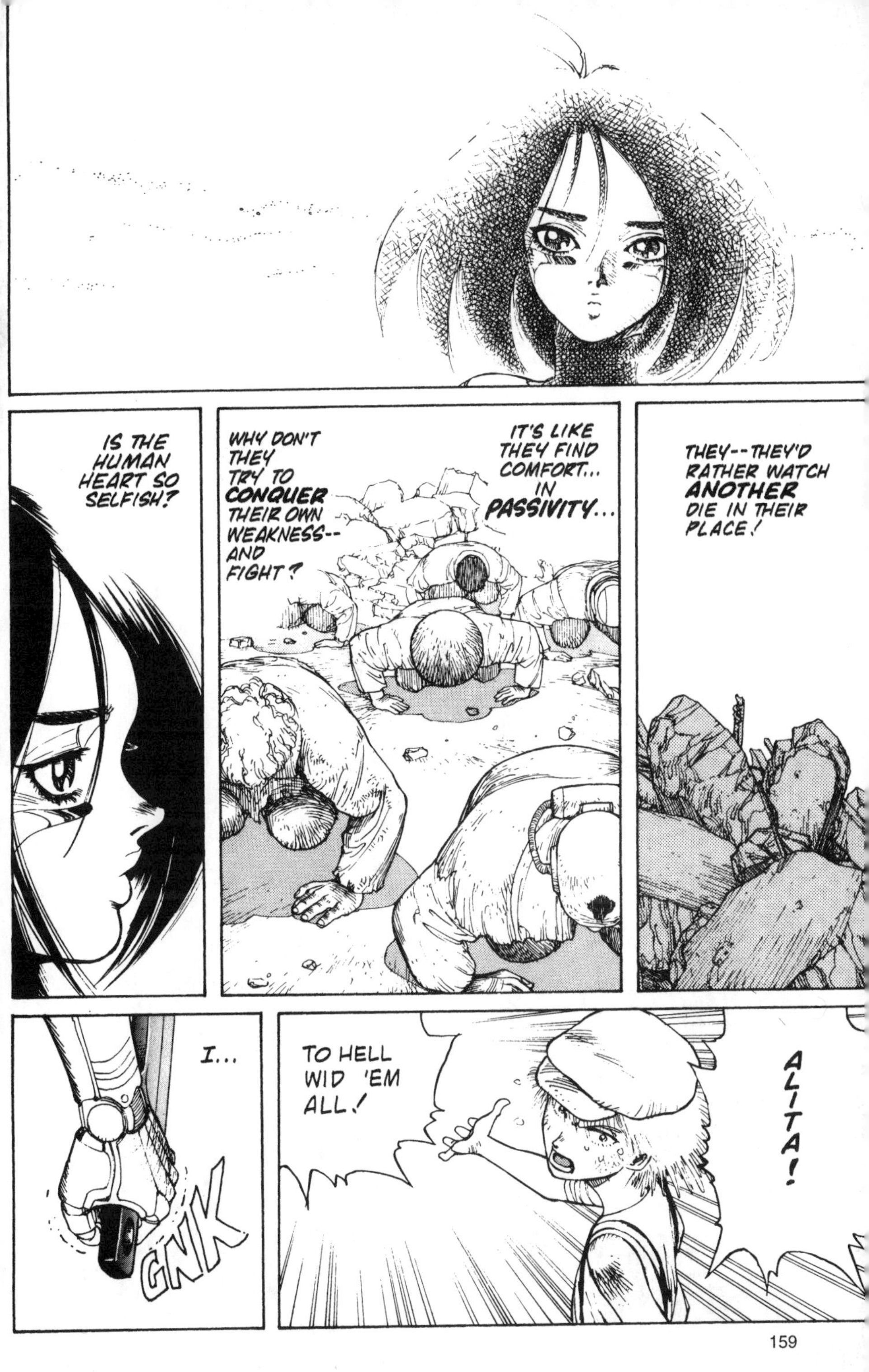
IS THE HUMAN HEART SO SELFISH?
WHY DON'T THEY TRY TO CONQUER THEIR OWN WEAKNESS-- AND FIGHT?
IT'S LIKE THEY FIND COMFORT... IN PASSIVITY...
THEY--THEY'D RATHER WATCH ANOTHER DIE IN THEIR PLACE!
I...
GNK
TO HELL WID 'EM ALL!
ALITA!

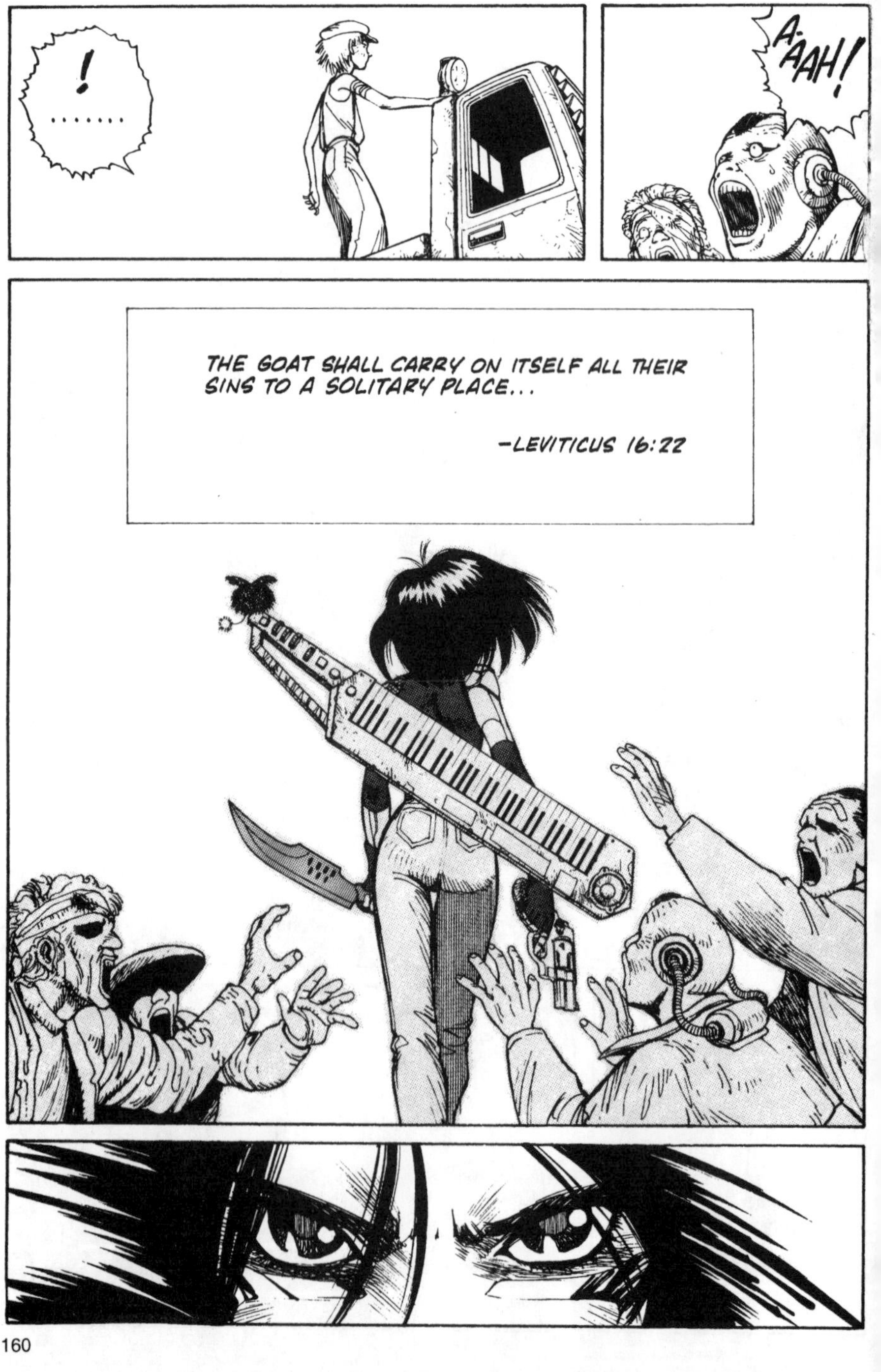
!
....
A-AAAH!
THE GOAT SHALL CARRY ON ITSELF ALL THEIR SINS TO A SOLITARY PLACE...
-LEVITICUS 16:22

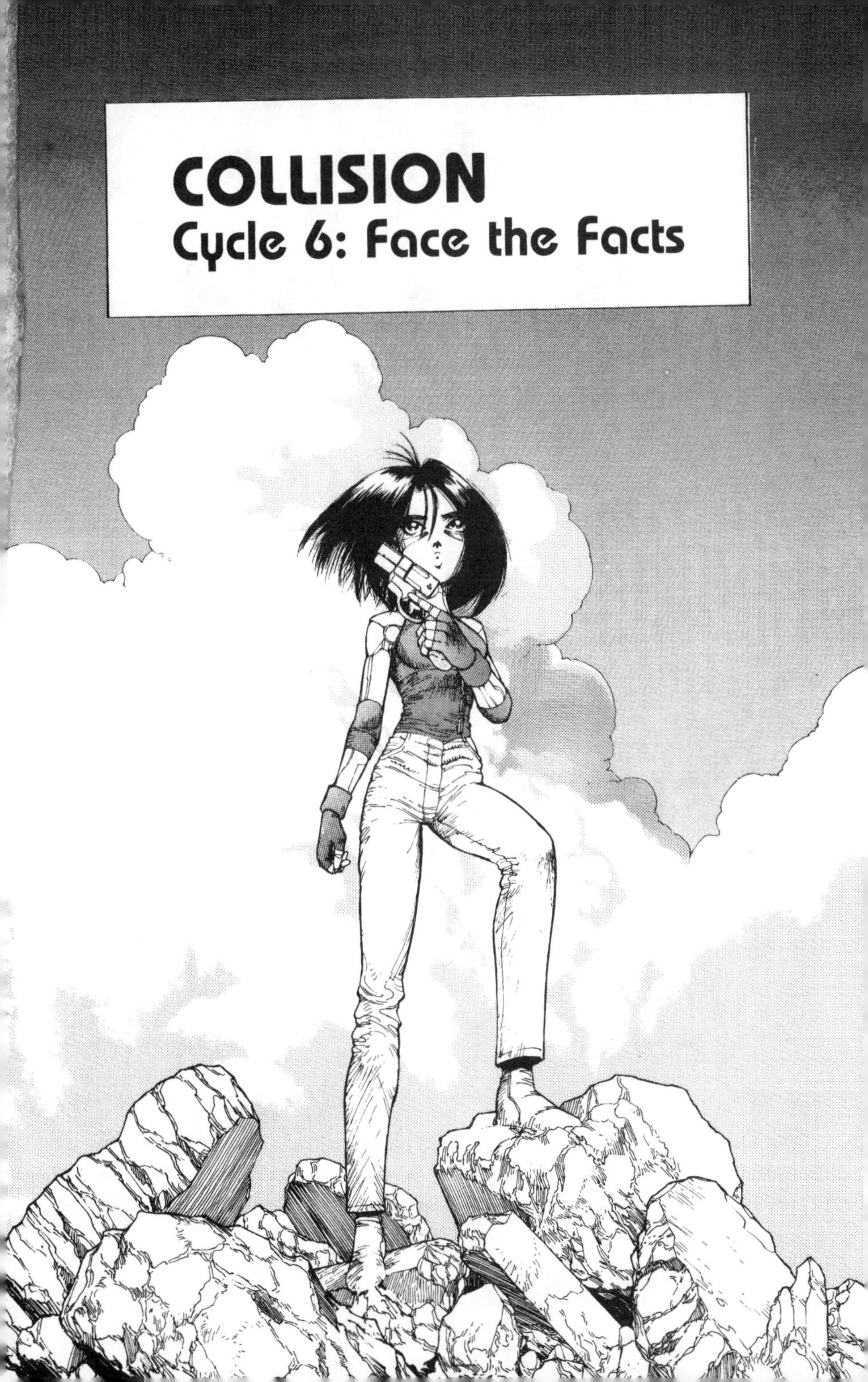
COLLISION
Cycle 6: Face the Facts

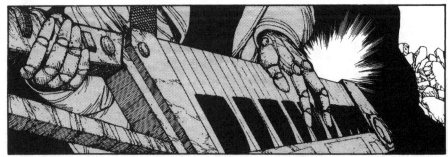

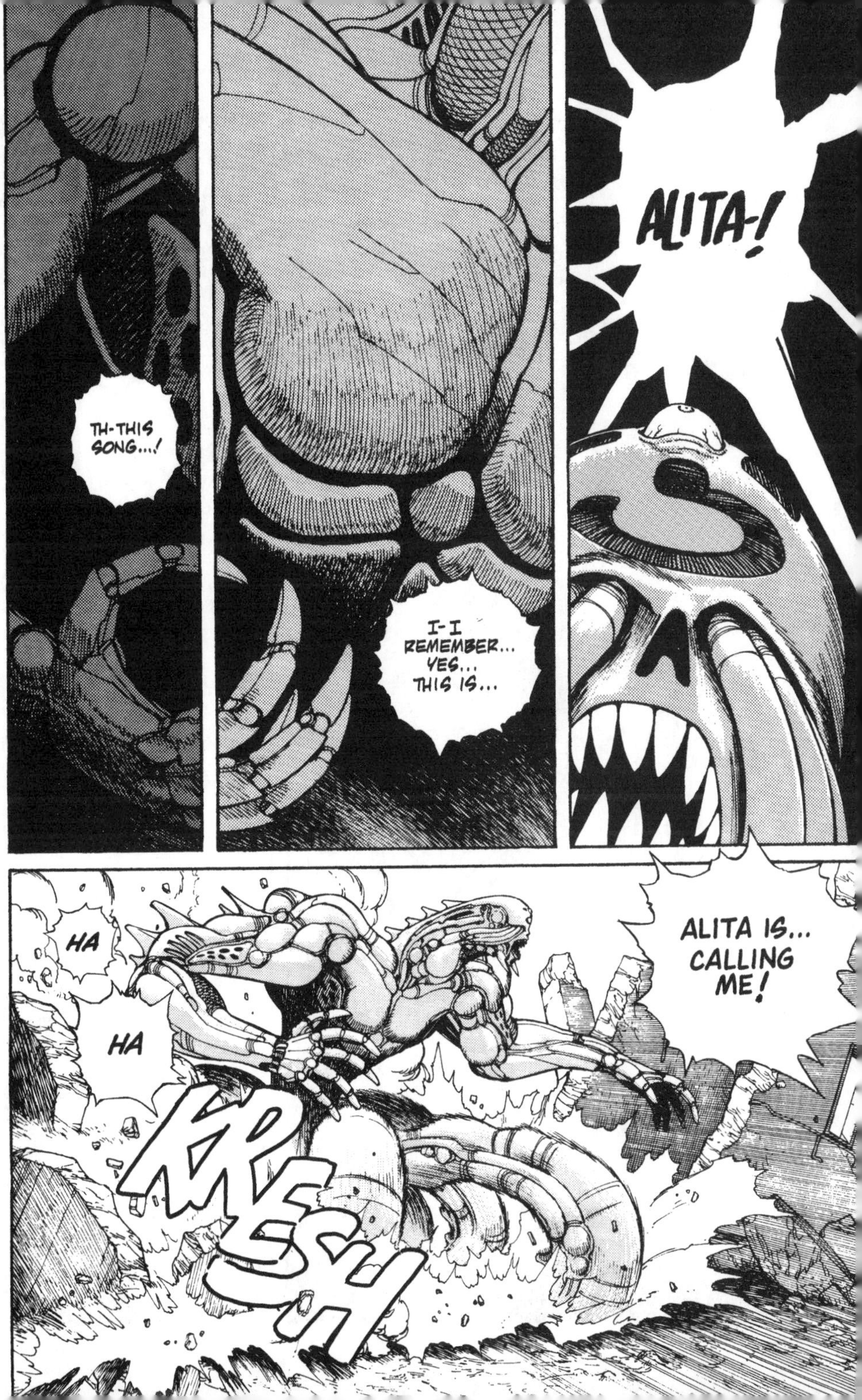
TH-THIS SONG...!
I-I REMEMBER... YES... THIS IS...
ALITA-!
HA
HA
KRESH
ALITA IS... CALLING ME!

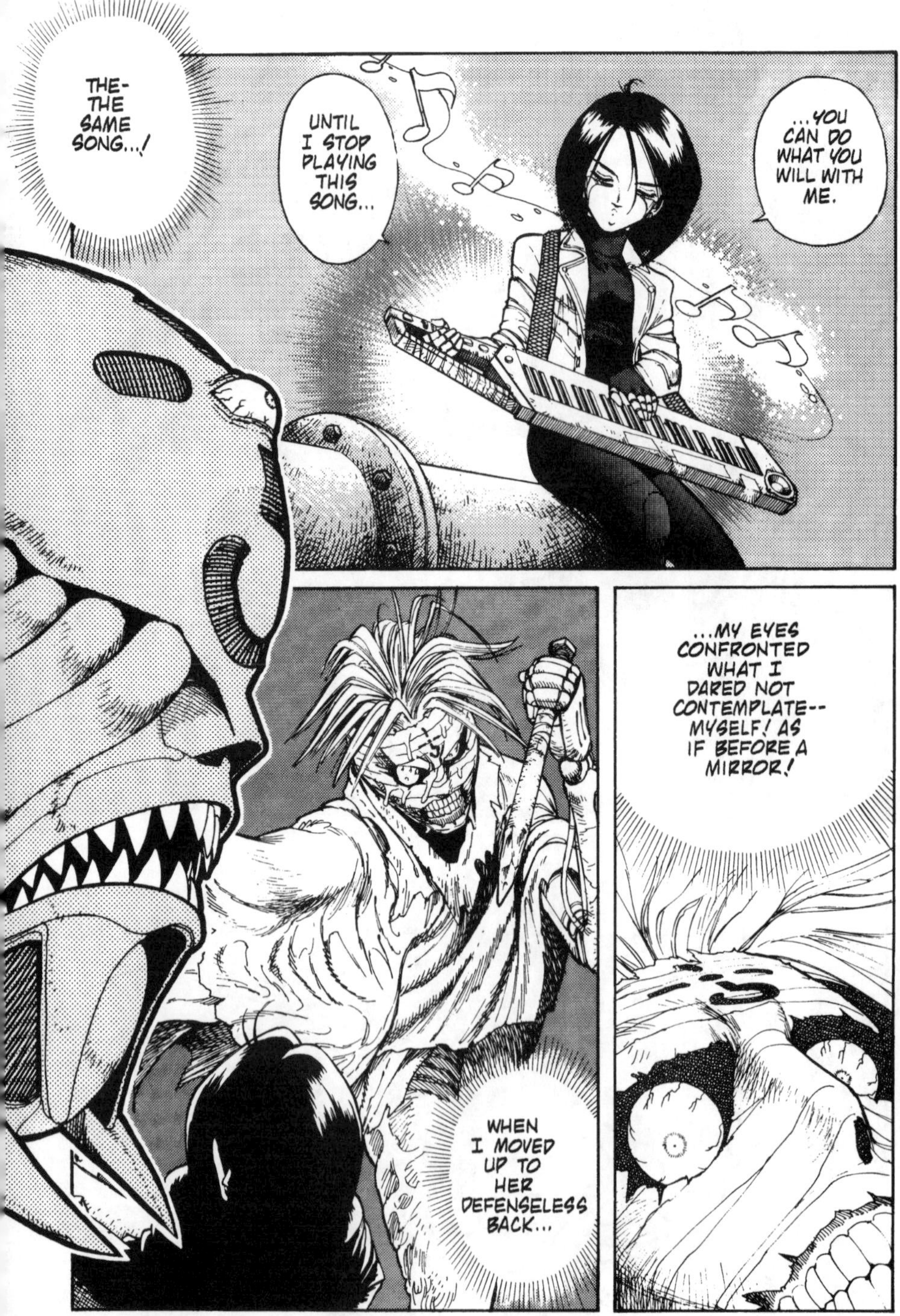
THE- THE SAME SONG...!
UNTIL I STOP PLAYING THIS SONG...
...YOU CAN DO WHAT YOU WILL WITH ME.
WHEN I MOVED UP TO HER DEFENSELESS BACK...
...MY EYES CONFRONTED WHAT I DARED NOT CONTEMPLATE--MYSELF! AS IF BEFORE A MIRROR!

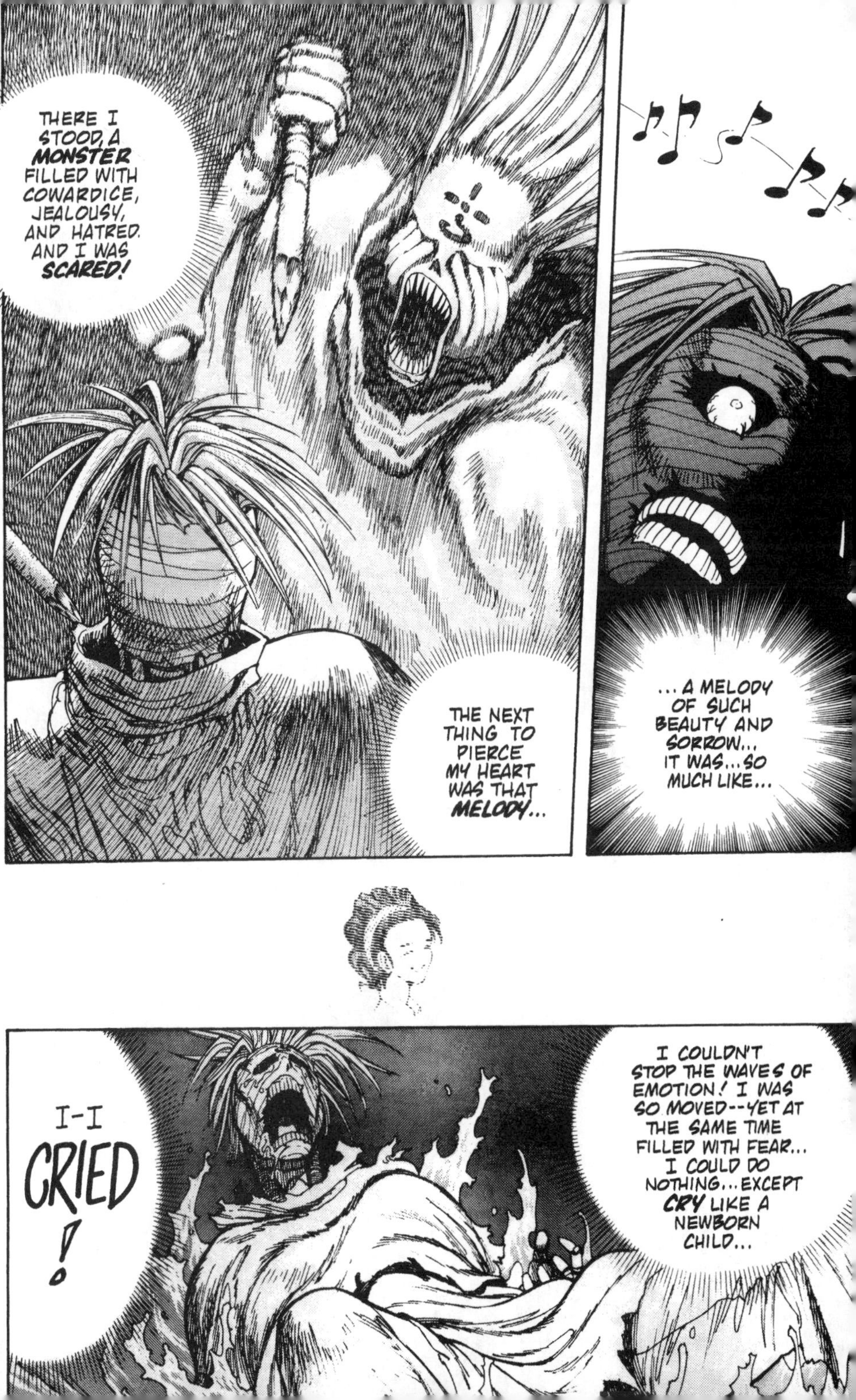
THERE I STOOD, A **MONSTER** FILLED WITH COWARDICE, JEALOUSY, AND HATRED. AND I WAS **SCARED!**
THE NEXT THING TO PIERCE MY HEART WAS THAT **MELODY**...
... A MELODY OF SUCH BEAUTY AND SORROW... IT WAS... SO MUCH LIKE...
I-I CRIED!
I COULDN'T STOP THE WAVES OF EMOTION! I WAS SO MOVED--YET AT THE SAME TIME FILLED WITH FEAR... I COULD DO NOTHING... EXCEPT **CRY** LIKE A NEWBORN CHILD...

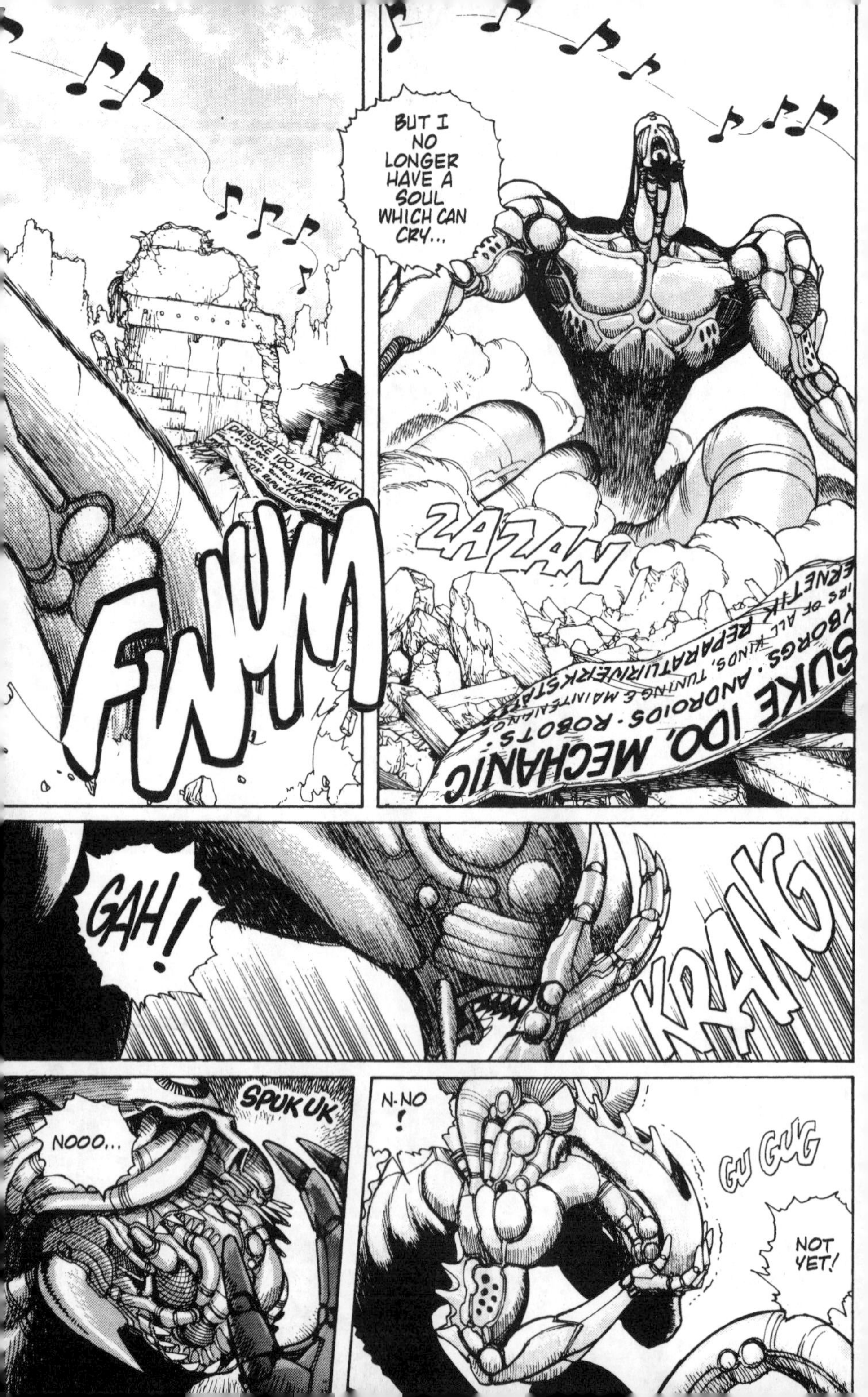

DAISUKE IDO, MECHANIC
FWUM
BUT I NO LONGER HAVE A SOUL WHICH CAN CRY...
ZAZAN
SUKE IDO, MECHANIC
GAH!
KRANG
NOOO...
SPUKUK
N-NO!
GU GUG
NOT YET!

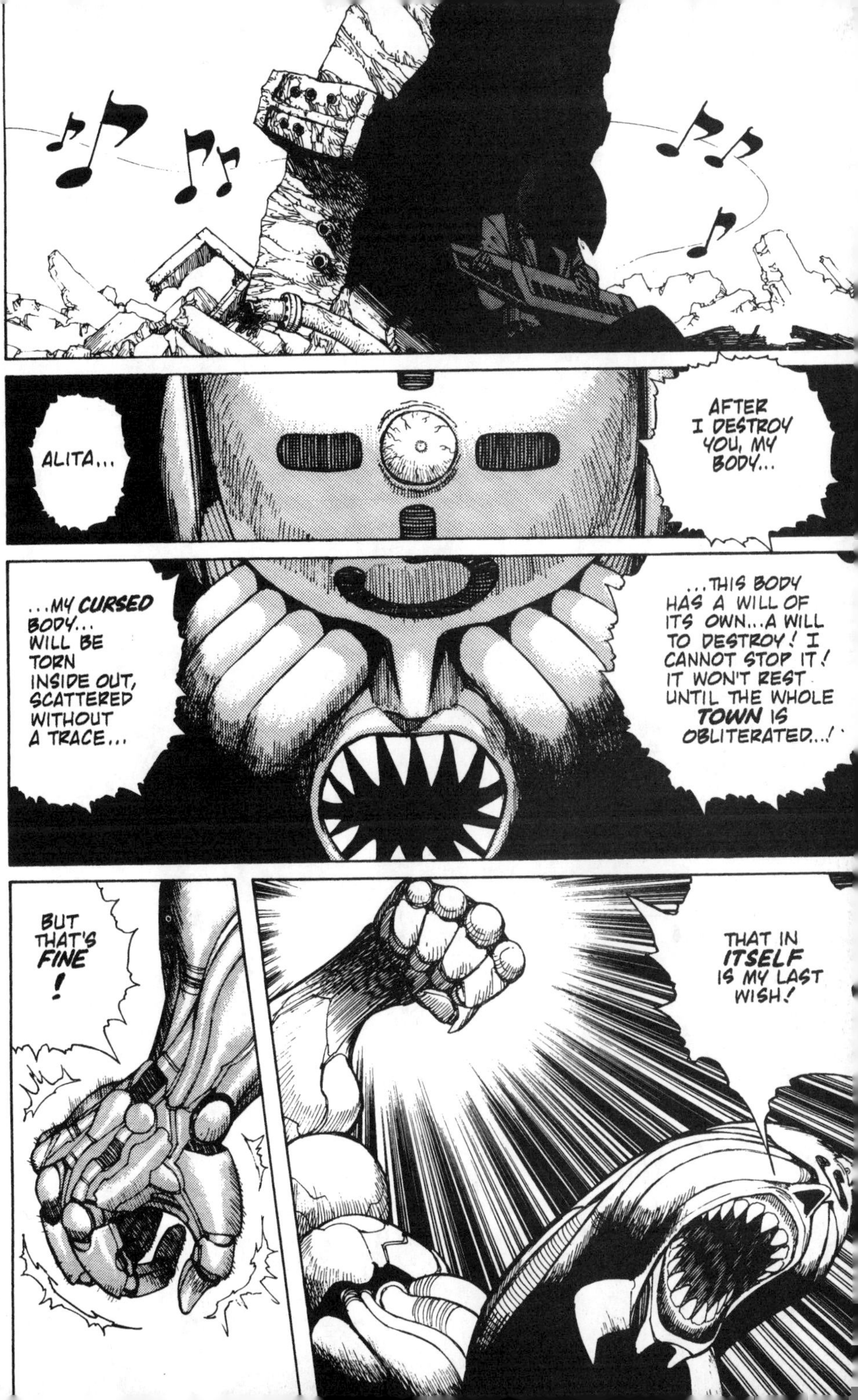
ALITA...
AFTER I DESTROY YOU, MY BODY...
...MY CURSED BODY... WILL BE TORN INSIDE OUT, SCATTERED WITHOUT A TRACE...
...THIS BODY HAS A WILL OF ITS OWN...A WILL TO DESTROY! I CANNOT STOP IT! IT WON'T REST UNTIL THE WHOLE TOWN IS OBLITERATED...!
BUT THAT'S FINE!
THAT IN ITSELF IS MY LAST WISH!

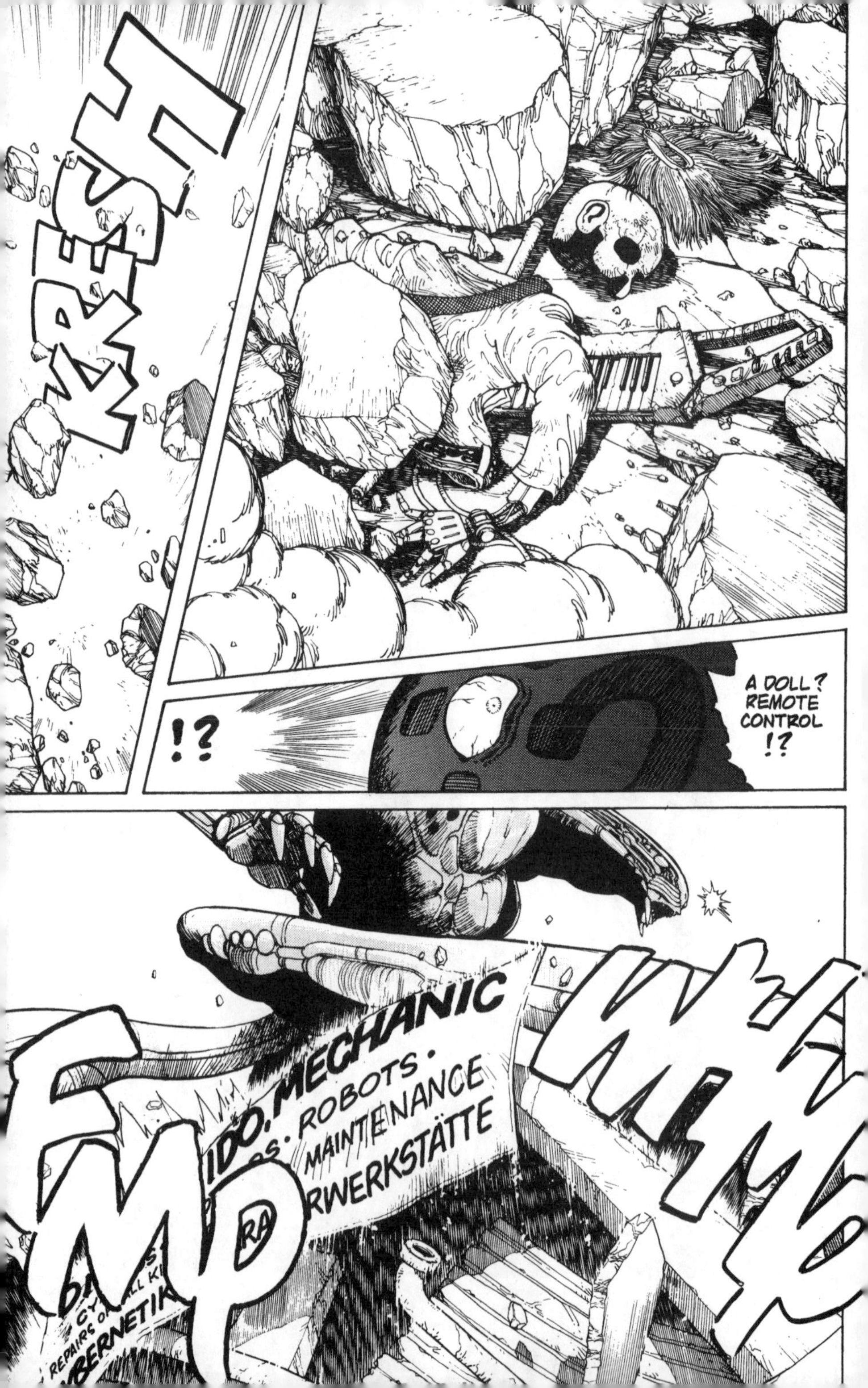

KRESH
!?
A DOLL? REMOTE CONTROL !?
IDO. MECHANIC
ROBOTS.
MAINTENANCE
RWERKSTÄTTE

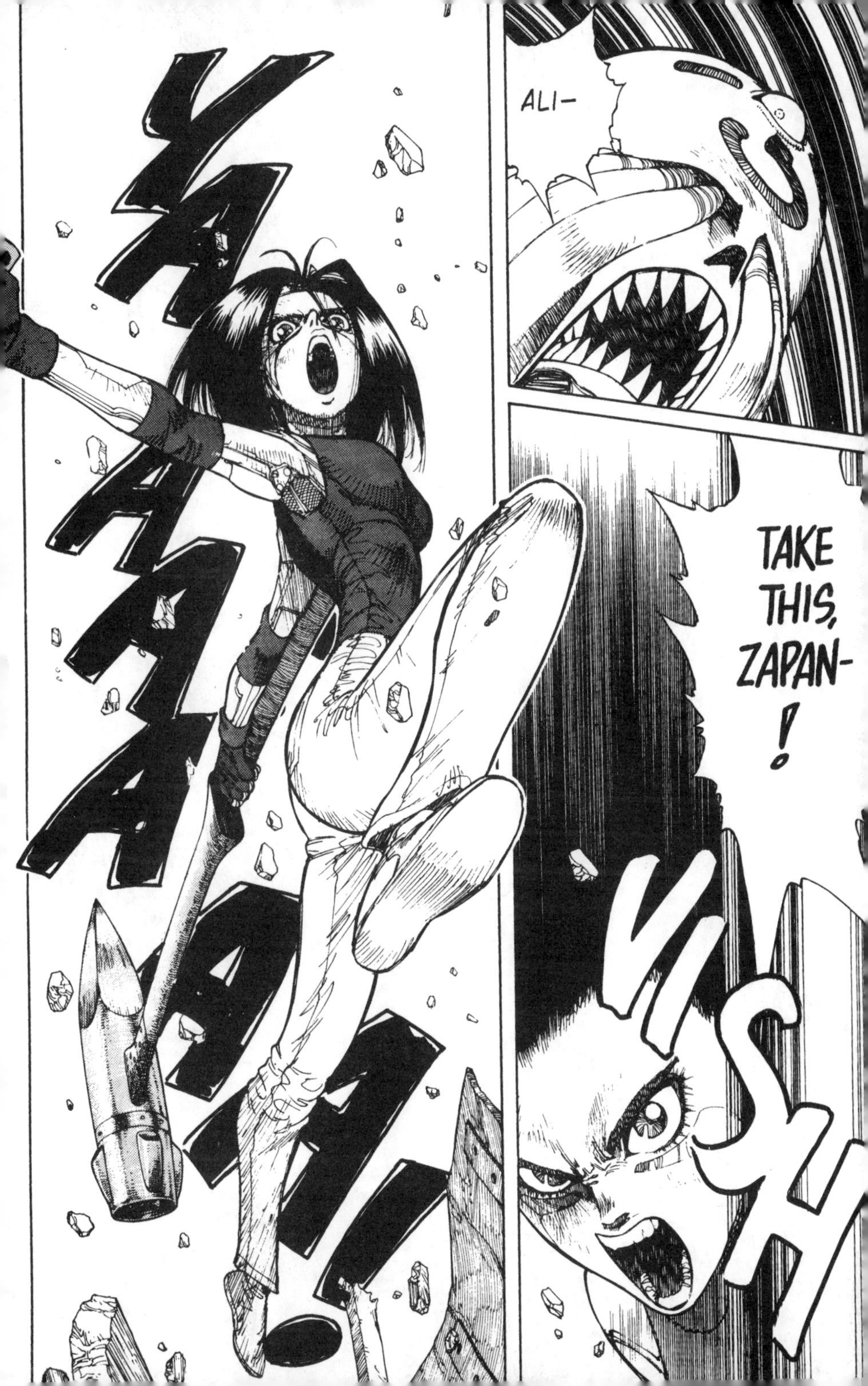
ALI-
TAKE THIS, ZAPAN-!

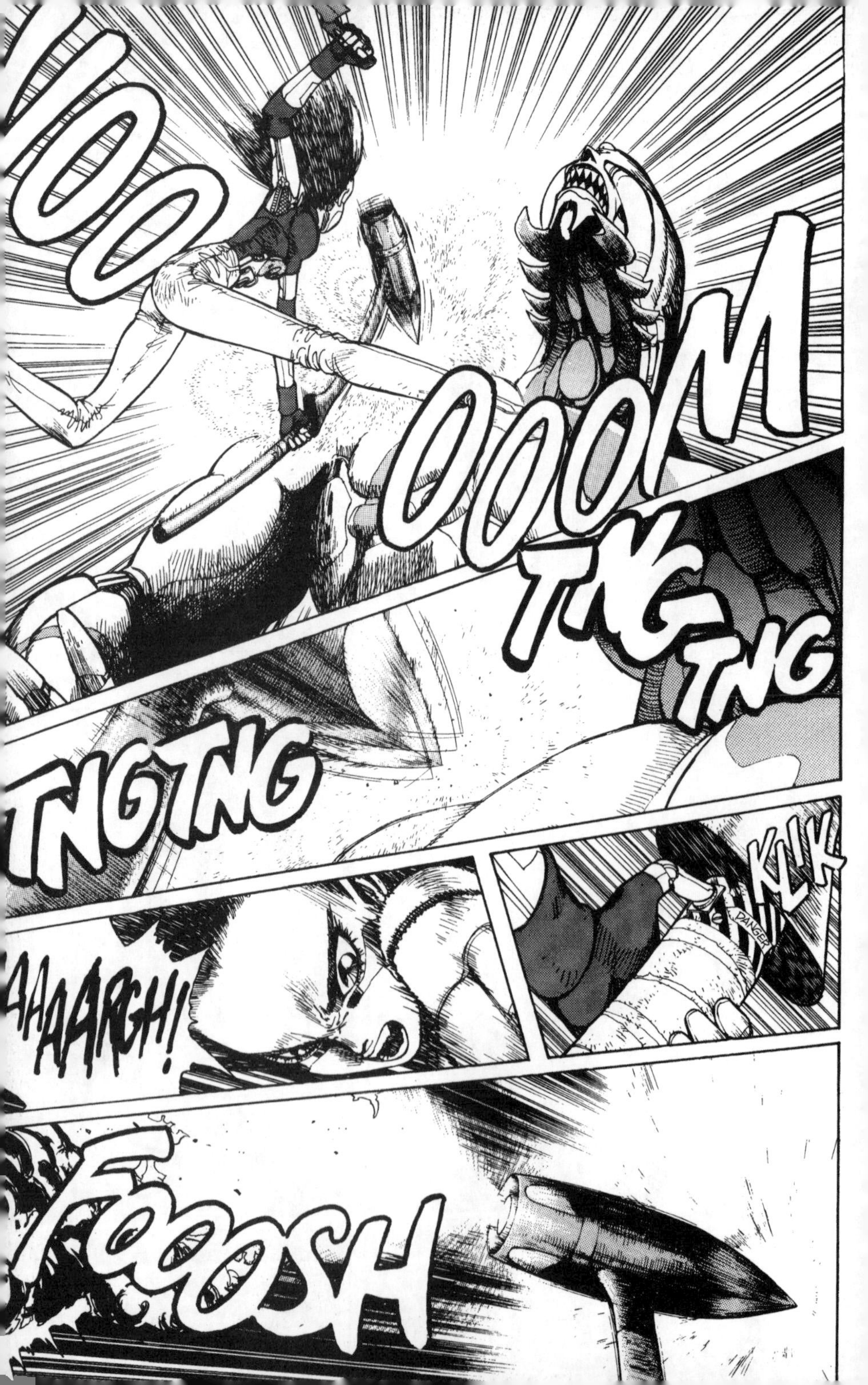
OOOOOOOM
TNG TNG
TNGTNG
AAAARGH!
KLIK
DANGER
FOOOSH

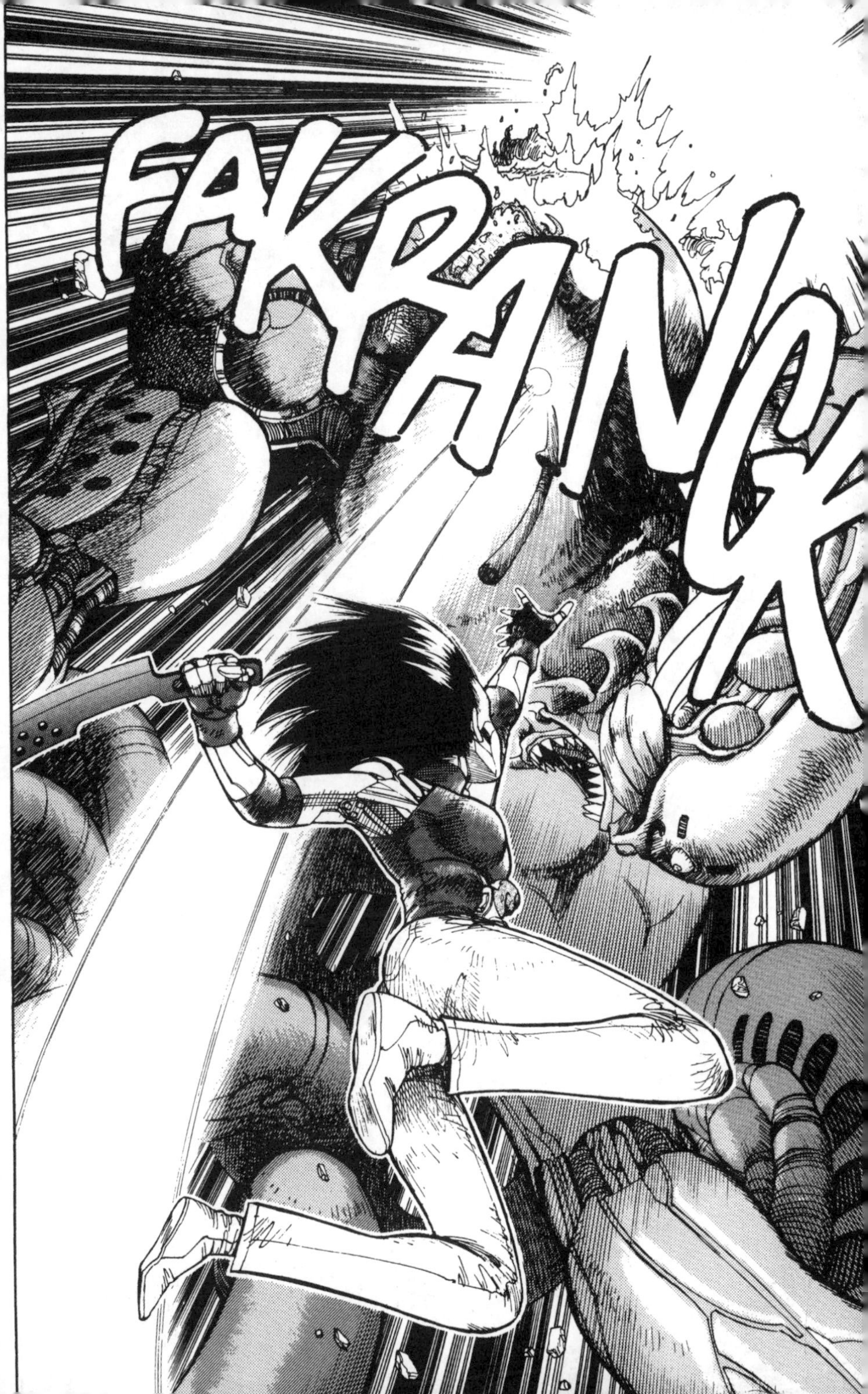
FAKRANCK

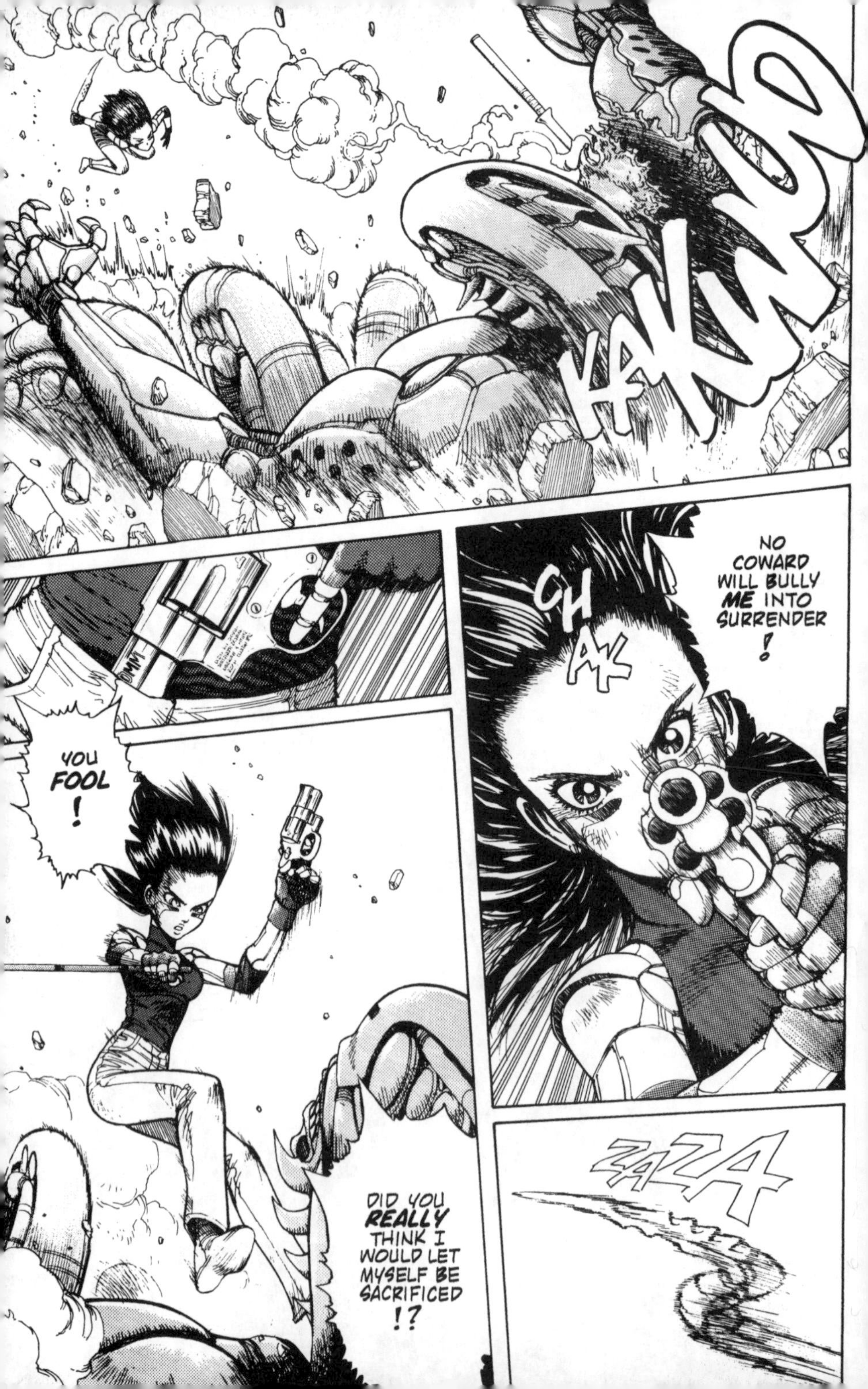
YOU FOOL!
DID YOU REALLY THINK I WOULD LET MYSELF BE SACRIFICED!?
CHAK
NO COWARD WILL BULLY ME INTO SURRENDER!
ZAZA

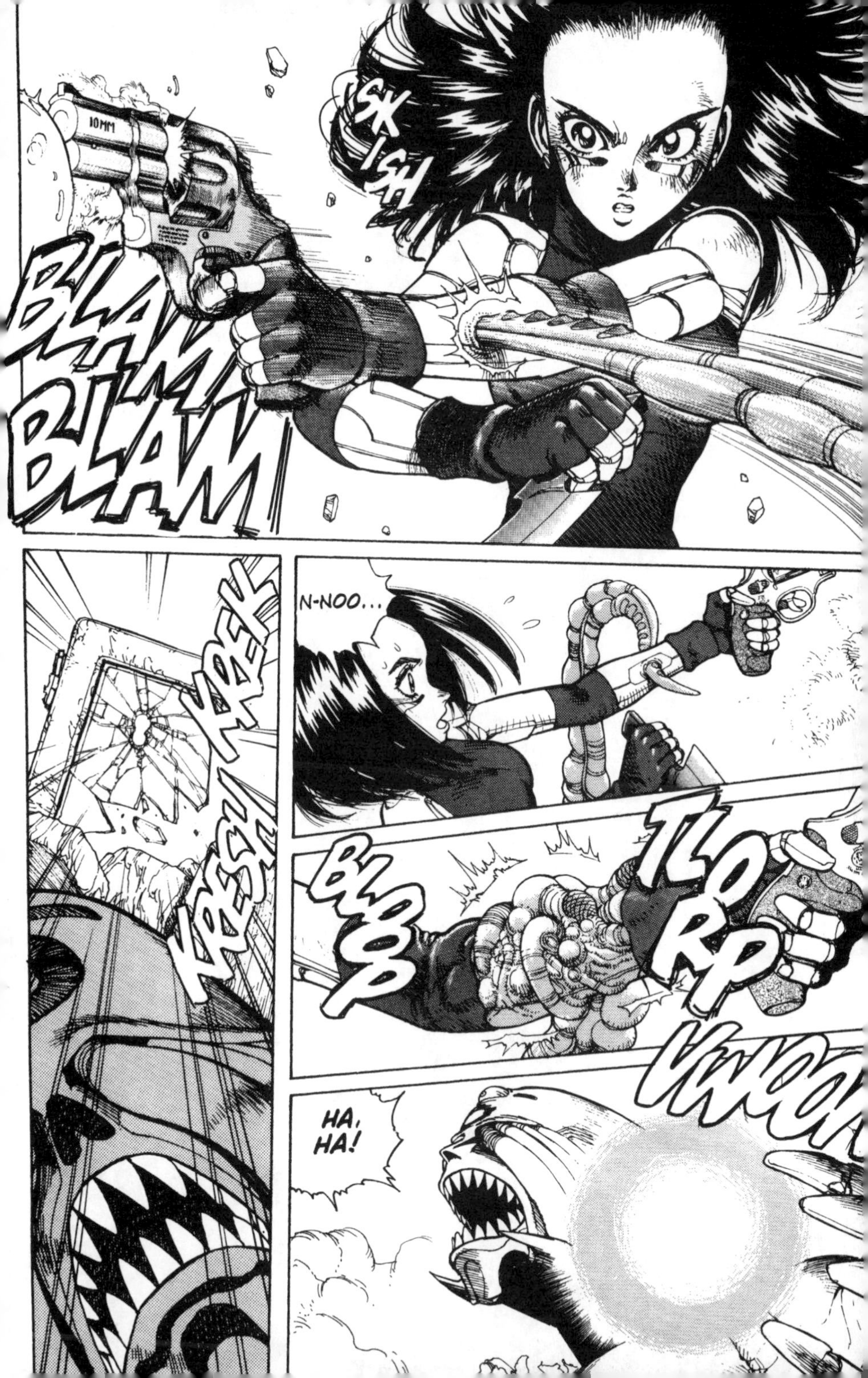
10MM
SK ISH
BLAM
BLAM
BLAM
KRESH
KRESH
N-NOO...
BLOOP
TLORP
VWOA
HA, HA!

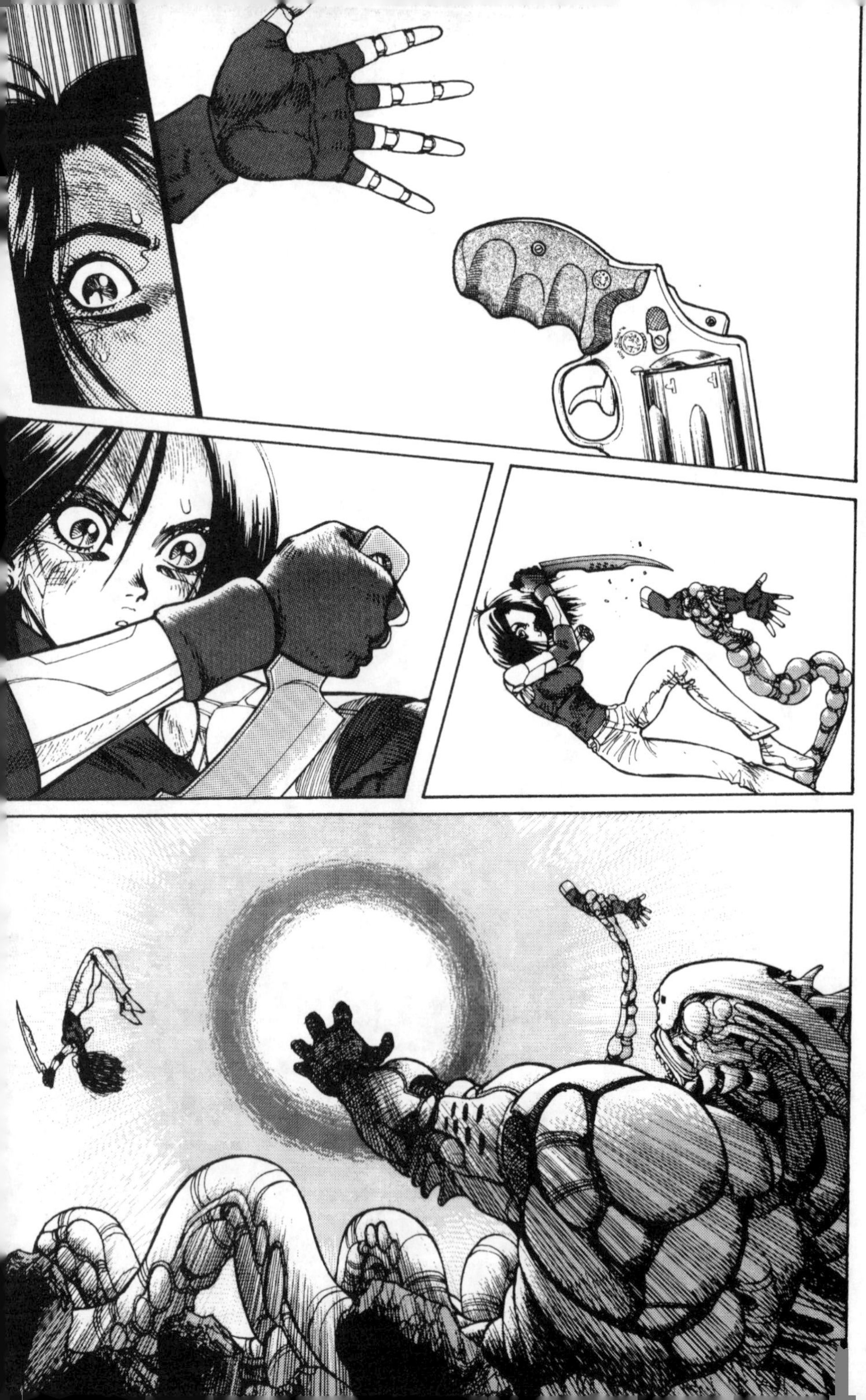

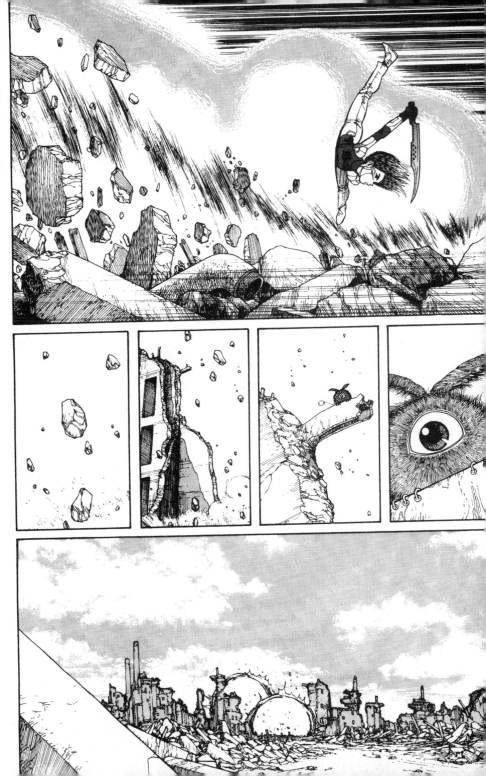

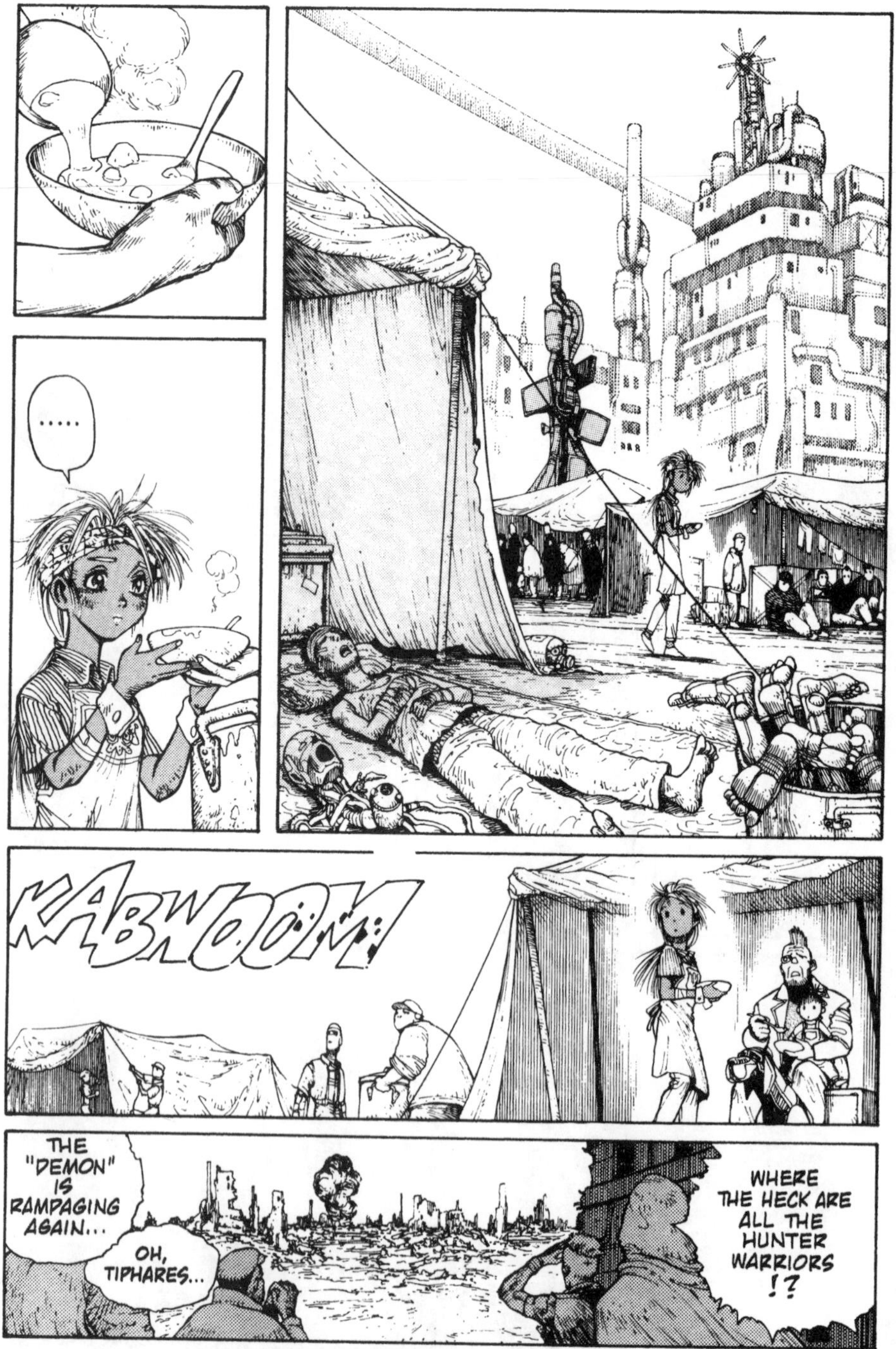
.....
KABWOOM
THE "DEMON" IS RAMPAGING AGAIN...
OH, TIPHARES...
WHERE THE HECK ARE ALL THE HUNTER WARRIORS !?

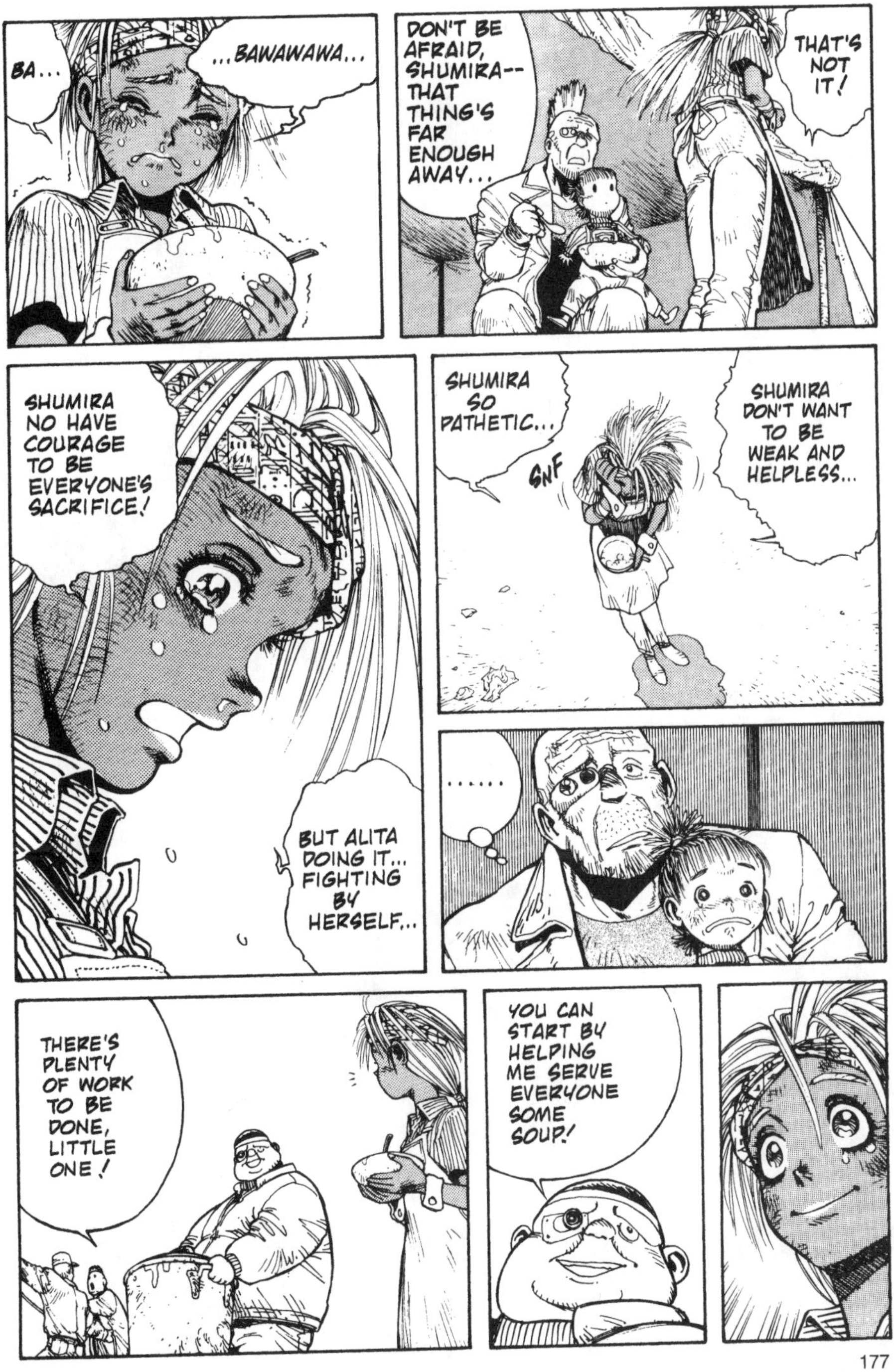
BA...
...BAWAWAWA...
DON'T BE AFRAID, SHUMIRA-- THAT THING'S FAR ENOUGH AWAY...
THAT'S NOT IT!
SHUMIRA NO HAVE COURAGE TO BE EVERYONE'S SACRIFICE!
BUT ALITA DOING IT... FIGHTING BY HERSELF...
SHUMIRA SO PATHETIC...
SNF
SHUMIRA DON'T WANT TO BE WEAK AND HELPLESS...
......
THERE'S PLENTY OF WORK TO BE DONE, LITTLE ONE!
YOU CAN START BY HELPING ME SERVE EVERYONE SOME SOUP!

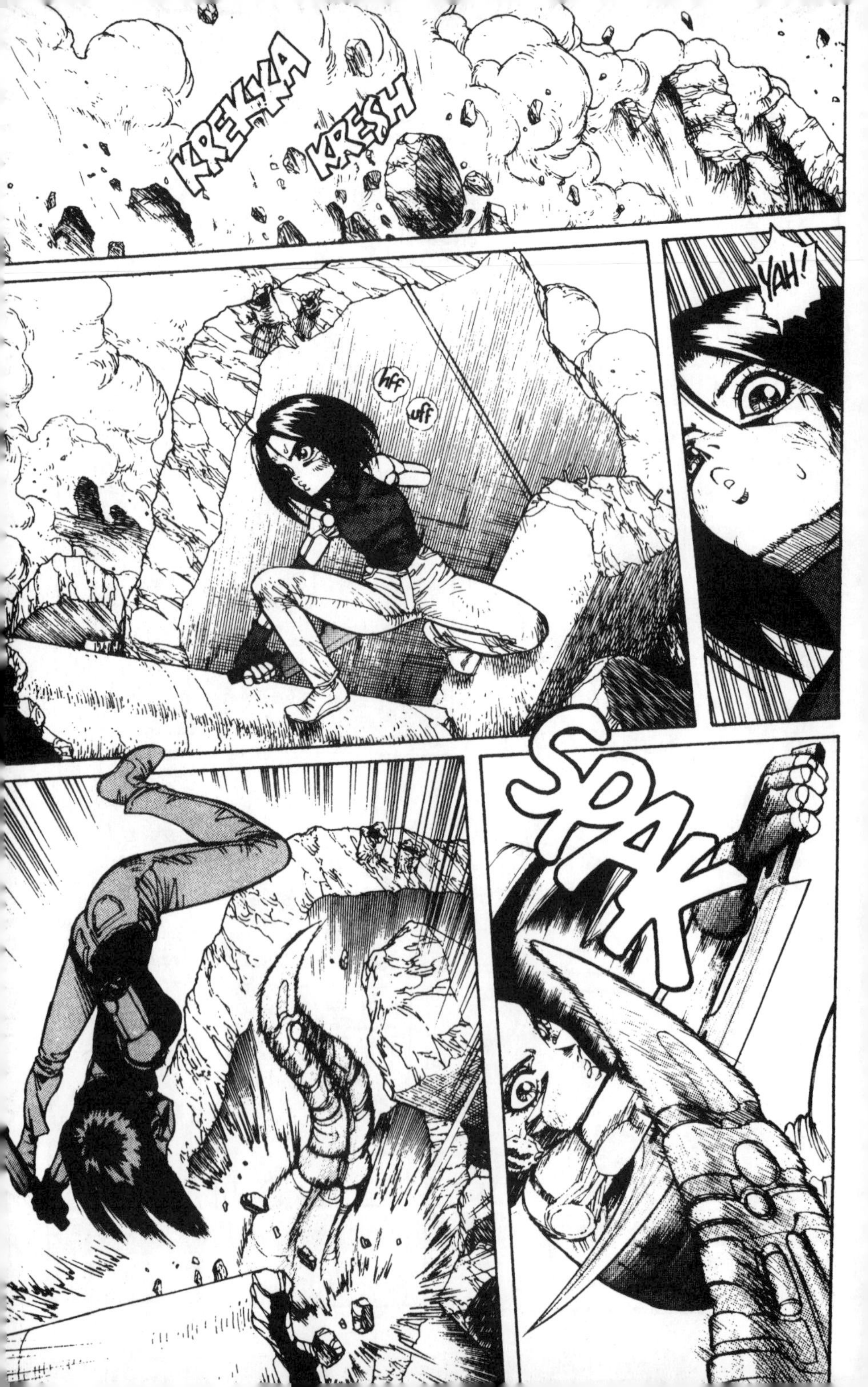
KREKKLA
KRESH
hff
uff
YAH!
SPAK

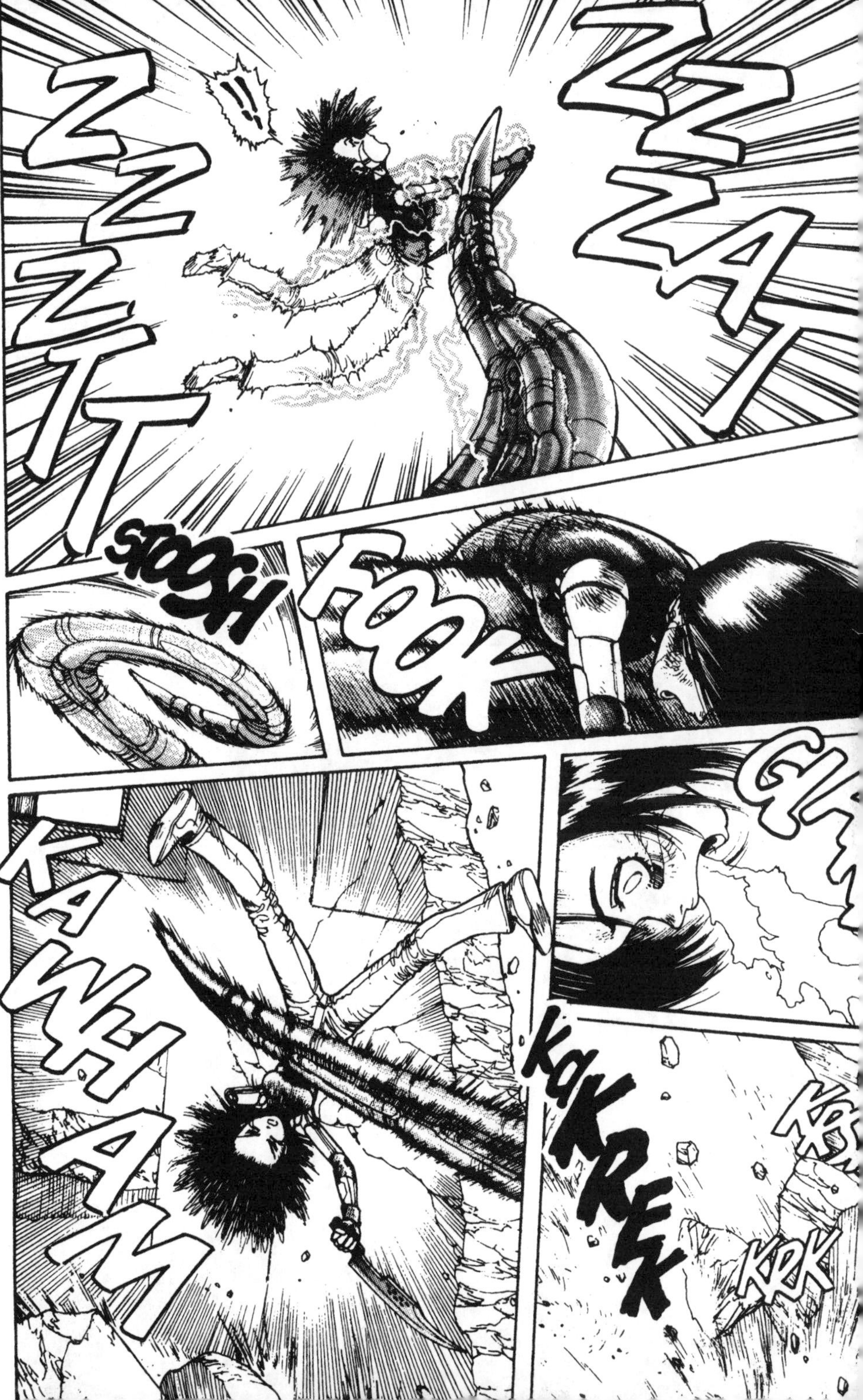
ZZZZT
!!
ZZZAT
STOOSH
FOOK
KAWHAM
KaKREEK
KDK

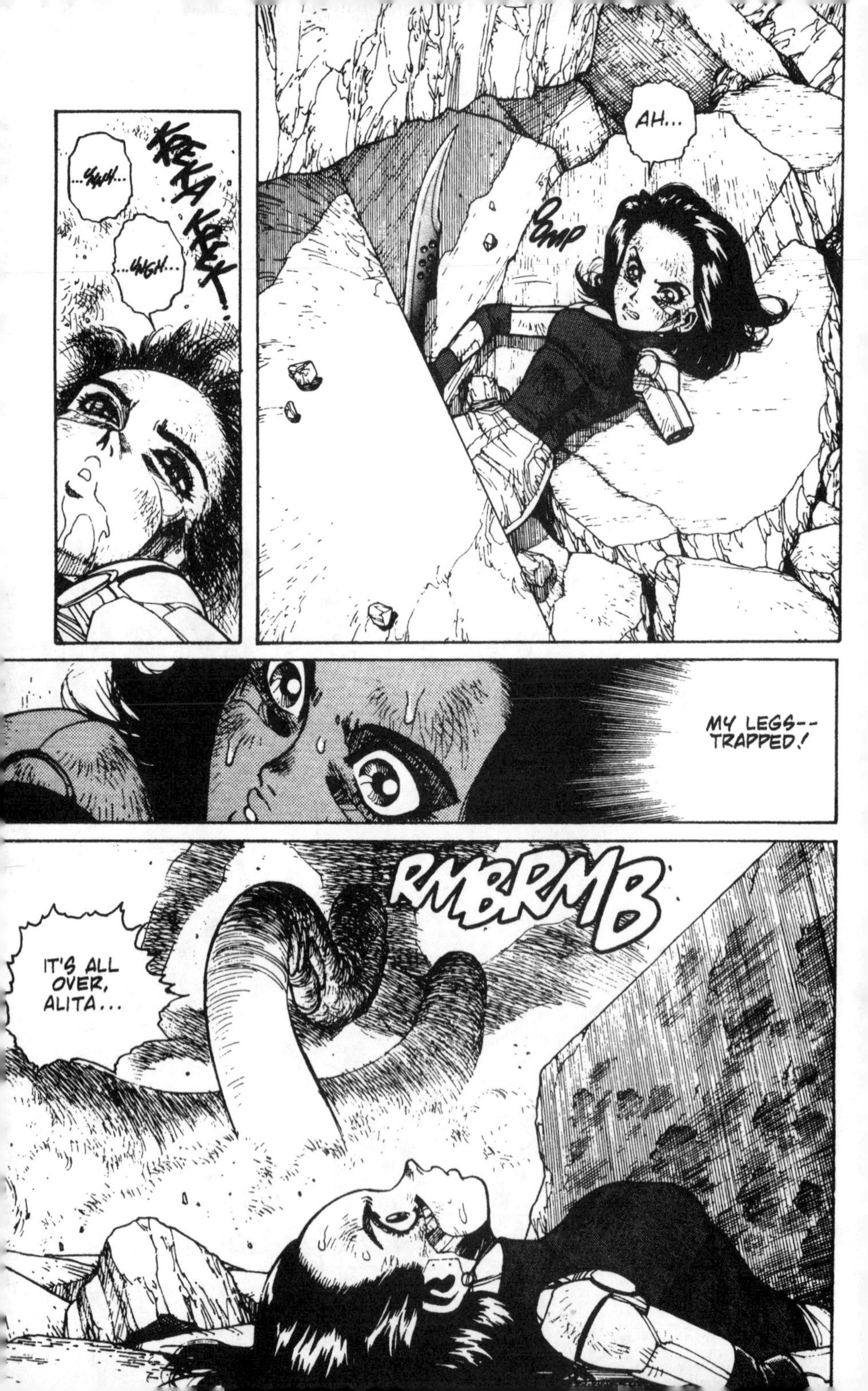
...UNGH...
AH...
THMP
MY LEGS--
TRAPPED!
RMBRMB
IT'S ALL OVER, ALITA...

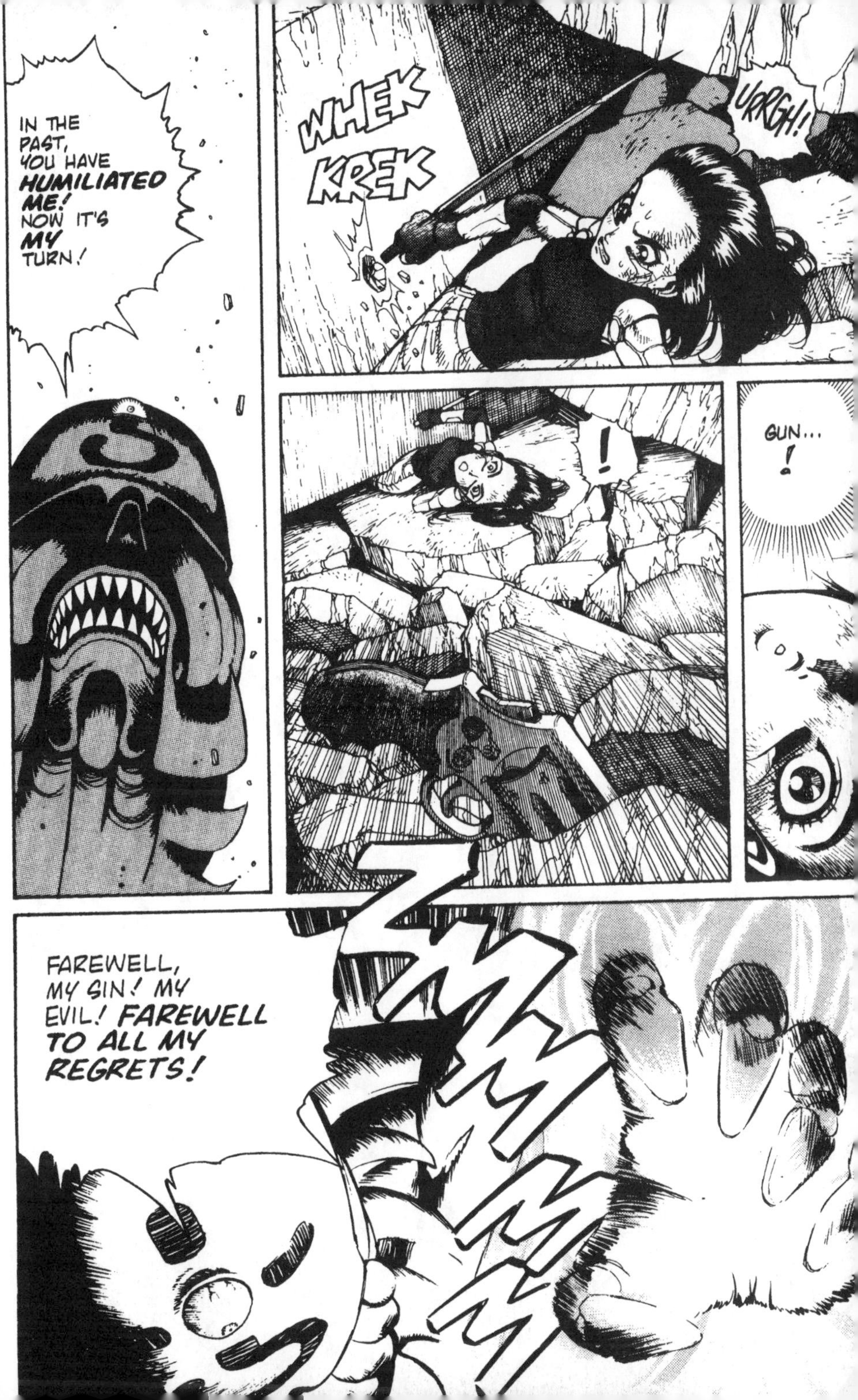
IN THE PAST, YOU HAVE HUMILIATED ME! NOW IT'S MY TURN!
WHEK
KREK
URRGH!
!
GUN... !
FAREWELL, MY SIN! MY EVIL! FAREWELL TO ALL MY REGRETS!

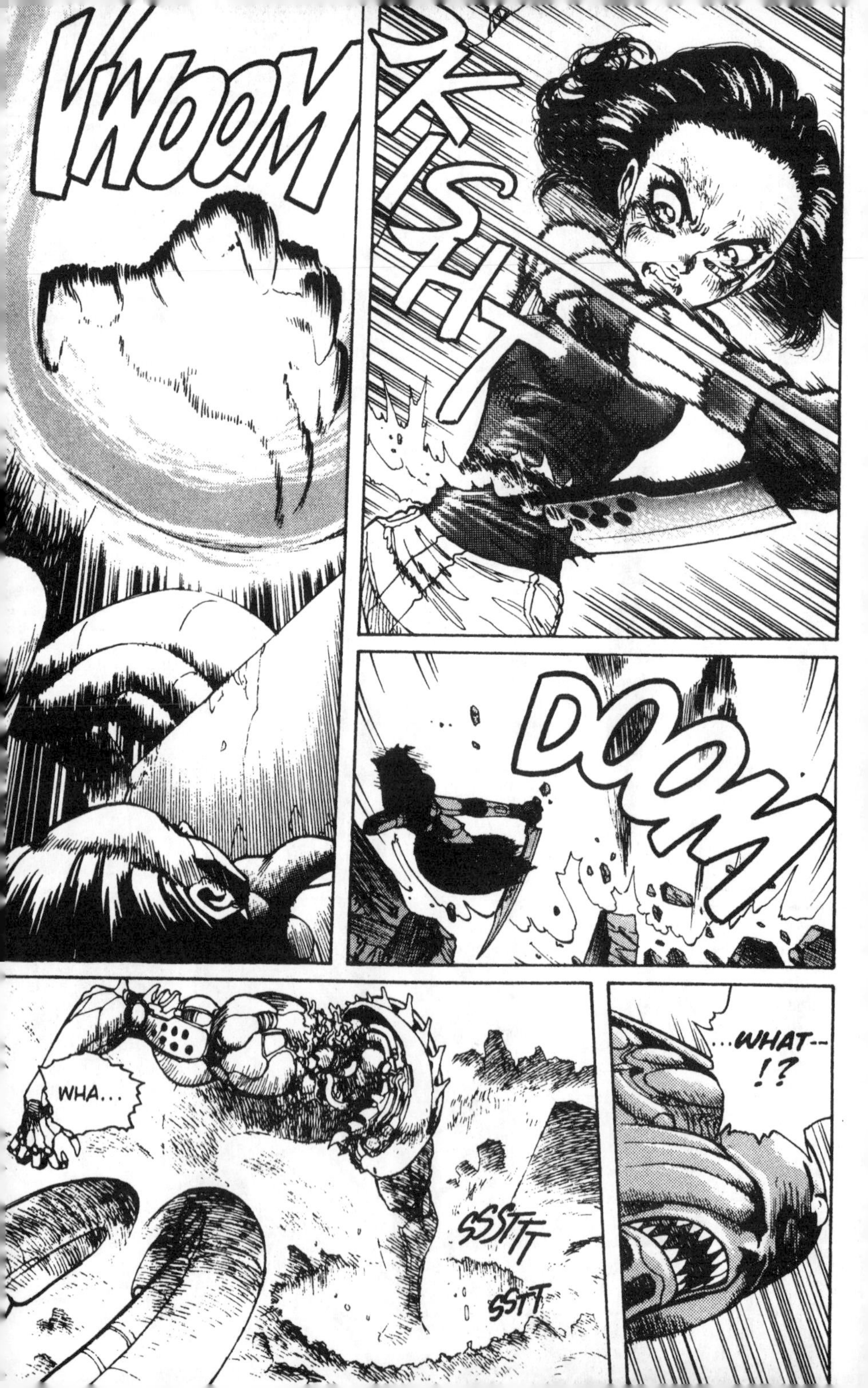
VWOOM
KRISHT
DOOM
WHA...
SSSTTT
SSTT
...WHAT--
!?

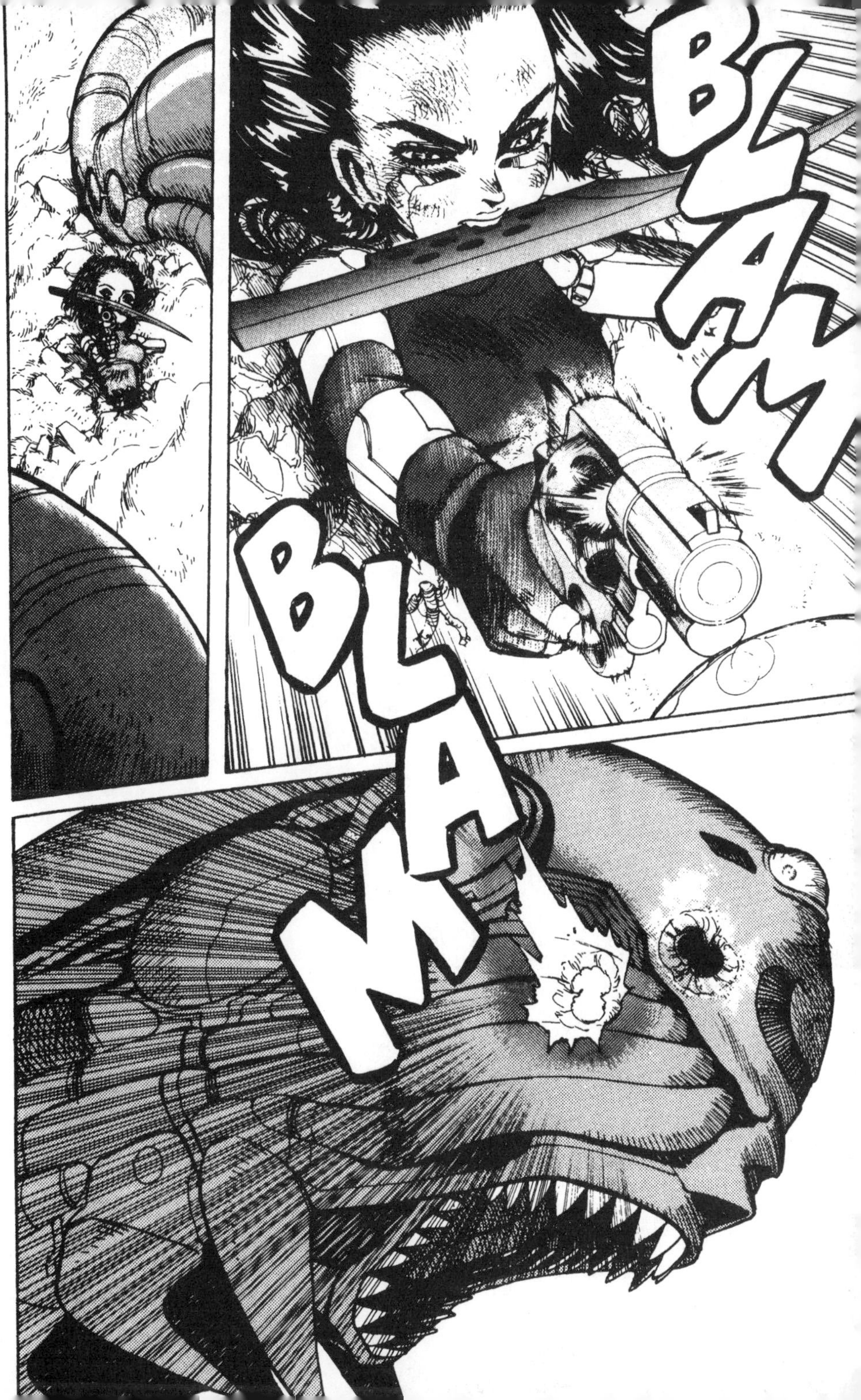
BLAM
BLAM

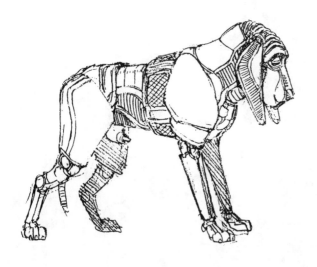

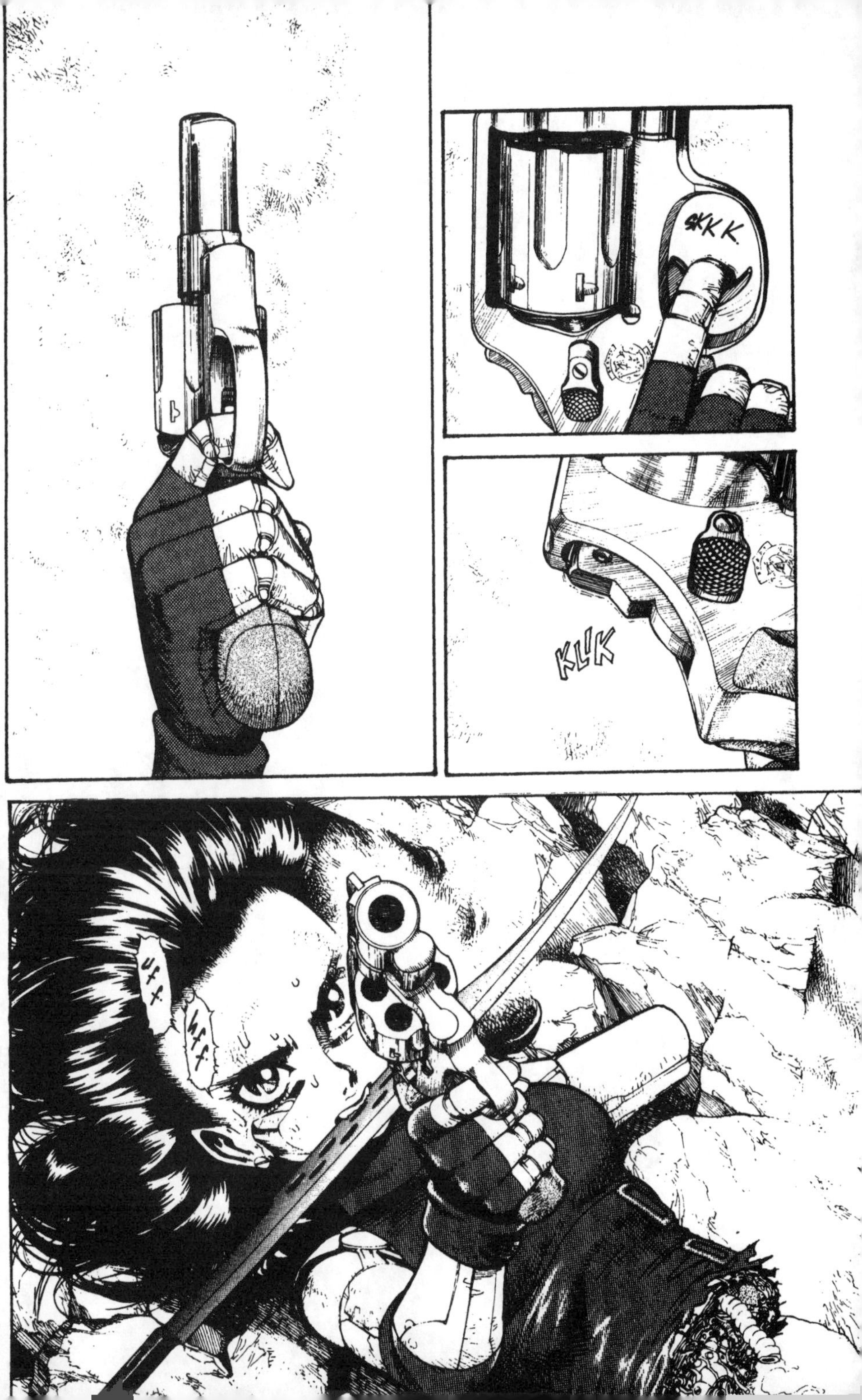
SKK K.
KLIK
UFF.
HFF.

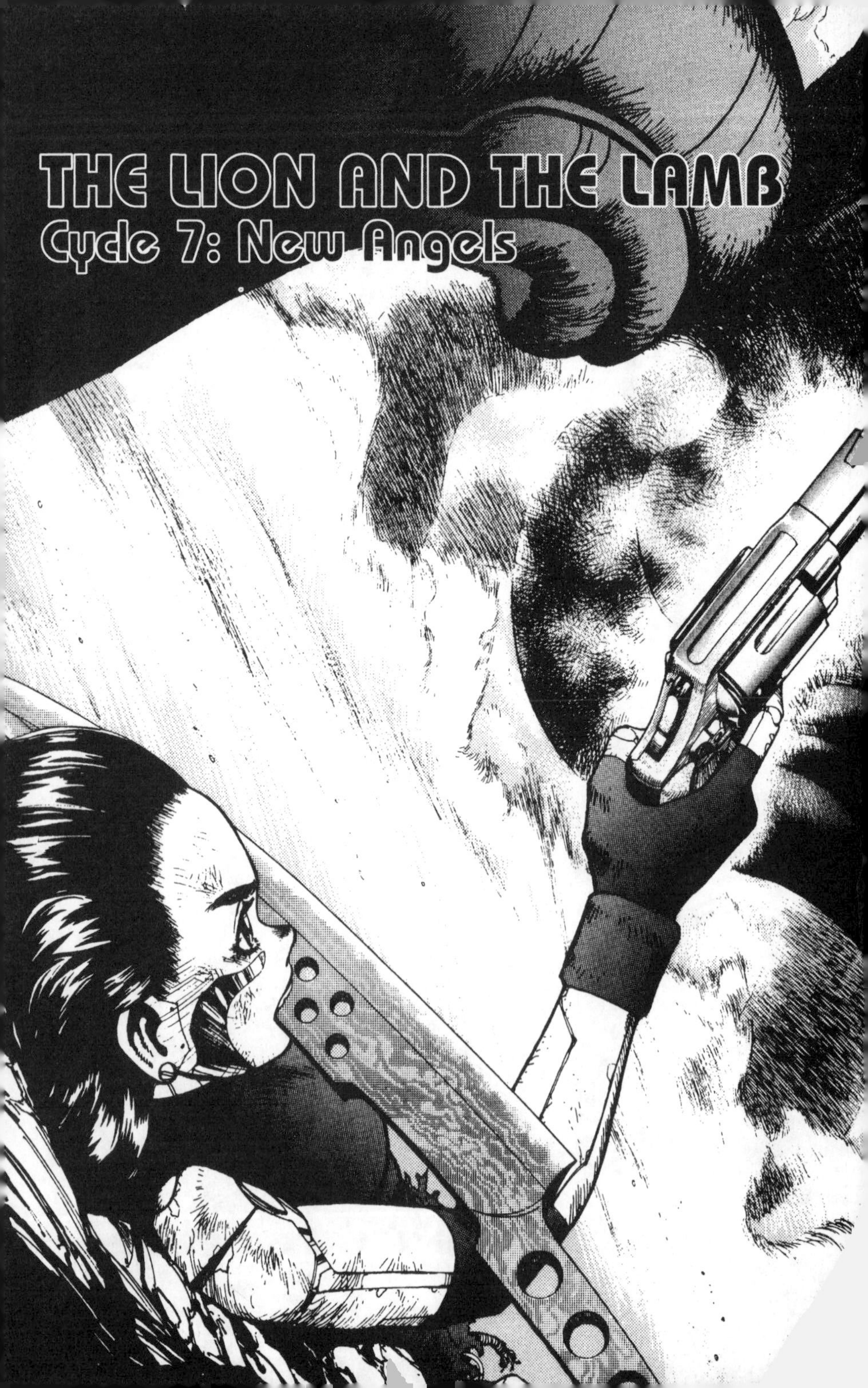
THE LION AND THE LAMB
Cycle 7: New Angels

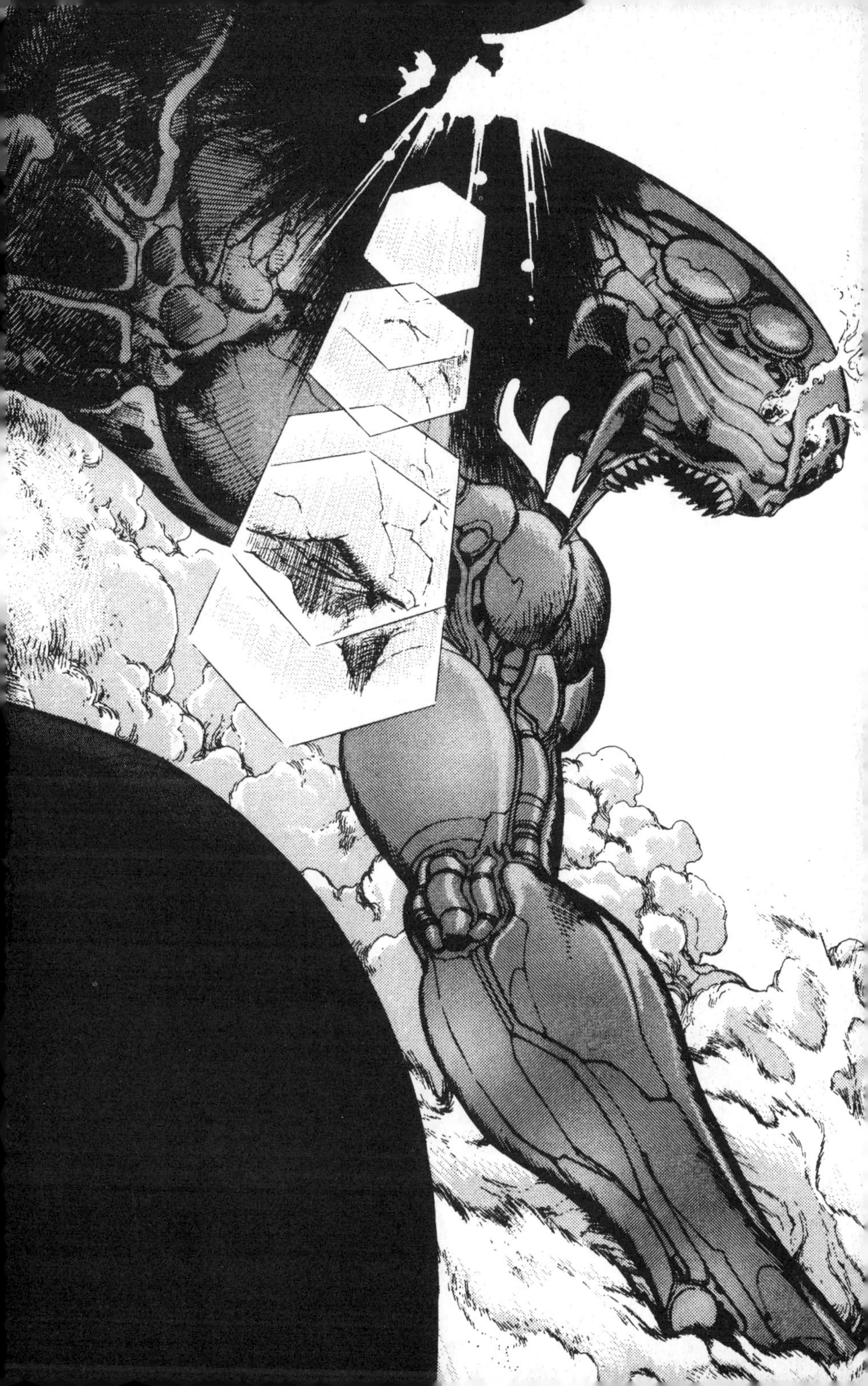

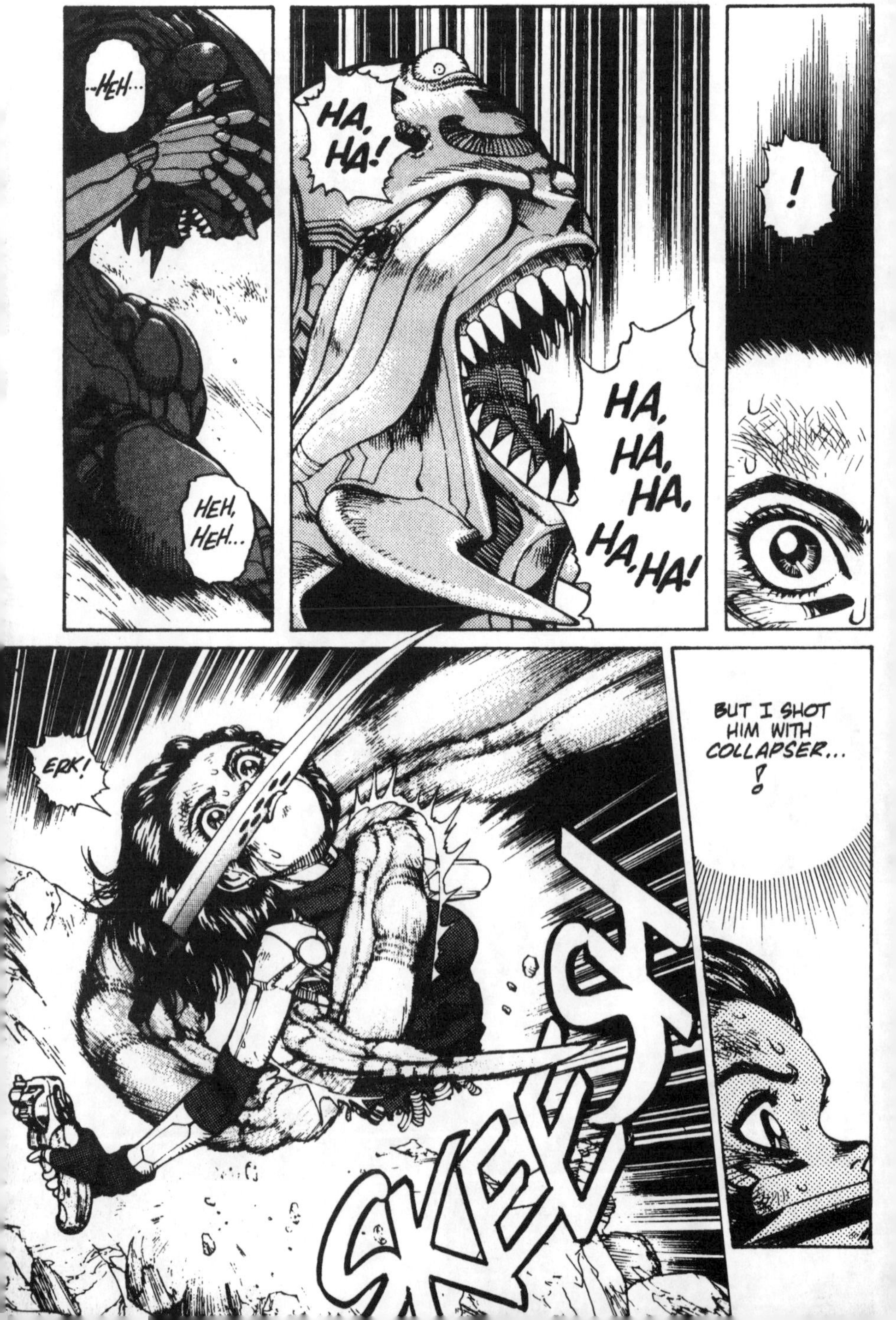
...HEH...
HEH, HEH...
HA, HA!
HA, HA, HA, HA, HA!
!
ERK!
BUT I SHOT HIM WITH COLLAPSER...!
SKEEST

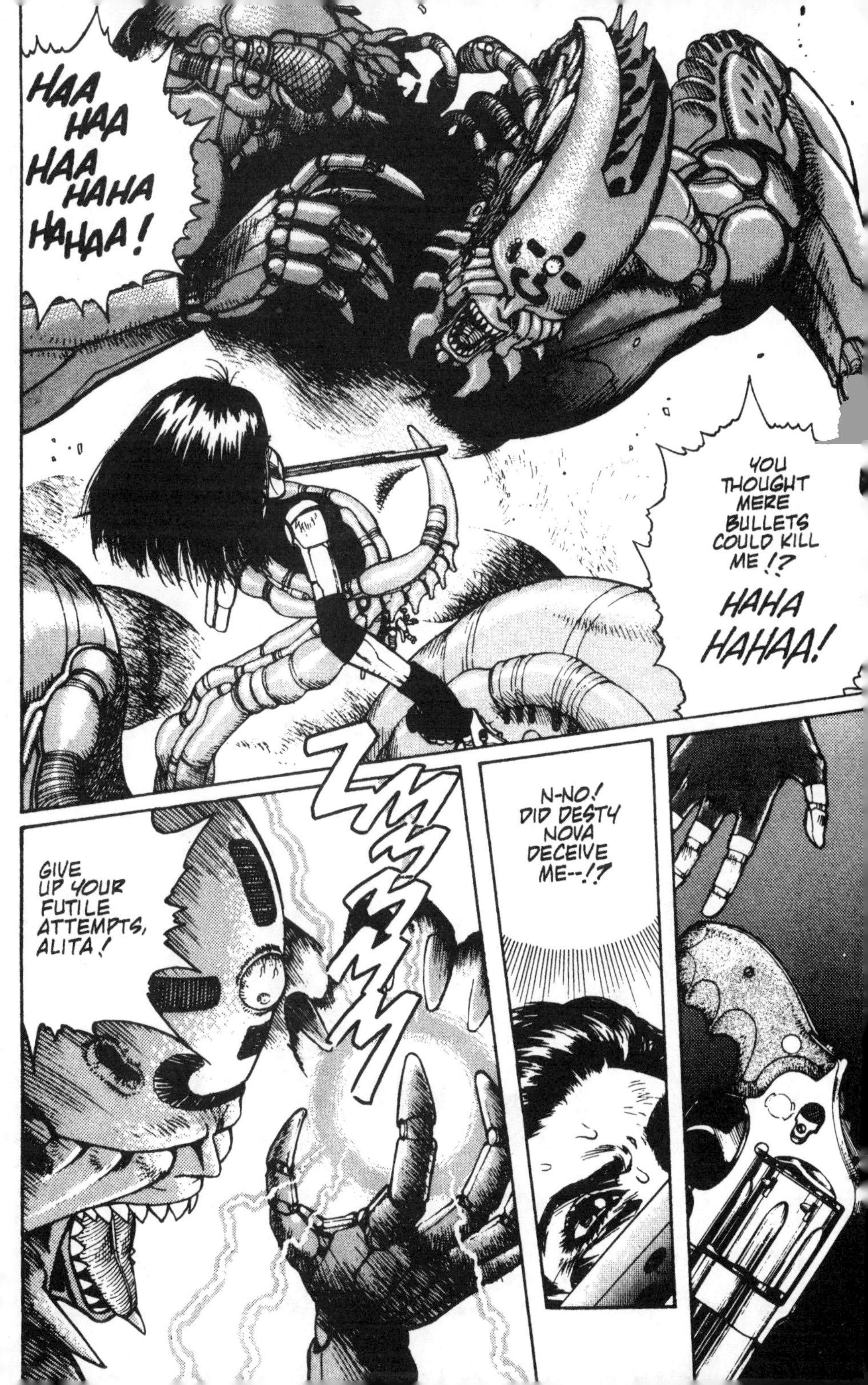
HAA HAA HAA HAHA HAHAA!
YOU THOUGHT MERE BULLETS COULD KILL ME!? HAHA HAHAA!
ZMMMMMM
GIVE UP YOUR FUTILE ATTEMPTS, ALITA!
N-NO! DID DESTY NOVA DECEIVE ME--!?

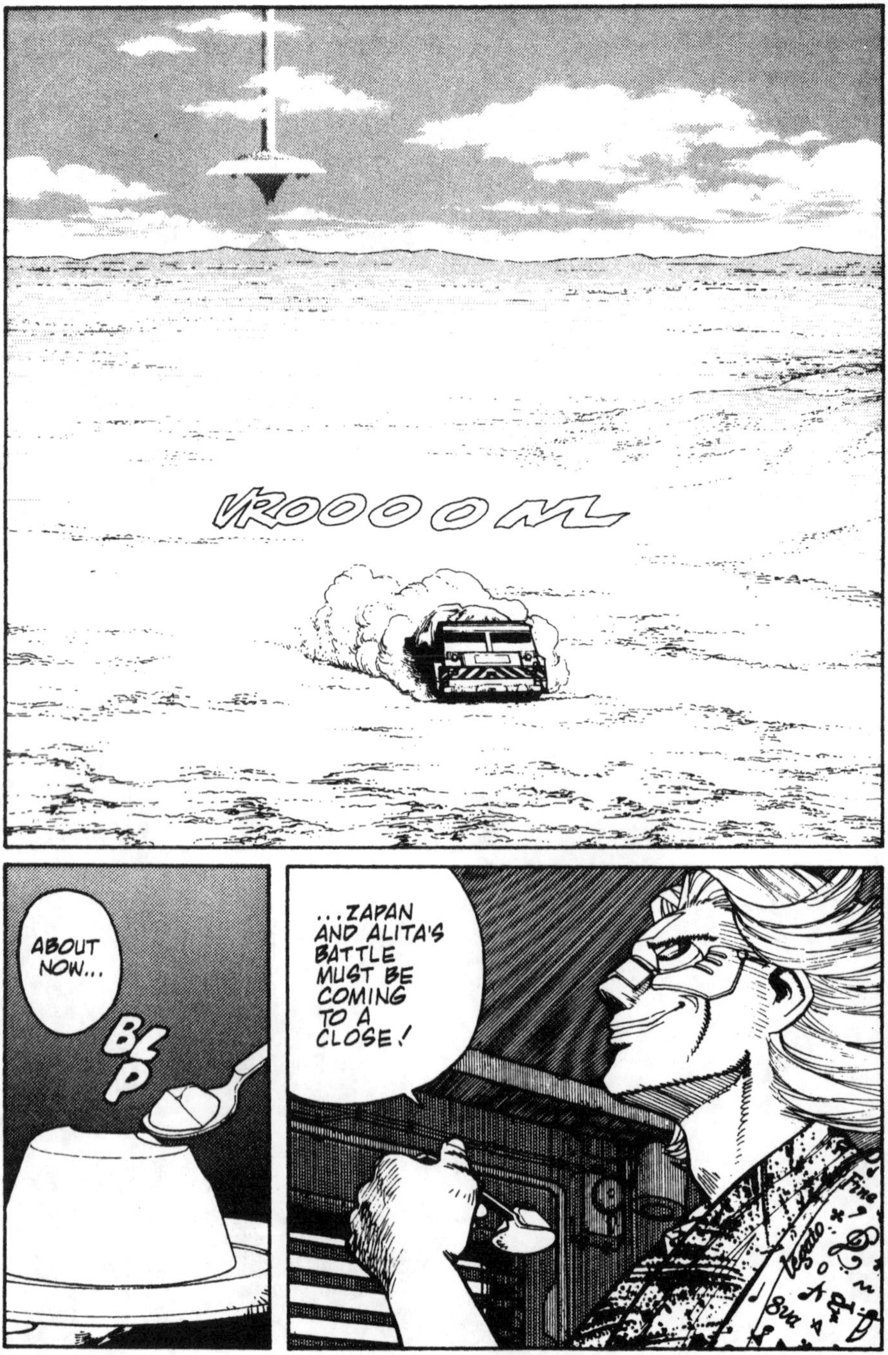
VROOOOM
ABOUT NOW...
BLP
...ZAPAN AND ALITA'S BATTLE MUST BE COMING TO A CLOSE!

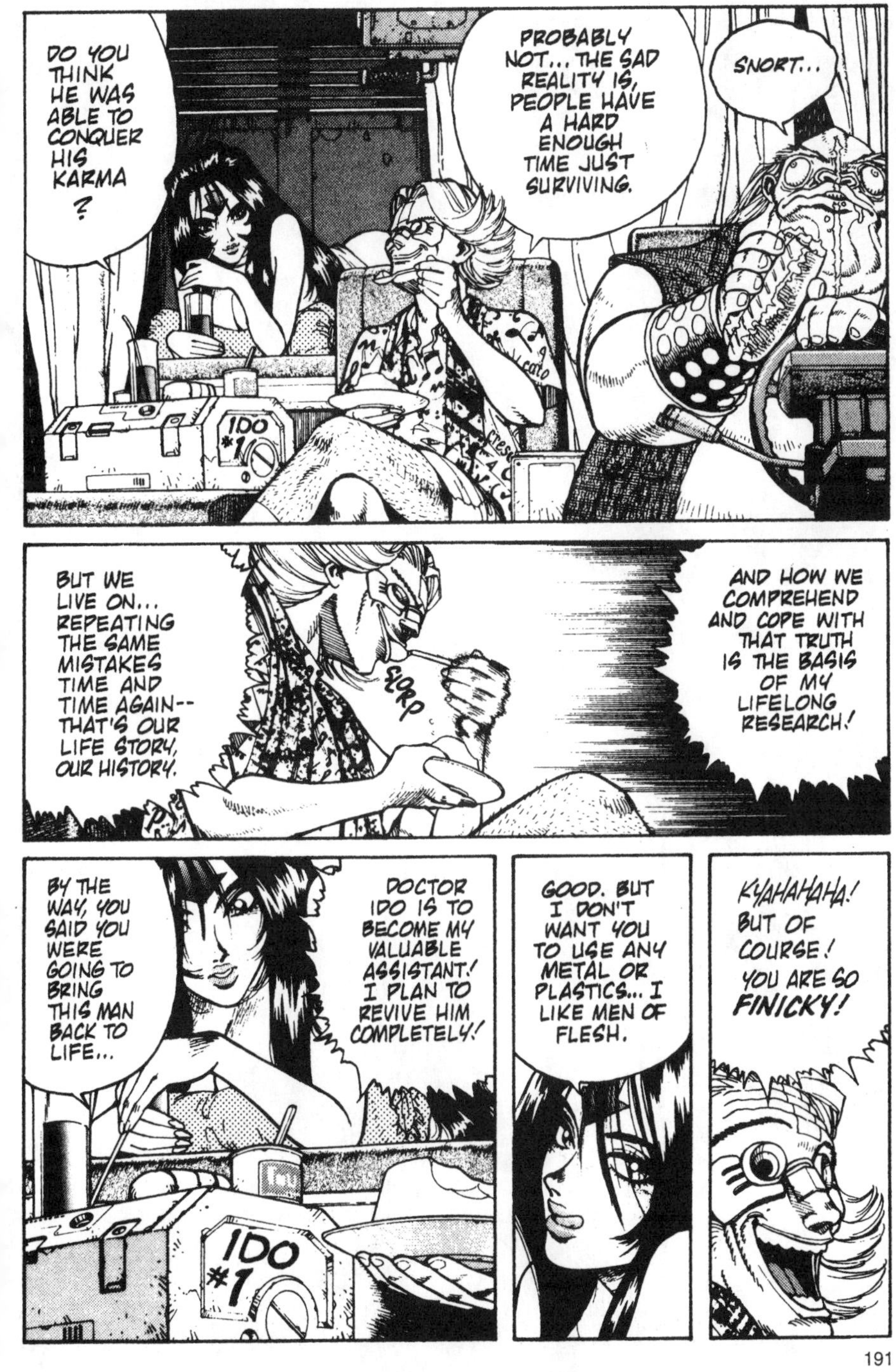
DO YOU THINK HE WAS ABLE TO CONQUER HIS KARMA ?
PROBABLY NOT... THE SAD REALITY IS, PEOPLE HAVE A HARD ENOUGH TIME JUST SURVIVING.
SNORT...
IDO #1
BUT WE LIVE ON... REPEATING THE SAME MISTAKES TIME AND TIME AGAIN-- THAT'S OUR LIFE STORY, OUR HISTORY.
SLORP
AND HOW WE COMPREHEND AND COPE WITH THAT TRUTH IS THE BASIS OF MY LIFELONG RESEARCH!
BY THE WAY, YOU SAID YOU WERE GOING TO BRING THIS MAN BACK TO LIFE...
DOCTOR IDO IS TO BECOME MY VALUABLE ASSISTANT! I PLAN TO REVIVE HIM COMPLETELY!
IDO #1
GOOD. BUT I DON'T WANT YOU TO USE ANY METAL OR PLASTICS... I LIKE MEN OF FLESH.
KYAHAHAHA! BUT OF COURSE! YOU ARE SO FINICKY!

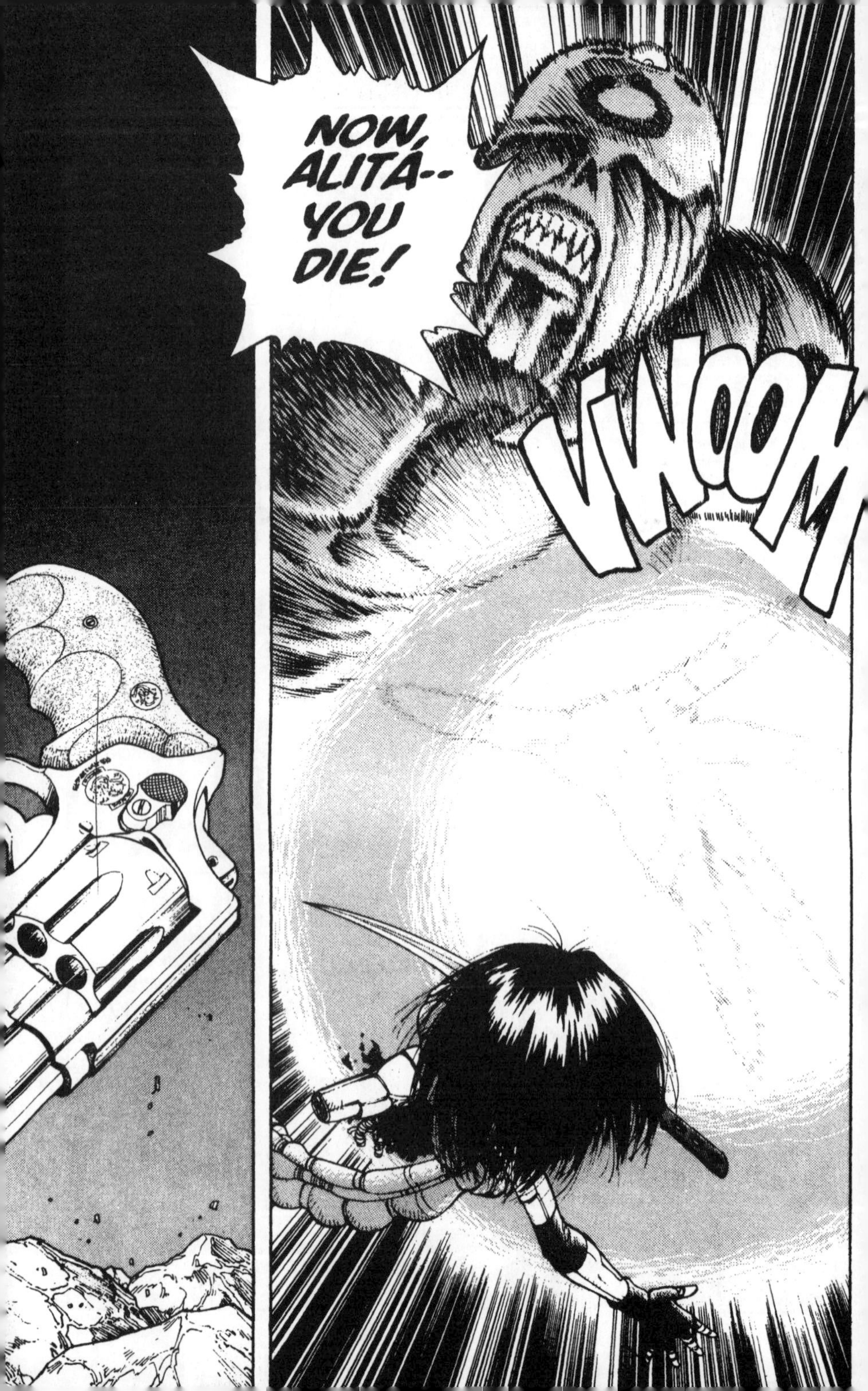
NOW, ALITA-- YOU DIE!
VWOOM

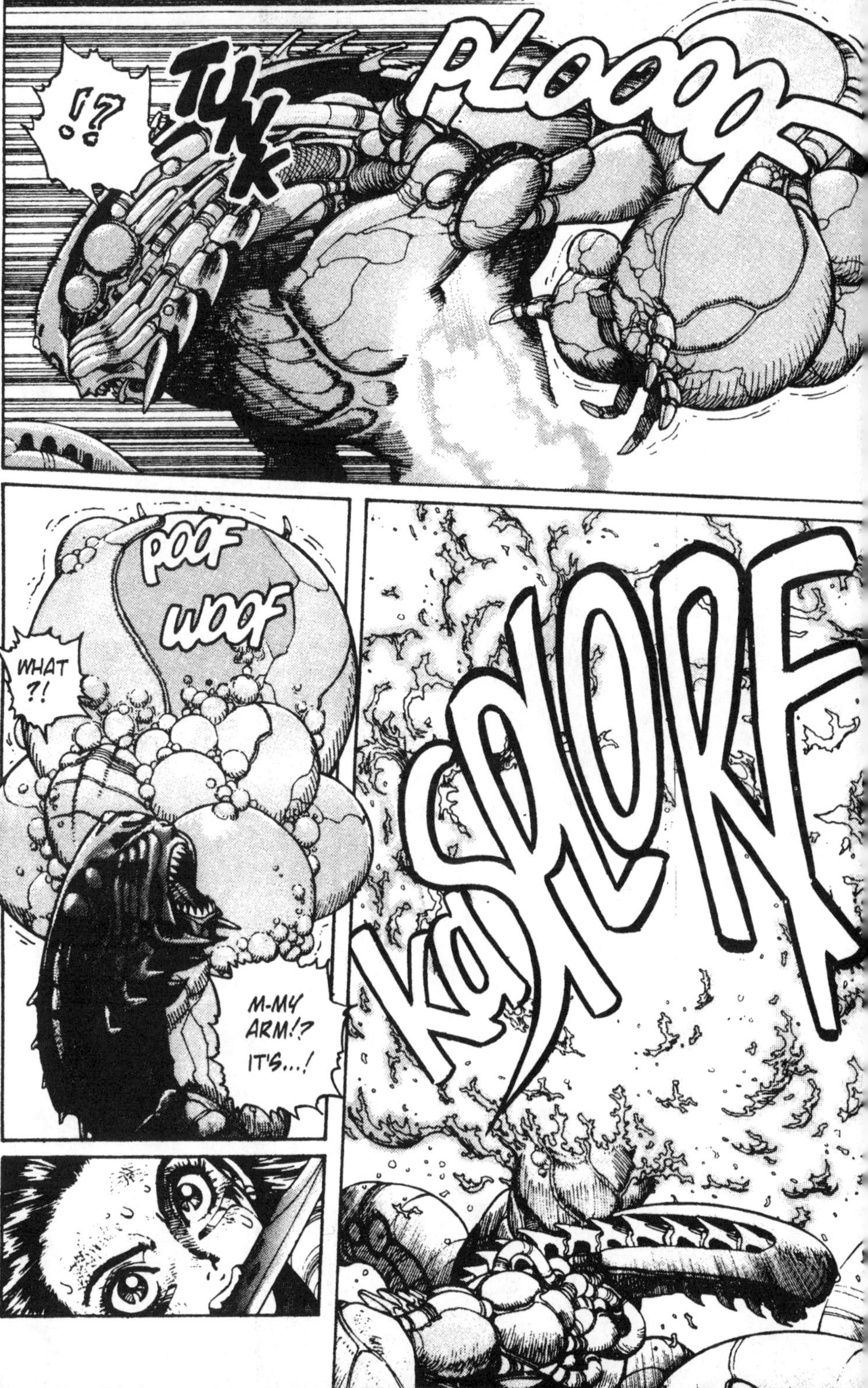
!?
TUNK
PLOOOO
POOF
WOOF
WHAT ?!
M-MY ARM!? IT'S...!
KASPLOOFF

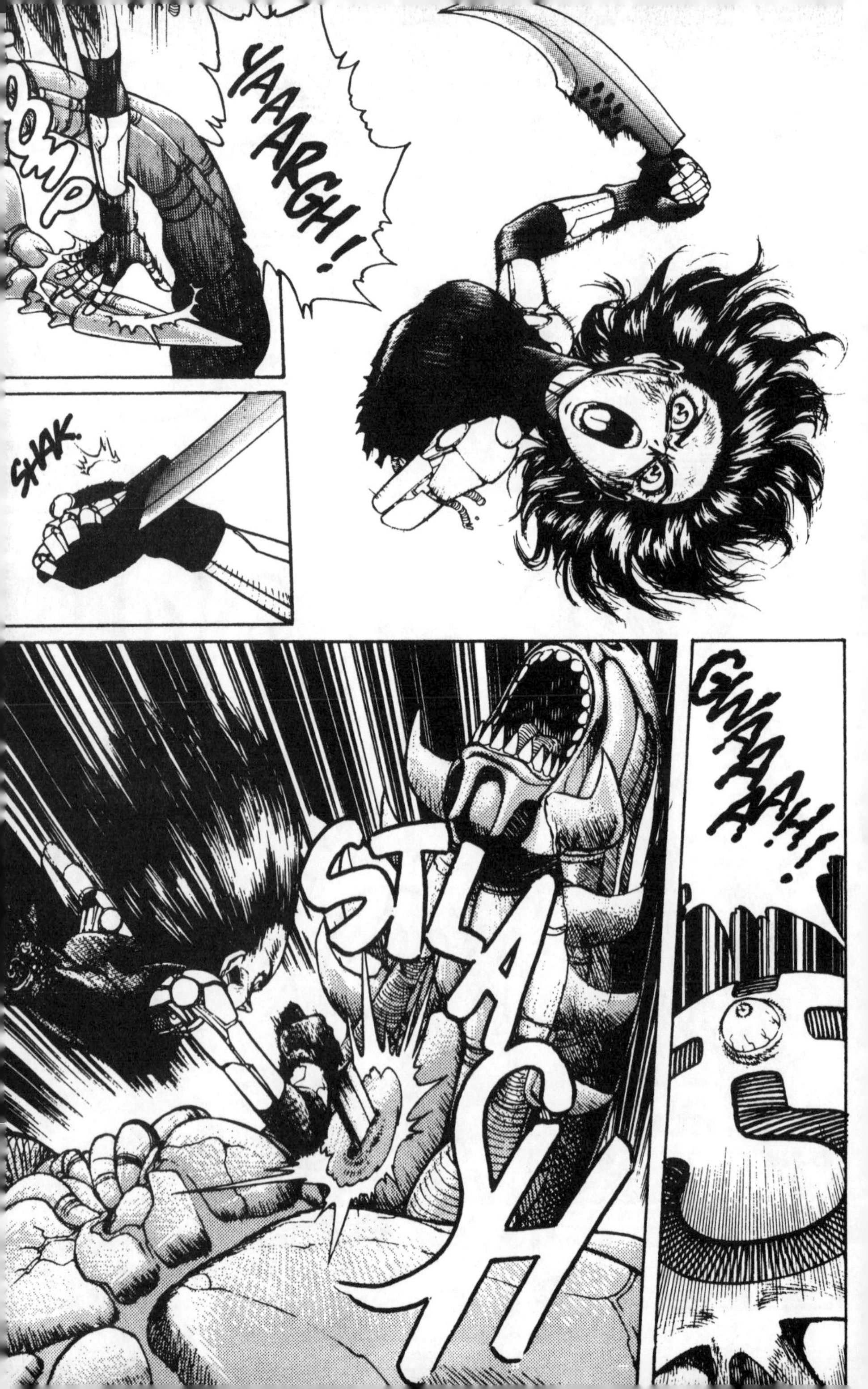

YAAARGH!!
THOMP
SHAK
GWAAAAH!!
SLASH

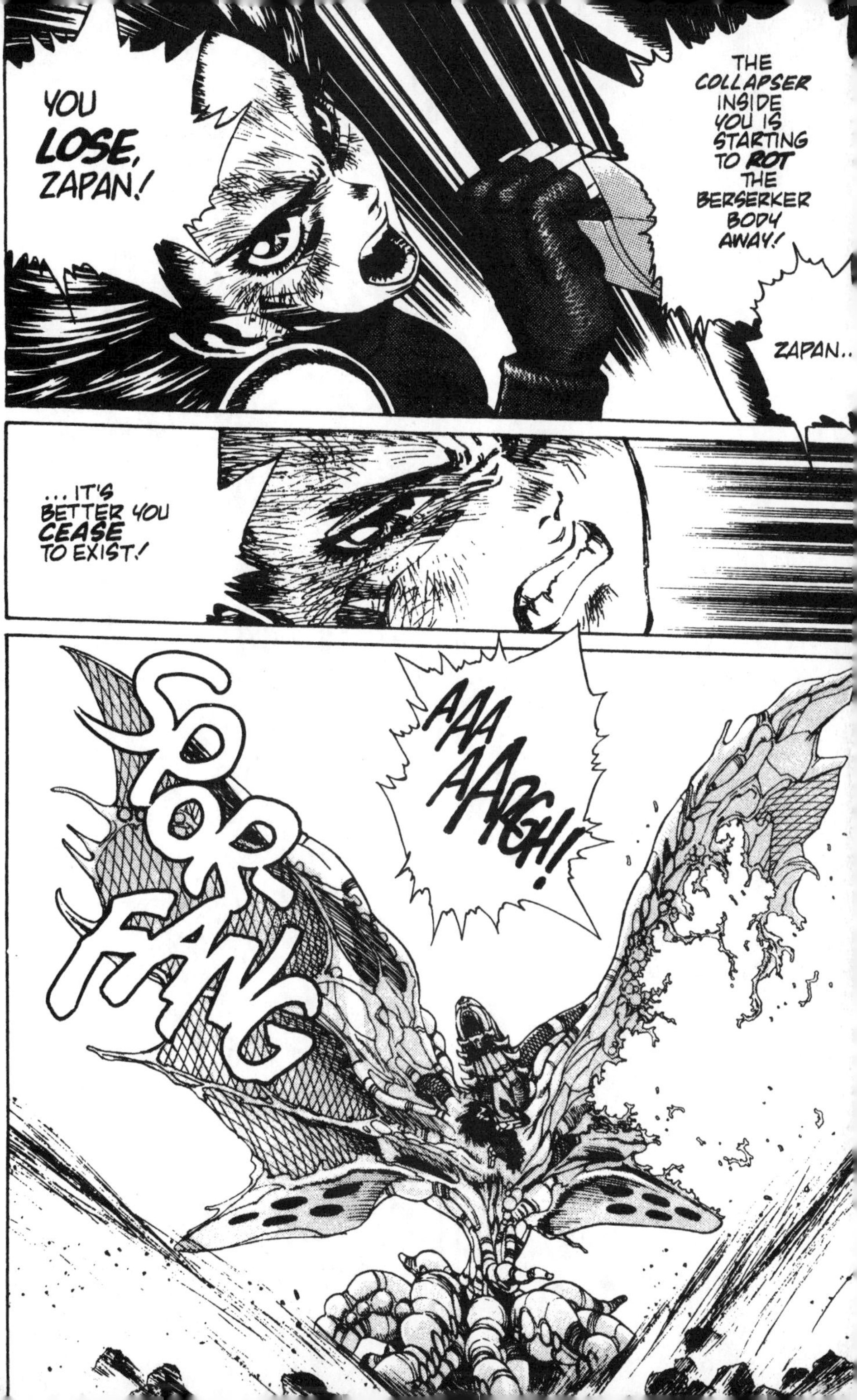
YOU LOSE, ZAPAN!
THE COLLAPSER INSIDE YOU IS STARTING TO ROT THE BERSERKER BODY AWAY!
ZAPAN..
...IT'S BETTER YOU CEASE TO EXIST!
SPOR FANG
AAAAAARGH!!

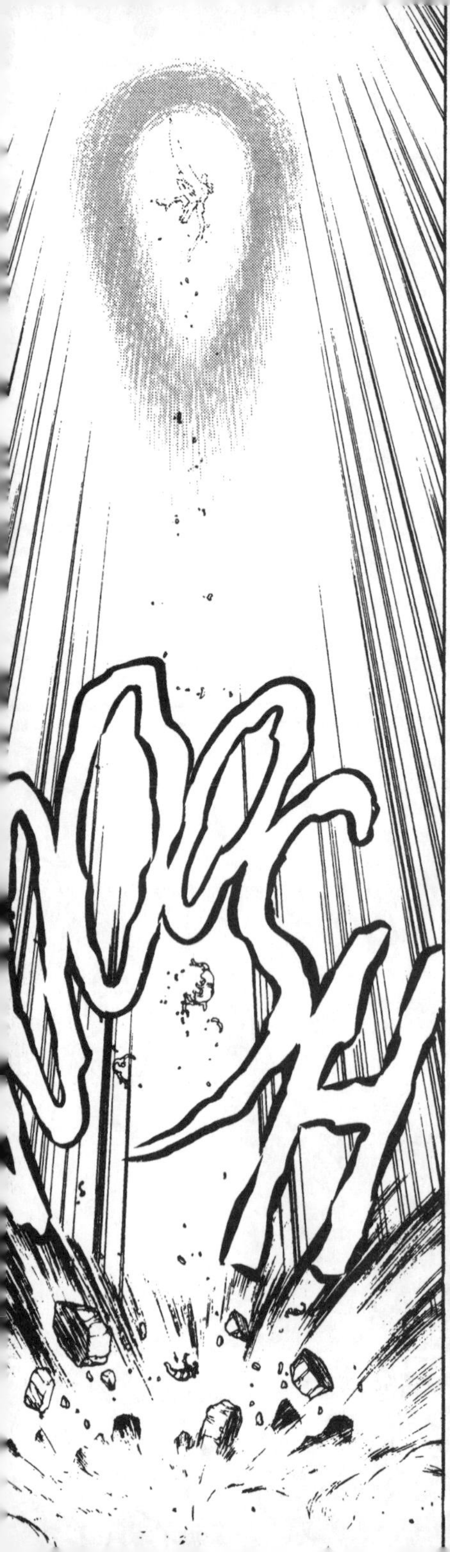

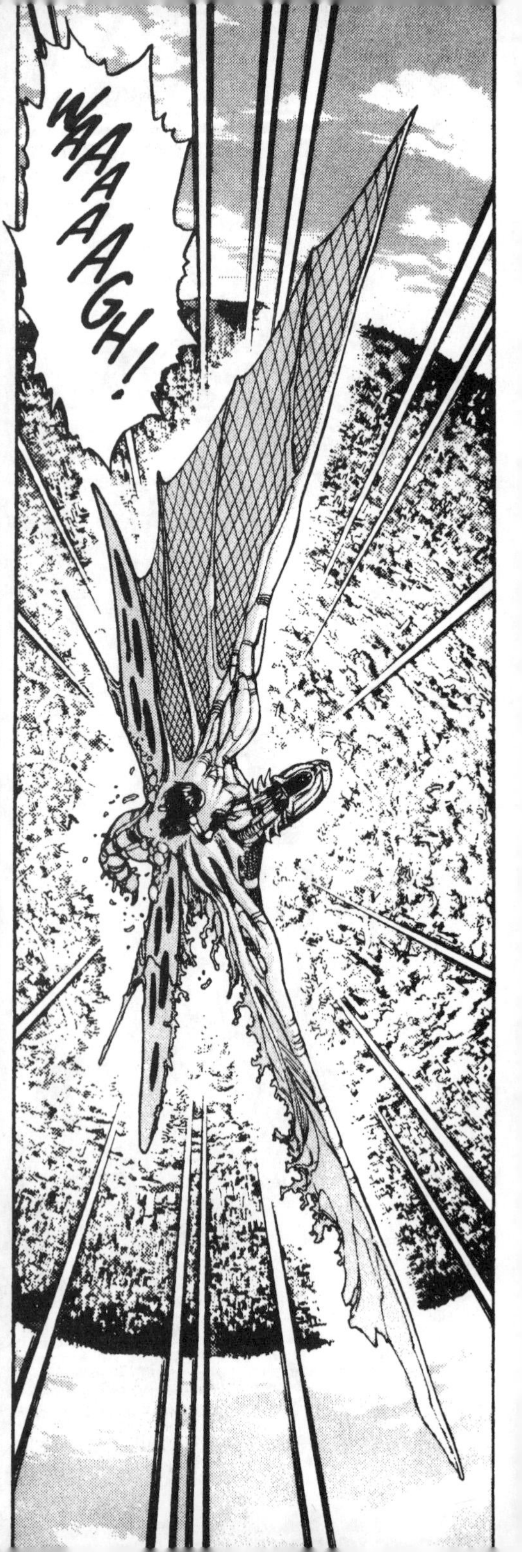
WAAAAAAGH!

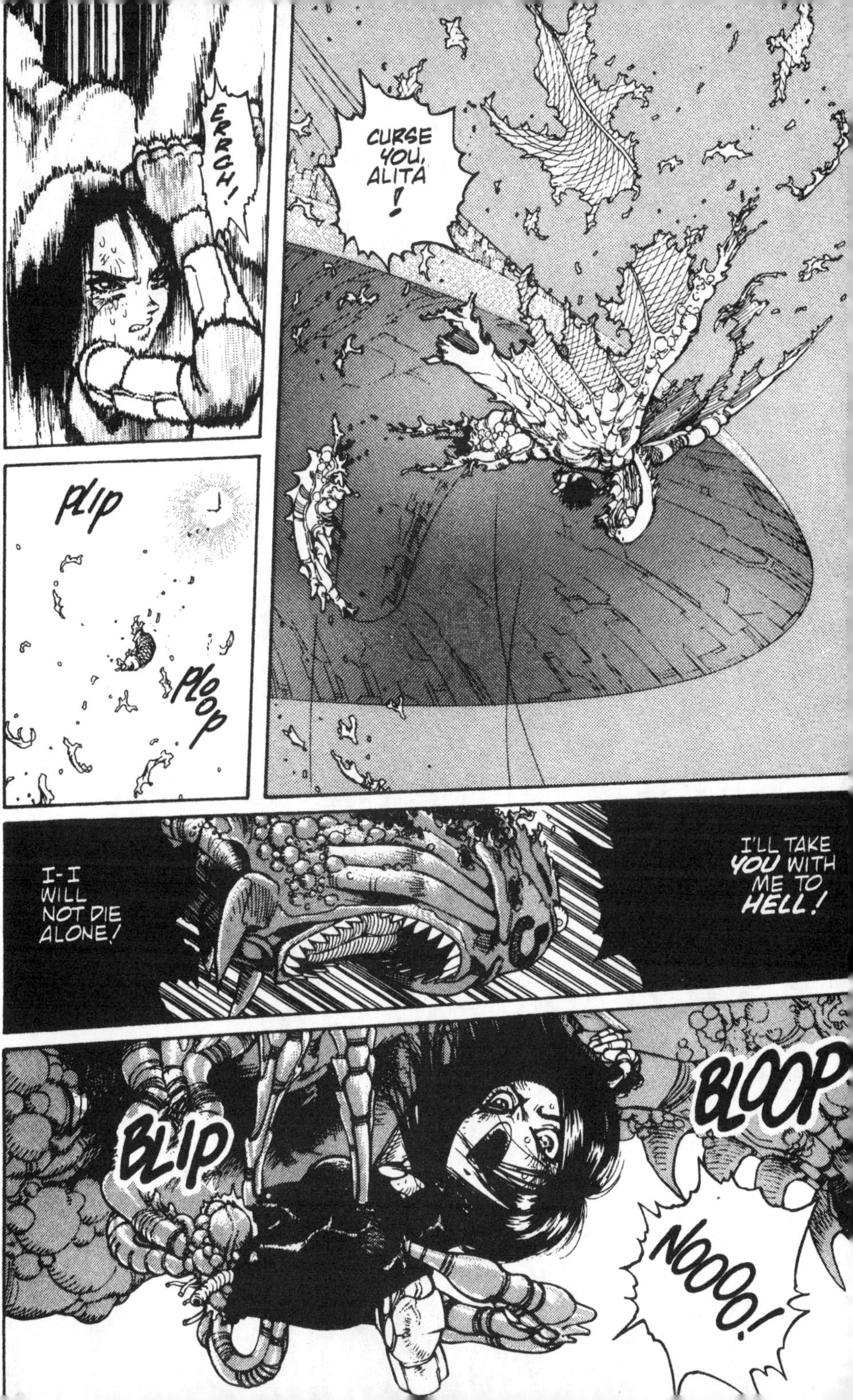
ERRCH!
CURSE YOU, ALITA!
plip
ploop
I-I WILL NOT DIE ALONE!
I'LL TAKE YOU WITH ME TO HELL!
BLIP
BLOOP
NOOOO!

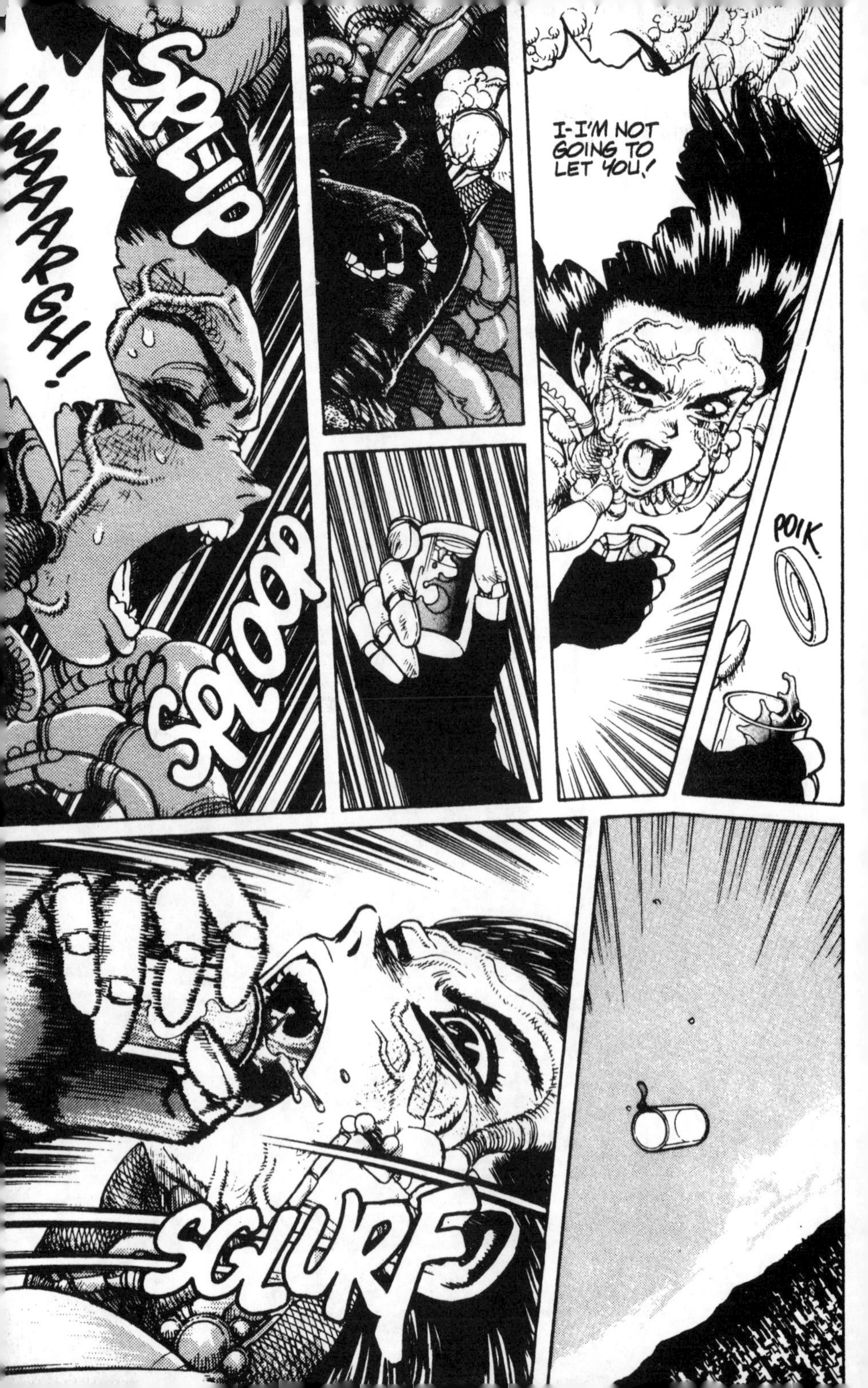

UWAAARGH!
SPLIP
SPLOOP
I-I'M NOT GOING TO LET YOU!
POIK.
SGLURP

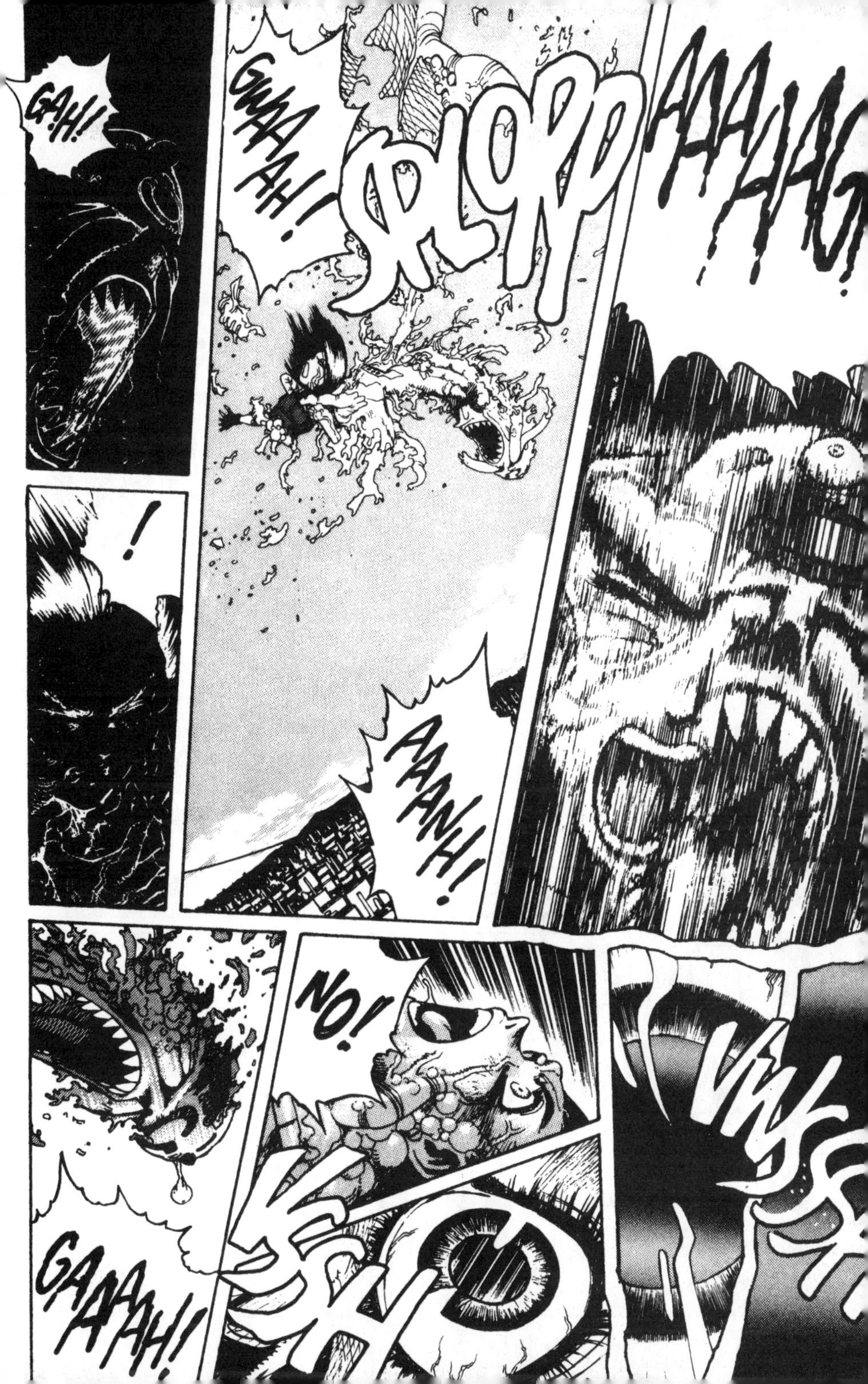
GAH!
!
GWAAAH!
SPLOOP
AAAANH!
AAAAG
GAAAAH!
NO!

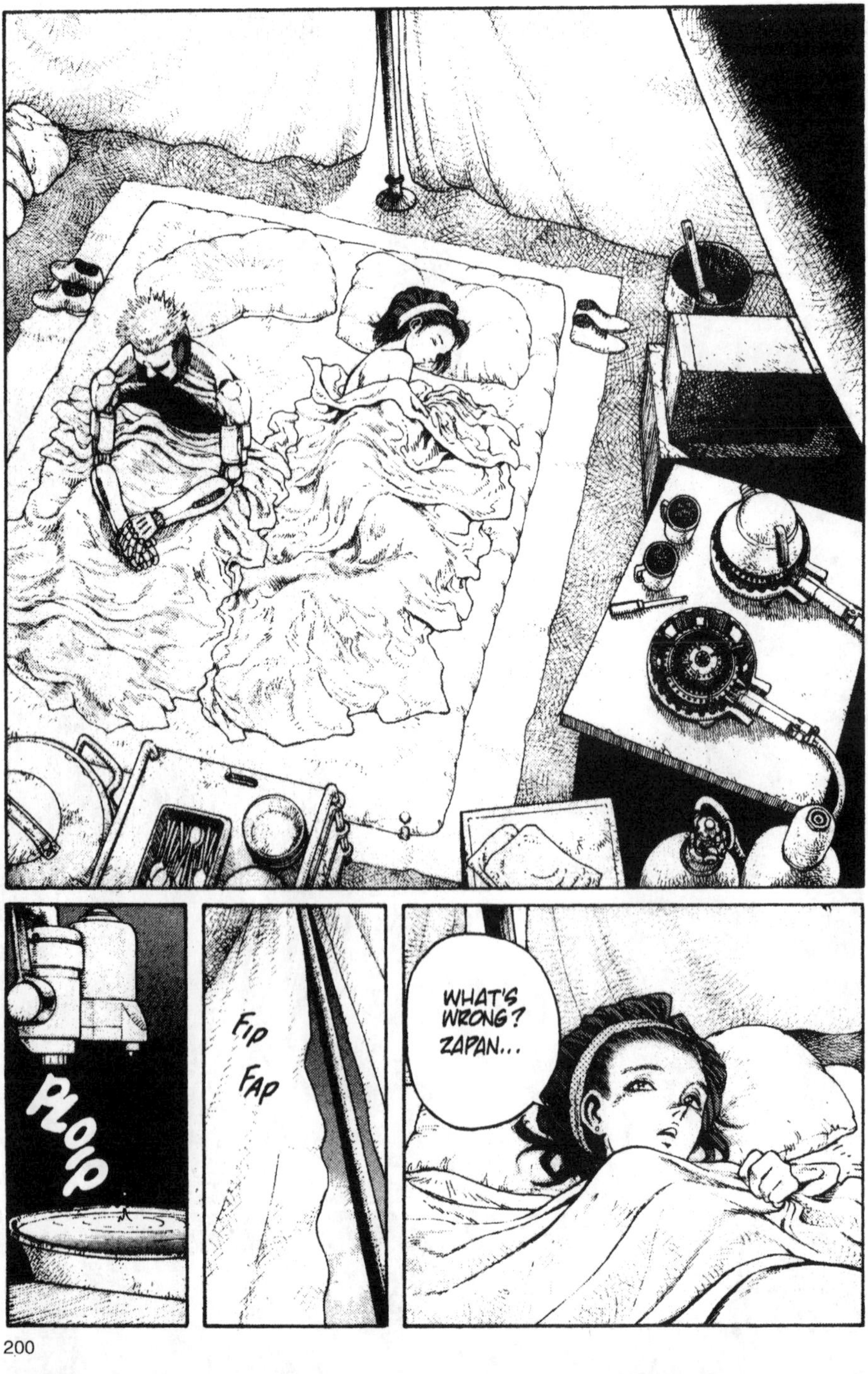
PLOIP
FIP
FAP
WHAT'S WRONG? ZAPAN...

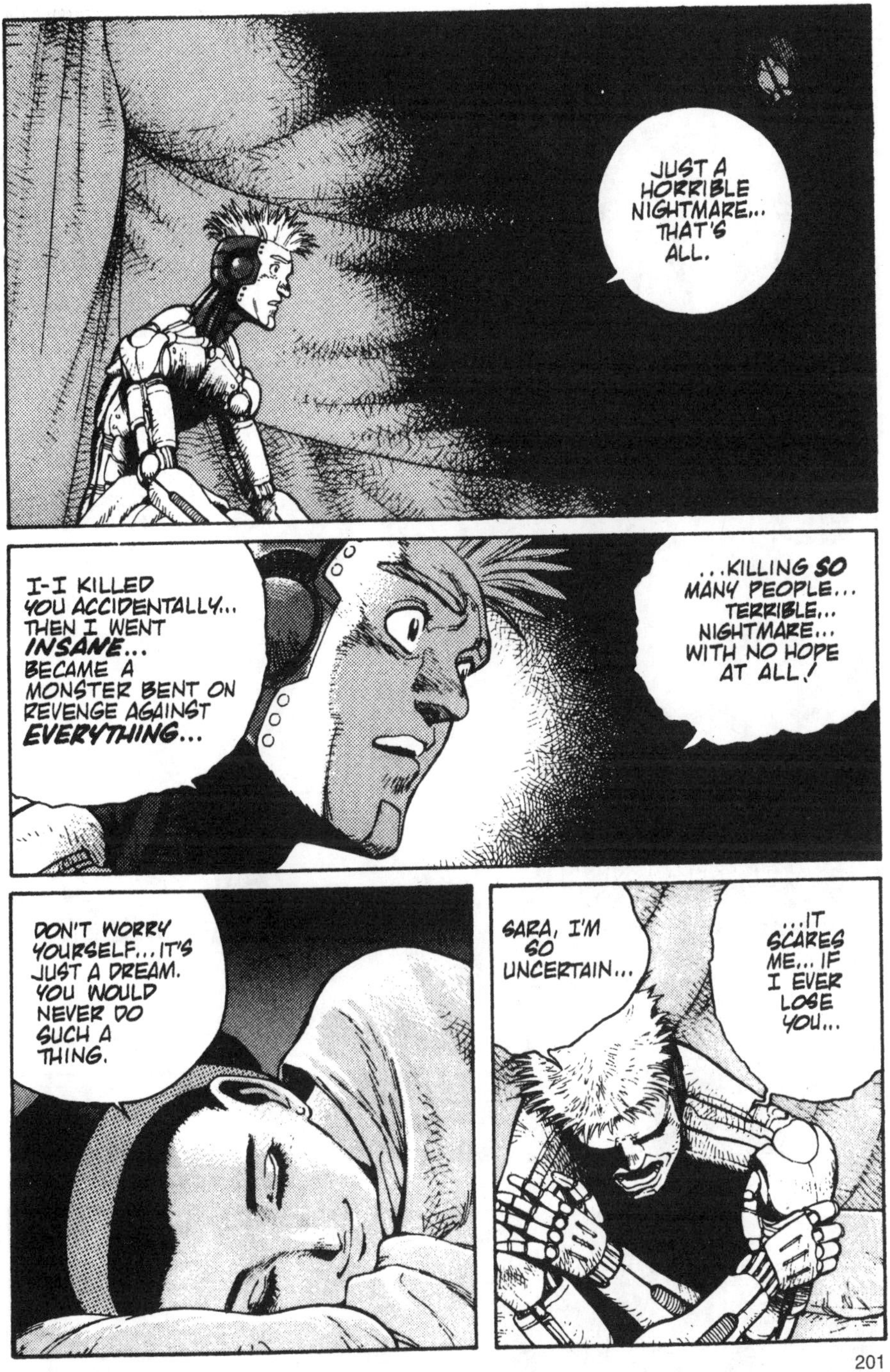
JUST A HORRIBLE NIGHTMARE... THAT'S ALL.
I-I KILLED YOU ACCIDENTALLY... THEN I WENT INSANE... BECAME A MONSTER BENT ON REVENGE AGAINST EVERYTHING...
...KILLING SO MANY PEOPLE... TERRIBLE... NIGHTMARE... WITH NO HOPE AT ALL!
DON'T WORRY YOURSELF... IT'S JUST A DREAM. YOU WOULD NEVER DO SUCH A THING.
SARA, I'M SO UNCERTAIN...
...IT SCARES ME... IF I EVER LOSE YOU...

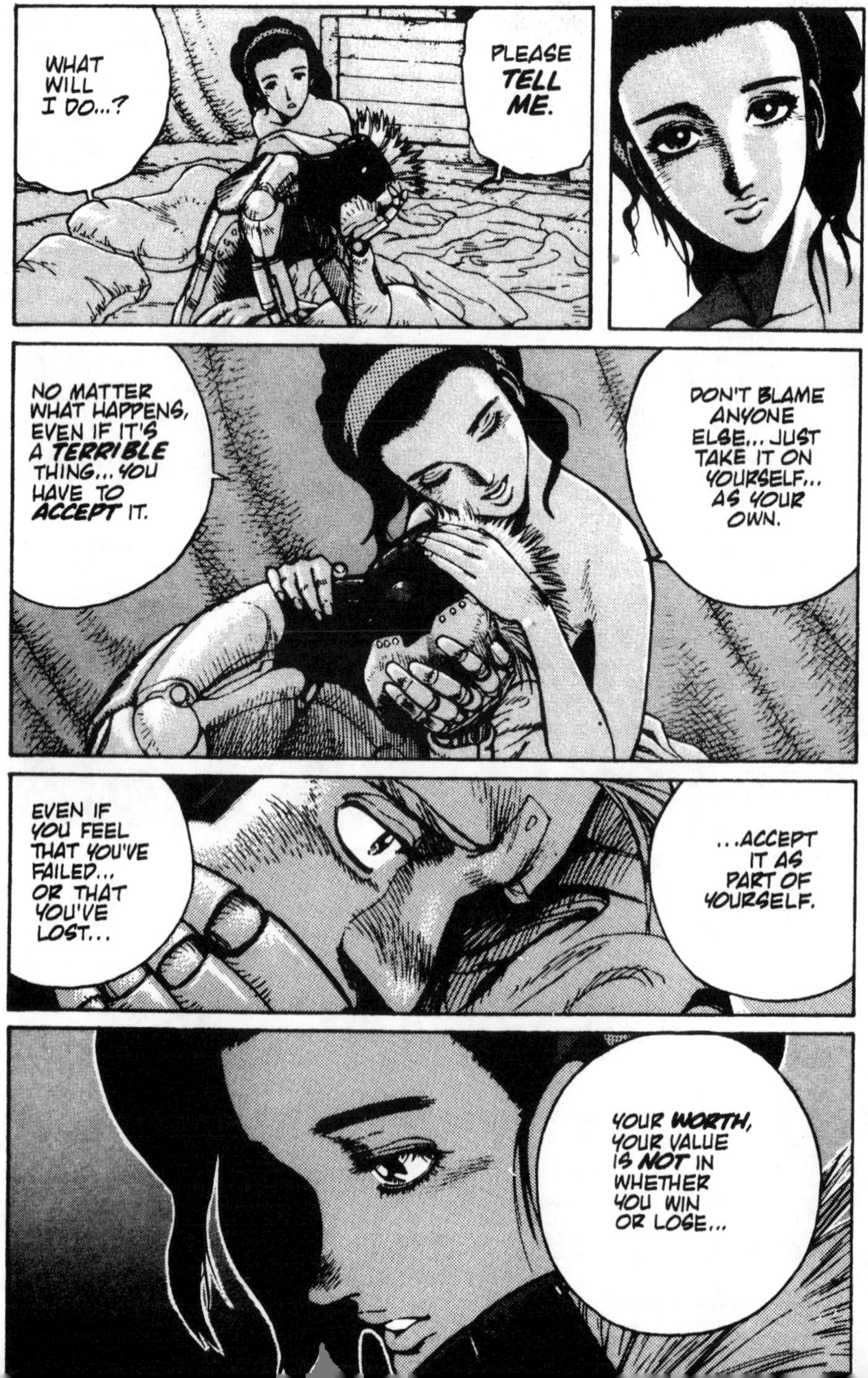
WHAT WILL I DO...?
PLEASE TELL ME.
NO MATTER WHAT HAPPENS, EVEN IF IT'S A TERRIBLE THING... YOU HAVE TO ACCEPT IT.
DON'T BLAME ANYONE ELSE... JUST TAKE IT ON YOURSELF... AS YOUR OWN.
EVEN IF YOU FEEL THAT YOU'VE FAILED... OR THAT YOU'VE LOST...
...ACCEPT IT AS PART OF YOURSELF.
YOUR WORTH, YOUR VALUE IS NOT IN WHETHER YOU WIN OR LOSE...

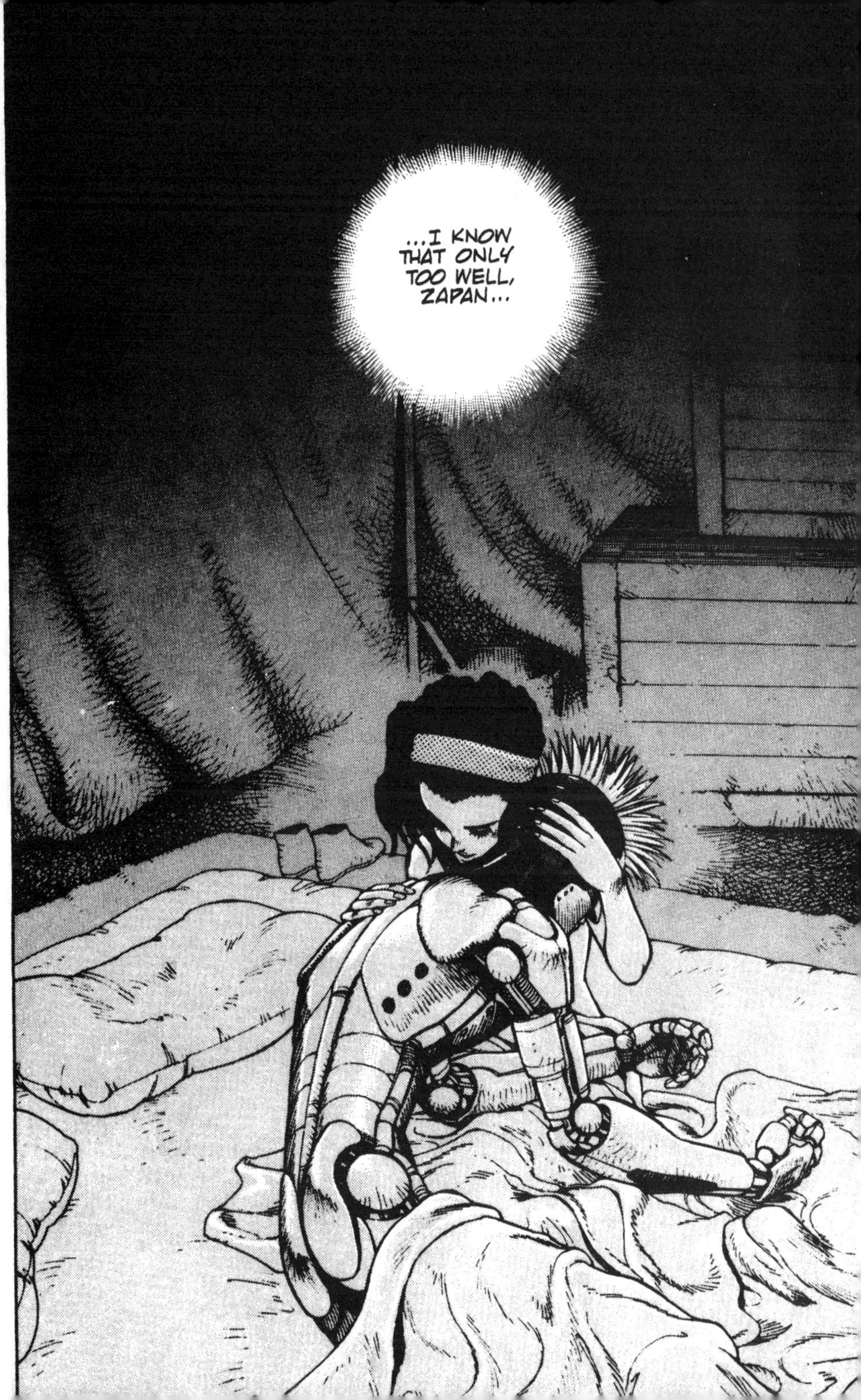
...I KNOW THAT ONLY TOO WELL, ZAPAN...

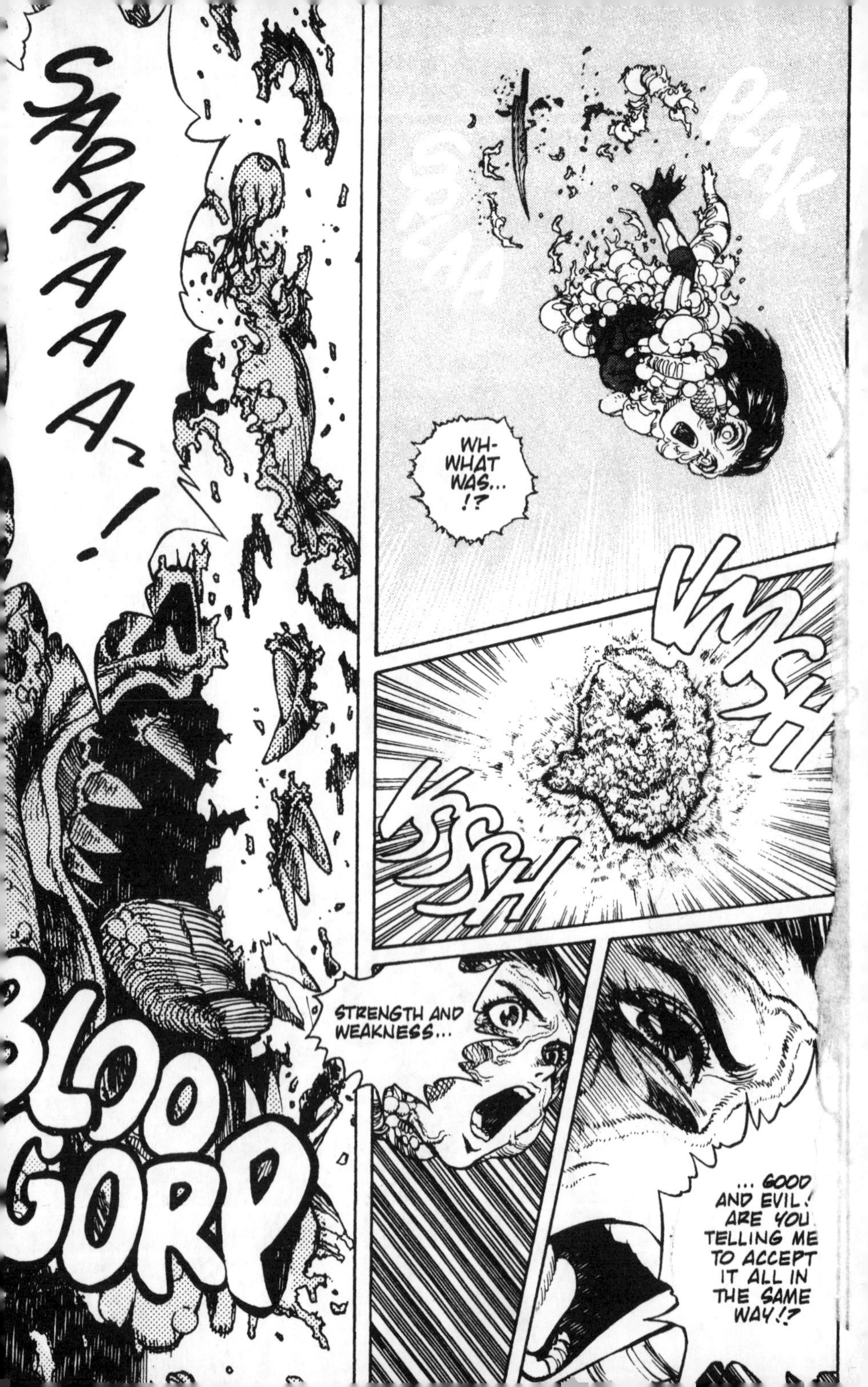
SARAAAAA—!
BLOO
GORP
WH- WHAT WAS... !?
STRENGTH AND WEAKNESS...
... GOOD AND EVIL! ARE YOU TELLING ME TO ACCEPT IT ALL IN THE SAME WAY!?

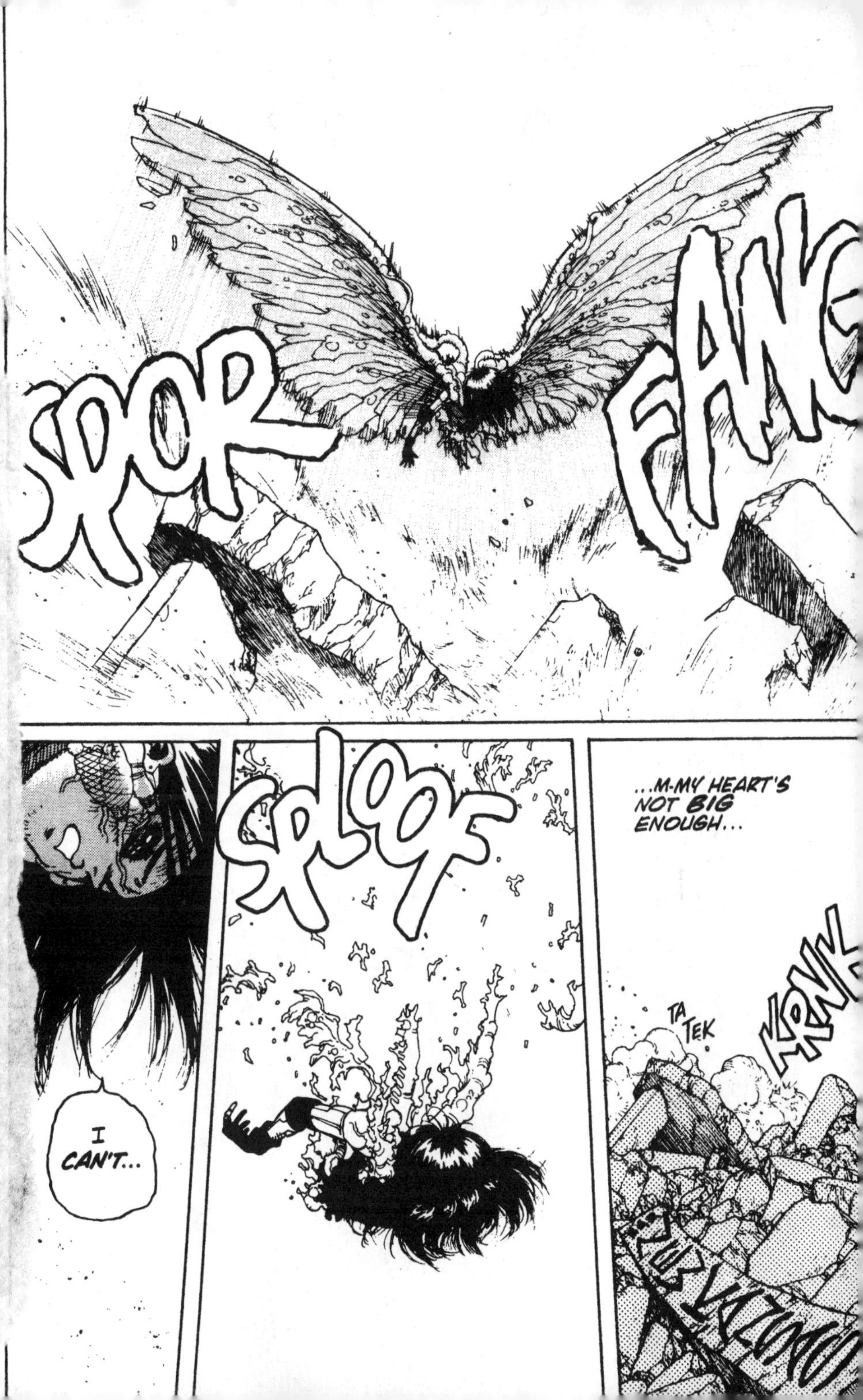
I CAN'T...
SPLOOF
...M-MY HEART'S NOT BIG ENOUGH...
TA TEK

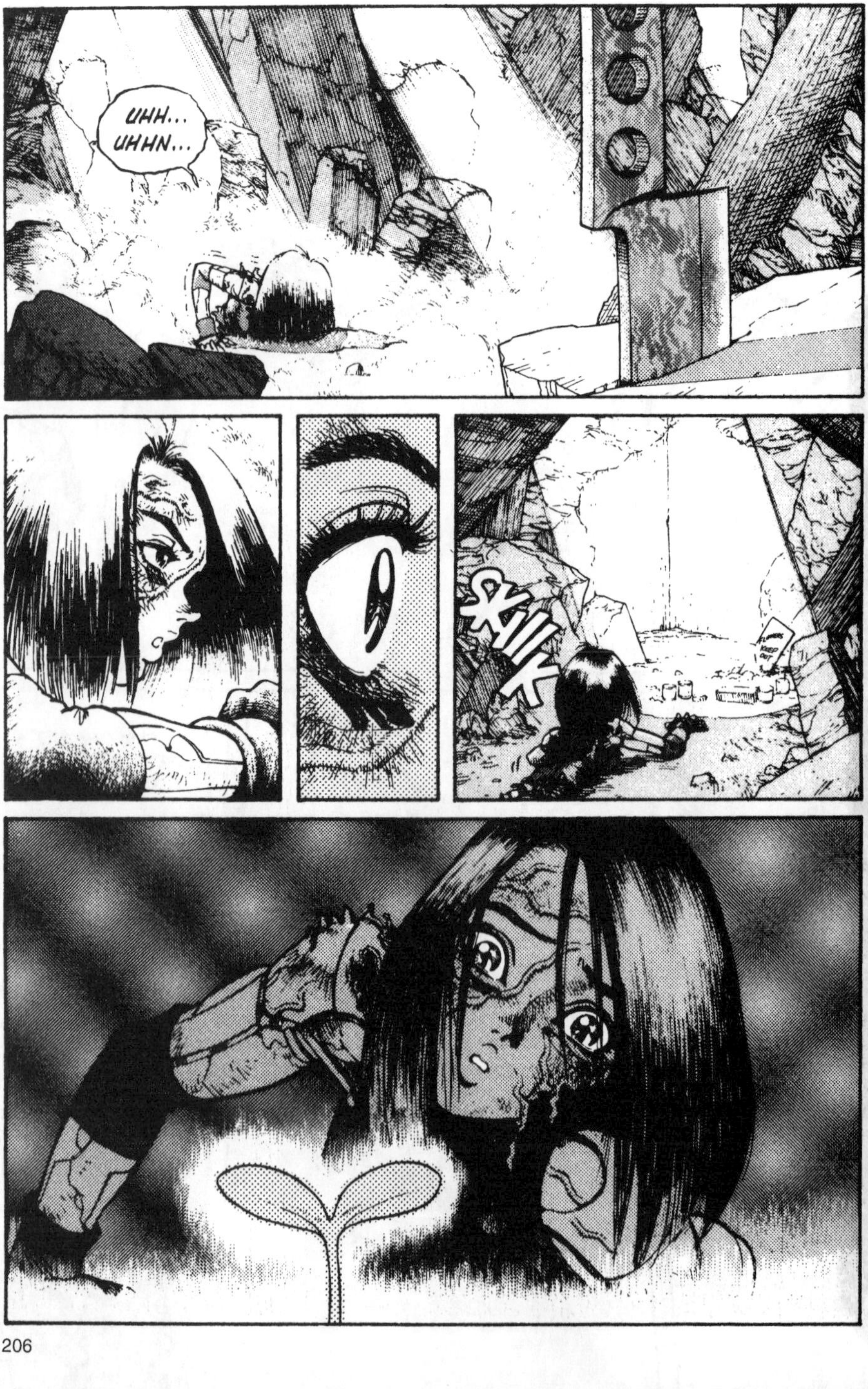
UHH... UHHN...
SKLIK
KEEP OUT

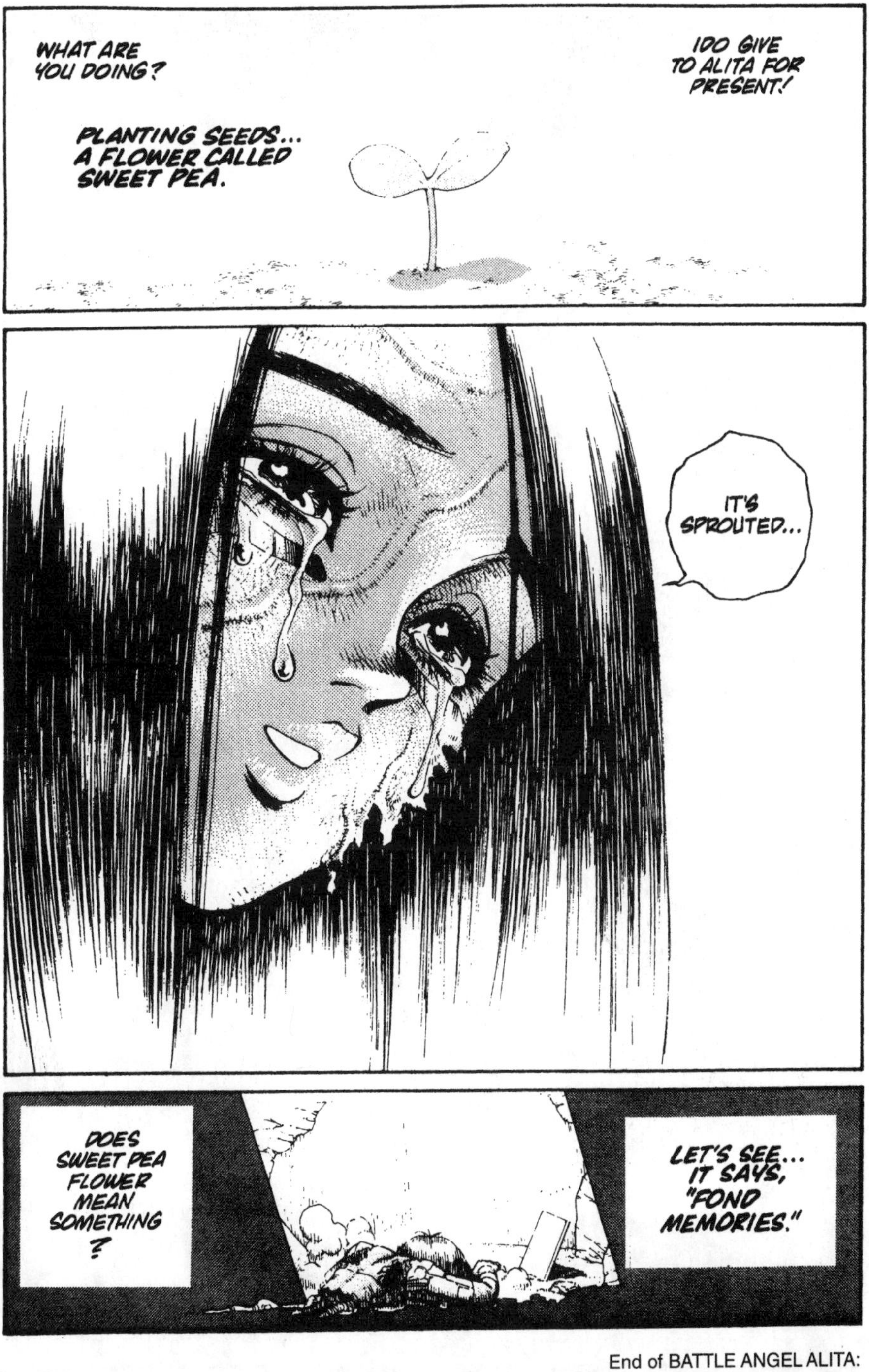
WHAT ARE
YOU DOING?
IDO GIVE
TO ALITA FOR
PRESENT!
PLANTING SEEDS...
A FLOWER CALLED
SWEET PEA.
IT'S
SPROUTED...
DOES
SWEET PEA
FLOWER
MEAN
SOMETHING
?
LET'S SEE...
IT SAYS,
"FOND
MEMORIES."

End of BATTLE ANGEL ALITA:
ANGEL OF REDEMPTION graphic novel.

ARMAGEDDON FILLS THE CRUMBLING SKY

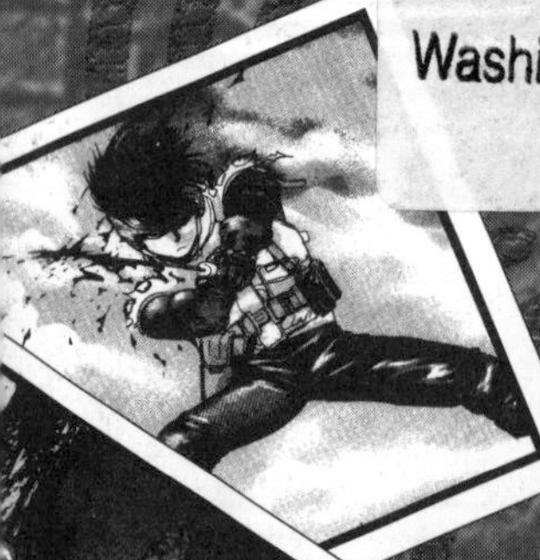

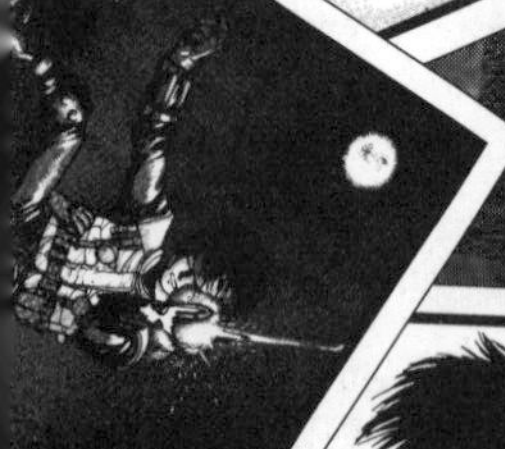

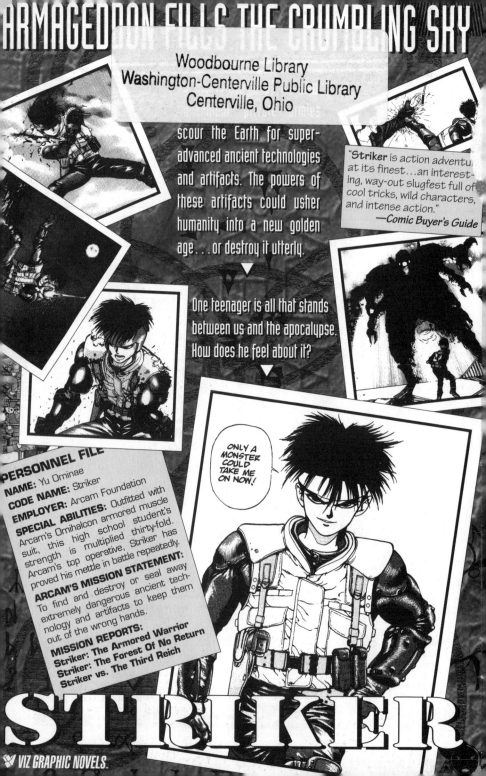

scour the Earth for super-advanced ancient technologies and artifacts. The powers of these artifacts could usher humanity into a new golden age. . . or destroy it utterly.

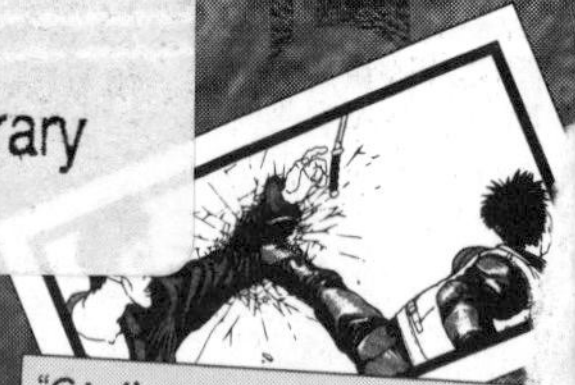

"**Striker** is action adventur at its finest. . . an interesting, way-out slugfest full of cool tricks, wild characters, and intense action."
—*Comic Buyer's Guide*

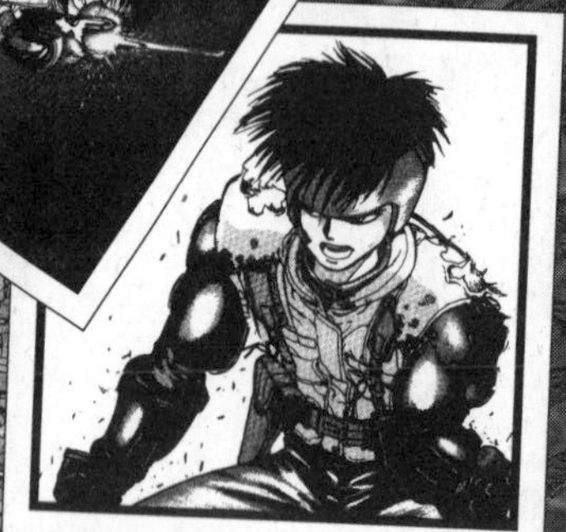

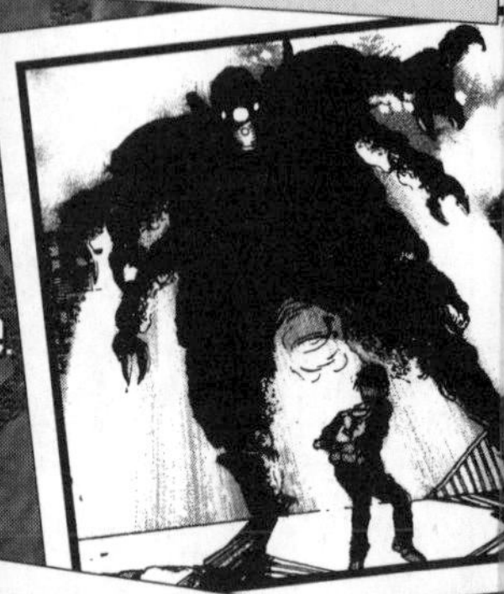

One teenager is all that stands between us and the apocalypse. How does he feel about it?

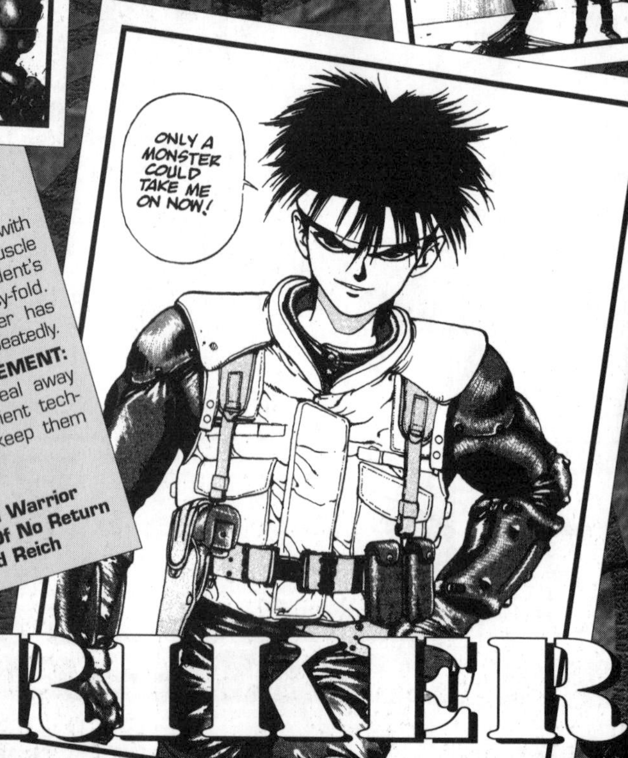
ONLY A MONSTER COULD TAKE ME ON NOW!

PERSONNEL FILE

NAME: Yu Ominae
CODE NAME: Striker
EMPLOYER: Arcam Foundation
SPECIAL ABILITIES: Outfitted with Arcam's Omihalcon armored muscle suit, this high school student's strength is multiplied thirty-fold. Arcam's top operative, Striker has proved his mettle in battle repeatedly.
ARCAM'S MISSION STATEMENT: To find and destroy or seal away extremely dangerous ancient technology and artifacts to keep them out of the wrong hands.
MISSION REPORTS:
Striker: The Armored Warrior
Striker: The Forest Of No Return
Striker vs. The Third Reich

STRIKER